The Gay Metropolis

FOR CHARLOTTE AND EMILY
AND
DANIEL AND THOMAS

....

AND IN MEMORY OF
BART GORIN,
TOM STODDARD,
ROD ROUTHIER, LOUIS BROWN,
MURRAY GITLIN, LARRY JOSEPHS, STORMY SABINE,
MIKE OSIAS, JOHN WALLACE, JAMES N. BAKER,
SCOT HALLER, GREG ROBBINS, LUIS SANJURJO,
RICHARD WHITE, RICHARD HUNT, JACK FITZSIMMONS,
SERAFIN FERNANDEZ, WALTER PERINI, PETER DAY,
AND
MURRAY KEMPTON

The Gay Metropolis

1940–1996

Charles Kaiser

A Harvest Book
Harcourt Brace & Company   SAN DIEGO   NEW YORK   LONDON

Also by Charles Kaiser

1968 IN AMERICA
Music, Politics, Chaos, Counterculture,
and the Shaping of a Generation

Reprinted by arrangement with Houghton Mifflin.

Library of Congress Cataloging-in-Publication Data
Kaiser, Charles.
The gay metropolis : 1940-1996 / Charles Kaiser.
p.   cm.
Includes bibliographical references and index.
ISBN 0-15-600617-0
1. Gays — New York (State) — New York — History. 2. Homo-
sexuality — New York (State) — New York — History. I. Title.
[HQ76.3.U52K35 1998]
305.9'0664'09747—dc21   98-15055

Printed in the United States

First Harvard edition 1998

A C E D B

Contents

Joseph, Mary, pray for those
Misled by moonlight, and the rose.

— W. H. AUDEN

Introduction

Adversity has its advantages.

A journalist once remarked to James Baldwin, "When you were starting out as a writer you were black, impoverished, homosexual. You must have said to yourself, 'Gee, how disadvantaged can I get?'"

"No," the novelist replied. "I felt I'd hit the jackpot."

This book tells the story of an amazing victory over adversity: how America's most despised minority overcame religious prejudice, medical malpractice, political persecution and one of the worst scourges of the twentieth century to stake its rightful claim to the American dream — all in barely more than half a century.

No other group has ever transformed its status more rapidly or more dramatically than lesbians and gay men. When World War II began, gay people in America had no legal rights, no organizations, a handful of private thinkers, and no public advocates. As recently as 1970, Joseph Epstein could write in *Harper's*,* "If I had the power to do so, I would wish homosexuality off the face of the earth." Only gay activists thought that statement was outrageous.

A quarter century later, gay people have completed the first stages of an incredible voyage: a journey from invisibility to ubiquity, from shame to self-respect, and, finally, from the overwhelming tragedy of AIDS to the triumph of a rugged, resourceful and caring community.

As the great architectural historian Vincent Scully pointed out, ours is "a time which, with all its agonies, has . . . been marked most of all by

* When Willie Morris was its editor.

liberation." In the Jefferson Lecture of 1995, "The Architecture of Community," Scully declared,

> I think especially of the three great movements of liberation which have marked the past generation: black liberation, women's liberation, gay liberation. Each one of those movements liberated all of us, all the rest of us, from stereotypical ways of thinking which had imprisoned us and confined us for hundreds of years. Those movements, though they have a deep past in American history, were almost inconceivable just before they occurred. Then, all of a sudden in the 1960s, they burst out together, changing us all.

America's best instincts have always been toward equality and inclusiveness. Especially in this century, the idea of a steadily widening embrace has been the genius behind the success of the American experiment. The main effects of these multiple liberations have been more openness, more honesty, and more opportunity — changes that have benefited everyone.

But despite all this progress, coming out to a parent remains the single most difficult thing a teenager can do on the eve of the twenty-first century. If you doubt that, consider the reaction of a Holocaust survivor to his son's announcement of his homosexuality:

"This," said the father, "is worse than the Holocaust."

Such incidents prove the terrible persistence of prejudice. Far too often, openly gay teenagers still face fierce harassment from their parents and their peers. But a handful of parents have changed their attitudes altogether. In 1994 the psychiatrist Richard Isay listened to these anguished words from a mother in New Jersey: "We know our son is gay," she said. "But he insists on dating girls and he wants to get married. What are we going to do?"

BARELY THIRTY YEARS AGO, most of society's glittering prizes were reserved for white heterosexual men. Today the job descriptions that the previously disenfranchised can reasonably aspire to include senator, law partner, rabbi, psychiatrist and corporate president. The only glass ceiling that remains is the one that some white executives still maintain by grooming successors who resemble themselves as much as possible.

Because it was the example of the black civil rights movement which made the gay liberation movement possible, it is especially appropriate that one of the most eloquent philosophers of liberation in the nineties is the Reverend Peter J. Gomes, a black gay Baptist with an "Anglican over-soul" who is the chief minister at Harvard University. He also happens to be a Republican who delivered the benediction at Ronald Reagan's second presidential inauguration.

Gomes outed himself to the Harvard community in 1991, after a conservative campus publication cited everyone from Freud to the Bible to prove that gay life was "immoral" and "pitiable."

"Gay people are victims not of the Bible, not of religion, and not of the church, but of people who use religion as a way to devalue and deform those whom they can neither ignore nor convert," Gomes declared. Then he identified himself as "a Christian who happens as well to be gay. . . . These realities, which are unreconcilable to some, are reconciled in me by a loving God, a living Saviour, a moving, breathing, healthy Holy Spirit whom I know intimately and who knows me."

Gomes offers an elegant argument that there is no intrinsic conflict between a Judeo-Christian God and a homosexual. In *The Good Book,* which Gomes published in 1996, he points out that when the Bible was written, its authors "never contemplated a form of homosexuality in which loving, monogamous, and faithful persons sought to live out the implications of the gospel with as much fidelity to it as any heterosexual believer. All they knew of homosexuality was prostitution, pederasty, lasciviousness, and exploitation. These vices, as we know, are not unknown among heterosexuals, and to define contemporary homosexuals only in these terms is cultural slander of the highest order."

Murray Kempton identified another ironic aspect of this debate. In 1994, he described the "early history" of the Anglican Church.

> Origin: a king's insistence on pursuing his freedom of choice in fleshly matters over the objections of the Bishop of Rome. The Book of Common Prayer, envy of the Romans: a masterpiece that would not exist if it had not been screened through Queen Elizabeth and found suitable for her doctrinal taste through its last amen. The King James Version: overseen by the most openly homosexual monarch in British history. Thus the founder of our church was a libertine, its ritual could only be authorized by a decision of a woman, its most enduring Bible is owed to the patronage of a homosexual, and yet its House of Bishops still has a fair quota of eminences disinclined to ordain women and gays.

The reconciliation of homosexuality and religion made possible by philosophers like Gomes has led to the founding of hundreds of gay synagogues and churches of every conceivable denomination. This development is among the most remarkable of all, because, as we will discover, it was the triumph of science over religion which made gay liberation possible in the first place.

THE EVENTS that opened the path for the twentieth-century revolution depicted in these pages began about 150 years ago. More than anything else, it was the rise of science in the middle of the nineteenth century which would eventually enable a handful of iconoclasts to challenge some of Western civilization's oldest assumptions about liberty and life.

It was a two-step process that began a fundamental reordering of Western thought. First, science had to be completely divorced from religion, to make it more truly scientific; then, a significant number of opinion makers had to begin to invest secular knowledge with as much importance as their ancestors had given the Sacraments. After that, *very* gradually, science became powerful enough to undermine some of the ancient dogmas of the Old Testament.

In the minds of many of his colleagues, Charles Darwin opened a crucial division between science and religion when he described his theory of evolution in the *Origin of Species* in 1859.* Sigmund Freud accelerated that separation with the invention of psychoanalysis, which gradually developed for some into an alternative to religion.

As Richard Isay has pointed out, Freud said "almost everything about homosexuality, including that it was biological, and that you couldn't change homosexuals into heterosexuals. But he also said it was caused by jealousy of siblings, and a number of interpersonal, early dynamic issues. He was not consistent." In 1937, Freud wrote, "Homosexuality is assuredly no advantage, but it is nothing to be ashamed of, no vice, no degradation, it cannot be classified as an illness." However, during the first two thirds of this century, most of Freud's disciples promoted the idea that homosexuality *was* a curable illness.

At the dawn of this new age, at the same time that Freud was researching *The Interpretation of Dreams,* his contemporary Magnus Hirschfeld was launching the first gay liberation movement of the modern era in Germany. In 1897 Hirschfeld distributed more than six thousand questionnaires to Berlin factory workers and university students. He concluded that 2.2 percent of all German men were homosexuals and published his findings in one of the twenty-three volumes of *Jahrbuch,* the

---

* In 1860, the bishop of Oxford made a brutal attack on Darwin's hypothesis. But after Thomas Henry Huxley responded vociferously on Darwin's behalf, the Church of England never made a formal challenge to science again.

first avowedly gay publication of the twentieth century. A few years later, Hirschfeld founded the Institute for Sexual Research, which collected twenty thousand books and thirty-five thousand photographs. He also organized the World League for Sexual Reform, which held annual conferences in Copenhagen, London and Vienna, between 1928 and 1932. He campaigned continuously for the repeal of paragraph 175, the law banning sodomy in Germany. A petition asking the Reichstag to annul that law attracted the signatures of Thomas Mann and Albert Einstein.

Hirschfeld conducted his research at a time when Weimar Germany nurtured a rich gay culture, which included costume balls and luxurious bars and nightclubs for gay men and lesbians. But after barely three decades, the Nazis would put an end to all of Hirschfeld's activities. Nazi toughs attacked him during public appearances. Four months after Hitler became chancellor in 1933, while Hirschfeld was out of the country, the Institute for Sexual Research was ransacked and its contents were burned in a public ceremony.

The fact that the Nazis seized power from a regime that had tolerated homosexuality would color American attitudes toward sexual permissiveness for thirty years afterward. American writers would regularly compare the Weimar period to the debauchery of ancient Rome — and then conclude that any culture that permitted gay life to flourish was obviously doomed to catastrophe.

The subject was further complicated by the fact that the Nazis themselves had tolerated openly gay men among their own leaders, even though "the official party apparatus had" assailed "all immorality, especially love between men" as early as 1928. This uneven tolerance ended in 1934, when Ernst Roehm, the gay commander of the Nazi S.A., and dozens of his allies were massacred during the Night of the Long Knives. Hitler said afterwards that these men deserved to die for their "corrupt morals alone," but the historian William L. Shirer wrote that the Fuhrer "had known all along . . . that a large number of his closest . . . followers were sexual perverts and convicted murderers."

What American journalists and historians neglected altogether was the vicious persecution that gay people suffered at the hands of the Nazis once Roehm and his friends had been eliminated. Historians of the Holocaust estimate that during the Third Reich at least ninety thousand homosexuals were arrested, more than fifty thousand were sent to prison and between ten and fifteen thousand ended up in concentration camps, where they were identified by pink triangles.

Most Americans considered Hitler's obliteration of the German Jewish population so horrifying that it did more to discredit anti-Semitism than any other single event. But Nazi oppression of homosexuals failed to increase sympathy for them in the United States or anywhere else.

ALTHOUGH World War II did nothing to improve the way most Americans viewed homosexuality, it would have a dramatic effect on the way thousands of lesbians and gay men viewed themselves. The United States Army acted as a great, secret unwitting agent of gay liberation by creat-ing the largest concentration of homosexuals inside a single institution in American history. That is why this volume begins with World War II.

People from all over the country who had assumed that they were unique learned that they were not alone. Soldiers and sailors also got a chance to sample gay culture all over the world — and discovered that large gay communities already existed in American ports of entry like San Francisco and New York City.

It was also during this war that the word *gay* became "a magic by-word in practically every corner of the United States where homosexuals might gather." (Some historians have traced the use of the word *gaie* as a syno-nym for homosexual all the way back to sixteenth-century France.)

In the postwar period, New York City became the literal gay metropolis for hundreds of thousands of immigrants from within and without the United States: the place they chose to learn how to live openly, honestly and without shame.

But the figurative gay metropolis is much larger: it encompasses every place on every continent where gay people have found the courage and the dignity to be free.

Some of the ordinary and extraordinary citizens who nurtured the spectacular growth of that larger metropolis are the main subjects of this book. While the women I have written about are among the most compel-ling characters in this saga, men gradually became my principal focus — because their story is also mine.

I

The Forties

"On any person who desires such queer prizes, New York will bestow the gift of loneliness and the gift of privacy."

— E. B. WHITE

"I think the trick is to say yes to life."

— JAMES BALDWIN

SANDY KERN grew up on Amboy Street, the Brooklyn block where the boys from Murder, Incorporated, used to shoot craps in front of Olesh's Candy Store. These were the Jewish mobsters of Brownsville before the war began. "We kids would stand and watch for the cops," Kern remembered, "and we would signal them. And when we didn't do it in time and the cops did raid them — they did it right in the street, of course — the cops would come, they would run away, these guys. And when the cops got to the site where they were playing craps, they would take all the coins that were on the floor and toss them up in the air, and the kids would scramble for the money."

Kern laughed at the vivid memory, a faraway moment when she already knew she was unlike everyone else, but didn't yet know how. "Of course the war stopped all that, and a lot of the guys never came back." She was twelve in 1941, when the Japanese bombed Pearl Harbor. "I always thought I was very, very *special,* because I was very different from everybody in the neighborhood. And I always imagined that there was a ray of light beaming down from the sky onto me. Following me all over because I was very special. And I didn't know why until we were in the midst of an air-raid drill.

"We used to have these regularly. It was in the evening. And the air-raid drill meant that all the lights had to be put out. Everything. As if there were actual enemy planes flying overhead. And all the lights would be doused, and the black curtains over the windows we had, and every light was either hidden, or covered, or turned off.

"So it was completely black. And I was sitting with my little girlfriend, whom I loved until it hurt me. I was so crazy about Minnie. We were the same age. She was about five foot eight, and she was beautiful in my eyes. My father was a pushcart peddler and made a few pennies a day. Her father was in construction, so he earned more money. All the lights went out and we were sitting in front of the stoop." She laughed again: "I'm remembering it all!"

"Anyway, it was black and dark, so I felt that I could put my arms around her. And oh! I was *so* happy. I was holding her in my arms. I never did that before. And I put my face in her hair, and I could smell her, and it was fantastic. I was never so open during the day when the light and everybody could see. I don't know why, but I sensed that I shouldn't display my affection for her. But in the dark, of course, I could do all that I wanted to do, and that's what I wanted to do: just hold her and smell her.

"I don't even know if I was kissing her. It was just fondling — holding her in my arms — when all of a sudden the sirens came on, which was the end of the make-believe air raid. And all the lights went on, and there I was still holding her in my arms — when a neighbor turned around and looked at us.

"And she said *that word* that I heard for the very first time in my life. She said, 'Are you a lesbian?'

"So! I remembered the word. We didn't have any dictionary at home — would you believe it? So the next day I ran to the library and I looked up the word *lesbian*. Oh boy. That's when I *really* felt special. Because I remember reading about the Isle of Lesbos. So I said, 'Well, I deserve!' I confirmed my feelings of being special. So, unlike many other lesbians, I was always very proud — and I always felt very special. But at the same time I knew somehow that I shouldn't tell everybody how I feel.

"That's when I started to read the literature about it. And I remember having read *The Well of Loneliness.* They didn't have it in the bookstore. I had to send away for it. I don't know how I found out about it. Maybe I read about it in the library when I was looking up the word *lesbian.* I wrote away to the publisher just for *The Well of Loneliness* and *The Unlit Lamp.* I got them both at the same time. And I didn't have to worry about receiving them at home because neither one of my parents could read English.

They came from Russia — Russian-Jewish — and they never learned how to read English. Before I went to school, I only spoke Yiddish.

"Minnie and I would walk together in the wintertime. I would have her hand in my pocket — we would hold hands in my pocket — and she loved it. And when we went to the movies, she always let me hold her hand." Then Minnie went away to camp for the summer. "My heart was broken! I used to write her letters, and in my letters I would cut my finger and bleed on the letter. I would be falling in love all the time. And each one was a bone-crushing kind of love!"

Kern laughed some more. "When I was very young, there was something strange going on with me. On the outside I was very tough. I was known as 'The Terror.' That was my nickname. I was the leader of the gang and I would beat up the tough guys and my territory was Amboy Street, and nobody could come onto Amboy if they lived someplace else. But inside I was afraid of people. And I was in love with all these women. And I would be composing all this music. My mother had this tall radio that stood on the floor. I would sit down on the floor and press my ear against the loudspeaker so I could feel *inside* the music. Inside it! Oh! And I would keep it very loud, and my mother would yell at me. But I was wild about the music.

"There was such a difference between how I was on the outside, compared to the way I was on the inside. I was in my secret world, which ran along with my real life. In my secret life I was a pianist-conductor-composer, and I wrote all this beautiful music and played all this wonderful music, and the women would just *swoon* over me. All this romantic music that came pouring out of my head and heart!"

ACROSS THE RIVER from Kern, Otis Bigelow lived in Manhattan. He, too, would never think of himself the same way again after the summer of 1942. Bigelow turned twenty-two that June. A striking native of Exeter, New Hampshire, where his father had been a master at the Phillips Exeter Academy, Bigelow was an only child.

After his father died, his mother sent him away to Rumsey Hall, a British-style school in Washington, Connecticut, where "Sir, yes, sir" was the required form and the students wore black ties to dinner.

At twelve Bigelow was already having sex with his classmates, but they didn't think their pastime had anything to do with being "gay" or "homosexual," words that they had never heard spoken. "In my world, in the thirties, it simply did not exist," Bigelow recalled.

Like millions before him, and millions after him, Bigelow believed he was simply going through "a stage. . . . It was just friends, you know, doing something for a friend. There was no masculinity or femininity involved. I thought for many years that it was fine, and that it was a substitute for girls. I always thought I would get married. I went out with girls and loved girls; they were interested in me and I in them and we got along beautifully."

His roommate at Rumsey, an admirer of Tarzan, taught Bigelow how to masturbate. "He loved to go off into the woods and tie me to a tree. Then I would say, 'Oh, Tarzan, Tarzan, where are you?' And he would come swinging through the trees and carry me away."

In 1934, Bigelow transferred to Exeter; two years later, his mother died, and he was devastated.

At Exeter, "There were a couple of guys who could actually see through me, both of whom I think turned out to be totally straight. They would say, 'Want to come down to my room?' And I would sneak down after lights out, we would fuck each other between the legs. That's what friends are for! It was just a friendly but mechanical act. More fun than doing it by yourself or doing it with a pillow — or a milk bottle. We tried everything." Later, in New York, he learned the forties slang for this kind of primitive sex: "first-year Princeton."

Once, at a bus station away from school, he was a little more adventurous. "I had gone to the movies and had taken the bus back and went into the john. There was a nice-looking fellow standing there and he took one look at me and took me into one of the booths and stood me on the john. I thought it was wonderful, but I had a terrible attack of conscience afterwards. I went home and scrubbed myself. I had never heard of such a thing."

Bigelow loved the theater, and he played all the leading ladies at Exeter until his voice began to change. In *Androcles and the Lion,* he was Lavinia and he had to kiss the handsome captain on the cheek. He told the director he didn't want to do it, but the director insisted that he follow the script. "So I did. It was a strange feeling."

When he graduated from Exeter in 1938, he ignored his uncle's admonition to go to college. Instead, he moved to New York, where he hoped to become an actor. While performing summer stock in Rye Beach, New Hampshire, Bigelow had met Gordon Merrick, an actor who had just graduated from Princeton. Bigelow and Merrick used to kiss, but nothing more. Although they shared an apartment when they reached New York, Bigelow was still planning to marry a woman. And quite quickly Gordon decided that he was "very into *not* being gay," Bigelow recalled.

Three decades later, Merrick wrote *The Lord Won't Mind,* one of the first gay novels to become a best-seller in the seventies, and he modeled one of its beautiful young men after Bigelow.* The other man sharing their apartment was Richard Barr, another Princeton graduate who went to work for the Mercury Theatre that fall and participated in Orson Welles's menacing broadcast of *The War of the Worlds.* Later, Barr became one of Broadway's most illustrious impresarios. He was Edward Albee's confidant and produced many of his most important plays, including *The Zoo Story, Tiny Alice* and *Who's Afraid of Virginia Woolf?* In 1968 he coproduced Mart Crowley's *The Boys in the Band,* and, eleven years later, Stephen Sondheim's *Sweeney Todd.* For twenty-one years, he was president of the League of American Theatres and Producers.

Bigelow would never be as famous as his roommates, but among gay men in New York he was a legend: a great many considered him the best-looking man in Manhattan. His life proved how far good looks and good manners could take anyone — regardless of gender or sexual persuasion.

Bigelow socialized with a group of gay men whom his contemporary, the playwright Arthur Laurents, derided as "the silver and china queens." Laurents described these gentlemen as "a class of gay from way back that was always as right-wing as possible, out of a desperate desire to belong. And they haven't changed. It's like gay couples who to try to emulate heterosexual couples. Nothing could be more stupid. I mean that one is sort of the husband and the other is sort of the wife and they have to have fidelity and all this kind of nonsense — instead of seeing how lucky you are if you're two men and have freedom."

Bigelow, Merrick and Barr selected an apartment on East 54th Street, sandwiched between the nightclub El Morocco and a store selling artificial limbs. A subway token still cost a nickel (as it had since the system opened in 1904); the rent for two rooms with a garden, plus kitchen and bath, was $45 a month; and a cluster of nearby restaurants offered shrimp cocktail, a small steak, dessert, and coffee for the grand sum of fifty cents. Instead of office buildings, Third Avenue was lined with brownstones, and it was dominated by the Elevated, whose rumblings Bigelow could hear from inside his apartment.

The nooks and shadows created by this shaft down the center of the avenue played a significant role in gay life in New York before the war: they

---

The New York Times scorned the book: a brief Sunday review predicted that it might "set homosexuality back at least twenty years." Bigelow also disliked it. (*New York Times Book Review,* April 26, 1970, and author's interview with Otis Bigelow, October 25, 1994)

offered a multitude of discreetly darkened meeting places right in the heart of the metropolis. "It was a little bit spooky," said Murray Gitlin, a Broadway dancer who remembered Third Avenue as "one of the only cruisy places" in the 1940s. "It was like being under palm trees on a summer night," Franklin Macfie quipped. "You could very easily feel you were in Rio!"

"The city smelled totally different than it does today," said Jack Dowling, who later worked for Colt Studios, one of the first emporiums of erotic photographs of attractive men. "There wasn't that much trash on the street, and the air had the wonderful smell of washed concrete. Downtown it smelled of diesel truck exhaust. The Village around West 11th Street, late at night, smelled of baking bread from commercial bakeries. All of the East Side, from the Thirties all the way up to the Sixties, was filled with rooming houses which had their own unique odors."

But Otis Bigelow never went "cruising" outdoors. His good manners, beautiful features and handsome clothes made him immensely sought after at all the most fashionable cocktail parties. And even though he continued to believe that he was destined to marry a woman, he led a very gay Manhattan life.

"I had a tuxedo and tails and all sorts of suits. What I wound up doing, pretty much, when I started, was living on my looks because it was terribly social in those days. Gay bars, no. I didn't go to those until later. But there were elegant bars like Tony's on Swing Alley on West 52d Street where Mabel Mercer sat and sang.

"There were a number of places where wealthy, youngish men had duplex apartments on Park Avenue, and pretty much any day if you dropped by at five o'clock there would be people there for cocktails and, more often than not, somebody would say, 'Well, I have tickets to the ballet and we can drop in on Tony's later.' I was polite and gorgeous, and I was always jumping up to get drinks for people. I had social graces.

"I might meet somebody at a cocktail party who would be staying at the St. Regis. I would walk him home, and he would say, 'Why don't you come up for a drink?' And then he would say, 'Well, why don't you stay over? We'll have breakfast and it'll be nice. Don't walk all that way home: you can sleep on my sofa.' Then there would be a little bit of this and that. It was friendly prep-school sex."

After a few weeks, a friend named Nicky Holden, whom Bigelow thought of as someone "on the fringes of society," introduced Bigelow to "an important acquaintance. It turned out to be an older man of thirty who owned a house on Beekman Place," Bigelow recalled, someone who had made his fortune in the printing business. "He was Jewish and not terribly attractive, but a wonderful man — a funny, witty, cultivated man. He started to invite me to dinner and take me to the theater." His name was Robert Goodhue and he drove a custom-built Packard V-16 convertible. "You cannot imagine what *that* was like! You could hardly turn around a corner it was so long! It was black with red trim and wire wheels and red leather and a rumble seat. After a couple of weeks, he said, 'I'd like to get out of town for the weekend. Would you like to go to Atlantic City?' Well, that's where you took somebody cheap. So I said, 'I don't think Atlantic City.' And he said, 'How about Williamsburg?' And I said, 'I'd love to.' It's funny — I did such a dramatic thing. He was so nice to me, and he used to like to kiss me, though I wouldn't let him kiss me on the mouth. He'd always say, 'You're so beautiful!' We got to Williamsburg and we had this marvelous great big double room. So I said, Well, he deserves it. And I like him. So this eighteen-year-old kid, being very sophisticated, said, 'Well, you've been so nice to me, would you like to see me as I really am?'" The answer was a very rapid "Yes!"

"So I took off all my clothes and let him do me. Well, he thought that was wonderful. I didn't mind. So that became something that we did once in a while when we got back from the theater." When their relationship ended, his patron dissolved into tears and handed his young friend an envelope that contained a check for one thousand dollars.

Bigelow carried the check around for months because he was afraid the bank might report him to his uncle — and he wouldn't know how to explain the check. After he enrolled in Hamilton College, he finally confided in a sympathetic dean, whom he thought was probably gay. The dean assured him he could rely on the bank's discretion, and Bigelow deposited the check in his account.

He immediately bought a 1933 Ford Roadster, "a wonderful car," for the huge sum of one hundred dollars. The other nine hundred was enough to provide him with plenty of spending money for the rest of his college career.

At Hamilton, Bigelow wrote a play, which John C. Wilson, a "class" producer, optioned. Wilson asked him to come to New York in the summer of 1942 to rewrite it. In Manhattan, Bigelow met Maury Paul, a portly gentleman from Philadelphia, who was the original Cholly Knickerbocker society columnist for Hearst. It was Paul who coined the term *café society* one night at the Ritz right after World War I, to describe the unprecedented new groupings of old money with new. Paul noticed that these disparate fun lovers had learned to be friendly in public, even though they would never invite one another to their homes.

"He was supposed to be so evil, but he never laid a glove on me," Bigelow recalled. "He was amused by me." One day Paul took him downstairs to the basement storage room of his apartment house, which was jammed with luxurious furs. "Pick out a coat!" Paul commanded. "I have fifty of them!" Bigelow chose a floor-length raccoon coat but promised to return it. "I don't want it back," the columnist shouted. "Keep it!" Another time the two of them spent an afternoon together at the Liberty Music Shop on Madison Avenue, listening to classical music. "I was just so thrilled by it. We came out with two packages of everything we had listened to and he gave one to me. It was my introduction to classical music — a lifelong pleasure. He was wonderful.

"Once when I went by to see him, there was the handsomest young man I had ever seen: beautifully dressed, beautifully groomed. He was the guy he was keeping. It was trade Maury had picked up, polished up, dressed up. Straight. He came in once or twice a week from New Jersey. Maury bought him a house. The young man was married and had a child. That was his arrangement. Strange man; as nice a man as you would ever want to meet."

Then Bigelow finally fell in love with a sailor: "the most beautiful person I ever saw. It was instant." He met Bill Miller at a party, and fifty years later Bigelow still remembered the moment. "A Frank Sinatra recording of 'I'll Be Seeing You' was playing on the phonograph. We went out and had dinner. So I was in love, and he was in love. He was stationed at the Brooklyn Navy Yard and we kind of spent that month together."

Bill Miller is also famous among his contemporaries as one of the most gorgeous men in 1940s Manhattan. Paul Cadmus drew him, George Platt Lynes photographed him, and everyone wanted him. Miller was by far the most powerful attraction Bigelow had ever felt. "We were at the Waldorf-Astoria in the suite of some wealthy man who invited us to stay over in the spare bedroom," Bigelow remembered. "We were in bed. I looked at Bill, and I thought, 'I can't live without him.' And that was that." Bigelow finally admitted to himself that he really was gay. "I had to face the fact that I had changed."

Bigelow's life was complicated somewhat by the fact that he had met a man named George Gallowhur earlier in the summer, another "older man" with a slightly higher public profile: a dashing thirty-seven-year-old industrialist who lived in a brownstone in Turtle Bay, an elegant group of houses surrounding a common garden in the East Forties. Gallowhur's neighbor across the rhododendron was Katharine Hepburn. A few doors down was Philip Johnson, the future architect. "George was family to me," Johnson remembered. "He was a rich boy around town who worked." Johnson described himself and Gallowhur as "chickenhawks" — gentlemen who preferred the company of younger men.

The striking, tall, blond Swedish American had made a fortune by inventing Skol, the first successful suntan lotion. While still a student at Princeton in 1926, Gallowhur drew attention to himself by crossing the Atlantic in a fifty-four-foot cutter. Afterward the undergraduate joked to *The New York Times* that he had considered asking for caviar when the skipper of an ocean liner turned off course to ask whether his tiny craft needed any assistance.

Paul Cadmus remembered Gallowhur as someone who "gave the appearance of being very, very businesslike and a straight American," but who actually "loved to go in for sailors and things like that." Gallowhur fell madly in love with Bigelow, who found him "stunning," but did not reciprocate his feelings. To entice the young undergraduate, Gallowhur made the young man an extraordinary offer.

Bigelow was about to enter his final year in the Naval Reserve Officer Training program at Hamilton. If the student would live with him, Gallowhur would purchase a ship. Then he would donate it to the Coast Guard — on the condition that Bigelow would become its captain. Bigelow was convinced that Gallowhur had the power to keep his promise, and to specify that Bigelow could not be sent to the Pacific.

Bigelow was still seeing Gallowhur when he met Bill Miller, "so I had to tell George I couldn't see him anymore." Gallowhur begged him to reconsider. "Let me give a dinner party for six people," the industrialist suggested. Bigelow could bring Bill, who would sit next to Gallowhur at dinner; afterward Bigelow could choose between them. "Give me a chance!" Gallowhur pleaded.

Bigelow agreed and brought Miller to Turtle Bay. After coffee had been served, Gallowhur took Bigelow aside. "Have you made your choice?" he inquired.

"Yes," said Bigelow. "It's Bill."*

---

*Two years later, Gallowhur married Nackey E. Scripps, the granddaughter of E. W. Scripps, the newspaper publisher. They were divorced in 1949. Three years later, Mrs. Gallowhur married William Loeb, the fiercely conservative publisher of the *Manchester Union-Leader* in New Hampshire. Upon Loeb's death in 1981, she succeeded him as the paper's publisher. George Gallowhur died in Miami Beach in 1974. He was sixty-nine.

Bigelow and Miller had only one more week together before Bigelow had to go back to college. "We were *so* happy," Bigelow remembered. "I went back to school and he went back into the Coast Guard." The sailor wrote Bigelow a single letter: he said he was "dead" without him, and Bigelow believed that Miller was shipping out.

In November, Bigelow returned to New York for Thanksgiving. He was glum, thinking that Miller might have already perished at sea. In Manhattan, he stayed with George Hoyningen-Huene, a famous fashion photographer for *Vogue* and *Harper's Bazaar*. Hoyningen-Huene had been born in St. Petersburg at the turn of the century, the son of a Baltic nobleman and the daughter of the American minister to the court of the czar.

The photographer was forty-two when Bigelow met him, and he kept himself fit with regular visits to the gym — a custom that would become almost universal among a certain class of gay men three decades later. After Bigelow had done some modeling for his host, Hoyningen-Huene tried to coax him into bed.

When Bigelow refused him, Hoyningen-Huene became furious, and started to shout: "You're doing all this moping around about that sailor Bill! Did you know that Bill has been living in Turtle Bay with George Gallowhur since about three days after you left?"

Bigelow was stunned. It was the "cruelest thing" he had ever experienced.

It was also his awakening.

FIFTY YEARS LATER, like many men of his generation, Bigelow resisted unpleasant memories of gay life in the 1940s — and deplored its more democratic style in the 1990s. After he finally acknowledged to himself that he was gay, he never worried about becoming an outsider because "gay society at that point was so hermetic and so safe and so wonderful. Everybody was very classy in those days. There was no trade. There were no bums." (He said so moments before he described Maury Paul's kept boy.) "Everybody that you met had a style of elegance. It was not T-shirts and muscles and so on. It was wit and class. You had to have tails and be polite. Homosexuality was an upscale thing to be. It was defined by class. There wasn't dark cruising."

On this subject, Bigelow was wholly misinformed. Across town from the Park Avenue swells who entertained him so lavishly in their duplex apartments, a completely different kind of gay life was thriving in Times Square. Obvious "fairies" (many of them heavily made-up) created their own flamboyant culture in the theater district. On either side of Broadway, there were gay bars, gay restaurants and even gay cafeterias. Automats were especially popular with the gay demimonde and even "the large cafeterias in the Childs chain" could be "astonishingly open," according to the historian George Chauncey. Some proprietors encouraged their reputation as "gay hangouts" to attract late-night sightseers.

Soldiers and sailors swarmed through this teeming crossroads, and gay men pursued them with abandon. Tennessee Williams loved to cruise Times Square with Donald Windham in the forties. Williams recalled making "very abrupt and candid overtures, phrased so bluntly that it's a wonder they didn't slaughter me on the spot." First the soldiers stared in astonishment; then they usually burst into laughter. Finally, after a brief conference, "as often as not, they would accept" the playwright's invitation.

Unlike the hermetic existence Bigelow enjoyed, which was protected by enormous wealth, ordinary lesbians and gay men led much more precarious lives. Because they had to be clandestine, the gay speakeasies that flourished in the twenties and thirties were usually very safe places to congregate. After Franklin Roosevelt ended Prohibition in 1933, the speakeasies were replaced by a constantly changing constellation of gay bars. These saloons tended to be more open, but that meant they were also subject to much more harassment. Even inside gay bars, plainclothes policemen would practice entrapment, actually displaying erections in the bathroom to trick customers into propositioning them — a practice that continued in New York until the end of the 1960s. Payoffs to policemen by bar owners were frequent and utterly brazen. Roy Strickland, who would become a very successful window designer for department stores, remembered the routine at the Old Colony, a popular cruising spot on West 8th Street in the forties. "You'd see a cop walk in and go toward the rear and meet with the proprietor, and the proprietor would put his hand out — obviously with cash in it — and the cop would walk out. That's the way these places kept open."

Cleanup campaigns were also quite common, especially just before elections, or the opening of world's fairs in 1939 and 1964. During one three-year period, fifteen thousand sex offenders were arrested for disorderly conduct in New York City. Sometimes they were referred to a rehabilitation center run by the Quakers.

The "respectable" (and deeply closeted) gay men whom Bigelow knew were honest about their homosexuality only among themselves; they were horrified by the brazen displays of the Times Square crowd. Despite enormous changes, the same syndrome is sometimes still apparent today, as closeted Park Avenue lawyers and wealthy Wall Street investment bankers cringe at the flamboyance of anyone less inhibited than themselves.

In the forties, money protected the wealthy from most forms of harassment. One of their favorite places to congregate in public was the old Metropolitan Opera House, on Broadway just below Times Square, where the presumed safety from police raids inspired outlandish attire. One opera lover was particularly famous for wearing his pants backward in the standing section — with the fly in the back — to permit a particular kind of ecstatic experience during the performance. Gay men also assembled in elegant men's bars like the Oak Room in the Plaza and, most famously, at the Astor, on Seventh Avenue at 45th Street. A red tie was sometimes worn as a secret signal, as well as matching tie and handkerchief ensembles. The balcony at the Sutton Theater was extremely active, and for a time a matron was employed to warn the patrons of incoming policemen.

The protocol at the Astor suggested the need for extreme discretion when wealthier gay men mingled with the rest of society. At the Astor's oval bar, gay men gathered on one side, heterosexuals on the other. While heterosexual patrons could touch each other as much as they wanted, whenever the gay customers became slightly outlandish, the bar's managers would immediately warn them to tone down their behavior.

Discretion was also the watchword within all of society's fancier families. "The sexual scene I'm sure was exactly the same, but it was much more discreet," said "Stephen Reynolds" (a pseudonym), the son of a wealthy New England manufacturer who first started visiting Manhattan in the late 1930s. Reynolds's family was extremely rich, and his father was unaffected by the Crash.

At the Choate School, Reynolds was in the same form as John Kennedy. "Nobody liked him very much," Reynolds recalled. "I wasn't crazy about him personally. But if I had known he was going to be president, I would have been so nice to him. It never crossed our mind. We voted him 'Most Likely to Succeed' because his father was ambassador to Great Britain, and we naturally thought, Well, he'll be taken care of. But we never dreamed he would be president. He was very loud and — I don't like to use the word, but I'm going to — very *common*. My family background is New England, and you know what they thought of the Kennedys. They thought they were pushy Irish. He had kind of fire engine hair — it all flew around — and he had a roommate called Lemoyne Billings." Billings, who happened to be gay, remained close to John and Bobby Kennedy all his life.

Before the war Reynolds used to come to New York from Yale for the weekend with $30, which would pay for a luxurious interlude. "On that, I would stay at the hotel, go to the theater, go up to Harlem. A restaurant was $1.25. A *good* restaurant. The Ambassador Hotel on Park Avenue charged me $7.50 a night for a nice room. And you'd go back with $2 or $3.

"We went to the Stork Club because Sherman Billingsley was so thrilled to have the college crowd that he didn't charge you anything. There was a band. And there was a thing called the Cub Room, which always had Walter Winchell in it and stars of the stage. The Cub was where you went if you didn't want to hear the music. We never sat there because we wanted to be where the band was.

"There were one or two extraordinary characters who maybe went so far as to wear natural nail polish, which we thought was terribly daring," Reynolds recalled. "Or they might wear a slightly outré shirt. But there were certain subjects one just didn't talk about. You just said, 'Oh, you know, he's difficult.' Or 'The family is having problems with him.' You certainly didn't say, 'He wears an evening dress,' I can tell you that."

Fifty years later, Reynolds was nostalgic for the understatement of the thirties and forties. "People didn't shove it down your throat," he remembered. "When I see two boys walking down the street holding hands, it doesn't offend me; I don't care if they walk around naked. But liberation carried to such an extent to where there's no law at all — I don't see how you can get the full enjoyment of it. It seems to me that there are no rules today at all. You can pretty much do what you want. Thank God there are a few people who have a little sense of manners and decency. But, by and large, people are sleeping together when they're fifteen and sixteen. I mean, that was unheard of in my day. If you had a girl who spent the night, you practically put a maid in the same room with her. I just wonder whether the kind of fun we had would be gone, if you're just permitted to do anything you want to."

Jack Dowling was a teenager in the forties. He had first gotten caught fooling around with another boy in the first grade. "We were at that early age when we knew it was something mysterious. It didn't occur to me that it was an inclination; it seemed perfectly natural. I knew it was a no-no for some reason, but I thought it was a no-no because of the sex, not because it was with another boy. I just thought you weren't supposed to have any kind of sex, or touch anyone, boy or girl."

The painter Paul Cadmus felt "the naiveté of the public was a great benefit if one didn't want to be exposed. I don't think I ever worried about exposure exactly — although I like reticence and I don't like flaunting. But then the world has gotten much more extreme.

"There were never magazines like *Screw*," Cadmus continued. "The only gay publication that I knew in those days was published in Switzerland, called *Der Kreis/Le Cercle*. It was bilingual; I think it had French and English. It published some of my drawings and paintings. George Platt Lynes used the pseudonym Roberto Rolf when the magazine published his photos. It printed very good art and had very good stories — not necessarily very gay things but generally homoerotic, I suppose. Not porn. It was quite a charming magazine actually. I would send them photographs of my drawings. It was mailed in a plain wrapper, but it was not junk. I think they published Thomas Mann."

"James Atcheson" (a pseudonym) left Harvard in 1938 to become a Broadway actor. "I grew up and came out in the theater, and there was a lot of it going on. I think the theater was perhaps less subterranean because it really didn't matter as long as you showed up on time for rehearsals and you were fun and you were talented. I don't think anyone gave a damn about people's private lives. They knew it maybe, or suspected it, but it didn't *really* matter. But you didn't go down wearing signs."

And any obvious gay reference on stage was quickly criticized by reviewers — and would continue to be, for the next thirty years. When Rodgers and Hart's *By Jupiter* opened in the fall of 1942, Richard Watts, Jr., was generally enthusiastic in the *Herald Tribune*. But he included this caveat: "What seems to me infinitely wearying [and] infinitely annoying is the attempted humor that is supposed to spring from homosexuality and kindred forms of degeneracy." He found those quips "dirty and offensive" and "the kind of thing that we might very well do without."

One of Atcheson's first acting jobs was in the Chicago company of *The Man Who Came to Dinner*, which starred Clifton Webb. "Webb was playing the part that Monty Woolley played in New York," Atcheson recalled. "I'm sure everyone knew about Clifton, but he would have been mortally offended if anyone said, 'You silly fag.' Nobody did that. One's private life was private. I think it was a little bit like that thing Mrs. Patrick Campbell said: 'My dear, I don't care what people do as long as they don't do it in the street and frighten the horses.' I think a lot of people in New York felt that way about their homosexual friends. I think that meant: don't be a roaring faggot and don't be a roaring bull dyke because that's offensive — not because of the direction of the sex drive, but because it's not subtle."

Atcheson was put off by some of the things the men he met wanted to do in bed — a sentiment he shared when he first met the legendary Tallulah Bankhead. "Oh God!" she replied. "I know just what you mean. After all, I've tried everything. If I go down on a man it chokes me and if I go down on a woman it gags me. If I get buggered it hurts me like hell and if I get fucked it gives me acute claustrophobia. So I've just gone back to reading, love!"

Shortly before the war, a young Harvard undergraduate named Leonard Bernstein made one of his first visits to Manhattan. On November 14, 1937, Aaron Copland, the great gay American composer, invited the budding musician to a birthday party at his New York loft on West 63d Street. The room was filled with gay and bisexual intellectuals, including Paul Bowles (then known only as a composer) and Virgil Thomson. When Copland learned that Bernstein loved his *Piano Variations,* he dared the Harvard boy to play them. "It'll ruin the party," said Bernstein. "Not *this* party," Copland replied, and the guests were mesmerized by Bernstein's performance.

During the next decade, Copland would become an important father figure for Bernstein, as well as his composition adviser. One of Bernstein's biographers, Humphrey Burton, believes Bernstein and Copland may also have been lovers. "He taught me a tremendous amount about taste, style and consistency in music," Bernstein said of his mentor. So many important New York musicians were gay, one wit dubbed the American Composers League the Homintern. Bernstein's exposure to gay life in Manhattan over the next couple of years convinced him that not everyone felt guilty about being homosexual, although he himself remained undecided about his ultimate orientation. Twenty years later, Bernstein would collaborate with three gay men to produce one of the most extraordinary Broadway musicals of all time.

THE DEGREE OF PROTECTION some American aristocrats enjoyed in the forties was demonstrated most dramatically by Sumner Welles, a confidant of FDR's (and a page boy at his wedding) who became undersecretary of state in 1937. Roosevelt relied on Welles as his main ally at the State Department, an arrangement that enraged Welles's superior, Secretary of State Cordell Hull.

In the fall of 1940, Welles was part of a huge Washington delegation that attended the Alabama funeral of House Speaker William Brockman Bankhead (Tallulah's father), who had died of a heart attack on September 15. On the special train back to Washington, Welles got very drunk and then

retired to his compartment. There, he repeatedly rang for the black porters attending the passengers and made brazen advances at several of
them.

One of the porters complained to his employer, the Southern Railway
Company, which was headquartered in Philadelphia. William Bullitt, who
had been FDR's ambassador to France, lived in Philadelphia. He heard the
story and immediately started to spread it. Bullitt was a friend of Hull and
an enemy of Welles, and he viewed Welles's indiscretion as the perfect
opportunity to get rid of the undersecretary.

Roosevelt too had heard rumors about the train incident and asked FBI
Director J. Edgar Hoover to investigate. In January 1941, Hoover made his
report to the White House: "Mr. Welles had propositioned a number of
the train crew to have immoral relations with them."

When Bullitt visited the president to urge him to fire Welles, Roosevelt
acknowledged the accuracy of the allegations against the State Department man. But he refused to do anything about them. He told Bullitt there
would be no publicity because the story was too scandalous to print. He
also said Welles would never behave this way again because he had taken
the precaution of assigning a bodyguard to watch over him day and night.
Bullitt said Hull considered Welles "worse than a murderer," but the
president insisted that he still needed his old friend at State.

Frustrated by Roosevelt's recalcitrance, Hull and Bullitt leaked the story
of Welles's indiscretion to a Republican senator, R. Owen Brewster of
Maine. Brewster then went to Roosevelt's attorney general and threatened
to hold hearings on the matter unless Welles was fired. Roosevelt could
not hold out any longer, and Welles announced his resignation on September 25, 1943, three years after the original incident.

Although the facts of the case were whispered about throughout Washington, the press never reported them. Apparently Roosevelt had been
right: the lurid details of what had happened were literally too scandalous
to print. Newspapers attributed Welles's resignation to his rift with the
secretary of state.

But Roosevelt never forgave Bullitt for forcing the resignation of his
friend. When Bullitt approached the president later to ask him to support
his run for mayor in Philadelphia, Roosevelt was furious: "If I were the
angel Gabriel and you and Sumner Welles should come before me seeking
admission into the Gates of Heaven, do you know what I'd say? I would
say: 'Bill Bullitt, you have defamed the name of a man who toiled for his
fellow men, and you can go to hell. And that's what I tell you to do now.'"

While a very famous man might occasionally enjoy the protection of his president, homosexuals barely had any public advocates in the forties. Even Roosevelt was not consistently broad-minded on this issue. When New York newspapers reported in 1942 that Senator David I. Walsh had allegedly visited a male brothel near the Brooklyn Navy Yard, Roosevelt told Senator Alben Barkley that the army handled this sort of thing by discreetly offering an offending officer the opportunity to commit suicide.

The National Association for the Advancement of Colored People was already well established, and some northern college campuses witnessed civil rights demonstrations protesting the treatment of African Americans, but gays remained outside any liberal's agenda — and remained there for the next three decades. Virtually every politician considered their orientation unspeakable and their cause indefensible. As a result, when the New York State Liquor Authority declared that the mere presence of homosexuals in a bar made it disorderly — and bar owners posted signs reading "If You Are Gay, Please Stay Away" — no one even tried to challenge them.

Before the Second World War it was easy to grow up in America without ever seeing any public reference to gay people. This invisibility was the sad product of society's toxic prejudice and a persistent self-hatred among homosexuals. "Biblical condemnations of homosexual behavior suffused American culture from its origin," the historian John D'Emilio observed. "A society hostile to homosexual expression shaped the contours of gay identity."

A SPECTACULAR BEEKMAN HILL murder case mesmerized the readers of Manhattan's tabloids in the fall of 1943. Fifty years before a young Virginia manicurist mutilated her husband, John Wayne Bobbit, with an eight-inch butcher knife, a similar act of passion produced one of Manhattan's most celebrated homicides — a case "so sordid," *Newsweek* reported, that "it shocked even the hardened police."* It also sparked the earliest extended discussion of homosexuality in the history of New York newspapers — including what *Time* magazine thought was the very first use of the word *homosexual* on the front page of *The New York Times*.†

Wayne Thomas Lonergan, "a tall, powerfully built and undeniably handsome youth" from Toronto, arrived in New York in 1939 at the age of twenty-one "with no more equipment than his good looks," according to

---

*The Inquiring Fotographer of the *Daily News* polled men in the street and got a unanimous reply: they would rather read about murder than about war news. (*Newsweek*, November 8, 1943)
†*Time* was mistaken. According to the Walt Whitman biographer David S. Reynolds, the *Times* started using the word homosexual in 1926. (*New York Times Book Review*, May 14, 1995)

a contemporary account. Almost immediately, he found a job pulling a rickshaw at the world's fair, a period perquisite for anyone too rich to explore the Flushing Meadow fairgrounds on foot. One of his first customers was William Burton, the forty-three-year-old playboy son of a Manhattan brewer who had accumulated a $7 million fortune. Once they had met, *Newsweek* noted, "Lonergan no longer worried about a job" and the two men quickly became "intimate companions."

Burton had attended the Yale School of Fine Arts and the Art Students League. He called himself a portrait painter, but he spent most of his time depleting his father's fortune. "He was a gay one," the *Journal-American* reported: "Cannes, Biarritz, San Sebastian — those were his playgrounds." Another article said he was "known to have lent several young men a helping hand." In Cannes, Burton had employed a Georgian prince as his chauffeur.

Unfortunately for Lonergan, his patron was in frail health. Barely a year after they met, Burton died of heart failure in his Ritz Tower apartment. Faced with imminent separation from Burton's fortune, Lonergan made a dramatic shift in his affections: he became the fervent suitor of his dead lover's daughter, Patricia.

Presumably because she had learned about Lonergan's affair with her deceased husband, Patricia's mother violently disapproved of this union, and she spirited her daughter off to California. But Lonergan followed both of them to the coast. In the summer of 1941, just four months before the bombing of Pearl Harbor, they eloped to Las Vegas.

Their marriage produced one son and endless rows, as Lonergan continued to see at least one wealthy male friend on the side. Less than a year after their marriage, Wayne and Patricia separated, and Wayne was cut out of her will. Lonergan tried to join the army, but he was classified 4-F after his draft board decided he was gay. Then he returned to his native Canada, where he managed to enlist as a cadet in the Royal Canadian Air Force.

On October 23, 1943, Lonergan flew to New York on a weekend pass. He stayed out all night Saturday and well into Sunday, club-hopping. Separately, his estranged wife Patricia did the same, arriving home at 6:00 A.M. after stops at El Morocco and several other watering holes. The *Times* reported that she wore a mink jacket, a black silk dress, black hat, nylon hose and black shoes. Her companion for the evening was one Mario Enso Gabelline, a forty-three-year-old man-about-town who later confided to New York detectives that he enjoyed beguiling married women by turning a "neat souffle," or making them "exceptional salads," an art he had "highly developed."

When Patricia got home, "She had torn off her girdle with her nylon hose still attached and had thrown them on the crescent-shaped chaise longue at the foot of her massive Empire bed," according to Meyer Berger's extraordinarily detailed account in the *Times*. At 8:45 on Sunday morning, Lonergan climbed the stoop of Patricia's "lavish" triplex at 313 East 51st Street. "It was quiet in Fifty-first Street, the quiet of the Sabbath," Berger reported. "The front door was open. Lonergan ascended the common stair case. The carpets took up his footfalls. He knocked at the master bedroom door. Mrs. Lonergan heard him and opened the door for him."

What happened next was never reported by the *Times*. But the unprintable details of Lonergan's confession quickly became known in all the better-connected boudoirs in Manhattan. In his obituary forty-three years after the crime, the *Times* reported only that "he admitted he had killed his estranged wife while she was inflicting 'great physical pain' on him" — but even that detail was omitted from contemporary accounts. The estranged couple fell into bed, where passion quickly turned into uncontrolled violence. While performing fellatio on her husband, Patricia tried to bite off his penis. Lonergan responded by attempting to strangle her. When Patricia began to gouge his face with her fingernails, he grabbed a huge candlestick and bludgeoned her to death. "I was in the army when that case broke," Gore Vidal recalled. "We thought it was a lot of fun in the military."

Although his uniform was covered with blood, Lonergan managed to return to the friend's apartment where he was staying for the weekend without attracting anyone's notice — not even the nanny who was in charge of his one-year-old son in the room next to his wife's bedroom, or the upstairs neighbor who nearly knocked when she heard "shrill screams" coming out of Patricia's bedroom, but instead decided to continue downstairs to the front stoop to retrieve the Sunday papers.*

Lonergan ordered breakfast from the servant at his host's East 79th Street apartment, but, lacking an appetite, he hid his unfinished plate in a corner sideboard, where it was later discovered. After the meal he went upstairs to apply make-up to the scars inflicted by his wife during their struggle. Then he cut up his blood-splattered uniform. He packed it in a bundle with a barbell borrowed from his host, then hopped on the 79th

---

*"I raised my hand to knock and then I thought better of it," Analise Schoenberg testified at Lonergan's trial. "The knowledge that this witness had stood within only a few feet of where Mrs. Lonergan was fighting for her life, and did not know it, seemed to awe the court room listeners," Meyer Berger reported in *The New York Times*, March 29, 1944.

Street bus to the East River. There he hurled the incriminating clothing into the Hell's Gate current. It was never recovered.

The murderer fled to Toronto, where he insisted he was innocent. New York detectives teased him back to Manhattan by promising him a visit with his infant son. In custody he offered what the police described as a "degrading" alibi to explain his uniform's disappearance: early Sunday morning he had picked up a soldier named "Maurice Worcester" and taken him to the apartment where he was staying for the weekend. When Lonergan made a pass at him, the soldier scratched his face. Then Worcester stole his uniform.

The alibi collapsed when the real Maurice Worcester appeared at the station house. Reacting to the relentless goading of his fellow factory workers, Worcester — a "respectable" married man with a wife and two children, who said he knew of no one else with his name — had come to clear himself of Lonergan's libel.

When Worcester was led into the room where Lonergan was being interrogated, the suspect showed no sign of recognition. "Have you ever seen this man before?" the assistant district attorney inquired.

"No," the befuddled suspect replied. Then Worcester's identity was announced. An hour later, Lonergan broke down and confessed. "After more than four days of merciless grilling, half-hysterical and trembling, the sex-twisted Cafe Society playboy admitted strangling [Patricia] to death, then bludgeoning her with a massive candlestick," the *Journal-American* reported. "'Yes. I did it! I did it!' he shouted in the District Attorney's office."

The victim's great grandfather, Frederick Housman, was philosophical about the tragedy. "You can't keep your eye on children and grandchildren and great-grandchildren all the time," he told the *New York Post*. "When they marry, one's responsibility ceases to some extent."

In its first story mentioning Lonergan's orientation, the *Times* reported on the top of the front page that Worcester had been unmercifully teased because Lonergan, "openly labeled in newspapers as 'homosexual' and 'bisexual,' pinned his murder alibi on a 'Maurice Worcester.' . . . The prosecutor's staff made a fine distinction in Lonergan's make-up after his confession. 'Bisexual would seem a better word,'" said the prosecutor.

With so many "sordid" details essential to the story, a fiercely competitive press could no longer resist the temptation to discuss what had hitherto been unmentionable. "For the first time in its haughty history," the paper of record "let words like *homosexuality* creep into its columns,"

Time magazine mistakenly reported. Two days after Lonergan's confession, Hearst's *Journal-American* printed a lengthy feature to clarify this perplexing condition for its "normal" readers. The article, which bore no byline, suggests the popular wisdom in 1943. Like most pieces published on the subject during the next twenty-five years, it gave a lurid picture of a deeply threatening sexual minority:

PSYCHIATRISTS GIVE VIEWS ON LONERGAN
REFER TO HISTORY IN DISCUSSION OF CHARACTER

Throughout the pattern of the Lonergan murder case are woven the deep purple threads of whispered vices whose details are unprintable and whose character in general is unknown to or misunderstood by the average normal person.

Well known, however, to both history and psychiatrists are the types of some individuals whose presence in the Beekman Hill slaying resulted in a rash of such loosely applied expressions as "twisted sex."

In the standard popular histories the activities of these individuals are glossed over, the damage they have done to numerous civilizations merely incorporated with descriptions of broader social declines.

And in the current history of our day, because of the sordid nature of the facts, little public light is shed upon the social cancer feeding in our midst.

Yet it is there, in all walks of life, a monster whose growth always prefaces social collapse of one kind or another — whether in ancient Rome or pre-Hitler Germany.

To present the fundamentals of the danger, a survey of opinion and analysis was sought from the city's outstanding psychiatrists.

Reluctant to be quoted individually, differing extensively on precise phraseology involved, all agreed on the following basic facts and conclusions.

Generally speaking and contrary to a popular conception, persons who engage in unnatural relationships with others of their own sex are not all of the same type although the law makes no distinction.

To experts in the medical profession, one of the two basic types is nothing more or less than a moral leper, deserving of condemnation because his actions are largely the result of his own decision.

This type, known as a bi-sexual or pervert, is a degenerate in the moral sense. While he can be helped at times by psychoanalytical treatment, his real cure depends upon his own desire to behave normally.

Such persons — both men and women — have nothing distinctive about their physical appearance or public behavior to set them apart. They are frequently very attractive to persons of the opposite sex.

Included in the type are often married persons, of the so-called sophisticated set. Possessed of too much money, jaded by normal activities, they turn to the unnatural for diversion.

Although married and frequently the parents of children, this type, when moneyed, spread their evil frequently through the adoption of "proteges," younger people willing to corrupt themselves in exchange for money and social position.

The latter, in turn, continue the cycle of degeneracy by either attracting imitators or seeking to corrupt others.

Because this basic type usually does have money and leadership, the behavior of its members tends to become a more or less accepted part of society, particularly in world centers like New York City.

Placed beyond the law through position, clever, unscrupulous, contemptuous of decent people, their influence is sinister and profound. No accurate estimate on their number can be determined.

Those of the second basic type, from a medical viewpoint, are far more to be pitied than condemned, are in need of treatment rather than the imprisonment so many receive.

Members of this type are known as sex inverts, or sex-variants, and are degenerate in the physical rather than the moral sense. Such persons are beyond self-help when their cases are pronounced.

The cause of their condition is widely believed to be an upset in the normal secretion into the blood stream of hormones governing secondary sexual characteristics and behavior.

All persons have both female and male hormones in their blood streams, with the more female hormones present, the more feminine the individual and vice versa. Great variations occur. When these variations reach a danger point, a person of one sex will begin to think, feel and act almost entirely like one of the opposite.

In such physiological disturbances, men will develop mincing walks, unnatural timidity and feminine emotions while women similarly affected become rough, aggressive and impatient of such womanly attributes as long hair.

These, then, were the words and phrases associated with homosexuality: "vice," "damage," "social cancer," "monster," "unnatural," "moral leper," "pervert," "degenerate," "evil," "unscrupulous," "contemptuous of decent people," and "sinister."

The piece neatly summarized the panoply of prejudices facing lesbians and gays a quarter of a century before the beginning of the modern gay liberation movement. And its class distinctions were a malignant version of Otis Bigelow's view of the wealthy world in which he lived. The assertion that "because this basic type usually does have money and leadership, the behavior of its members tends to become a more or less accepted part of society" suggests just how much protection wealthier gays did enjoy in Manhattan, as long as they remained discreet. Finally, the veiled reference to the gay liberation movement in pre-Nazi Germany (and its alleged connection to the rise of Hitler) is another typical refrain. Writing a year earlier in the *Herald Tribune,* Richard Watts, Jr., decried *By Jupiter*'s "dubious joking about sexual decadence, which the Germans, too, used to think was funny when Hitlerism was being born."

A few months later, *Time* echoed the *Journal-American.* The news weekly ran a picture of Lonergan above the caption "Was he born or made?" *Time* opined, "Contrary to popular legend, homosexuals are not necessarily physically abnormal, though sometimes a glandular disturbance is involved." Seduction in childhood is "the commonest precipitating cause. Other causes: 1) a tendency to varied and primitive sexual outlets; 2) an inherited tendency . . . Lonergan would seem to fall into the varied and primitive sexual outlet group."

"The majority of people just thought we were the worst characters in the world," remembered William Wynkoop, who was twenty-seven in 1943. "But among those who were enlightened, we were sick. Sick and abnormal."

On April 17, 1944, Lonergan was sentenced to thirty-five years to life in prison. After he was sent to Sing Sing he tried to get access to his wife's estate, but a surrogate judge ruled that because of his life sentence he was "civilly dead." During his first few years in prison, Lonergan sent humorous Christmas cards to his former gentleman callers. Ten years after Lonergan went to jail, his twelve-year-old son, who changed his name to William Anthony Burton, inherited $7 million from the estate of his great-grandfather, Max Bernheimer. In 1965, Lonergan challenged his confession on the grounds that it had been coerced. He testified that someone whom he could not see had repeatedly struck the back of his head with the heel of a hand during the ten hours preceding his confession. He also said he was "appalled" by the publicity describing him as a homosexual and had agreed to plead guilty to manslaughter in exchange for a promise that the nasty leaks to the press would end. Lonergan said he "made up" his confession because an assistant district attorney told him it was required to get a judge to accept the manslaughter plea, but once he had signed the incriminating statement, the promises of leniency were forgotten. In 1967, he was paroled and immediately deported to Canada. He died of cancer in Toronto in 1986.

THE IDEA that some forms of homosexuality were caused by hormonal imbalances was widely accepted before the war. Roy Strickland, a native of Huntington, Long Island, was twenty in 1938 when his sister decided he needed medical treatment. "Just after I'd graduated from high school I'd gotten a job as a beach attendant at this club in Huntington and met this very attractive young chap who was five years younger than I," Strickland recalled. "And one rainy Saturday, Morton and I had gone to the movies, and I was holding hands with him up in the balcony. My sister came into the theater, and that night she came up to my room.

"'Roy,' she said, 'what does this mean? I saw you holding hands with Morton in the movies.'

"Well, I told her," Strickland continued. "I said I was very fond of this fellow and we liked to be together. We'd had no sex yet, but we loved to be together. We'd walk along the beach at night singing popular songs and go skinny dipping and that sort of thing.

"She said, 'I think you need some help.' So she arranged for me to go to a doctor who had arrived in Huntington from Hitler's Austria. He heard my story, and he said, 'Roy, I will advise you to stop seeing this chap, cultivate the friendship of girls, and I'm going to give you male sex hormones.' Which he did. For six sessions, my sister paying twenty-five bucks a session, which she could ill afford. In those days it was a hell of a lot of money.

"This was the standard procedure. He was going to turn me from a homosexual into a heterosexual by sticking that damn thing up my rear end. So, after six sessions I finally went to my sister, and I said, 'Look, this is doing me *absolutely* no good. It's only making me hornier.' And she didn't even know what the word meant. But I did stop the shots."

Long before he met Morton, Strickland knew he was gay: like so many other men and women he was aware that he was different from most of his friends at a very early age. "I knew it from when I was three or four or five years old. I used to love to try my mother's hats on and go up in the attic and put on old dresses that she had. And I enjoyed playing with the girls on the block rather than baseball with the boys. In high school, I didn't go out for baseball or football or basketball. I went out for tennis and loved to swim.

"I always knew I was gay and I didn't fight it. While I was still in high school, a chap who lived two doors above us — this fellow was a *real* basketball star and track star — came one day, and said, 'Roy, do you want to go up in the woods and shoot some crows?'

"He had a BB gun. So we went into the woods, and we didn't shoot any crows. But we had sex, and it was absolutely incredible! Then he said, 'Would you like to meet me at the doctor's one evening?'

"I said, 'Sure,' and he told his family he was going to the library.

"He was a bit older. And I went down and met him at the house of a doctor who was there in Huntington. I did this fairly often that winter, and it was quite an experience. Because the doctor had been married, had children. His wife had died, and his family had moved away. But he loved to entertain young men.

"He did not participate in it. He stood by the bed and told us what to do. And supplied Vaseline. Simply incredible experience. We went about once a week. That was my visit to the library in the evenings. It was really quite amazing.

"And then I learned from this chap that I was not the only one he was taking down there. He was taking four other guys, two of whom were basketball stars in high school. Simply amazing. Later I heard that this guy had married and fathered a couple of children — this guy who had taken me to the doctor's."

NOTHING WOULD HAVE a greater impact on the future shape of gay life in America than the explosive growth of the United States Army during World War II. Six months after the Japanese attack on Pearl Harbor, 14,000 men were entering 250 different training centers every day. The wartime draft* pulled all kinds of men together from every hamlet and metropolis. The army then acted like a giant centrifuge, creating the largest concentration of gay men inside a single institution in American history. Volunteer women who joined the WACS and the WAVES enjoyed an even more prevalent lesbian culture.

The army's attitude toward homosexuals during World War II created a new kind of official stigmatization. But it also provided gay men and lesbians with a dramatic new vision of their diversity and ubiquity. To a few, it even suggested how powerful they might one day become.

The combination of friendship and discrimination experienced by homosexuals in uniform created one of the great ironies of gay history: this mixture made the United States Army a secret, powerful, and unwit-

*Actually enacted by Congress at FDR's request in September 1940

ting engine of gay liberation in America. The roots formed by this experience would nourish the movement that finally made its first public appearance in Manhattan twenty-four years after the war was over. World War I did not have a comparable effect because it was not the same kind of mass experience in America; by the end of our relatively brief involvement in Europe, only 1,200,000 American troops were stationed in France. During World War II, about twenty million Americans were in uniform.

World War II gnawed away at all kinds of ancient taboos. Most importantly, although it was fought with a religious fervor, this conflict probably did more to loosen the religious constraints on a puritan society than any previous event. And for many who came of age in this era, the awesome force of the atomic bomb encouraged the notion that twentieth-century man was now just as powerful as God. The war would also give the generation that fought it an extraordinary sense of accomplishment — a feeling that bordered on nobility — since the Nazi defeat was universally viewed as a magnificent achievement.

Because the war brought women into factories and offices for the first time in large numbers to replace the men who departed for the front, it was at least as important to the eventual liberation of women as it would be to the liberation of gays. The overwhelming success of women who became workers and soldiers, and gay men who became warriors, proved the falseness of centuries-old stereotypes.

To win their rightful place inside the armed forces, gay men theoretically had to evade a whole new set of barriers. Before 1940, the army and navy had only prosecuted acts of sodomy, rather than attempting a systematic exclusion of homosexuals from their ranks. It was only after the beginning of the draft in 1940 that the psychiatric profession began a campaign to convince the Selective Service System to perform psychiatric as well as physical examinations of all draftees.

In *Coming Out Under Fire,* a superb study of homosexuals who served in the American military during the Second World War, Allan Bérubé reports that the psychiatric establishment used an economic argument to convince the War Department of the need for psychiatric screenings. The government had spent more than $1 billion caring for the psychiatric casualties of World War I; in 1940, these victims still occupied more than half the beds in veterans hospitals.

On the eve of the Second World War, three members of the American Psychiatric Association's Military Mobilization Committee became the key advisers to army generals on this question. Winfred Overholser, Harry

Steckel, and Harry Stack Sullivan, coeditor of the journal *Psychiatry,* argued that the country could save millions by excluding potential psychiatric cases before they became patients in veterans wards. Sullivan was extremely well known and widely admired within the Washington psychiatric community. He also happened to be a gay man who lived with his lover in Bethesda, Maryland.

Thus began an unholy alliance between the War Department and psychiatry, a specialty still disdained by much of the medical profession. The war provided psychiatrists with a unique opportunity for legitimization: the official imprimatur of the federal government. This affiliation would help them shed their reputation as members of a fey discipline. Now they would be able to act as robust patriots, eager to prevent the encroachment of perverts on the nation's armed forces.

Ironically, Sullivan's original plan for psychiatric screening did not include any reference to homosexuality. Understandably, Sullivan believed homosexuals should be "accepted and left alone," a position that made him a dissident in his own profession. And Overholser tried to convince the military that homosexuals should be handled by psychiatrists rather than prison guards. "The emotional reaction of the public against homosexual activity is out of all proportion to the threat which it represents to personal rights, or even to public order," he told the navy. But Overholser also believed the public could not think rationally about the subject because it was "so overlaid with emotional coloring that the processes of reason are often obscured."

Unfortunately, as Bérubé explains, Sullivan and his colleagues "had carved out the territory on which others would build an antihomosexual barrier and the rationale for using it." Sullivan's belief in the relative insignificance of "sexual aberrations" in establishing mental illness was undermined as his plan was digested by the Washington bureaucracy. By the middle of 1941, the army and the Selective Service both included "homosexual proclivities" in their lists of disqualifying "deviations."

At a series of government-sponsored seminars at Bellevue Hospital in Manhattan in 1941, psychiatrists expanded on their theory of homosexuality as a mental illness. Homosexuality was discussed as "an aspect of three personality disorders: psychopaths who were sexual perverts, paranoid personalities who suffered from homosexual panic, and schizoid personalities" who displayed gay symptoms. In 1942, army mobilization regulations were expanded to include a paragraph entitled "Sexual Perversions." It was written by Lawrence Kubie, a Manhattan psychiatrist who was famous for his treatment of show business patients tormented by doubts about their sexual orientation — from Clifton Webb to Tennessee Williams and Moss Hart.

EVERY ARGUMENT made against the admission of lesbians and gays to the military in the nineties has its own echo in the forties, including the idea that effeminate men would become "subject to ridicule and joshing, which will harm the general morale and will incapacitate the individual for Army duty."

"Malingerers" were those who pretended to be gay to avoid duty at the front; "*reverse* malingerers" — a term invented by military psychiatrists — described gay recruits who pretended to be heterosexual so they could perform their patriotic duty. By 1943 doctors had devised the Cornell Selectee Index, which used "occupational choice" questions to screen out dancers, window dressers, and interior decorators because they would have difficulty with their "acceptance of the male pattern."

The media periodically spread this new official prejudice. The *Washington Star* noted that navy psychiatrists would "be on the lookout for any number of mental illnesses or deficiencies that would make the recruit a misfit," including homosexuality, and *Time* reported that "How do you get along with girls?" was one of the questions "machine-gunned" at the inductee during his physical.

These press reports produced all kinds of unlikely fears. When Murray Gitlin enlisted in the navy, he was "very afraid that they would undress me during the physical examination, and they'd know, looking at me, that I was gay. That's how innocent I was. Well they didn't — and they couldn't have cared less."

Two factors discouraged nearly all gay men from using their status as members of a sexual minority to avoid the military: the fear of a permanent stigma, because the reason for exclusion was recorded on draft records available to future employers, and an overwhelming desire to participate in the defining experience of a generation. Charles Rowland was drafted at the age of twenty-five. He knew "an awful lot of gay people, but nobody, with one exception, ever considered not serving. We were not about to be deprived of the privilege of serving our country in a time of great national emergency by virtue of some stupid regulation about being gay."

"Leo Aultman" (a pseudonym) was twenty-three in 1941; he enlisted eight months before the bombing of Pearl Harbor. "I wanted to go in," said Aultman, who grew up in Cincinnati and settled in Manhattan when the war was over. "You had real villains, and if you were Jewish, they were

sizable villains. And you had heroes. Roosevelt was a great man. And
Churchill was a great man. Also, it was *the* experience of my generation.
And I wanted to get away from home. It was a big deal to get away: a big
adventure.

"I remember a man who did get out while I was still in basic training,"
Aultman continued. "A man from Cincinnati, who got out based on
family need. He said, 'Sure I want to avenge Pearl Harbor.' But he wanted
out. He was not gay; he was a straight man who was a coward, who wanted
to make money, and who didn't want to be in the army. I thought he was
awful."

Aultman had been in love with a man named Alan for four years before
he went into the army: "There was no one ever more beautiful in my
whole life. *Ever!* I always felt very lucky to have attracted that man. He was
Nijinsky and I was Diaghilev. I was very lucky to have that leaper." After
Aultman enlisted, he and Alan got together one more time when Aultman
came home to Cincinnati for a twelve-day leave.

"We spent three days in a hotel room — a rather seedy hotel — and I
couldn't leave because if I were seen, I would be in terrible trouble with my
folks, who didn't know I was home yet. So I stayed in there with my
clothes off for three days, and he'd go down and sneak a sandwich. It was
just *heaven!* It was like being enslaved to this thing we were doing constantly. It was a total cure.

"The war was on now: it was 1942. I think there was a radio in the room,
but I don't think we listened. We had so much to talk about. We were very
idealistic. You know, it was Ingrid Bergman and Humphrey Bogart time
— *Casablanca.* We're going off, and we might never see each other again."

Two years later Alan was posted to Iceland and he sent Aultman a Dear
John letter. "I was in France," said Aultman. "Alan loved this person, and
what was he going to do? The man didn't even know about it. I was so
hurt. You know, *saving* myself! My eggs were all in his basket. I didn't write
him for a long time, but I kept getting letters. And then I got sick and I
wrote him. And I just wished him luck. I said, 'I can't talk to you. I just
can't!' All I wanted to do was to go back to big Al. And now I had nothing
to go back to."

Aultman became a captain by the end of the war, but unlike some other
veterans he never felt pride in his success as a gay man in the army. "Pride?
No. There was fear, uncertainty; also the feeling of not being quite fit for
what you were doing. You're softer; you didn't have the macho. I felt in
danger. I felt in jeopardy. I always felt vulnerable, that somebody might
catch up with me. I thought I was passing: softly passing. I couldn't drill as

well as anyone else, I wasn't as good on the athletic field or in the morning exercises. I could do other things. I excelled where I could excel. Here's a smart Jew — but he can't down the beers in the canteen, you know. I was considered snobbish — which I didn't really want to be. I didn't play craps; I didn't get into big poker games; and I didn't go out and fall down drunk. I felt I really didn't belong there in the army because I didn't have the muscles and I didn't have the mind-set for it. And I think maybe that's why I worked so hard — to stay with it, to hang in."

Those who got in generally fell into one of two categories: either they had long ago learned to mask their sexual identity in civilian life, or they were too young to have realized that they were gay. And despite the elaborate new regulations developed to discriminate against gays in the army, the only obstacle many of them encountered at the induction center was the "Do you like girls?" question.

George Buse remembered, "One of the worst of the stereotypes was the lie that all homosexuals are effeminate — and you're not really a man, you're more like a girl. So a lot of us at that time who were gay had to prove our manhood. So I joined the toughest, most masculine military organization in the country — and that was the Marine Corps. 'The Marine Corps builds men.'"

Of the eighteen million men examined for military service, fewer than five thousand were excluded because of their sexual orientation. No records were kept on the exclusion of lesbians. Once inside, many gay soldiers were astonished to discover how common their orientation was. Charles Rowland's first assignment was in the induction station at Fort Snelling, which was "instantly called the seduction station," he said. "I found that all of the people I had known in the gay bars in Minneapolis–St. Paul were all officers who were running this 'seduction station.' Recruits would be lined up by the thousands every morning outside our windows. All of us would *rush* to the windows and express great sorrow that all these beautiful boys were going to be killed or maimed or something in the war."

Aultman had met only one other gay man (besides Alan) during his first four years in the army. But then he visited Seventh Army Headquarters in Deauville, France, in 1945. "I never saw so many gays in my life as that weekend in Deauville," he recalled. "When I went to the theater, they were yoo-hooing and waving. It was incredible! A *flaming* crew of gays running that outfit." But he did not identify with them at all; their flamboyance made him uneasy. "I resented them. I did not want to be considered their equal. I'd been in the field. They'd been living a very soft life, probably with boas in their closet.

"On my way back I stopped to see Liechtenstein. I went to the movies and I met a *beautiful* soldier, who really didn't know I was after him. But we went for a walk in this gorgeous park. And I scored. Yeah. I got even with Alan again." Aultman's first gay experience with a stranger in uniform had taken place earlier when he was posted in California. "I was a second lieutenant and I took a four-day pass by myself to get laid. I went to Carmel, California. So lovely. And there was a whole crew of guys there from the cavalry. Which never went overseas because there was no need for a cavalry. But they looked great: jodhpurs and the boots and the whole thing. And there was one who eyed me and I eyed him, and he said he had a room.

"When we got there, he said he had to have ten dollars. I said, 'Oh?' He said, 'Well, I have a date tonight with a girl, so give me ten bucks. Okay?' And I said, 'All right' — because he was very attractive. And then he said, 'I'm not taking my boots off.' And I felt really cheap. He just lowered his trousers. And it was not mutual at all. I just did it and I hated it. And I had to wash afterward, and he said, 'Hey, if you want to go again, I'll get undressed for fourteen.' And I said, 'Not for *two* dollars.' And I left. I felt very demeaned. And I never paid again. Ever."

ALLAN BÉRUBÉ DISCOVERED that the extreme stress of battlefield conditions occasionally permitted gay men to express their affection for one another without any inhibition. Jim Warren's boyfriend was shot while trying to eliminate a machine-gun nest on Saipan.

"They brought him back and he was at the point of death. He was bleeding. He had been hit about three or four times. I stood there and he looked up at me and I looked down at him, and he said, 'Well, Jim, we didn't make it, did we?' And tears were just rolling down my cheeks. I don't know when I've ever felt such a lump and such a waste. And he kind of gave me a boyish crooked grin, and just said, 'Well, maybe next time.' I said, 'I'm going to miss you. And I'll see your mother.' There were maybe seven or eight people standing there, and I was there touching his hand and we were talking. Somebody said later, 'You were pretty good friends,' because I had been openly crying, and most people don't do this. I said, 'Yes, we were quite good friends.' And nobody ever said anything. I guess as long as I supposedly upheld my end of the bargain everything was all right."

Ben Small's boyfriend was hit moments after he said good night to him in his tent.

"This plane came overhead and all we heard was explosions and we fell to the ground. When I got up to see if he was all right, the thrust of the bomb had gone through his tent and he was not there. I went into a three-day period of hysterics. I was treated with such kindness by the guys that I worked with, who were all totally aware of why I had gone hysterical. It wasn't because we were bombed. It was because my boyfriend had been killed. And one guy in the tent came up to me, and said, 'Why didn't you tell me you were gay? You could have talked to me.' I said, 'Well, I was afraid to.' This big, straight, macho guy. There was a sort of compassion then."

On another occasion, Small witnessed an injured lieutenant being evacuated from the Philippines. The men "all went to the plane to see him off that night. It was an amazingly touching moment when he and his lover said good-bye because they embraced and kissed in front of all these straight guys and everyone dealt with it so well." It was "a little distilled moment out of time" when the men's prejudices were suspended and gay soldiers "could be a part of what this meant."

FOR THOSE WHO failed their physicals for the regular army but remained eager to participate in the war, the American Field Service provided an attractive alternative. Stephen Reynolds, who flunked his vision test, first learned about the Field Service through an article in *Life* magazine, which described its role as a volunteer ambulance corps for the Allies.

"I got in my car and I went down to the Ritz Hotel in Boston. Fortified by three martinis, I went into the lobby and dialed the State Department. Eventually I got a woman on the phone and I told her I wanted to inquire about the American Field Service. She said, 'Where are you calling from?' and I said, 'I'm calling from Boston.' She said, 'Where are you?' And I said, 'I am in the lobby of the Ritz Hotel.' And she said, 'Well, I come from Boston. Go out of the lobby, turn right, and about four houses down you'll find the AFS office.' It was three minutes from the Ritz. So I walked over, lurched up some stairs, and found an old man with a pad in front of him who asked my name. It turned out that he was a great friend of my father, so my application was accepted."

Many volunteers purchased their own ambulances: front-wheel drive

Chevrolets, which were indispensable equipment in the Egyptian desert. "The British army didn't have front-wheel drive. And they were crossing the desert. And they got stuck."

In January 1942, Reynolds boarded a ship in Manhattan. "Our destination was Egypt. The volunteers were kind of a mishmash — many 4-F who couldn't get into the American army, and a generous sprinkling of 'the boys.'

"We did all the front line work for the British army — *all of it*. We had the highest casualty rate of any organization in the Second World War. We were small, but we had the most captured and killed and wounded. My great friend Arthur Jeffries wallpapered his ambulance. It had all kinds of roses in it. He was part of a group affectionately known as the Taffeta Twelve. We wore uniforms, most of them custom-made. Many of us wore two or three gold identity bracelets. It was somewhat outrageous. That nut who wrote *Auntie Mame* was in: Patrick Dennis was his name. He was kind of boring. He got married to a very nice girl and then he ran off with a Mexican boy. He died in Mexico City, I think. That'll give you just a rough idea."

In the desert, there was terror and loneliness — and, Reynolds believed, something in the food to suppress the passions of troops cooped up in foxholes. "One day Cecil Beaton came out to photograph the troops. As he got out of the staff car, someone heard him remark,

"'My dear! It's beige!'

"We ate bully beef in vast quantities," said Reynolds. "I don't know how I lived through that sleeping in a foxhole in the desert with fleas and rats. The first day we got to the desert I modestly inquired about the lavatory facilities and they threw a shovel at me. We were allowed one pint of water a day, with which we had to wash, make tea, shave. You shaved in tea is what you did."

But then there was also rest and recreation in Cairo.

"When we were on leave, we lived like princes. You could stay at the Shepherd's Hotel for $5 a night in Cairo. And then drinks were cheap. There were twenty thousand troops in Cairo who were not allowed to sleep with the women because they would get syphilis — it was an army order! *You cannot!* Twenty thousand men would walk around two or three blocks — clomp, clomp, clomp. And it was like selecting a necktie: you just said, '*That* one.' We were terrible. There was a restaurant called Le Gavroche. It was a very good French restaurant. And the bar was adrift with guardsmen — Coldstream, Irish. And you'd say, 'What do you want?'

And for one pound — which was $5 — you could have anything you want. My God! We had a very good time. We laughed and screamed. I was miserable some of the time. I was terribly lonely. I was away too long.

"I had a lot of Egyptian friends. And the Egyptians all entertained every night. They had dances and parties and champagne and caviar. When you think the Germans were less than fifty miles away and the Egyptians lived as if they were on the edge of the volcano! You'd see Farouk, the king, all the time. He was a fat slob. He had an American girlfriend and I'm told he used to screw her in the swimming pool. I think that's probably true. I remember there was a woman called Princess Latfellah. She gave a huge dance — about three hundred of us — and she had a big tent. Suddenly she threw a switch and on every bloom in this huge garden there was a lightbulb. You would have thought we were in Paris. Caviar! You would have never thought there was war."

One of Reynolds's best friends in Egypt was Burt Shevelove, who later wrote the book for the Broadway musical *A Funny Thing Happened on the Way to the Forum.* "He was the loveliest man who ever lived. He had a sensational sense of humor. We used to call Hitler 'Helen.' And we'd be in the desert, and there'd be a lot of German planes, and we'd say, 'Helen's angry today. God, she's mad!' I remember one night we were walking down the streets of Cairo. And the king of Greece came toward us. He was plastered with medals, had a red band around his hat, and he had a fly whisk, which many of us did. And as we passed by, Burt said, 'Too much! Back to wardrobe!'"*

Later, Reynolds would serve in Italy, France, and Germany. "I worked with the Coldstream Guards for a couple of weeks. And they were the most wonderful boys. Mostly kids. They were all square. But we got to Perugia, and we were stationed in the Perugina chocolate factory. And the Coldstream were there. We were all walking through the streets. Then they saw a woman's hat shop, and they said, 'Let's go in.' And they all put on women's hats with their uniforms — just to be campy. So many of those wonderful boys were killed."

On leave in Paris, Leo Aultman was astonished when he found himself inside the Boeuf sur le Toit: "It was a *great* gay nightclub. Beef on the roof! You walked in, and suddenly you realized the *size* of homosexuality — the total global reach of it! There were hundreds of guys from all over the world in all kinds of uniforms: there were free Poles dancing with Ameri-

---

*Reynolds also heard about the Wayne Lonergan case while he was in Egypt because the names of several of his Manhattan friends appeared in Lonergan's address book — and all of them were contacted by the police after Lonergan's arrest.

can soldiers; there were Scotsmen dancing with Algerians; there were Free French; there were Russians. It was like a U.N. of gays. It was just incredible. I mean there were men dancing with each other! I had never seen that before in my *life!* There was lots of singing at the bar, and lots of arms around each other's shoulders. For me, it was sort of like a V-E Day for gays — before the real V-E Day."*

AROUND THE WORLD, the army's extensive sponsorship of drag shows was its most unlikely official encouragement of any aspect of gay culture. Though not every drag performer was gay, it gave those who were a secret opportunity to communicate with one another — and with their comrades-in-arms in the audience. James Atcheson played the heroine in *She Was More to Be Pitied Than Censured,* a showboat melodrama. "My God!" he recalled. "My dance card filled up very quickly. I said, 'Isn't this nice.'"

The army set up a special school at Fort Meade to promote theater arts for soldier entertainment. Its most successful production was the Irving Berlin all-soldier show, *This Is the Army,* which played a thousand performances in front of two and a half million GIs around the world. Then it became a movie with Ronald Reagan and George Murphy. "It has everything except girls," the *New York Herald Tribune* reported, "and the terrible truth is that you don't miss them."

Most ironically, the army sponsored numerous all-male productions of *The Women,* Clare Boothe Luce's brilliantly bitchy 1936 Broadway melodrama. Turned into a movie by the gay director George Cukor in 1939, *The Women* would be essential viewing for many gay men for the rest of the century. The cattiness of its characters made it a model for the camp culture embraced by one segment of gay male society. Mrs. Luce visited backstage with the cast of one of the army's all-male productions. The headline in *Life* (a magazine invented by Henry Luce at his wife's suggestion) read "MEN IN KHAKI TAKE OVER THE WOMEN."

"Despite their hairy chests, size-12 shoes and bulging biceps," the soldiers "did a good job with the play," *Life* reported. "This play shows that, after all, there is very little difference between men and women," Mrs. Luce told *Life's* correspondent. Naturally, the story made no reference to the gay subtext of the production, but the ten accompanying photographs captured it perfectly.

Arthur Laurents, who would become a celebrated playwright after the war, was a soldier at Fort Aberdeen, Maryland, when Mrs. Luce attended a

*Victory in Europe

performance. "I was wandering through the woods and I saw this sign. I can see it to this day, 'An All-Male Soldier Cast in John Frederic's Hats in *The Women.*'

"As I tell it, I sound sophisticated, but it was really like Alice in Wonderland down the rabbit hole," Laurents continued. "I could not believe any of this. They did *The Women* with all these guys and they had bras and they walked around in underwear and they had the big scene with Crystal in the bathtub. She stood up and had a jockstrap on. But it was done straight. The only one who wasn't was the one who played Sylvia, the Rosalind Russell role, who really was a bitch, and that was obviously the real McCoy. Even I knew that. But nobody said boo. And they played it very seriously: 'How dare you take my husband!' Clare Boothe Luce ran up on stage, took a bow, and said: 'Crystal has the prettiest back of any Crystal I've ever seen.' Of course I thought nobody in the world knew about this production but me. It never occurred to me that they would do anything like that. God! The army was a strange place."

Even Dwight David Eisenhower, the supreme commander of Allied Forces in Europe, put his official imprimatur on these transvestite performances. "You are not fighting with machine guns — but your job is just as important," he told the all-male cast of the Yard Bird Review in Algiers. "As long as you are doing your job well — and you are doing it extremely well — you will be rendering a service and a great one, to your fellow soldiers and your country."

BACK IN MANHATTAN, the steady influx of thousands of men and women in uniform created scores of new locales with homoerotic undertones — everywhere from the balconies of 42d Street moviehouses to six-year-old Franklin Macfie's living room on the Upper West Side. In 1943 young Franklin was living with six older sisters and three older brothers. "My sisters were all teenagers and older than teenagers during the war. It was very sexy to me because they were all so pretty. In my eyes, they all looked like Rita Hayworth and Betty Grable. They had tons of boyfriends, and the house was like the USO. There were always uniforms sitting in the living room waiting for the girls, and I was bounced on their knees, being as cute as I knew how to be."

Macfie also went to Central Park with his sisters: "The lawns were littered with absolutely lovely girls in summer dresses and sailors and soldiers, you know, lying and not quite making love but being very close to making love. Necking and so on. By the tennis courts, when I was very young, we often saw people fucking because the back of the tennis courts was very hidden." Dimouts and blackouts made the parks particularly amorous after dark.

JERRE KALBAS was twenty-four in 1942. She was working on the assembly line at the Ford Instrument Company in Queens, and she didn't know how to do "*anything* feminine. I couldn't carry a purse. I had a paper bag with my comb in it and my cigarettes in it and my change; I didn't even think to get an envelope." Then she met Patty, a professional dancer ten years her senior who looked a lot like Gertrude Lawrence — tall and slender — and they wore their hair the same way. At seventeen Patty was dancing all over Europe: "She even doubled for Garbo in *Mata Hari*. Garbo sent her roses. But Patty's mother sent them back."

Kalbas moved into Patty's house on Hicks Street in Brooklyn Heights, and often they dined out on popovers at Patricia Murphy's popular restaurant nearby. "Patty was a very bright girl. She could do anything! At the time we could get parachutes for $3. She took them and dyed them green. And those were our drapes in the apartment." Patty was also "ultrafeminine," and she went to work on Kalbas. "I was walking like a truck driver, and she was making me into a lady. There were no nylons available because of the war, and she taught me how to use make-up to draw stockings on my legs. She even drew the lines on her legs, but I wouldn't do that — that was going too far!"

The spirit of war opened lives up in all kinds of surprising ways. "People sort of did with their gay behavior what they did with everything else. Which was take chances and risks and try to enjoy things because who knows where you might be sent tomorrow," Stuart Loomis remembered. "Manhattan parties got to be a little bit wild," said Bob Ruffing, "because this war spirit was starting to invade everything."

"During the war, when I think of my own sleeping around, my hair stands on end," remembered the composer Ned Rorem. "The *thousands* of people I went to bed with! Much of that had to do with being a teenager, but it had to do with the war too. Although I was not in the army, I'm sure that had a lot to do with the military."

When Arthur Laurents was stationed in New York, he wrote radio propaganda for civilians. "New York in wartime was the sexiest city in the world," said Laurents. "*Everybody* did it — in numbers. And everybody drank. Bill Holden and I were in the army together, and on payday we'd have a contest to see who could drink the most martinis. And once I drank fifteen. Can you imagine that? I can't." During basic training, an MP made a pass at Laurents. "We did it, but I was terrified. I mean, it was like a cop.

And again, I was totally bewildered. And felt it was wrong. This is why later I went into analysis.

"There were two great bars in Manhattan," Laurents said. "The Oak Bar at the Plaza and the bar at the Savoy Plaza. Oh, the cream of the crop. All you had to do was just go. You wouldn't get in if you didn't have a uniform on. I felt guilty, I wanted to change — and I loved it. I never had so much sex in my life. It was incessant." Gore Vidal agreed: "Everybody was released by the war; people were doing things they hadn't dreamed of in the villages from whence they came. Under the right circumstances, everyone was available."

Donald Vining was a pacifist who admitted his homosexuality to his draft board because his mother needed his support, and he could not afford to be placed in a camp for conscientious objectors. Twenty-four years old when America joined the war, Vining kept a diary in which he recorded affairs with soldiers, sailors, marines, and civilians. Many of these encounters occurred at the Sloane House YMCA in Manhattan, where he worked as a desk clerk. In 1942, he wrote, "Just as I put on my robe to leave the shower room, in comes a nice-looking well-built boy. Something destroyed my usual timidity and I walked right up and ran my hands over him. 'Do you mind?' I asked, without a quaver in my voice. 'No,' he said casually, as he went on drying himself. I would have had him come to my room, but he had a double room with a fellow, who came to hunt him up."

In the forties, young men never felt any sense of menace on Manhattan streets or subways. "We never thought of such a thing," said Stephen Reynolds. "There was nobody sleeping on the streets. It was glamour without danger. We dressed, which is a simple thing. You never went to the theater unless you had a black tie on. And then if you went to the Stork Club and saw Gertrude Lawrence, you'd faint. A star!"

Reynolds also made frequent visits to Harlem to hear Lena Horne perform. "We would go to these nightclubs, with huge brass bands, and we'd be maybe six white people there and *six hundred* blacks, and nobody was nervous. We didn't feel like we didn't belong there. We would smell something funny, and people would say, 'That's a reefer.' We thought the musicians were all smoking it. But I never heard of anybody saying, 'Well, I'll try one.' Certainly not in my group."

HARLEM'S ANNUAL DRAG BALL at the Fun Makers Social Club was a hit in 1944. "The men who don silks, satins and laces for the yearly masquerades are as style-conscious as the women of a social club planning an annual charity affair or a society dowager selecting a debutante gown for her favorite daughter," *Ebony* magazine reported. "Lawyers, undertakers, truck drivers and dishwashers minced across the stage to compete for cash prizes." And at Lucky's Rendezvous, black and white men mingled happily in an atmosphere "steeped in the swish jargon of its many lavender customers." On upper Madison Avenue, the Mount Morris Baths in Harlem was already an interracial cruising spot, and it would remain popular for another four decades.

Philip Johnson found his first serious lover in Harlem — an extremely handsome café singer named Jimmie Daniels. Johnson met Daniels during one of his excursions uptown with the composer Virgil Thomson. The architect was enchanted by Daniels, whom he later referred to as "the first Mrs. Johnson." There would be three more "Mrs. Johnsons" after him.

Daniels was "a most charming man," Johnson recalled six decades later. "I still look back with greatest pleasure. I was the envy of all downtown. It was so chic in those days — it was what one did if one was really up to date. Those were the days when you just automatically went to Harlem. I had an older friend living in a midtown hotel, and he had an open Chrysler. And every evening when it was still light, we'd go up there. We knew that Harlem was the only place there was any freedom.

"We went to the house of an English lady who lived with a black actress — lesbians," Johnson continued. "And in that house Jimmie also lived as a boarder. So it was comfortable and familial. There was also a husband around. I'd spend the night there. I tried to have him downtown; it didn't work so well. They'd say, 'I'm sorry we're full tonight' — a totally empty dining room. Even in New York City in the 1930s."

"He was a beautiful, beautiful kid," Johnson recalled. "I was always interested in younger people." Daniels was eighteen and Johnson was twenty-five. The affair ended after a year: "A terrible man stole him away — who had better sex with him, I gather. But I was naughty. I went to Europe and I would never *think* of taking Jimmie along. I had rather an upper-lower-class feeling about him. I didn't realize it at the time, but it must have galled him. Everything that I was doing that was interesting, he wouldn't be included. Terrible way to treat anybody."

Virgil Thomson was so impressed by Jimmie Daniels's "impeccable enunciation" that he decided to write an opera "sung by Negroes." The result was *Four Saints in Three Acts,* with a libretto by Gertrude Stein.

Daniels had sung in clubs throughout Europe during the thirties, and he became a fixture of New York nightlife. In 1939, he opened Jimmie Daniels' at 114 West 116th Street, an establishment that *The New Yorker* described as a "model of dignity and respectability" by "Harlem standards." Ten years later Daniels was the host at the Bon Soir on West 8th Street, where "blacks and whites [and] gays and straights mingled without a trace of tension," according to the historian James Gavin. Barbra Streisand, Phyllis Diller, and Kaye Ballard all eventually performed there.

Johnson traveled to Germany regularly during Hitler's rise to power, and he became infatuated with the Nazis. Fifty years later, the architect said he had been attracted by the Third Reich's "general aura." His sympathies first became widely known in 1941 when William L. Shirer, a radio correspondent for CBS, published his *Berlin Diary,* an instant best-seller. Shirer wrote that the German Propaganda Ministry had forced him to share a double room at the Polish front in 1939 with "Phillip [*sic*] Johnson, an American fascist who says he represents Father Coughlin's *Social Justice.* None of us can stand the fellow and suspect he is spying on us for the Nazis."

One of Johnson's saviors was Lincoln Kirstein, who was at the center of New York's gay intellectual elite for more than half a century. Kirstein was the extremely wealthy heir to the Filene's department store fortune. He had been Johnson's contemporary at Harvard, where Kirstein started a literary quarterly, *Hound and Horn,* whose contributors included T. S. Eliot, Ezra Pound, Edmund Wilson, and E. E. Cummings. During the same period, he was also a founder of the Harvard Society for Contemporary Art, a precursor of the Museum of Modern Art in Manhattan. In 1933 he persuaded George Balanchine to leave Russia for America, and together they created what became the New York City Ballet.

In 1944 Kirstein wrote a "To Whom It May Concern" letter to try to bolster his friend's sagging reputation:

> I, Pvt Lincoln Kirstein, have known Pvt. Philip Johnson for fifteen years. When he left the Museum of Modern Art to join Huey Long, I did not speak to him again until a few months prior to my induction into the Army, February, 1943.
>
> In his most rabidly fascist [*sic*] days, he told me that I was number one on his list for elimination in the coming revolution. I felt bitterly towards him, and towards what he represented.
>
> Since being in the Army, I have seen Pvt Johnson frequently; both of us having been stationed at the Engineer Replacement Training Center,

Fort Belvoir, Va. I am convinced that he has sincerely repented of his former facist beliefs, that he understands the nature of his great mistake and is a loyal American . . .

I am a United States Citizen, born Rochester, N.Y. May 4th 1907. I am of Jewish origin.

This statement was not solicited by any person, and is made unknown to Pvt. Johnson.

Kirstein's letter is one of the earliest examples of the incipient "gay network" of Manhattan taking care of one of its own. Eventually, Kirstein would become famous as one of the most important art patrons of the twentieth century. His salon included W. H. Auden, Glenway Westcott, and Monroe Wheeler, among many others.

In 1937, he met the painter Paul Cadmus, who pioneered his own style of "magic realism." Cadmus believed Kirstein championed Johnson later on mostly because he thought he was a good architect. "Lincoln's always been very supportive of good art," said Cadmus, "even when it wasn't popular. He didn't give a damn about what other people liked."

When Kirstein met Cadmus, the talented painter had a gentle charm and a magnificent face, and many of their friends believed that Kirstein immediately fell in love with him. Cadmus said Kirstein fell in love with his *work*; in any event, the painter never reciprocated Kirstein's romantic feelings. "Quite soon after he met me, he met my sister," Cadmus remembered almost six decades later. "I think he met her twice, and then he came to see me one day, and he said 'Paul, I want to marry Fidelma.'

"'But you hardly know her,'" Cadmus replied. "'And she's not like me.'"

But Kirstein was insistent. "'I know what I want, I want to marry Fidelma.'"

"'Please don't suddenly surprise her like this,'" said Cadmus. But "very shortly afterwards," Kirstein took Fidelma to the Plaza and proposed to her, and she soon accepted, although the engagement spanned three years. The marriage lasted until Fidelma was institutionalized for mental illness many years later, but Kirstein continued to sleep with men all his life. Partly through Fidelma, he also kept Cadmus close to him until Kirstein died in 1996. Kirstein also bought many of Cadmus's canvases, and eventually wrote a book that was an homage to the painter's work. In the 1970s, Kirstein built Cadmus a house on the grounds of his Connecticut estate. There, Cadmus lived with his lover, Jon Andersson, and the two of them took care of dinners for Kirstein and his weekend guests every Saturday for years — sort of a friendly catering service.

"He had glamour of course," said Cadmus. "Very dynamic. He knew everybody. He used to have very good parties with people like Callas and Nelson Rockefeller." At a memorial service at the New York State Theater — a building that Kirstein had chosen Philip Johnson to design — Cadmus described his friend as a "benevolent hurricane."

During the war, Cadmus began to send food packages to E. M. Forster in England, after the painter's close friend Margaret French told Cadmus that Forster had seen his work in *Time* or *Newsweek* and greatly admired it. They began a correspondence that blossomed into a fine friendship. "He was not shy with me," Cadmus remembered. "He was very astute always. He was no ninny. And he was very scornful of people who didn't enjoy going to Niagara Falls or the Grand Canyon. He thought those were wonders that people should see. He enjoyed visiting them very much."

Later Forster came to America and visited Cadmus and French in Provincetown, where she and her husband, Jared, had rented a house for the summer. "I and George Tooker were their guests for the summer there," said Cadmus. Provincetown was not particularly gay. "It wasn't like it is now. We weren't there for that. We were there to be at the beach and for working."

Then Cadmus visited Forster in his rooms in Cambridge. "I sat on the window ledge drawing his portrait as he read *Maurice* to me" — the gay novel that was first published many years after Forster's death. "In two sessions, I guess he read the whole book to me. I loved it. He had no intention of publishing it because of his relationship with his policeman friend. That would have been very damaging to him and [the policeman's] wife."

Like Forster, Cadmus considered himself a moralist: "I admire the virtues of long-term friendships and all the things that Forster writes about: tolerance, sympathy, and kindness."

MURRAY GITLIN was working in the terminal cancer ward of the Brooklyn Naval Hospital and dreaming about becoming a dancer when he got out of the navy. "On nights off I would come into Manhattan. Servicemen — all of us in uniform — were treated like royalty. You were given tickets to movies and concerts." When he was eighteen he went to Radio City Music Hall "alone, in my uniform. I wasn't what you'd call a hot sailor. I was too fat. Anyway, I sat there, and this tall blond man came — not old — and sat next to me.

"I felt something and I began to tremble. And he put his hand on my thigh, and I thought to myself, Well, I've got to do something. So he kept fooling around. In the orchestra of the Music Hall! I believe the movie was *Abe Lincoln in Illinois.* So he asked me if I would like to come to his hotel room, and I said yes. It was called the Hotel America, on 47th, between Sixth and Seventh. It was like a hotel that Tennessee Williams would have stayed in, in New Orleans — louvered doors and very rinky-dink. I was as nervous as a cat. And when we got to the hotel, he said, 'You wait down here for a few minutes and I'll go up.' He told me the room number, and then he said, 'You can come up and I'll let you in.' I said, 'Great.' And then I went up and I knocked on his door and he opened the louvers and we hugged one another and kissed. And I said, 'I love you!' He turned out to be a cocktail pianist from Asbury Park. There was nothing unusual about him. He was very corn-fed and very middle of the road. For me it was a great release and a great experience. And we saw one another several times after."

In the East Fifties near Lexington Avenue, the friendly woman owner of the Cloisters served excellent food and enjoyed playing matchmaker for her numerous gay patrons. William Wynkoop remembered, "If you went in and there wasn't a vacant table, she would say, 'Oh, as you can see, every table is taken. Would you mind sitting down with somebody else?' Another single male. And I met three or four guys there that way."

Wynkoop's future lover Roy Strickland was working at Grumman Aircraft on Long Island when he was invited to a Manhattan cocktail party with forty other gay men in 1942. "We were in a building overlooking the garden of the Museum of Modern Art. When one of the fellows I met found out I was from Huntington, he said, 'Well, you must go over to Fire Island a lot.' I said, 'Fire Island, what's that?'"

The man recommended Ocean Beach, which had a gay hotel before Cherry Grove and the Pines became the island's principal gay outposts. The following summer Strickland wrote away to the Ocean Beach Chamber of Commerce for a list of hotels. He chose Sis Norris's (named for its owner), which had a bar overlooking the bay and a clientele that included a number of Russian ballet dancers.

"One day I was walking down the beach and I looked up in the sand dunes, and here was a guy standing there completely stark, buck naked," Strickland recalled. "And I thought, Well, I'm going up and investigate. I went up and we got together. We had sex in the dunes on a blanket. This was my first experience on the beach. It was wonderful: the hot sun beating down and the sound of the waves. Afterwards we started talking, and he said, 'What do you do?' He was a bit older than I. And I told him I worked at Grumman's. He said, 'Well, what do you want to do after the war?' And I said, 'I think that I would like to move to New York, and I'd like to get into display work. I think I could do as nutty windows as they do at Lord & Taylor's and Bonwit Teller's and R. H. Macy's, and McCreery's.' We chatted some more. And then when I was about to leave, he said, 'Well, look me up after the war. I'm display director at Bonwit Teller's.' I nearly died."

Strickland did look up his new friend when the war was over, and he still remembered him. "Unfortunately, he had no opening. But he sent me with a note to R. H. Macy, to the woman in charge of display there, and she hired me. I just realized that I would be much happier as a gay person, living in New York."

Jules Elphant used to camp out for the weekend just outside of Lido Beach on Long Island. "In those days you didn't have anybody there. It was just wild. And it was great. It was isolated and people could go sunbathing nude and bathing nude and nobody ever thought about it. It started to get bad when a lot of drag queens started doing shows on weekends on the beaches. They started performing, and some straight people happened to see it and they started bringing their friends. Once that happened, forget it. Before you knew it, there were too many people coming down and that started to ruin Lido Beach."

Stephen Reynolds remembered going out to Cherry Grove right after the war. "I was aghast," he said. "I thought it was very amusing. I loved it. But if I had a house out in Fire Island and I looked down on the beach, and two men were fucking I would call the police. Now, of course, if you say such a thing as that, they say, 'What do you mean? You're prejudiced!' Well I don't go along with that. I mean, if I saw a man and a woman fucking I would call the police, and if I saw two men fucking, I would do the same. But I was brought up a different way."

Paul Cadmus spent many happy hours gazing at the sailors who flooded Riverside Park: "A lot of my 'gay life' was visual mostly. Not all of it, but more than I wanted. I was rather timid, I guess. I kept most of my dreams about sailors to myself. I used to like watching them, thinking what a good time they were having."

ALTHOUGH THE ARMY trained its officers to be on the lookout for men with "feminine bodily characteristics," or who demonstrated "effeminacy in dress and manner," there were no instructions to exclude masculine women from the armed forces. Johnnie Phelps, a woman sergeant in the army, thought, "There was a tolerance for lesbianism if they needed you.

The battalion that I was in was probably about ninety-seven percent lesbian."

Sergeant Phelps worked for General Eisenhower. Four decades after Eisenhower had defeated the Axis powers, Phelps recalled an extraordinary event. One day the general told her, "I'm giving you an order to ferret those lesbians out. We're going to get rid of them."

"I looked at him and then I looked at his secretary, who was standing next to me, and I said, 'Well, sir, if the general pleases, sir, I'll be happy to do this investigation for you. But you have to know that the first name on the list will be mine.'

"And he kind of was taken aback a bit. And then this woman standing next to me said, 'Sir, if the general pleases, you must be aware, that Sergeant Phelps's name may be second, but mine will be first.'

"Then I looked at him, and I said, 'Sir, you're right. They're lesbians in the WAC battalion. And if the general is prepared to replace all the file clerks, all the section commanders, all of the drivers — every woman in the WAC detachment — and there were about nine hundred and eighty something of us — then I'll be happy to make that list. But I think the general should be aware that among those women are the most highly decorated women in the war. There have been no cases of illegal pregnancies. There have been no cases of AWOL. There have been no cases of misconduct. And as a matter of fact, every six months since we've been here, sir, the general has awarded us a commendation for meritorious service.'

"And he said, 'Forget the order.'

"It was a good battalion to be in."

Allan Bérubé notes that "an extraordinary aspect of WAC policy" was to encourage officers to try to "mold the lesbian desires of WACs into qualities that made better soldiers. Such advice grew out of psychiatrists' attempts to apply their concepts of transference and sublimation to the interpersonal dynamics of military life. Trainees who had 'potential homosexual tendencies'" could be deterred from sex "by encouraging them to sublimate their desires into a 'hero-worship type of reaction. . . . By the strength of her influence [an officer] could bring out in the woman who had previously exhibited homosexual tendencies a definite type of leadership which can then be guided into normal fields of expression, making her a valued member of the corps.'"

A lecture prepared by the Surgeon General's Office and delivered to WAC officers included the statement that "every person is born with a bisexual nature." Any WAC might gravitate "toward homosexual practices because of her new close association and the lack of male companionship which she had known in civilian life."

As the nation's manpower needs mushroomed, the armed forces were constantly adjusting their regulations governing the treatment of homosexuals. The balance of power in determining how they should be handled shifted back and forth between psychiatric consultants and hard-line military bureaucrats. Part of the time psychiatrists encouraged reform by opposing routine court-martials and imprisonment for homosexual soldiers; at other points in the debate they supported "the stigmatization of homosexuals with punitive rather than medical discharges," according to Bérubé, because they worried that heterosexual soldiers would pretend to be gay if they knew that could get out with an honorable discharge.

A 1943 policy published by Secretary of War Henry L. Stimson provided an exception for a soldier who had a homosexual experience but was not a "confirmed pervert."* After psychiatric examination and if "he otherwise possesses a salvage value," this type of offender was to be reclaimed and returned to duty after "appropriate disciplinary action." But periodic witch-hunts continued, and gay soldiers were routinely interrogated to obtain the names of anyone else they believed was gay.

In 1944 a new directive required hospitalization for suspected homosexuals. And it was no longer necessary to commit sodomy to be targeted as an undesirable. As Bérubé noted, "Now merely being homosexual or having such 'tendencies' could entrap both men and women, label them as sick, and remove them from the service." A psychiatrist interviewed each suspect, and a Red Cross worker wrote up his life history and contacted his family. If he refused dishonorable discharges, he could be court-martialed and imprisoned.

Leo Aultman met a man who had been hospitalized for six months because he had "gone down" on a private — "and it was very important to him to get the boy off. The boy was straight, very beautiful, and very amenable to being seduced. I don't think he felt remorse about what he had done. They decided not to court-martial" the man who had seduced the private. "But he got a dishonorable discharge."

All those who received a dishonorable discharge paid a huge price when the war was over: they were automatically denied the lavish benefits of the GI Bill, which financed the educations and subsidized the mortgages of

---

*A similar provision survived into President Clinton's "reform" of regulations governing gays in the military, which went into effect in 1994.

millions of other veterans. However, at least in the case of Aultman's friend in the hospital, his dishonorable discharge had no effect at all on his employment prospects.

"Nobody asked to see it," said Aultman, who received an honorable discharge. "Nobody asked him and nobody ever asked me. But it was an ugly thing to have done to you."

When the army moved toward a policy of hospitalization for suspected homosexuals, it created an unprecedented opportunity for psychiatrists to study large numbers of gay men in one place. Many military psychiatrists were very surprised to discover that many gay men saw themselves as part of a superior elite — just as Otis Bigelow did — and rejected the idea that they were degenerates.

One of the oddest projects was aimed at developing a new method to detect homosexuals. It involved inserting tongue depressors into the throats of 1,404 psychiatric patients. Researchers found that 89 percent of those diagnosed as sexual psychopaths "and who had 'admitted fellatio' did not show a 'gag reflex' due to 'the repeated control of the reflex during the act of fellatio.'" The study couldn't explain why one third of the drug addicts in the study also showed no gag reflex.

Although psychiatrists believed they were improving the plight of gay soldiers by lobbying for hospitalization rather than imprisonment, their efforts would have a decidedly negative effect on gay life in America over the next three decades. Practically everything psychiatrists urged the army to do — "forced hospitalization, mandatory psychiatric diagnoses, discharge as sexual psychopaths, and the protective sympathy of psychiatrists" — reinforced the notion that homosexuals were sick.

A handful of psychiatrists who studied the gay experience in the armed forces reached remarkably enlightened conclusions. But this minority view received very little publicity, and negligible support from colleagues.

Immediately after the war, Clements Fry and Edna Rostow examined the records of 183 servicemen. These Yale researchers concluded that the military had rarely enforced its official discharge policy and permitted most gay personnel to remain in the army and navy.

Inside, most soldiers kept their sexual behavior secret. They had performed just as well as heterosexuals "in various military jobs," including combat. The researchers also found no reason to believe that homosexuality alone "would make a man a poor military risk. . . . Homosexuals should be judged first as individuals, and not as a class." Their report even suggested that military officials should "examine the question as to whether the military service should be interested in homosexuality as such, or only in the individual's ability to perform his duties and adjust to military life."

This study was the first in a Pentagon series that contradicted the military's official prejudice. A Defense Department committee in 1952 and the Navy's Crittenden Board in 1957 both rejected the idea that gays represented exceptional security risks. But like the report of Fry and Rostow, these studies and nearly all the others devoted to homosexuals in the military were either suppressed or destroyed. In 1977, the army announced that its files revealed "no evidence of special studies pertaining to homosexuals," and the navy couldn't locate any either.

In an unusual article, *Newsweek* reported in 1947 that the typical gay serviceman "topped the average soldier in intelligence, education and rating. . . . As a whole, these men were law-abiding and hard-working. In spite of nervous, unstable and often hysterical temperaments, they performed admirably as office workers. Many tried to be good soldiers." The Yale report might have been the source of this information, but it wasn't credited in the piece.

A study conducted in 1989 by the Defense Department's Personnel Security Research and Education Center concluded that sexuality "is unrelated to job performance in the same way as is being left- or right-handed." It too was suppressed until 1989 when Gerry Studds of Massachusetts, the first openly gay man in Congress, made it public. An additional PERSEREC report concluded that personnel discharged because they were gay were better qualified and had fewer personal problems than the typical heterosexual in the military.

WHEN THE WAR finally ended in Europe in the spring of 1945, Stephen Reynolds was stationed in Germany. "It was the most depressing day on earth," he remembered. "I don't know why. I was on a run. I was with someone in the ambulance. We were in Bavaria, and we stopped by the road for tea. And an American truck came roaring around the corner, and he said, 'The war is over.' We said, 'What?' He said, 'The war is over.'

"So we got in the car. My brother had been killed in the war. And there was no excitement. If we'd been in a city, there would have been an orgy. But we were out in the field in some ghastly place. And it just didn't mean anything. Nobody celebrated. There was no way to celebrate."

But a few months later, when Japan surrendered after the United States dropped the second atomic bomb in August, Reynolds was back in Manhattan. And there he witnessed pandemonium: "That was a *huge* celebration. I was very young then. I was invited to the Colony for supper. It was the first time I'd ever been there. After that I went there a lot — it was the most marvelous restaurant in New York City. And the Windsors were there — they had a lot to celebrate. *That* was a wild night. There was great jubilation."

IN THE LATE 1940s, thousands of lesbian and gay soldiers who had poured through New York City on their way to Europe settled in Manhattan, bolstering what was already the largest gay community in America. In 1945, they founded the Veterans Benevolent Association, one of the first gay organizations ever incorporated in New York State.

The group met monthly and then twice a month on the fourth floor of a building on Houston Street near Second Avenue. Jules Elphant attended its meetings right from the start, when he was twenty-two. "A lot of it was uncomfortable because in those days we just didn't talk about being gay," Elphant remembered. "Of course in those days we weren't 'gay.' I think we were just 'queer.' Or 'sissies.' *Sissy* was the word that took care of everything, but so many of us were so far from being sissies. I always found myself in a macho-type way."

The association's dances attracted nearly two hundred men. The dances also attracted a couple of the veterans' wives, including the woman married to James Lang, who founded the association and did most of the work that kept it together until 1954. "The women were all straight, but they knew their husbands were gay and they just went along with the husbands," said Elphant.

"Once we dressed in bathing suits," he continued. "Everyone was introduced as Miss So-and-So. I was very uncomfortable with that. But I whipped up my own red, white, and blue costume — I was Miss Patriot. And I met a lot of interesting people because of that — 'Oh, you've got such powerful legs.' This was one of the first socials I went to, and it brought me out. Suddenly I made more friends that way.

"Sex was one of the things of course that made us part of the group. But sex was not the basic reason for it. It was social — they wanted to be together with people [like themselves] so they could relax more." All the members were white, with lots of Jews, Irishmen, and Italians. And there were plenty of couples. "We also had a 'Stitch and Bitch gang' — for sewing and gossiping. I was doing beaded fruit. I've been doing it for years. It's expensive, but it's wonderful therapy.

"We had actual business meetings of the veterans association. We discussed general subjects and we had speakers — and a legal adviser. Occasionally someone was having problems in their job and we would discuss what we could do about it. Of course, the best thing you could do was keep your mouth shut. And try to stay out of problems. That was the easiest way in those days. When we were at our jobs, we had to be careful. I had to be careful. I didn't show any signs of pansyism or anything like that. But other people who do have a little more feminism within themselves did have problems."

Elphant liked the association's big gatherings because "you would get to meet two or three that you'd become interested in. . . . that's how I met my lover in 1946. When I first joined, he was one of the young people at a house party. He was seventeen, and he was interested in me and I didn't even know it. I was so shy about things. And somebody had to come over and tell me, 'Do you know Richard is interested in you?' And so I got friendly with Richard. We were inseparable after that for quite a while. On and off, we were together thirty-four years. But we never lived together."

IN 1947, AMERICA was shocked by a contradiction of one of its most strongly held prejudices — the idea that great athletes could never be homosexuals. William "Big Bill" Tilden was a national hero, a larger-than-life tennis player who had been the American champion from 1920 to 1925 and a three-time winner at Wimbledon. Along with Babe Ruth, Red Grange, Johnny Weissmuller, Jack Dempsey and Bobby Jones, he was one of the giants of the golden era of American sports.

But at the age of fifty-three Tilden was sentenced to five years probation in Los Angeles after pleading guilty to a charge of contributing to the delinquency of a fourteen-year-old boy. "You have been the idol of youngsters all over the world," said the sentencing judge. "It has been a great shock to sports fans to read about your troubles." Later his probation was revoked when the police found him with a seventeen-year-old boy, and Tilden was forced to serve seven and a half months in jail.

TWO BOOKS PUBLISHED at the beginning of 1948 — a short novel and a giant scientific treatise — sparked a huge debate about sex in America. Both of them were controversial partly because they were so nonjudgmental. Precisely because each volume emphasized the sheer ordinariness of being gay, in the coming decades they would play a crucial role in a very long campaign to convince Americans that homosexuality wasn't really an illness at all.

The longer and more important book did more to promote sexual liberation in general and gay liberation in particular than anything previously published between hard covers. Because it was a dense scientific study, the publisher ordered an initial printing of only 5,000 copies. But just weeks after it first reached bookstores, there were an amazing 185,000 copies in print.

Sexual Behavior in the Human Male, by Alfred Charles Kinsey and his associates Wardell B. Pomeroy and Clyde E. Martin, was an 804-page tome, nine years in the making, which drew its conclusions from detailed interviews with twelve thousand Americans. No one had ever seen anything like it before. Crammed with tables and graphs, its statistics startled nearly everyone, including its authors. The accuracy of those numbers has been debated continuously ever since they were first published. But while the book's estimates about the prevalence of different kinds of sexual behavior captured most of the headlines, over the long term those numbers were much less important than the authors' radical approach to their subject.

What made Kinsey's book revolutionary was its insistence that scientists had to divorce their judgments about sexuality from the "religious background" of the culture that had dominated "patterns of sexual behavior" for many centuries. "Ancient religious codes are still the prime source of the attitudes, the idea, the ideals, and the rationalizations by which most individuals pattern their sexual lives," Kinsey declared.

In his introduction, Dr. Alan Gregg wrote that "no aspect of human biology in our current civilization stands in more need of scientific knowledge and courageous humility than that of sex. . . . As long as sex is dealt with in the current confusion of ignorance and sophistication, denial and indulgence, suppression and stimulation, punishment and exploitation, secrecy and display, it will be associated with a duplicity and indecency that lead neither to intellectual honesty nor human dignity."

Because he adopted a disinterested tone and divorced all of his judgments from the traditional Judeo-Christian influences, Kinsey helped Americans to think about sex in a completely different way. "To each individual, the significance of any particular type of sexual activity depends very largely upon his previous experience," the fifty-three-year-old zoologist explained.

> Ultimately, certain activities may seem to him to be the only things that have value, that are right, that are socially acceptable; and all departures from his own particular pattern may seem to him to be enormous abnormalities. But the scientific data which are accumulating make it appear that if circumstances be propitious, most individuals might have become conditioned in any direction, even into activities which they now consider quite unacceptable. . . . There is an abundance of evidence

that most human sexual activities would become comprehensible to most individuals, if they could know the background of each other individual's behavior.

The questionnaire about homosexual activity was incredibly detailed, posing more than 120 queries, ranging from "frequency" and "age preferences" (and "reasons for age preferences") to "positions involved (including 69)" and "blackmail, active and passive." Kinsey's most surprising conclusion was that "at least 37 percent of the male population has some homosexual experience between the beginning of adolescence and old age." He described himself as "totally unprepared to find such incidence data," but he added that the data about homosexual activity had been "more or less the same" in big cities and small towns all across the country.

Kinsey had been a professor of zoology since 1920 and director of the Institute for Sex Research at Indiana University since 1942. He conducted hundreds of the interviews himself, and many of his subjects remembered him as a charismatic figure. Kinsey interviewed Otis Bigelow over several days at the Pennsylvania Hotel in Manhattan.

"You started out shy, but after fifteen minutes you could tell him *anything,*" Bigelow remembered. "He was a father — God the father figure. If you told him you had licked someone's toes, he was fascinated to find out about it. And he was nonjudgmental. He wouldn't have been able to get things out of people unless he was the person that he was." After spending a couple of days with Kinsey, Bigelow decided that if the doctor had asked him to jump out of the window so he could observe his reactions going down, "I probably would have. He was a godfather in a good way. Somebody that you would trust with your life — and you did, of course, in those days."

Kinsey was fascinated with Bigelow because he had kept a list of all the men he had slept with. "I think it was around five hundred. I would say, 'That one was in September in the 34th Street–Lexington Ave. john.' That's what one did in those days — you'd have four or five in an hour, if you were attractive and had some nerve."

Paul Cadmus, who also met Kinsey in the late forties, remembered him as "gentle and quiet — and a little bit formidable because he was so terribly serious. One didn't think of him as laughing or smiling very much. He took homosexuality just as calmly as he did his work with wasps. He interviewed me about my sex life — how many orgasms, how big it was, measure it before and after. He interviewed your friend at the same time. He interviewed Jerry French at more or less the same time to see what he had to say about our relationship." Cadmus believed Kinsey was gay, but never suspected that the scientist had acted on that impulse, so the painter arranged for two friends to give the researcher a demonstration of gay lovemaking. "I think he viewed it probably very calmly," Cadmus said. "We had a date with him and these two friends after the little exhibition, and he came to dinner at our house." After dinner, Kinsey suddenly felt ill. "We had to put him in a hot bath and give him cognac. But he was all right after that. I don't think he stayed very late after dinner."

In the report, Kinsey introduced his famous zero-to-six scale (completely heterosexual–to–completely homosexual), which left most people somewhere in between. Thirty-seven percent of the men interviewed for his study had reached orgasm with another man at least once after puberty. Kinsey estimated that twenty-five percent of the male population had "more than incidental homosexual experience or reactions for at least three years between the ages of 16 and 55," and ten percent were "more or less exclusively homosexual." Four percent were "exclusively homosexual throughout their lives, after the onset of adolescence."

But the conclusions he drew from these statistics were even more devastating to traditional prejudices than the numbers themselves:

> In view of the data which we now have on the incidence and frequency of the homosexual, and in particular on its co-existence with the heterosexual in the lives of a considerable portion of the male population, it is difficult to maintain the view that psychosexual reactions between individuals of the same sex are rare and *therefore abnormal or unnatural, or even that they constitute within themselves evidence of neuroses or even psychoses* [emphasis added]. If homosexual activity persists on as large a scale as it does, in the face of the very considerable public sentiment against it and in spite of the severity of the penalties that our Anglo-American culture has placed upon it through the centuries, there seems some reason for believing that such activity would appear in the histories of a much larger portion of the population if there were no social restraints.

This statement was obviously another attempt to encourage tolerance. However, its unsupported speculation that without discrimination, the number of homosexuals might actually increase (rather than simply making them less unhappy) contained the seeds of a provocative argument. Many gay rights opponents still use this idea to promote prejudice against homosexuals — to prevent their numbers from multiplying. However, scientific evidence that homosexuality is primarily hereditary has accumulated steadily during the past decade.

Kinsey urged a reconsideration of the treatment of homosexuals because homosexual activity turned out to be so much more common than anyone had believed before he made his estimates:

> The judge who is considering the case of the male who has been arrested for homosexual activity should keep in mind that nearly 40 percent of all the other males in the town could be arrested at some time in their lives for similar activity. . . . It is not a matter of individual hypocrisy which leads officials with homosexual histories to become prosecutors of the homosexual activity in the community. They themselves are the victims of the mores, and the public demand that they protect those mores. As long as there are such gaps between the traditional custom and the actual behavior of the population such inconsistencies will continue to exist.

"Homosexuality was thought to be a very rare phenomenon," said Evelyn Hooker, who would do some groundbreaking research of her own a few years later. Before Kinsey, "There was nothing in the literature that concerned well-functioning gay males . . . Kinsey gave great hope." Gay people realized for the first time "that they were not a tiny minority but actually a very sizable proportion of the population."

ALTHOUGH the *New York Times* would do quite a lot to impede the cause of gay rights over the next three decades, it greeted the Kinsey Report with respect. The sensitive job of reviewing the book fell to Dr. Howard Rusk. A favorite of the *Times*'s publisher, Arthur Hays Sulzberger, Rusk wrote a regular column for the Sunday paper (and later founded the Rusk Institute of Rehabilitation Medicine).

Rusk may have been sympathetic to the book because he wasn't a psychiatrist. Therefore, nothing in it challenged any of the basic tenets of his profession. Rusk wrote that the "end results" of the report "should be healthy. They should bring about a better understanding of some of our emotional problems, and the bases for some of our psychiatric concepts. . . . It presents facts that indicate the necessity to review some of our legal and moral concepts. It gives new therapeutic tools to the psychiatrist and the practicing physician. It offers a yardstick that will give invaluable aid in the study of our complex social problems" as well as "data that should promote tolerance and understanding." He also predicted that "after decades of hush-hush," the new book was certain "to create an explosion."

Some of the initial criticism of the book was quite mild, but it built steadily through the spring. At a forum of the American Social Hygiene Association in Manhattan in April, Carle Zimmerman, an associate professor of sociology at Harvard, suggested that "we have the right to ask the backers of the report what they plan for the future, since they indicate throughout the work that they are dissatisfied with the prevailing sex norms." Helen Judy Bond, head of the department of home economics at Columbia University's Teachers College, advocated "a law against doing research dealing exclusively with sex" because "sex is only part of the sum total of the behavior of each human being."

In June the attacks grew harsher. Henry Van Dusen, head of Manhattan's Union Theological Seminary, called Kinsey's statistics evidence of a "degradation in American morality approximating the worst decadence of the Roman era," while the president of Princeton compared the report to "the work of small boys writing dirty words on fences."

But no one was angrier than the psychiatrists, because Kinsey's conclusions struck at the heart of their notion that all gay men and lesbians were sick. By suggesting that homosexuality alone should not be considered evidence of psychosis or neurosis, Kinsey had implied that the entire psychiatric profession was guilty of massive medical malpractice.

Lawrence Kubie was the prominent Manhattan psychiatrist who six years earlier had expanded the army's mobilization regulations to include a paragraph on sexual perversions. Now he led the attack on Kinsey's conclusions. *Time* contended that Kubie had "stuck a scalpel into the heart" of Kinsey's whole project by accusing him and his assistants of giving human memory "a precision it does not have: 'they recognize that we can forget, but not that we can misremember.' The statistics based on the interviews add up all right . . . but may be an 'accurate recording of inaccurate data.'"

Moss Hart, one of Kubie's many celebrity patients, dedicated *Lady in the Dark,* his musical about psychoanalysis, to Kubie. The actor James Atcheson was sent to Kubie by Clifton Webb. "He was a celebrity fucker," said Atcheson of the doctor. Kubie lost interest in the young actor as soon as he implied that his father wasn't wealthy. "Oh, I don't think there's anything very much the matter with you," the psychiatrist declared. Then Atcheson mentioned that his grandfather was a name partner in one of Manhattan's most famous law firms. "Kubie turned really brick red and gave me a look of total hatred," Atcheson remembered. "Because I was onto him. He was also a money snob, you see. And very sinister. But there are people still alive who thought he was God."

Some of Kubie's sharpest comments were aimed at Kinsey's conclusions about gays and lesbians: "The implication that because homosexuality is prevalent we must accept it as 'normal,' or as a happy and a healthy way of life, is wholly unwarranted." This was undoubtedly his conviction, but it was also the inevitable point of view of a man with numerous patients who were paying him large sums to alter their sexual orientation.

"Kubie ruined Tennessee," said Arthur Laurents. "He really did. Because Frankie Merlo was a wonderful man who held Tennessee together, and Kubie broke them up." Then Merlo got lung cancer, and Williams returned to him. "But a little late," said Laurents. "Frankie was a very nice man." The widow of one of Kubie's theater patients described the doctor as a "Rasputin type" and a control freak. He even insinuated himself into his patients' social lives, explaining that out-of-office observations would assist him in deciding the proper course of treatment.

After Moss Hart married Kitty Carlisle, they spent their honeymoon in Bucks County, Pennsylvania, where they were both performing in *The Man Who Came to Dinner*. An old friend who visited them there remembered, "All the so-called men were sitting around the pool, and Moss said, 'Why don't we take our suits off?' I was in analysis at the time, and I thought, 'This is not right. This is the groom. Something has gone askew here.' Moss was a very kind man, crippled with an obvious problem."

At the beginning, Kinsey dismissed the criticism from Kubie and his colleagues. In a speech at the Commodore Hotel in Manhattan on June 4, 1948, he reiterated that "most of the sexual behavior called abnormal in our particular culture is part and parcel of our inheritance as mammals, and is natural and normal biologically." But Kinsey's work would continue to inspire violent attacks throughout the coming decade.

John D'Emilio points out that the Kinsey Report was important for gay people because it enhanced their sense of belonging to a larger group. "By revealing that millions of Americans exhibited a strong erotic interest in their own sex," it encouraged everyone still struggling with his own sexual preference to accept his inclinations. In this way, Kinsey gave "an added push at a crucial time to the emergence of an urban gay subculture."

THE OTHER BOOK published in January 1948 that would help thousands of gay people change the way they thought about themselves was Gore Vidal's third novel, *The City and the Pillar*. His book told the story of Jim Willard's obsessive love for Bob Ford, a childhood friend who makes love with him once when they are teenagers — an experience Jim can never forget.

The novel, written when Vidal was twenty-one, features remarkably modern portraits of Hollywood and Manhattan. A New York party includes gay writers, painters, composers, and athletes — "even a member of Congress" — as well as a Hollywood actor with whom Jim has had an affair. "In the old days [the actor] would never have gone to such a party," Jim notes. "But now he was indifferent, even defiant."

Another guest at the party mentions that the war "has caused a great change. Inhibitions have broken down. All sorts of young men are trying out all sorts of new things, away from home and familiar taboos." His companion says, "Everyone is by nature bisexual" and "nothing is 'right.' Only denial of instinct is wrong."

The Hollywood scenes feel equally authentic, probably because Vidal used to hitchhike there during the war from an army hospital in Van Nuys where he was recovering from the rheumatoid arthritis he developed while stationed in the Aleutian Islands. Vidal especially enjoyed hanging out at the Metro-Goldwyn-Mayer studios. "You'd sit in the commissary, and Lana Turner would sweep by," he remembered. Meanwhile, his mother was having an affair with Clark Gable. "She thought she was going to marry him too," Vidal recalled. "Which proved not to be the case. But I saw a lot of Gable then."

Laurents had a four-year affair with Farley Granger, who starred with John Dall in *Rope*, the 1948 Hitchcock thriller for which Laurents wrote the screenplay. Dall was also gay, as was a third actor in the film whom Laurents had also dated. "The studios didn't care what anybody did about anything so long as it was kept private," said Laurents. "There was wholesale fucking of all kinds in Hollywood then." During his affair with Granger, Sam Goldwyn's wife, Frances, asked Laurents to tea. "You know, you're Farley's best friend," she said. "I would like to ask a favor. He takes out Miss Shelley Winters in public. We don't care about what he does in private. But Miss Winters is too old and too vulgar for him. And if he insists on taking out a girl, could he please take out Ann Blyth?" — who also happened to be under contract to Goldwyn.

Loosely inspired by the Leopold and Loeb murder case of 1924, *Rope* is about two young psychopaths who decide to murder a friend for the fun of it, and it is replete with homosexual overtones. "Hitch wanted Cary Grant and Monty Clift, and they both turned it down," Laurents remembered. "And he said to me, 'Well, of course I knew they would because they're afraid — because of their own sexuality.' And it was the truth. Hitchcock knew I was living with Farley, and he loved that. He loved what he thought was sexual perverseness." Later, Laurents remarked, "I don't think the censors at that time realized that this was about gay people. They didn't have a clue what was and what wasn't."

Laurents remembered the sexual scene in Hollywood right after the war this way: "It didn't matter whether you were straight or gay or bisexual. If a new attractive person came to town, the other stars felt free to call up and say, 'Come on over and let's fuck.' And they did. They all did . . . I remember a New Year's Eve party at Sam Spiegel's where you walked in and Jennifer Jones was sitting on David Selznick's lap, and he was nursing her breast. That's the only way I can put it. And on one side in the corner was an actor standing up fucking a starlet. And people were saying, 'Hello, how are you? Have a drink! Oh, what a good party!' Hollywood then was very sexual. It is not now. Now it's about grosses. No one can stay in that town and not go downhill."

BEFORE THE PUBLICATION of *The City and the Pillar,* Vidal had been acclaimed for his first two novels. But Orville Prescott, the daily critic at the *Times,* told Vidal's editor that the subject of this third work disgusted him. "I will not only not review it, but I will never again read a book by Gore Vidal," Prescott told Nicholas Wreden at E. P. Dutton. Prescott kept that promise for Vidal's next five books. As a result, Vidal says he was forced to turn to the theater, movies, and television in the coming decades to earn a living. "I was quite aware by my second book that I was going to make a choice," said Vidal. "And I am a rather short-tempered person and don't put up with the sort of canting bullshit of Americans very easily. Sooner or later I was going to explode on the subject. I perhaps did it too soon, before my knives were sharp enough. But I did it anyway." Like the Kinsey Report, *The City and the Pillar* was a largely nonjudgmental account of the gay experience. And though it was panned by the Sunday *New York Times* and ignored by many other newspapers, it quickly became a national best-seller. The *Times* ran just one advertisement for the book. Vidal believes the paper refused to accept any more after it learned the novel's subject. The ad copy betrays the ambivalence of his own publisher toward the topic. "A frightening glimpse of the submerged world," read the headline. It went on to promise, "Never before in American letters has there been such a revealing and frank discussion of the sexually malad-justed, of those of the submerged world which lives beneath the surface of normality. . . . With sensitive understanding, Gore Vidal deals a powerful blow to hypocrisy and sensationalism in facing an existing social condi-tion."

Vidal said, "The fact that it was a commercial success kept me going as a writer — at least they kept publishing me. But everything I wrote was denounced or greeted with just silence. While I was getting marvelous reviews in England for the same books that were being ignored or attacked in America." But he never regretted writing a gay novel so early in his career: "Of course not. I mean I was made for battle."

Vidal hoped to show "the normality of this particular act," and his matter-of-fact tone was a dramatic departure for a work of gay fiction. But in one respect, his book was exactly like its predecessors. In its original version, *The City and the Pillar* ended with a catastrophe. When Bob rebuffs Jim's effort to repeat their previous lovemaking experience, Jim murders him in his hotel room.

This conventional conclusion aroused the indignation of many gay writers, including Tennessee Williams and Christopher Isherwood, who thought the book — and the public — deserved a less disastrous finale. "You spoiled it with that ending," Williams told Vidal. "You didn't know what a good book you had." Christopher Isherwood agreed. Isherwood was the British novelist whose short stories about Berlin in the thirties became the basis for the musical (in the sixties) and the movie (in the seventies) called *Cabaret*. He read *The City and the Pillar* in Lima, Peru, at the end of 1948. He wrote to Vidal to praise the book as "certainly one of the best novels of its kind yet published in English. It isn't sentimental, and it is extremely frank without trying to be sensational and shocking." He also predicted it would be "widely discussed and have a big success, well-deserved."

But then he took Vidal to task, with words that hinted at the awakening of an important new consciousness:

> This brings me to your tragic ending: Jim's murder of Bob. Dramatically and psychologically, I find it entirely plausible. It could have happened, and it gives the story a climax. . . . What I do question is the moral the reader will draw. This is what homosexuality brings you to, he will say: tragedy, defeat and death. Maybe we're too hard on these people — maybe we shouldn't lock them up in prison; but oughtn't they to be put away in clinics? Such misery is a menace to society. . . . Now as a matter of fact, it is quite true that many homosexuals are unhappy; and not merely because of the social pressures under which they live. It is quite true that they are often unfaithful, unstable, unreliable. They are vain and predatory, and they chatter. But there is another side to the picture, which you (and Proust) don't show. Homosexual relationships can be, and frequently are happy. Men live together for years and make homes and share their lives and their work, just as heterosexuals do. This truth is peculiarly disturbing and shocking even to 'liberal' people, because it cuts across their romantic, tragic notion of the homosexual's fate. Cer-

tainly, under the present social setup, a homosexual relationship is more difficult to maintain than a heterosexual one (by the same token, a free-love relationship is more difficult to maintain than a marriage), but doesn't that merely make it more of a challenge and therefore, in a sense, more humanly worthwhile? The success of such a relationship is revolutionary in the best sense of the word. And, because it demonstrates the power of human affection over fear and prejudice and taboo, it is actually beneficial to society as a whole — as all demonstrations of faith and courage must be: they raise our collective morale.

No one has ever offered a more elegant explanation of why gay liberation would be valuable — and important — for everyone.

II

The Fifties

"In that era of general good will and expanding affluence, few Americans doubted the essential goodness of their society."

— DAVID HALBERSTAM

"Undergraduates seemed uniformly committed to playing parts from a fifties script, according to which paternal white men benignly ruled a prosperous country devoid of serious conflict."

— MARTIN DUBERMAN

"We are not living in experimental times. . . . We are not producing real tragedy. On the other hand we are not producing real satire either. The caution prevents it, all the fears prevent it, and we are left, at the moment, with an art that is rather whiling away the time until the world gets better or blows up."

— LEONARD BERNSTEIN, 1953

"The fifties was the bad decade."

— GORE VIDAL

Most americans who lived through the fifties — the triumphant warriors of World War II and their teeming progeny — remember this decade with affection. Millions of returning GIs (with honorable discharges) received subsidized college educations, good jobs in a growing economy and cheap mortgages for their new houses in the suburbs. Inflation was low, gasoline was cheap — less than thirty-five cents a gallon — and white middle-class American families became the best-fed, best-dressed and best-sheltered bourgeoisie in the history of the world. By the end of the decade, millions of Americans seemed as self-confident as

Detroit's consummate symbol of conspicuous consumption: a 1959 Cadillac with four headlights, dual exhaust pipes and towering tail fins.

Mass entertainment was careful to promote the values of what remained a remarkably puritan and (publicly) innocent place. Even after the loosening effects of World War II, sex and death remained unmentionable, abortion was illegal, divorce was difficult for anyone who couldn't afford a quick trip to Nevada, the segregation of public schools was still legal, and the Lord's Prayer was a morning staple in most of those public schools. The suburban family with three children, a barbecue, and a two-car garage was good for business — and almost no one was questioning the notion that whatever was good for General Motors was also good for the United States.*

Conformity of every kind was king.

The establishment of the Hays Office in 1934 ensured the strict censorship of Hollywood movies. Every picture needed its seal of approval; without one, filmmakers risked a disaster at the box office because of a boycott ordered by the Catholic Legion of Decency. The code's purpose was clearly stated: "No picture shall be produced which will lower the moral standards of those who see it. Hence the sympathy of the audience shall never be thrown to the side of crime, wrongdoing, evil or sin" and "correct standards of life . . . shall be presented" because "correct entertainment raises the whole standard of a nation. Wrong entertainment lowers the whole living conditions and moral ideals of a race."

The function of the official censors "was to protect us from the truth and to saddle us with comfortable illusions," Gerald Gardner wrote in his history of the Hays Office. The censors would "root out all signs of the disagreeable facts of life, and many of the agreeable facts as well."

Adultery and murder could never go unpunished; drug addiction could never be glamorized (nor the profits emphasized); a child could never be kidnapped, unless returned unharmed; and no film could "infer that casual or promiscuous sex relationships are the accepted or common thing." Furthermore, "Lustful and open-mouthed kissing" was prohibited, and passion had to be "treated in such manner as not to stimulate the baser emotions." Obscenity "in words, gesture, reference, song, joke or by suggestion, even when likely to be understood by only part of the audi-

---

*After Eisenhower picked the General Motors executive Charlie "Engine" Wilson to become defense secretary, Wilson actually said, "We at General Motors have always felt that what was good for the country was good for General Motors as well," but most people remembered it the other way. (David Halberstam, *The Fifties,* 118)

ence" was also forbidden. Abortion could "never be more than suggested," and whenever it was referred to, it had to be condemned.

Banned words and phrases included *chippie, fairy, goose, madam, pansy, tart in your hat* and *nuts*. Even *hell* and *damn* were excised from many scripts until the sixties. And, needless to say, "sex perversion or any inference of it" was strictly forbidden. (When the censors of the thirties ordered Charlie Chaplin to eliminate "the first part of the 'pansy' gag" in *Modern Times,* he immediately complied.)

As the fifties progressed, television gradually supplanted the movies as the dominant form of popular entertainment — and TV was even more puritanical than the cinema. Although network television still featured serious drama and even symphony orchestras in the fifties, producers were pressured to appeal to a steadily lower common denominator. But for everyone who could identify with the flickering black and white images of this exploding new medium — pictures of idealized white suburban families on "Leave It to Beaver," "Ozzie and Harriet," and "Father Knows Best" — the fifties felt like a wonderful time to be alive.

"I Love Lucy" became a gigantic hit, watched by as many as fifty million people by the middle of the decade — but first Lucy had to overcome the vehement opposition of CBS executives in gray flannel suits. The network and its confederates at Philip Morris, which sponsored the show, were certain that the casting of Lucy's real-life Cuban husband would be a catastrophe. They wanted their idea of an all-American man (with an all-American accent) to play that part. No one would believe Lucy could be married to a Cuban bandleader. "What do you mean?" Lucy demanded. "We *are* married!" Eventually CBS relented, but there was still strong opposition after some top entertainers screened the first pilot in New York. "Keep the redhead but ditch the Cuban," Oscar Hammerstein recommended.

Lucy's real-life pregnancy caused a new crisis at CBS. Ultimately the network permitted her condition to be written into the show, but only after realizing that it wouldn't be practical to keep her hidden behind counters and couches at all times. Nevertheless, the word *pregnant* could never be spoken, even after Lucy was allowed to suffer from morning sickness.

These battles with the bosses at CBS illustrate an essential fact of life in the fifties: in this era the American establishment was uncomfortable with *all* public manifestations of sexuality, not just homosexuality. *The New York Times,* the daily bible of the liberal elite, was particularly squeamish. The historian George Chauncey considered the decade an "utter anomaly" because a larger percentage of the American population was married than at any other time in the nation's history.

The gap between the carefree comedy served up every week by Lucy and Desi and the reality of their rocky marriage mirrored the gulf between real life in America and the white-bread TV version that Americans gobbled up. Unpleasant realities of any kind — from infidelity to racism — were all unfit subjects for programs designed to sell great American products like Marlboros, Alka Seltzer, Geritol and Johnson's baby shampoo.

According to Lucille Ball, "Half of the nicest girls in Hollywood" were having an affair with her husband. And Desi Arnaz, Jr., remembered learning "to relate to 'I Love Lucy' as a television show and to my parents as actors on it. . . . There wasn't much relationship between what I saw on TV and what was really going on at home. Those were difficult years — all those funny things happening on television each week to people who looked like my parents, then the same people agonizing through some terrible, unhappy times at home."

THESE POSTWAR TENDENCIES toward conformity and obedience were sharply reinforced by the dreadful morality play staged throughout the decade in congressional hearing rooms and federal courts. In a frightening replay of the Red Scare that had gripped the country after the First World War, Americans in nearly every profession learned that the penalty for even momentary nonconformity could be the termination of their careers — sometimes decades after their alleged indiscretions.

Congressional Republicans — joined by quite a few Democrats — began their anti-Communist crusade in earnest after Mao Tse-tung defeated Chiang Kai-shek in 1949, and President Harry Truman was accused of "losing China." Ruthless investigators decreed that even the oldest and briefest flirtation with the Communist party should be incapacitating for nuclear physicists and Hollywood screenwriters alike. For members of Hollywood's elite, the cost of continuing their careers often included the annihilation of some of their colleagues — because only those who revealed the ancient party memberships of their former "comrades" were deemed fit to continue in their chosen professions.

Joseph McCarthy was a Wisconsin Republican who was first elected to the Senate in 1946. A heavy drinker and compulsive gambler, the Senate press gallery named him America's worst senator three years after his election. In February 1950, McCarthy pretended to have a list of 205 Communists working in the State Department and known to the secretary of state. It was the first in a long series of charges for which no serious evidence would ever be forthcoming.

The Communist witch-hunt conducted by McCarthy and his cohorts is the nightmare remembered by most liberals who lived through this period. But a parallel persecution of lesbians and gay men began in 1950, with devastating effects. And just as the Lonergan case had inspired the first extended discussion of homosexuality in print, this new "scandal" would again stimulate extensive coverage of the subject in the New York press.

What one liberal columnist described (ironically) as Washington's "homosexual panic" began after a State Department official shocked a congressional committee by disclosing that ninety-one employees had been dismissed between 1947 and 1949 because they were homosexual — far more than had been fired for being suspected Communists.

This 1950 bombshell inspired two congressional investigations and a spate of jokes about "cookie-pushers" inside the nation's diplomatic corps. The *Washington Post* reported that a man on line for the movies provoked titters just by mentioning his employment at State, while an Alan Dunn cartoon in *The New Yorker* carried this caption: "It's true, sir, that the State Department let me go, but that was solely because of incompetence."

The scandal at State also revived an explosive World War II rumor that was constantly repeated without any public evidence to support it. According to Washington insiders, Adolf Hitler had maintained a secret list of homosexuals in high government posts all over the world, and used it to blackmail them at will. The list had supposedly fallen into Stalin's hands after the Russian army entered Berlin in 1945.

This rumor fit perfectly with the main intellectual justification for the persecution of homosexuals in government jobs — the prevailing notion that they were more vulnerable to blackmail than their heterosexual counterparts. But when the *New York Post* columnist Max Lerner researched an unprecedented twelve-part series on the "Washington Sex Story," he made a remarkable discovery: "At no point, whether I talked with State Department officials, Civil Service Commission officials, or Senators, was I able to track down a single case" of a homosexual being blackmailed. "Almost in every case, when I had kept pushing my questions, I was told 'Well, Hoover says they're more vulnerable.'"

The irony of J. Edgar Hoover's role in this harassment was lost on the typical newspaper reader. Many Americans were unaware that the FBI director had what appeared to be a homoerotic relationship for forty-four years with his top assistant, Clyde Tolson — though the mystery of whether the relationship was actually consummated remains hidden from history. Hoover's biographer Richard Gid Powers described the relationship as "spousal" and "so close, so enduring, and so affectionate that it took the place of marriage for both bachelors." Every morning, the FBI chauffeur picked up Hoover at his house, then Tolson at his. Then the chauffeur would let them out before they reached the office, so they could walk the last few blocks to headquarters together.

The director was too powerful and much too feared for most reporters to speculate about the implications of this arrangement during his lifetime, although *Life* magazine did publish a rather suggestive photograph of Hoover and Tolson on vacation, riding together in a golf cart. Truman Capote, bolder than most journalists, described Hoover as a "killer fruit," a "certain kind of queer who has Freon refrigerating his bloodstream."* But the presidents who were his theoretical bosses were almost uniformly terrified of him. For example, after a story by Ben Bradlee in *Newsweek* suggesting that Lyndon Johnson was searching for Hoover's successor, the president called a press conference to announce that Hoover would retain his position for life.

Max Lerner was a liberal iconoclast, a son of Russian immigrant parents, who had graduated from Yale and taught political science before and after becoming a columnist for the *New York Post*. His twelve-thousand-word series in 1950 was a breakthrough for daily journalism in America. Never before had anyone treated the subject of homosexuality so extensively and seriously in a New York newspaper.

While he was careful to write, "No one argues the question of homosexuals in the government service should be ignored," Lerner broke ranks with almost all of his contemporaries by arguing that it was necessary to distinguish between different kinds of homosexuals — and "which posts they must be kept out of."

Lerner interviewed Kinsey and made it clear that the scientist's findings were a major reason for the reporter's groundbreaking approach. "More drastically than anything that has happened in our time, [Kinsey's figures] have revealed the gap between our moral and legal codes and our actual behavior," Lerner wrote.

Hoover may have been too frightening to mock, but Lerner had a field day interviewing the hapless Washington detective who had electrified a congressional committee with his testimony identifying 5,000 Washington residents as homosexuals — including 3,750 employed by the federal gov-

*This sentence may have been Capote's only literary quarry from his romance with an air-conditioning repairman.

ernment. It turned out that 5,000 was *not* the actual number of people who had been apprehended and charged with disorderly conduct, but a rather creative extrapolation.

Lieutenant Roy E. Blick had produced his official estimate this way: first he took sixty percent of the men arrested, and added the names of all the friends whom they had identified as homosexuals. Then he took the other forty percent of the list and multiplied it by five. "It's 60–40," he explained. Lerner wrote: "This adventure in higher mathematics had exhausted both of us . . . I reflected grimly, thinking back to the reverent way in which Senators and security officers used Blick's estimate of 5,000 homosexuals in Washington, with 3,750 in the government. This was how a statistic got to be born."

Ben Bradlee was a young *Washington Post* reporter in 1950 — "low, low, low general assignment" — and Roy Blick was part of his beat. "Blick specialized in young apple-cheeked police recruits who did the worst things in the world," Bradlee recalled. "They hung around the cans in Lafayette Square and in first-run movie theaters. They'd hang out in the john and wave their tallywackers around and see if anybody was interested. The newspapers at that time were not modern. Shall we put it that way? And if they got a senator's aide, or especially someone in the CIA or the State Department, it was just too good to be true.

"Blick was a poisonous man," Bradlee continued. "He loved it and he relished it. At first he hadn't gotten any ink at all in the vice squad because nobody was particularly interested in rubbing out prostitution or little after-hours clubs. They were all terribly sad stories — most of the guys probably married. Even if you weren't in any way enlightened, you felt there was something terrible about this. There was entrapment, and the joy that this asshole Blick took out of it was wrong.

"He was a nasty little man."

In 1950, "The lack of sensitivity or awareness was total," said the newspaperman. "We're not talking about unenlightenment or enlightenment, we're talking about ignorance." Bradlee hated these stories: "I couldn't get off from this sort of thing" — and they were one reason he ended his first stint at the *Post* in 1951. After he returned fourteen years later, he became the executive editor — and one of the most celebrated journalists of his generation.

Lerner urged his readers to distinguish between men who might have had occasional homosexual experiences and what he called "the compulsive" who was unable to control his impulses. He also pointed out that "alcoholics, reckless and compulsive gamblers, or sexual adventurers who get themselves into frequent scrapes with women" were just as vulnerable to blackmail as any gay person. Lerner compared the new campaign to eliminate homosexuals from all government posts to the attitude of the Soviets and Big Brother in George Orwell's *1984.*

"When the security officers of government agencies start firing people because their sexual habits seem strange it is a case of the sick being pursued by the sicker," Lerner wrote. "For while homosexuals are sick people, the ruthless campaign against them is symptomatic of an even more dangerous sickness in the social atmosphere. . . . The communist regime in Russia takes command not only of the political thinking of its people, but also of their private lives, including their sex habits."

This emphasis on the sickness of the homosexual hardly sounds progressive four decades later. But at the time, it was not only the attitude of almost every psychiatrist; it was also the way most homosexuals viewed themselves.

Ironically, while no one gave Lerner any proof that Communists were successfully blackmailing homosexuals, there were rumors about congressional investigators threatening to blackmail American homosexuals if they refused to discuss their previous ties to the Communist party. When the renowned choreographer Jerome Robbins testified before the House Committee on Un-American Activities in New York City in 1953, he disclosed his own three-year membership in the party and named eight other former party members. Some of his friends believe that Robbins agreed to testify only after committee investigators threatened to expose him as a homosexual.

The day after Robbins testified, Peter Kihss wrote in *The New York Times,* "While other witnesses denounced the committee for staging what they called a 'circus' and relying on 'stool pigeons,' Mr. Robbins said he was testifying because 'I think I made a great mistake before, entering the Communist party, and I feel I'm doing the right thing as an American.'"

Robbins denied that he testified after a threat to expose him as a homosexual. But Victor Navasky wrote in *Naming Names,* a history of the McCarthy period, that Robbins's testimony was "so compliant . . . it had the aura of social blackmail." Ring Lardner told Navasky, "I don't know whether it's true or not, but if you were Jerome Robbins, wouldn't you like to have people believe that's the reason you did it?"

"He wasn't threatened with exposure," said Arthur Laurents, who was unable to get his passport renewed during this period because of his own former connections with leftist organizations. "It was very simple. I knew him very well at that time. It was the same thing as with Kazan. They wanted movie careers. That was it. He wanted to do *The King and I,* and he did. Jerry said, 'It won't be for years until I know whether I did the right thing.' I said, 'Oh, I can tell you now. You were a shit.' But I wasn't so pristine myself. I worked with him afterwards and I knew he'd been an informer."

When Laurents first arrived in Hollywood after the war, he found it "wildly exciting intellectually: there were really bright people and all the cream of the European refugees, like Thomas Mann." But after the black-listing period, most of those people left the movie business for good. "The blacklist destroyed Hollywood," Laurents said.

James Baldwin described his own homosexuality with frankness and ambivalence in *Giovanni's Room,* the novel he published in 1956. The book came out of "something which tormented and frightened me: the question of my own sexuality," Baldwin explained many years later. One reason he wrote it was to eliminate the nagging problem that other closeted writers faced in the fifties. Baldwin said the book "simplified" his life because it "meant that I had no secrets. You couldn't blackmail me. You didn't tell me, I told you."

Coming out of the closet gave Baldwin the freedom that thousands of his contemporaries would not experience until they emulated him two, three, or four decades later. Of course, thousands of others would never emulate him at all.

"It's only the twentieth century which is obsessed with the details of somebody's sex life," Baldwin said on another occasion. "I don't think the details make any difference. Love comes in very strange packages. I love a few men and I love a few women. I suppose it's saved my life."

Alfred A. Knopf had published Baldwin's first novel, *Go Tell It on the Mountain,* in 1953. A semiautobiographical account of a poor boy growing up in Harlem during the 1930s, the book was a critical success. "I'd been a boy preacher for three years," said Baldwin. "That is what turned me into a writer really. . . . My father frightened me so badly I had to fight him so hard, nobody has ever frightened me since."

But when he submitted *Giovanni's Room* a couple of years after his first big success, Knopf rejected it. "I guess they were scared," said William Cole, who was Knopf's publicity director — and the first person to bring Baldwin to the publisher's attention. "Homosexuality wasn't on the books in those days and they turned it down," Cole recalled. When he learned the young author's second novel had been rejected, Cole was "horrified."

BELIEVING THAT HOMOSEXUALS in the federal government could become a potent new campaign issue, right-wing Republicans greeted the

State Department's disclosures gleefully. John O'Donnell, a rabid right-winger, wrote in his syndicated column that the "primary issue" was that "the foreign policy of the United States, even before World War II, was dominated by an all-powerful, supersecret inner circle of highly-educated, socially-highly-placed sexual misfits in the State Department, all easy to blackmail, all susceptible to blandishments by homosexuals in foreign nations."

O'Donnell also reported that of the first 2,500 letters McCarthy received in response to his campaign against the State Department, "A preliminary sampling of the mail shows that only one out of four of the writers is excited about the red infiltration into the higher branches of the government; the other three are expressing their shocked indignation at the evidence of sex depravity."

Republican National Committee Chairman Guy Gabrielson mailed a newsletter to seven thousand party workers to alert them to the new "homosexual angle" in Washington. "Sexual perverts . . . have infiltrated our government in recent years," wrote Gabrielson, and they were "perhaps as dangerous as actual communists." He said the Republican party had a special responsibility to spread the news because "decency" constrained the media from "adequately presenting the facts." This occasion was the first of many over the next four decades when the Republican party would try to exploit anti-gay prejudice to win votes on election day.

Senator Kenneth Wherry, a Nebraska Republican, issued the first of two Senate reports on the "pervert problem." He told Max Lerner, "You can't hardly separate homosexuals from subversives. Mind you, I don't say every homosexual is a subversive, and I don't say every subversive is a homosexual. But a man of low morality is a menace in the government, whatever he is, and they are all tied up together. . . . There should be no people of that type working in any position in the government."

JOE MCCARTHY HIMSELF never did much to exploit the gay issue, perhaps because of the swirling rumors about the Wisconsin senator's own bisexuality. On January 14, 1952, Drew Pearson, the liberal investigative columnist, made the following entry in his diary:

[Maryland Democratic Senator] Tydings has an amazing letter which a young army lt. wrote to Senator Bill Benton of Connecticut telling how McCarthy performed an act of sodomy on him after picking him up in the Wardman Park Bar. The letter was sent to Benton about January 1, but two weeks have gone by and apparently nothing has been done. Tydings and I, knowing how McCarthy operates when he knows a witness is against him, thought we had better interview the lt. immediately. So Tydings got Benton on the phone in New York. Benton was evasive and appears to have done little. Therefore, Tydings thought I should arrange for Jack [Anderson] to go to New York.

However when I called Benton as a precautionary measure, he told me that the White House had stepped in and that the lt. was being handled by the FBI. I am a little skeptical as to how the FBI interviews certain witnesses, especially with James McInerny, head of the Justice Department Criminal division, playing cozy with McCarthy for the last two years.

Two days later, Pearson wrote in his diary, "This is the third report on McCarthy's homosexual activity," but when the FBI interviewed the young lieutenant in New York, he denied writing the letter to Tydings, and "claimed it was planted by another homo who was jealous."

Like Hoover, McCarthy was never publicly accused of being gay during his own lifetime. But Lerner pointed out in the summer of 1950 that McCarthy seemed uncertain about how to handle the homosexual issue. "The portrait of the Wisconsin Senator as a tortured Hamlet is novel enough to stir some reflections about what may have caused his paralysis of action in the face of a sure-fire issue. . . . The answer is when you try to use the twisted sex issue as a weapon for twisted political purposes, there is a danger of a boomerang."

In one of his frequent attempts to be "one of the boys" with reporters who covered him, McCarthy once remarked, "If you want to be against McCarthy, boys, you've got to be a communist or a cocksucker." Then the senator roared with laughter. To journalists like Pearson that must have sounded like a bizarre double entendre.

Ben Bradlee believed "there was a lot of time spent investigating" the possibility that McCarthy was gay, but "nobody ever came close to proving it. What a wonderful solution to this problem it would have been." McCarthy's appointment of Roy Cohn as his chief counsel rekindled all the private speculation about the senator's sexuality, especially after Cohn threatened to "wreck the Army" if it failed to give special treatment to his close friend David Schine. In a speech on the Senate floor, Ralph Flanders, a Vermont Republican and a McCarthy enemy, said the Army-McCarthy hearings needed to get to the "real heart" of the matter — the "mystery concerning the personal relationships of the army private, the staff assistant, and the senator." And when Cohn himself became a witness before the committee, Arkansas Democrat John McClellan asked him if he had "any special interest in Mr. Schine."

"I don't know what you mean by 'special interest,'" Cohn replied. "He's a friend of mine."

But the transfixing moment for millions of American television viewers occurred when the army's counsel, Joseph Welch, interrogated former FBI agent James Juliana about a photograph that had been cropped to imply that Schine was close enough to Secretary of the Army Robert Stevens to be alone with him at an air force base. The altered picture was supposed to disprove the idea that Cohn and Schine might want to blackmail the army. Welch discovered that the original photo had been "shamefully cut down" to eliminate the other men near Schine and Stevens, thereby creating an unwarranted impression of closeness between them. "Did you think this came from a pixie?" Welch demanded of Juliana. "Where did you think that this picture I hold in my hand came from?"

"I have no idea," Juliana replied. Then McCarthy interrupted, "Will counsel for my benefit define — I think he might well be an expert on it — what a pixie is?"

"Yes," said Welch. "I should say, Mr. Senator, that a pixie is a close relative of a fairy. . . . Have I enlightened you?"

The audience in the hearing room exploded with laughter. McCarthy managed to smile for the live cameras, but Cohn was grim-faced. As the historian Neil Miller pointed out, Cohn had become "an easy target for the kind of gay baiting he himself had practiced," and he soon resigned and returned to New York to practice law. Inspired by Cohn's devotion to Schine, Lillian Hellman referred to Cohn, Schine, and McCarthy as "Bonnie, Bonnie and Clyde."

Cohn was a homosexual, and he became quite promiscuous, but he always denied that he was gay, even after he began to surround himself with a coterie of young men in public. His lifelong cultivation of a tough-guy image may have been partly motivated by his desire to disguise his sexuality from others — and perhaps, on some level, even from himself.

"Anybody who knows me, and knows anything about me or who knows the way my mind works or knows the way I function . . . would have an awfully hard time reconciling that with any kind of homosexuality," Cohn told the reporter Ken Auletta. "Every facet of my personality, of my, ah, aggressiveness, of my toughness, of everything along those lines is just totally, I suppose, incompatible with anything like that."

Years after Cohn had worked for McCarthy, Gore Vidal enraged Cohn when they appeared together on a New York television program. Vidal remembered saying, "The only thing I really found attractive about McCarthy was of course the fact that he was homosexual — and was extremely tolerant of having them around him." Cohn's hands started to twitch, and he said, "'Well, you would, of course.' And I said, 'I am sure you would too.'"

Then Vidal asked, "'How is Mr. Schine?'

"And [Cohn] said, 'He's all right. He's out in California.'

Vidal said, "'We regarded the two of you as the Damon and Pythias of the homosexual movement.' Well, by then he was shaking all over in a ghastly way."

Despite Cohn's apparent crush on Schine, there is no evidence that they had a sexual relationship. "In Schine's case, he denied it," said "Bill Gillman" (a pseudonym), a young lawyer who saw Cohn frequently during the last ten years of his life. On the other hand, Cohn refused to answer Gillman when he asked about the sexuality of Hoover, or Cohn's close friend Cardinal Spellman.

Ethan Geto, a gay activist and Democratic political operative in New York City, remembered the televised confrontation between Vidal and Cohn as one of those "thrilling moments." As Geto remembered it, Vidal seemed about to ask his adversary directly if he was gay, and Cohn fled from the show during a break. "Gore Vidal was great," said Geto. "Roy Cohn, who had dominated every debate he was ever in, was so cowed, so shaken, and so rattled. He turned ashen!"

In the 1970s, Geto was having dinner with Doug Ireland, a New York journalist, at Uncle Charlie's, a popular gay restaurant on Third Avenue. When Ireland spotted Cohn at a nearby table, surrounded by attractive young men, he went over to speak to him.

"Roy, it's great to see you!" said Ireland. "Especially here in a gay restaurant. It shows you're really surfacing!"

And Cohn jumped up from the table and said, "This is a gay restaurant?"

Bill Gillman said Cohn "did not acquire a coterie of effeminate men around him. The guys that hung out with him were a bunch of jocks, frankly, and they spent more time watching football. I doubt that they ever went to a fashion show. He didn't think of himself as gay. He thought a gay person at that time was a hairdresser or a poodle walker. It reminds me of the retired Wall Street lawyer down in North Carolina who says, 'Hell, I'm not gay, I just like to suck cock. You and all your fancy friends that go to decorating shows — now that's gay!'

"Being gay was only one part of Roy's life," Gillman continued. "I certainly don't think it was the most important thing. He was probably gay the hour before he went to bed. The rest of the time he was many, many other things. He was a lawyer, an employer, a son, a nephew, a friend. He was a very busy man."

"Roy was a lot of different people in one," said Stanley M. Friedman, the Bronx political leader who became one of Cohn's law partners in 1978.* "Roy was whatever the situation called for. He could sit with royalty. And he could sit with gangsters. And everybody was comfortable with him. Roy did all the categories."

Friedman questioned the idea that Cohn needed to be powerful to compensate for his sexual orientation. "You're presupposing that Roy grew up gay," said Friedman. "If I'm right, he was a tough guy before he was gay — because we know he was a tough guy when he was a kid. I have a hunch he was a mean SOB tough guy before he knew he was gay. Because when do you become aware that you're gay? I think he would be in the category of being a late bloomer. I'm guessing. When you were born in the late twenties or early thirties, which is my generation — I was born in thirty-six — it was a disgrace to be gay. There's something wrong with you. You're an embarrassment to your family — you're a 'sissy,' you're a 'fairy,' you're a 'pansy.' Whatever the appropriate words were of that era.

"I think he wanted to be powerful from the very beginning because he had a father who he considered to be influential, but not strong, and he had a mother who was strong, but without influence," Friedman contin- ued. "And he thought he could be as good or as powerful or as influential as they were, plus some. He enjoyed being sought after; being feared, respected. I think he saw what it meant to 'make' a judge. He saw what it meant to be able to use a judge, to be able to influence people's lives, to control people's property. To dictate things that happened — laws that would be passed. Did he need that to make up for some defect which he believed that he was impaired with? We don't know that, because we didn't have the luxury of growing up with him."

AT THE END of 1950, the Senate Subcommittee on Investigations issued a lengthy report on the "pervert problem." These were some of its conclu- sions:

---

*Friedman said he "probably" did not know that Cohn was gay at that time — and that "most people thought I was crazy to want to work with him." (Author's interview with Stanley M. Friedman, November 30, 1994)

Homosexuals and other sex perverts are not proper persons to be employed in government for two reasons. First they are generally unsuitable, and second, they constitute security risks. Aside from the criminality and immorality involved in sex perversion such behavior is so contrary to the normal accepted standards of social behavior that persons who engage in such activity are looked upon as outcasts by society generally . . .

Law enforcement officers have informed the subcommittee that there are gangs of blackmailers who make a regular practice of preying upon the homosexual. These blackmailers often impersonate police officers in carrying out their blackmail schemes. . . . There is an abundance of evidence to sustain the conclusion that indulgence in acts of sex perversion weakens the moral fiber of an individual to a degree that he is not suitable for a position of responsibility. . . . Eminent psychiatrists have informed the subcommittee that the homosexual is likely to seek his own kind because the pressures of society are such that he feels uncomfortable unless he is with his own kind. Due to this situation the homosexual tends to surround himself with other homosexuals, not only in his social, but in his business life. Under these circumstances if a homosexual attains a position in government where he can influence the hiring of personnel it is almost inevitable that he will attempt to place other homosexuals in government jobs.

The committee noted approvingly that the Civil Service Commission had stepped up its efforts against homosexuals, and acted in 382 "sex perversion" cases during the previous seven months versus a total of only 192 during the three years before that. The senators also berated the Washington, D.C., Police Department for failing to turn over automatically the names of the 457 government employees who had been arrested in "perversion cases" during the previous four years. And it noted that Washington's municipal judges had promised to halt the "slipshod practice" under which most homosexuals were booked on charges of disorderly conduct, and then allowed to make "forfeitures of small cash," instead of being brought to trial.

News of this homosexual scourge was spread across the nation by Lee Mortimer, a columnist for Hearst's New York *Daily Mirror,* who wrote a series of *Confidential* books that combined Kinsey's statistics with the Senate's conclusions. "Homosexuality became an epidemic infecting the nation," wrote the historian John D'Emilio. Mortimer said "10,000 faggots" had avoided detection by the FBI and that the government was "honeycombed in high places with people you wouldn't let in your garbage-wagons."

Most damaging of all to gay government employees was a new execu-tive order signed by President Eisenhower shortly after his inauguration in 1953. For the first time, "sexual perversion" was listed as sufficient and necessary ground for disbarment from federal jobs. During the next sixteen months, at least 640 homosexuals were removed from govern-ment employment. That number probably understates the real figure be-cause many were allowed to resign without being forced to disclose their sexuality.

The fear fostered by congressional investigators created a hideous ri-valry among the executive departments. Federal agencies competed with one another to prove which one was the most vigilant in its campaign to root out "perverts" and subversives. In 1954 *The New York Times* actually published a "U.S. Agency Box Score on the 'Security Risks.'" It showed 1,057 "security" dismissals from seven agencies in 1953, as well as 40 fired as "alleged loyalty risks." Every year in the early fifties, the State Department fired more than twice as many homosexuals as it did suspected commu-nists. During the three and a half years ending in July 1953, 381 employees at State lost their jobs because they were gay, compared to 150 who were considered security risks for other reasons.

JOSEPH ALSOP, the scion of a prominent Connecticut Yankee family and a distant relative of the Roosevelts, was one of the few known victims of a Soviet attempt to compromise a prominent American homosexual. A famous Washington newspaperman for almost fifty years, Alsop spent his entire life in the closet. But his humiliation in the Soviet Union was well known to a number of Washington insiders.

During a visit to the Soviet Union in 1957, Alsop was seduced by a male agent of the KGB, with whom he had sex in his hotel room. Because American visitors to Moscow were routinely warned about Russian at-tempts to entrap important tourists of all persuasions, Alsop's blunder was surprising.* Perhaps it resulted from his well-known weakness for copious amounts of fine wine.

But Alsop's behavior contradicted the popular notion that homosexuals were easier to blackmail than heterosexuals. Instead of succumbing to the Soviet attempt to intimidate him, he immediately reported the incident to his editors and to the Central Intelligence Agency. His editors declined his

*Allen W. Dulles, who served as director of the Central Intelligence Agency, said, "So long as there is sex it is going to be used in espionage." He declined to say whether the CIA used such techniques, but acknowledged that "we recognize the existence of sex and the attraction of sex." (*New York Times,* July 21, 1962)

offer to stop writing his column. The CIA made him write a detailed report about the incident, and then forwarded a copy to Hoover at the FBI. But neither his editors nor the agency leaked the incident to Alsop's enemies right away, and the columnist never altered the anti-Soviet slant of his columns.

For the rest of Alsop's life, the Washington establishment behaved very much as it did immediately after Sumner Welles tried to seduce a railroad porter. It kept the columnist's transgression a secret from the public while selectively using it against him in private.

In 1959, Alsop attacked President Eisenhower for permitting a nuclear "missile gap" to develop between the United States and the Soviet Union. Though this charge was used with considerable success by John Kennedy during the 1960 presidential campaign, like many of Alsop's speculations about the communist menace, it was eventually proven to be completely false.

Eisenhower's aides were furious about Alsop's accusation. The president's press secretary, James Hagerty, told one of the columnist's friends on the *New York Herald Tribune* that the administration was planning to lift Alsop's White House press pass. "The guy's a pansy," said Hagerty. "The FBI knows all about it."

A memorandum written by Hoover revealed that Eisenhower's attorney general, William Rogers — who later served as Richard Nixon's secretary of state — had visited the FBI director to discuss the Alsop matter. "The Attorney General . . . commented that he was going to see that certain individuals were aware of Alsop's propensities . . . but he would not take the responsibility for such information going any further," Hoover wrote in a memorandum to the file. Thirty-six years later, Rogers refused to comment on his meeting with Hoover.

In 1961, Alsop married Susan Mary Patten. A year later, a KGB agent defected to the United States and told the CIA that the Soviets "had the goods" on Alsop. But the CIA knew that Alsop was a good friend of President Kennedy, so it removed this item from its report about the KGB man. John and Robert Kennedy both knew about the blackmail attempt anyway. And they were happy to go on protecting their friend from any public embarrassment.

In 1970, the Russians renewed their campaign against Alsop. They sent pictures of the incriminating incident to two writers they considered Alsop's enemies — the humorist Art Buchwald and the columnist Charles Bartlett. Buchwald was a fierce opponent of the Vietnam War, while Alsop was one of its strongest supporters. An unsigned note accompanying the pictures asserted that they had been taken by the Israelis, and that was why Alsop was such a strong supporter of the Jewish state.

Fifteen years later, Buchwald told a *Washington Post* reporter that he had torn the pictures up as soon as he received them. "I don't give a damn what a guy's sexual proclivities are," said the columnist, "as long as they don't involve me." Bartlett mailed his copies to Alsop, with a note reading, "I thought you should have these. I'm not signing this because I don't want it to be an embarrassment to us when we meet." A couple of days later, Alsop asked Bartlett if he had sent him the pictures. After Bartlett confirmed Alsop's suspicion, Alsop never mentioned the subject again.

Alsop did consider a public confession about the incident, to make any future blackmail attempt impossible. But a friend talked him out of the idea, saying that it would embarrass his wife and stepchildren.* Alsop separated from his wife in 1972, and toward the end of his life he became more open about his homosexuality with some of his younger friends. But no one ever wrote about his proclivities until after his death in 1989.

ALMOST EVERY New York City newspaper reference to lesbians and gay men in the fifties was connected to a crime. "Perverts Called Government Peril," "Inquiry by Senate on Perverts Asked," and "Perversion Cited in Security Unit": these were all headlines in *The New York Times*.

A feature story in *Coronet* in September 1950 reported that "psychiatric case histories bear eloquent testimony to the thousands of warped lives that follow in the wake of associations with perverts. . . . Some male sex deviants do not stop with infecting their often-innocent partners: they descend through perversions to other forms of depravity, such as drug addiction, burglary, sadism and even murder. Once a man assumes the role of homosexual, he often throws off all moral restraints."

Most local newspaper stories on this subject concerned periodic clean-ups of gay bars and sweeps of the streets of Times Square. "23 More Undesirables Are Seized in Times Square as Round-Up Spreads" was the headline over a four-column-wide picture on the front page of the *Times* one Sunday during the summer of 1954. It showed the back sides of five identically clad young men leaning against the booking table at the West 47th Street station house. Each one wore a black T-shirt, blue jeans turned up three inches at the bottom, sneakers, and "wide leather motorcycle

---

*This advice was typical of Washington. When Massachusetts Congressman Barney Frank first discussed the possibility of disclosing his homosexuality publicly, most of his powerful heterosexual friends urged him to remain in the closet.

belts, ornamented with artificial, glittering 'gems'" — a uniform, the article reported, that had "become almost standard."

The arrests were part of "the spreading campaign to rid the city of unsavory individuals on its streets." With the subtlety typical of the times, Deputy Chief Inspector James B. Leggett explained that the raids were necessary because "the rise of organized young hoodlums and the patent increase of homosexuals on the city's streets had brought a wave of rape, muggings and other crimes of violence often culminating in murder."

Most of those arrested pled guilty to disorderly conduct and paid $2 fines. "One of the immediate results of the police campaign appeared to be that many of the bars, usual hangouts of the undesirable persons, were oddly deserted last night in contrast to the normal Saturday crowds," the *Times* reported. At the end of the decade, Lee Mortimer closed several gay bars in Manhattan by repeatedly listing them in his column in the *Daily Mirror* and taunting the police into raiding them.

There was a thriving hustler scene on the streets surrounding Times Square in the fifties and early sixties. "In those days it wasn't as scummy," remembered "Sam Baron" (a pseudonym), a young journalist who had grown up in the Bronx and first discovered the wiles of 42d Street in the mid-fifties. "There was a safer feeling about it. The boys were teenagers on into their twenties, a mix of whites and some Puerto Ricans. Not a lot of blacks. They cost $5; $10 was expensive. The thing that astonished me was, I couldn't believe that these beautiful, magnificent specimens of manly beauty would be so pliable and agreeable in bed."

"The hustlers were mostly at the Silver Dollar bars," Jack Dowling recalled. "There was one on Sixth Avenue and 43d Street that had a wonderful selection of hustlers and gay guys, gay older men looking for hustlers, whores, sailors — sort of like the mood of the story 'Tralala' in *Last Exit to Brooklyn*. It was also known that if you wanted to get picked up or pick somebody up and it involved money, you went to the Astor Bar, but you went in a suit and tie. If the hustler wanted some decent money and dinner, he went to the Astor Bar. On the street $10 was a lot, but not in a bar."

GAY LIFE in New York City in the 1950s was by turns oppressive and exhilarating, a world of persecution and vast possibilities. Plainclothesmen tried to entrap men, even inside gay bars in Manhattan, and uniformed officers harassed women dressed like men because women were legally required to wear at least one article of women's clothing whenever they appeared in public. Knowingly serving a drink to a gay person automatically made a bar disorderly under state law, and it was illegal for two men to be on a dance floor together without a woman present.

Blackmail of the closeted was a constant danger, and in some cases criminals impersonated corrupt policemen to extort money from the frightened. A man robbed by someone he had brought home for sex never reported such an incident to the police. And gay murder victims were among the police department's lowest priorities. Joe Schoener, an Associated Press reporter at police headquarters during the fifties, recalled how the New York press treated gay murders. "When a dead man was found murdered inside an apartment, we would all go to the scene to wait for the coroner," Schoener remembered. "Then we would wait for him to examine the victim. If the coroner came out, and said, 'Loose sphincter,' that meant the victim was gay. Then we would all leave — because that meant there was no story."

FROLICKING IN THE FIFTIES in Central Park and on the gay beach at Riis Park, Sandy Kern was an attractive young woman with a shy smile, a compact body, thick black hair, and powerful legs. But she never thought of herself as good-looking: "I always felt ugly. I never felt gorgeous at all." Forty years on, her passionate account of the outlandish escapades of her youth was tempered by a wry amusement at the absurdity of life.

Sandy Kern was not her real name; she had it legally changed because she despised her father. She chose "Sandy" because it sounded androgynous — so she could use it to try to pass as a man. "Kern" was in honor of Jerome, one of her musical idols. Kern's lawyer for the name change was Pauli Murray, an African American activist who first challenged segregation on an interstate bus in 1940. When Kern met her, Murray was just out of law school. In the fifties, Murray was a lawyer at the famous Manhattan firm of Paul, Weiss, Rifkind, Wharton and Garrison. In 1977, after her graduation from the General Theological Seminary in New York City, she became the first American black woman to be ordained as a priest in the Episcopal Church. To the public, Murray was a well-known civil rights activist. To Kern, she was "the first black lesbian lawyer that ever was."

In 1947 Kern graduated from Thomas Jefferson High School and got a job working in the garment district for $30 a week. Like many other young New York Jews of this era, her main political concern was equality for black people. "I felt sorry for them. I lived in poverty, but they lived even worse. So my main objective was to get them out of their hell and make things better for the black people." When a "very black" man named Oscar asked her for a date, she was immediately intrigued. "I thought to myself, God, I could get back at my father if I had this black guy come to the apartment to pick me up for a date." She laughed at the memory of her rebelliousness. "You know, all white and Jewish neighborhood — and Oscar.

"My father nearly had a coronary. Oh God! I was a very, very bad kid."

After just two dates, Oscar told her he was in love with her. But Kern was not interested. "It's not because you're black," she explained. "I'm a lesbian.

"He said, 'What!? You're a lesbian? What a fucking waste!'"

Oscar sent Kern to see a social worker who was his cousin. The social worker told Kern she had a "very good friend" who used to be a lesbian but had cured herself. The ex-lesbian lived in Greenwich Village, and Kern became very excited because she had never been there. "And when I heard *the* Village, I used to think of little private cottages with beautiful little gardens with white picket fences. But I knew that's where lesbians were — because of what I would read from time to time about the Village."

It was 1949. Kern was twenty and still a virgin. "These women that I loved and I had fantasies about — the sex was hardly present. It was just the purity of love: you know, with music and the moonlight and the blue sky."

So she drove to Thompson Street and met "Linda Savage" (a pseudonym) the "reformed" lesbian, who, it turned out, hadn't changed quite so much as her social worker friend believed she had.

"I was very nervous. I remember my impression of the apartment was awful. It was a five-flight walk-up. And even though on Amboy Street we lived in what I considered to be poverty, this place was worse. There was no steam heat. Oh, it was disgusting! But I was very excited about meeting her, and she was looking at me, I knew, in a way that . . . hmmm. And she was very beautiful. She looked like a heavy version of Madeleine Carroll" — the blond star of Alfred Hitchcock's *Secret Agent* and *The Thirty-Nine Steps*.

Savage was a governess who worked for a wealthy family. "It might have happened at the first meeting; it certainly happened by the second: this so-called straight woman seduced me." After the third meeting, they were living together. "I took my records, my hi-fi, my books, and my toothbrush. All in the back of my car.

"I always felt very caged up in Brooklyn. Because I knew I couldn't express my feelings there. But in the Village I was a freed uncaged tiger! I loved it."

Audre Lorde was a self-described "black lesbian feminist warrior poet" who also lived in the Village in the fifties. "We knew we were outside the pale," said Lorde, who four decades later would become the poet laureate of New York State in 1991. "We were dykes. A lot of us were artists. We hated typing. We didn't want straight jobs. We were the fringe. And that was because of the fifties. It was like the gay girls version of the beatniks."

The historian Joan Nestle remembered, "Just going to the bar meant taking on fifties America. It meant being a woman who was different from the protected woman, the domesticated woman. It felt subversive just going out in the streets at two o'clock in the morning, knowing that I was going to a place that was illegal."

Sandy Kern's new girlfriend was forty — exactly twice her age. Although she was not in love with Savage, Kern was enjoying herself because she realized for the first time that "sex is beautiful," instead of "the filthy horrible thing that I thought it was. And we were very good partners. I felt here was this big woman, and I was satisfying her. I felt so strong, you know: like a big-time operator!"

When Savage went away to Switzerland for the summer with the family that she worked for, Kern "met a lot of young, gorgeous women. Bars were all over the place in those days. They kept opening and closing. They were raided and there would be a signal: when they knew that the cops were coming, the lights would flash on and off.

"I would run away because I used to dress in drag and I would bind my breasts. My underpants were men's — I hated the women's stuff. And I didn't want to be in court, because I knew they would put me in prison, because there was a law against cross-dressing in those days. My friends have all been to prison. They were never held, of course. They were booked and then let go.

"In those days it was terrible. I looked obviously like a lesbian. Never like a boy. They would call filthy names and even throw things at me. I remember once in Prospect Park a gang of young hoodlums ran after me and my lover. . . . We had to run for our lives."

But none of this ever stopped her from being who she was: "Even in the daytime I would try to pass as a boy." She came to hate being a secretary in the garment district, so she found a job in Long Island City, in Queens, at an optical frame company. "It was great! I was polishing these frames and using the men's bathroom, and I really thought that I was passing."

Kern's life got a lot more complicated after Savage discovered that her lover was cheating on her. "Oh, my God, she was a violent woman! She did terrible things to me. She said, 'Hell hath no fury as a scorned woman!' She reported me to the police department because I didn't pay my parking tickets. Then she reported me to the IRS. She broke my most cherished records. My Rachmaninoff — the Second Piano Concerto was my favorite in all the world, and she stomped on it! With Rachmaninoff himself playing the piano."

Kern fell in love with another woman named "Cathy" (a pseudonym) and moved to a new apartment on Bank Street. She didn't tell her first lover her new address, but Savage found out about Kern's new girlfriend and followed her home. "Somehow Savage made a duplicate key of the apartment that I was living in. And she would let herself in when my current lover was there, and it was terrible. My current lover was terrified of her."

Savage said, "'This city is not big enough for the both of us. You have to leave. Otherwise I'm going to kill you *and* your lover.' And I believed her. She was crazy. I was such a dumb kid. And so I have to leave. Where am I going to go? So, she sent me away to California." Kern laughed at the memory of her innocence. "I was a very naive person."

One reason for Kern's willingness to leave was that Cathy "didn't like being a lesbian. And she decided she's going to try to become straight. So she met this guy who was also gay, and he didn't want to be gay either. I think the two of them met at Julius's" — a venerable Village saloon that still attracts a motley clientele on West 10th Street. "They decided that they were going to get married. So she left me to marry him in 1953."

Seven months later, Cathy tracked Kern down in Los Angeles. "She was pregnant, and she says to me, 'We couldn't do it. He couldn't do it, and I couldn't do it, and I want to come back to you.' I said, 'Are you crazy? I'm not gonna take you with a belly. I'm not going to be responsible for a child.' This was in the fifties, and I was terrified. And I'm not going to bring up a child in a homosexual atmosphere.

"You know, being a lesbian was terrible, and I wasn't going to bring up an infant who's going to follow me and be like me. I was terrified of that because I wasn't feeling special anymore. I really hit reality after all these years — that it was no good thing to be a lesbian. Because of all the harassment in the streets and the bars closing, being raided and run by Mafia. It was just an ugly world, and I certainly wasn't going to be responsible for bringing a child into that world."

Kern and Cathy took a Greyhound bus back to New York and moved in with Kern's mother on Amboy Street (her father had died before she moved to California). A few weeks later Kern was in the hall outside the delivery room at Sydenham Hospital in Harlem — "pacing with the other husbands" — when the doctor came running to her:

"'Sandy!' he says. 'It's a girl, it's a girl, it's a girl!!' Oh, God, I was so happy. We had tried to abort the baby. But we were both *so* innocent. We had no idea about abortions. And thank God, the baby was born. We decided to call her 'Rosemary' (a pseudonym). When I looked at her the first time there in the hospital, I thought that she looked exactly like me. You know, 'cause, her father is Jewish — she had that Jewish look. And we brought her home, and I did everything but feed her from my breast. She was like my own daughter. I was crazy about her. I worked and supported them — until Rosemary was about four years old.

"Then I started to get frightened because I knew she was going to be starting school soon and I didn't want her to have any hassles from the other kids: 'Who's that lady living with your mother?' You know, all that horrible stuff. So I decided to leave. And also — I didn't want her to start emulating me. It was the biggest mistake of my life, leaving, but in those days I wasn't going to take any chances. So for her benefit I left, and we were *both* brokenhearted, that kid and I. I feel tearful. She used to come and visit me every weekend. I had a motor scooter then. So I would take her on rides with me. We had a great time.

"Today Rosemary is thirty-eight years old. I see her all the time. She has a little factory. She manufactures children's clothes. And I work for her — I work for her as a salesperson, on a volunteer basis. And Rosemary now has her own son. So I'm like a grandma. He's eight years old. I still see Cathy. But after I left her, she never got involved with a woman again, or a man."

DESPITE ITS MANY HARDSHIPS gay life in New York City in the fifties still offered more possibilities than it did anywhere else. Like San Francisco on the opposite coast, the city was a magnet for artists and iconoclasts of all sexual persuasions, a spiritual safe haven for Americans who felt like strangers in their own land everywhere east of the Bay Bridge or west of the Hudson. During the fifties, New York's cosmopolitan appeal was only enhanced by America's passionate embrace of the conventional.

Gay life acted like a bracing undertow, exerting a powerful opposite pull beneath waves of conformity. Because being a rebel is almost always an essential part of accepting one's homosexuality, it was both especially difficult and especially satisfying to be gay in an age like this. Beneath the prevailing waters there was a thriving world of creativity and indulgence which resembled nothing on network television. The sterility of mass culture made the life of an outsider particularly attractive to writers, artists, actors and painters. Stress often feeds the sublimation that produces a vibrant culture, and this synergy was conspicuous in the plays, poems, books, and canvases produced all over Manhattan.

Many gay historians have claimed a connection between homosexual orientation and artistic avocation. However, Edward Sagarin, the first American historian of gay life in the fifties, argued that homosexuals are hardly confined to the arts. He suggested that artists were simply more likely to leave behind hints about their sexuality than "scientists, businessmen, [and] political leaders" — men and women who "not only leave no such evidence," but are forced to engage in "vehement denial and deliberate misinformation."

One reason that lesbians and gay men often make great artists may be that being gay and creating art both require similar strengths: the ability to create an original world of one's own, and a willingness to jettison the conventional wisdom in favor of one's own convictions. Sagarin wrote that "homosexual creativity" is "often freed from conventional thought, with imagination unbound and unfettered — and sponsored by the need for perfection to overcome the doubt of oneself." Notable gay nonconformists who struggled against the fifties tide included poets like Allen Ginsberg, Audre Lorde, John Ashbery, and Frank O'Hara; painters as diverse as Paul Cadmus, Jasper Johns, Robert Rauschenberg, and Ellsworth Kelly; the composers Leonard Bernstein, Ned Rorem, John Cage, and Aaron Copland; and playwrights and screenwriters like Gore Vidal, William Inge, Arthur Laurents, Edward Albee, and Tennessee Williams.

THE FIFTIES were the magical age of musical comedy in America. Broadway was lit up by *The King and I, Guys and Dolls, The Pajama Game, Damn Yankees,* and *My Fair Lady.* But the most original production in this medium, the first "tragic musical comedy," was the creation of Leonard Bernstein, Jerome Robbins, Arthur Laurents, and Stephen Sondheim: four gay Jewish men, all working at the very top of their craft. Bernstein was married and the father of three children, but Laurents considered Bernstein "a gay man who got married. He wasn't conflicted about it at all. He was just gay." Sondheim refused to characterize Bernstein's sexuality. But he felt that Bernstein's family was very important to him. "The *idea* of family was deeply rooted: patriarchy. It had nothing to do with pretending to be heterosexual or anything like that."

Jerome Robbins got the idea for the musical after a gay actor named Montgomery Clift asked the choreographer how he should play a modern Romeo. Robbins's original conception was for something called "East Side

Story," and he called Bernstein at the beginning of 1949 to pitch it to him. "Jerry R. called today with a noble idea," Bernstein wrote in a diary he published eight years later, "a modern version of Romeo and Juliet set in slums at the coincidence of Easter-Passover celebrations. Feelings run high between Jews and Catholics. . . . But it's all much less important than the bigger idea of making a musical that tells a tragic story." In an entry dated four weeks later, he added: "Prejudice will be the theme of the new work . . . the music will be serious music. Serious yet simple enough for all people to understand." In that ambition, Bernstein would be magnificently successful.*

The project was shelved later that year, partly because Bernstein and Robbins discovered that the "Catholic-Jewish, Irish-Jewish" situation had changed after the war, and partly because Arthur Laurents was ambivalent about writing the book for the musical. "I didn't want to write Abie's Irish Rose with music," said Laurents.

The musical came back to life five years later when Bernstein ran into Laurents at the Beverly Hills Hotel swimming pool. When they noticed a headline in the *Los Angeles Times* about gang fights between Mexicans and "so-called Americans," they suddenly realized that their moment had arrived. Back in New York, Robbins became "wildly excited" because this was the "living, breathing reincarnation of the Romeo story, and it was topical." Now, for the first time, it became *West Side Story.*

Laurents recruited Sondheim for the project after an audition at which Sondheim played a whole show he had written in school. Sondheim was initially unenthusiastic about the musical because he was asked to be only colyricist with Bernstein; and now Laurents was ambivalent about working with Robbins because of his testimony before the House Committee on Un-American Activities. But the surge of electricity created by their collaboration obliterated every misgiving.

Bernstein adored working with Sondheim: "We thought the same way; we were word people and note people . . . I could explain musical problems to him and he'd understand immediately, which made the collaboration a joy. It was like writing with an alter ego. To me, it was like Gilbert and Sullivan, like Strauss and von Hofmannsthal." And Bernstein was amazed by Laurents's generosity. When the decision was made to add a new song called "Something's Coming," Bernstein and Sondheim stole from Laurents's dialogue, in which he had written, "Something's coming,

---

*Later evidence suggested that the diary entries were not contemporary, but a creative reconstruction made several years later. (Humphrey Burton, *Leonard Bernstein*, 187)

it may be around the corner, whistling down the river, twitching at the dance — who knows?" Bernstein said, "We raped Arthur's playwriting. I've never seen anyone so encouraging, let alone generous, urging us, 'Yes, take it, take it, make it a song.'" Sondheim decided later that some of his lyrics sounded ridiculous coming out of the mouth of a Puerto Rican girl, especially "I feel pretty." On the other hand, in "Gee, Officer Krupke," he was hip enough to include the first sung reference to marijuana in an American musical hit.

"I remember all my collaborations with Jerry in terms of one tactile bodily feeling," said Bernstein. "Composing with his hands on my shoulders. I can feel him standing behind me saying — four more beats there, or no, that's too many, or yeah — that's it!" Robbins fondly recalled "the amount of fuel that we fed each other, the ideas and chemistry between us, each one taking hold of something and saying, 'Hey, I think I can do that,' or saying, 'No, don't write it as music, we can do it better in book' — or 'Don't do it in song, I can do it better in dance.' The continual flow between us was an enormous excitement."

Originally, Robbins wanted only to direct the show, and he planned to get someone else to do the choreography. But his collaborators insisted that he do both jobs — because they believed he was the greatest choreographer in America.

Laurents contributed a compact, clever book, which included an invented slang that would take young America by storm after Hollywood brought the work to a mass audience — especially the word *cool*. "I twisted syllables and did all sorts of things because the show needed a language," Laurents told Sondheim's biographer Craig Zadan. "It was lyric theater and if you used actual language it would have been flat." Bernstein was writing much more sophisticated music than Broadway was accustomed to, while Robbins figured out how to translate gang wars into beautiful ballets. The exacting choreographer often dominated the creative process. Bernstein wrote to his wife, Felicia, during rehearsals, "Jerry continues to be — well, Jerry: moody, demanding, hurting. But vastly talented."

Robbins said, "The idea was to make the poetry of the piece come out of our best attempts as serious artists: that was the major thrust." But despite all the talent they brought to bear on the project, they alternated between great expectations and intimations of catastrophe. "I thought it would run three months," said Laurents. "I thought it was a sure turkey. But we were doing what we wanted to do." Sondheim remembered everyone saying, "It's such a shame you can't hum the music."

Six weeks before rehearsals were scheduled to begin, *West Side Story* almost vanished from the stage forever after one of its original producers, Cheryl Crawford, withdrew from the show. "We thought at that point that it would not get on," said Bernstein. "Everybody told us to stop. They all said it was suicidal. I don't know how many people begged me not to waste my time on something that could not possibly succeed. After all, how could we do a musical where there are two bodies lying on the stage at the end of the first act and everybody eventually dies? A show that's so filled with hatefulness and ugliness?" (Actually, not everyone dies. In a crucial modification of the Shakespeare original, Laurents allowed Maria to live.)

The producer Harold Prince was in Boston rehearsing another show with his partner Robert E. Griffith when they heard about the crisis in Manhattan, and the two of them decided to keep *West Side Story* alive. Their gamble seemed worthwhile when it opened in Washington to fabulous reviews — and Bernstein bumped into a weeping Supreme Court Justice Felix Frankfurter during the intermission.

Despite the triumphant opening, Sondheim remained unhappy because he had only a cocredit for the lyrics. In a remarkable act of magnanimity, Bernstein removed his name as colyricist to placate his young collaborator. "It was extremely generous," Sondheim remembered.

But Laurents remained dissatisfied because the line above his book credit still read, "Based on a conception of Jerome Robbins." Laurents recalled, "The next day I went to Robbins and I brought up what Lenny had done for Steve. And I said, 'You know, Jerry, obviously they think conception means this whole thing of juvenile delinquency and the gangs and the color thing. So I think you should remove that credit.' So he said, 'Well, let me think about it.' The next day he said, 'You're right, but it means too much to me.' So that's when I learned: once an informer, always an informer." By the time the show opened in New York, none of the other collaborators was talking to Robbins, according to Laurents. But out of all their struggles, they had produced a masterpiece.

These four young artists absorbed the romance, energy, anger, and pathos of the streets of New York; then they managed to make all those elements pulsate through every moment of the musical. Sondheim's lyrics were moving, clever and funny; Laurents's spare book managed to tie everything together unobtrusively, while Robbins's choreography also functioned as brilliant storytelling.

Bernstein's music was *West Side Story*'s sublime achievement. His synthesis of Broadway, jazz, Latin rhythms, and Aaron Copland perfectly captured the city's astonishing spirit. "The purity of the music was most important," said Laurents.

The actor Alan Helms remembered announcing at a Christmas party shortly after *West Side Story* opened that the person who obviously deserved the most credit for the show was Steve Sondheim.

"A man tapped me on the shoulder and said, 'You're wrong,'" Helms recalled. "'The man who deserves most credit is Arthur Laurents.'"

"How would you know?"

"I'm Steve Sondheim," the man replied.

Thousands of gay Americans fell in love with *West Side Story* when they were children in the fifties. And for legions of kids of all persuasions, the show provided them with their first concrete notion of romantic love. To many gay adults coming of age in the sixties, the romance, violence, danger, and mystery so audible on the original cast album all felt like integral parts of the gay life they had embraced. The lyrics of "Somewhere" in particular seemed to speak directly to the gay experience before the age of liberation. In 1996, it was one of the songs chosen for the first mass gay wedding of two hundred couples in San Francisco, presided over by the city's mayor, Willie Brown.

But none of the collaborators (or their 1950s contemporaries) ever suspected there was anything gay about their very heterosexual love story. (Coincidentally, Larry Kert, who starred as Tony, was also gay.) "It was never an issue that we talked about," said Murray Gitlin, who fell in love with the show when it opened. "I never thought about it as gay."

"There is one sensibility all four of us share which is much more important and really *does* inform the work," said Arthur Laurents. "We're all Jews. Think about it and what it means. Creative work is undoubtedly the sum of the creators but certain elements take a bigger role than others at different times. *West Side* can be said to be informed by our political and sociological viewpoint; our Jewishness as the source of passion against prejudice; our theatrical vision, our aspiration, but not, I think, by our sexual orientation." Gore Vidal agreed that the sexuality of the authors was irrelevant to their work: the fact that they were gay didn't mean that they couldn't do "boy-girl stuff. I mean boy-girl stuff is no different from boy-boy stuff."

Sondheim reacted angrily to the suggestion that there might be anything gay about the lyric of "Somewhere." He said, "If you think that's a gay song, then all songs about getting away from the realities of life are gay songs."

On one level, this debate simply highlights the similarities between the experiences of Jews and homosexuals in New York City: two oppressed minority groups who have struggled mightily, and very successfully, to travel out of invisibility and assimilation to proud self-declaration.

Regardless of whether the collaborators' portrayal of prejudice was shaped more by their gayness or their Jewishness, together they had created the most vibrant musical portrait of twentieth-century Manhattan ever mounted on the New York stage — an achievement that remains unrivaled four decades later. The show has been performed tens of thousands of times in almost every major city in the world. "What we did was to aim at a lyrically and theatrically sharpened illusion of reality," Laurents explained. What they achieved was a show that remains remarkably ageless.

When the show opened on September 26, 1957, the New York critics were enthusiastic. "The radioactive fallout from *West Side Story* must still be descending on Broadway this morning," Walter Kerr wrote in the *Herald Tribune*. He praised "the most savage, restless, electrifying dance patterns we've been exposed to in a dozen seasons." In the *Times*, Brooks Atkinson called it "a profoundly moving show . . . as ugly as the city jungles and also pathetic, tender and forgiving. . . . Everything contributes to the total impression of wildness, ecstasy and anguish. This is one of those occasions when theater people, engrossed in an original project, are all in top form. . . . The subject is not beautiful, but what *West Side Story* draws out of it is beautiful."

It was not, however, a big commercial success. It was *too* hip and *too* smart — too far from "I Love Lucy" and too close to the sensibility of the urban sophisticate. "It was a big hit with theater people but not with the audiences," said Sondheim. "It never sold out for very long," said Harold Prince. "It's an important show, but most shows that are important are not smash hits," Prince said. The smash hit on Broadway that year — the one that took most of the awards and made the most money — was *The Music Man*, the musical comedy whose "Seventy-six Trombones" were perfectly in tune with the white-bread taste of the fifties. Only after Hollywood had produced a broader and coarser *West Side Story* with Natalie Wood did the show become a box office smash. "The picture failed for me," said Laurents. But it was the movie and its soundtrack that finally brought big profits to its creators.

IN HIS 1954 short story, "Two on a Party," Tennessee Williams offered a succinct description of the way the artistic demimonde viewed everyone outside the world they inhabited. This passage relates how Billy (in real life, the poet Oliver Evans) and Cora (Marion Black Vaccaro) enjoyed cruising sailors together:

> It was a rare sort of moral anarchy, doubtless, that held them together, a really fearful shared hatred of everything that was restrictive and which they felt to be false in the society they lived in and against the grain of which they continually operated. They did not dislike what they called "squares." They loathed and despised them, and for the best of reasons. Their existence was a never ending contest with the squares of the world, the squares who have such a virulent rage at everything not in their book.

Within this self-consciously bohemian milieu, there was intense sexual and intellectual cross-pollination — not just among gay artists, but also between them and their more experimental heterosexual colleagues. In this era before the gay liberation movement, sexual nonconformists often felt less pressure to label themselves as exclusively homo- or heterosexual. With less political importance attached to one's self-identification, it may have been easier to be bisexual, especially because most sexual encounters were dealt with so circumspectly.

Michael Butler was the extremely good-looking son of the founder of Butler Aviation, a Chicago businessman who occasionally dabbled in politics, and an internationally famous polo player. He was also a close friend and bad-boy companion of John Kennedy. In the sixties, he would become famous as the producer who brought the musical *Hair* to Broadway and to stages across America and around the world.

Butler is a self-described member of a tiny minority: those adults who are equally attracted to men and women.* In the early 1950s, he first became enamored of three-way romantic relationships after an extended affair with one of Hollywood's biggest male stars and the actor's wife.

In 1955 Butler married the nightclub singer Marti Stevens. After flying to England on their honeymoon, Butler bought a black Rolls-Royce Coupe de Ville convertible with gold trim from a British relative; then the bridal couple motored through Europe. "We mostly got married to get away from our families," said Butler, although they also enjoyed each other's company.

By the time they had reached Venice, Butler's friends sensed that he was bored, so they introduced him to Rock Hudson. There was immediate chemistry between them. "Rock was a simple guy: very sweet," said Butler. For the next two weeks the two of them drove around Italy — and

---

*Butler and Ethan Geto were the only people I interviewed who fit into this category.

flaunted their new affair from Butler's Rolls-Royce convertible. Mean-while, Marti Stevens went off to visit her close friend Marlene Dietrich.

Word of Hudson's Italian liaison quickly reached his Hollywood han-dlers, who were horrified by his lack of discretion. They ordered him to take the next ship back to America — without Butler. "He always said I stood him up," said Butler, "because he didn't give a shit about the studio." But Butler stayed in Europe, and visited Deauville with Michael Todd. There, Butler met a new lady whom he went "bonkers" over and took her to the Hôtel du Cap d'Antibes outside Cannes.

Jack Kennedy was also touring Europe that summer with Jacqueline, although he was still recovering from his latest back operation. According to Butler, Kennedy left his wife to meet Butler in the south of France, and the two of them went sailing in the company of Butler's new girlfriend on his 120-foot gaff-rigged schooner. "It was just the three of us," said Butler. "You can imagine what happened. It was a scene. Jackie always thought *I* was the troublemaker. But Jack was also presidential timber in that cate-gory. He was still on crutches from the operation, but that didn't stop him. He was something extra-special. I really loved him."

In Newport a year later Butler and Kennedy repeated the same arrange-ment on another sailing trip with another "very famous" woman. "It was a good arrangement for us," Butler said.

Gore Vidal, a child of the fifties, has always insisted "there are no homosexual or heterosexual persons, only acts . . . I never in my life accepted that these two categories existed. And when they began on 'gay sensibility' back in the sixties and seventies, I said, 'Well, if you think there is such a thing, what does Roy Cohn have in common with Eleanor Roosevelt?' Other than they liked their own sex."

The novelist, essayist, and biographer Edmund White is similarly skep-tical about the notion of a gay sensibility. "What we can discuss . . . is the gay *taste* of a given period," he wrote in *States of Desire*. "A taste cultivated (even by some heterosexuals) or rejected (even by many homosexuals). What we can detect is a resemblance among many gay works of art made at a particular moment — a resemblance partially intended and partially drawn without design from a shared experience of anger or alienation or secret, molten camaraderie." Elsewhere, White argued that "any discus-sion of a group's sensibility (the 'black sensibility'? the 'Jewish sensibility'?) is too general to be useful."

Vidal thought the fifties were a time when "you got very good at pro-jecting subtexts without saying a word about what you were doing."

His proudest achievement in this regard was to imply a homosexual relationship between Ben Hur and his Roman rival in William Wyler's film.
Vidal said Wyler permitted his subterfuge on the condition that he kept
Charlton Heston ignorant of his mischief.* The censors were not "rocket
scientists," said the screenwriter Jay Presson Allen. "If a director was subtle
enough and clever enough, he got away with it," she said. One of the
greatest on-screen contortions occurred when Rock Hudson pretended
to be a gay man in *Pillow Talk* to try to get Doris Day into bed. It was
"tremendously ironic," said Armistead Maupin. "Here was a gay man
impersonating a straight man impersonating a gay man."

Tennessee Williams's iconoclasm was very much on display when Vidal
took him to lunch with Jack and Jacqueline Kennedy in Palm Beach a
couple of years before JFK became president. According to Vidal, "At one
point . . . the Bird [Williams] muttered in my ear, 'Get that ass!' I said,
'Bird, you can't cruise our next president.' The Bird chuckled ominously.
'They'll never elect those two. They are much too attractive for the American people.' Later, I told Jack that the Bird had commented favorably on
his ass. He beamed. 'Now, that's *very* exciting,'" the future president said.

The painter Larry Rivers was "so convinced of being heterosexual I
could be homosexual." So the first time he met Frank O'Hara in 1950 at a
party given by John Ashbery, he started kissing the New York poet behind
a curtain. "From the earliest moments of our friendship we were enthusiastic about each other's work," Rivers remembered, and in 1957 they
collaborated on a series of lithographs which combined O'Hara's poetry
with Rivers's images. This partnership did not "exclude all sorts of sexual
undercurrents," Rivers recalled. "'What are you working on?' was inter-
woven with 'What are you doing later on?'" It was also the sort of era
when someone as talented as O'Hara could go "pretty quickly from a
Christmas job selling postcards at the Museum of Modern Art to being
one of its most outstanding curators."

To O'Hara's biographer, Rivers explained: "I was in a rather conventional tradition of men who are mainly heterosexual . . . who when they
get with men who are homosexual act as if they are allowing themselves to
be had. So he would get me aroused enough by a blow job for me to get a
hard on and then screw him in the ass. That was about what it was about.

---

*Heston also portrayed Michelangelo in *The Agony and the Ecstasy,* but he told the filmmaker
Jeffrey Friedman that he "knew for a fact" that Michelangelo was *not* a homosexual. (*The
Advocate,* March 19, 1996)

. . . One night I'd be with him and the next night I'd be with a woman. It got to be funny.

"I was also introduced to the ever-critical pipe-smoking lay analyst Paul Goodman, who told me I must be sick for refusing to go to bed with him," Rivers said. "'But, Paul, you're married. You have a beautiful wife and child. What future would there be for me?'"

Gore Vidal recalled a romantic adventure with Jack Kerouac. "I wouldn't go to bed with an actor or with a writer," said Vidal. "Or with anyone well known. But that doesn't mean I haven't. As everybody in the world knows, I fucked Kerouac. He rang me [in August 1953] and said, 'I got this friend. He's a junkie and he killed his wife, and he wants to meet you.'" The friend was the writer William Burroughs. "So we met at the San Remo," an Italian restaurant and bar that was one of the great gay-straight Greenwich Village meeting grounds of the fifties. "Then Jack got so stoned, Burroughs was disgusted with Jack, and he left," Vidal continued. "Then Jack and I end up in the Chelsea Hotel. His idea, may I say. Though he was quite attractive that night. Relatively. He describes it all in a book called *The Subterraneans,* in which I am Arial Lavalina, the author of *Recognition in Rome.*"

Here is Kerouac's version of the evening in *The Subterraneans:*

repairing the three of us to 13 Pater a lesbian joint down Columbus, Carmody, high, leaving us to go enjoy it, and we sitting in there, further beers, the horror the unspeakable horror of myself suddenly finding in myself a kind of perhaps William Blake or Crazy Jane or really Christopher Smart alcoholic humility grabbing and kissing Arial's hand and exclaiming "Oh Arial you dear — you are going to be — you are so famous — you wrote so well — I remember you — what —" whatever and now unrememberable and drunkenness, and there he is a well-known and perfectly obvious homosexual of the first water, my roaring brain — we go to his suite in some hotel — I wake up in the morning on the couch, filled with the first horrible recognition, "I didn't go back to Mardou's at all . . ."

Vidal believes the handful of artists whose "deviant" orientation was known to the critics all paid a significant price for their openness. "It is hard now to realize what a bad time of it Tennessee used to have from the American press," Vidal wrote.

During the forties and fifties the anti-fag battalions were everywhere on the march. From the high lands of *Partisan Review* to the middle ground of *Time* magazine, envenomed attacks on real or suspected fags never let up. A *Time* cover story on Auden was killed when the managing editor of the day was told that Auden was a fag. From 1945 to 1961 *Time* attacked with unusual ferocity everything produced or published by Tennessee Williams. "Fetid swamp" was the phrase most used to describe his work. But, in *Time*, as well as in time, all things come to pass. The Bird is now a beloved institution.

"So why all the fuss?" Vidal asked.

In order for a ruling class to rule, there must be arbitrary prohibitions. Of all prohibitions, sexual taboo is the most useful because sex involves everyone. To be able to lock up someone or deprive him of employment because of his sex life is a very great power indeed, and one seldom used in civilized societies. But although the United States is the best and most perfect of earth's societies and our huddled masses earth's envy, we have yet to create a civilization, as opposed to a way of life.

Jack Kerouac was the first person Allen Ginsberg came out to at Columbia in 1946 — "'Cause I was in love with him," Ginsberg remembered. "He was staying in my room up in the bed, and I was sleeping on a pallet on the floor. I said, 'Jack, you know, I love you, and I want to sleep with you, and I really like men.' And he said, 'Oooooh, no ...' We'd known each other maybe a year, and I hadn't said anything."

Within a year, Ginsberg said he had slept with Kerouac "a couple of times."

Neal [Cassady], his hero, and I were lovers, also, for many years. . . . At the time Kerouac was very handsome, very beautiful and very mellow. . . . As a slightly older person and someone who I felt had more authority, his tolerance gave me *permission* to open up and talk. . . . He wasn't going to hit me. He wasn't going to reject me. . . . He was going to accept my soul with all its throbbings and sweetness and worries and dark woes and sorrows and heartaches and joys and glees and mad understandings of mortality, 'cause that was the same thing he had. . . . The basic thing about him was Character, with a capital C . . . an enormous mellow, trustful tolerance and sensitivity. And that's why he's such a great writer and observer. He held everything ever, as sensitive young fellow, even my fairy woes.

But Ginsberg did not consider Kerouac to be primarily gay.

He had mixed feelings at different times, but I think it would have been abusive of his character to point an accusing finger and say, "You're a fairy!" There is a certain tendency among gay people . . . to plaster labels over everybody, including themselves, instead of seeing the nameless love that everybody is. Just as there was a tendency among macho heterosexuals to plaster labels, so there was a counter-balancing tendency among homosexuals to overreact to that and camp too heavily, so that he was sensitive about being put down as a fairy, which he wasn't.

In his classic, *On the Road,* Kerouac originally included a scene in which Dean Moriarty had sex with a traveling salesman who is taking him to Chicago in a Cadillac. According to Ginsberg, "That was eliminated from the book by Malcolm Cowley . . . and Jack consented to that. So Jack actually did talk about it a little in his writing."

But Kerouac, Ginsberg and the rest of the Beats, as they called themselves, were far more important for what they stood for than for whom they slept with. Their celebration of nonconformity planted the roots of the rebellion against a monochrome society that would flower into the counterculture in the coming decade. And in this postwar period, they were the first group of American writers ever to portray homosexuality as hip — a huge step forward for all those who continued to accept society's definition of this orientation as an illness, a crime, or both. "It took an enormous amount of courage to openly declare yourself to be a lesbian or a gay male," the historian Martin Duberman remembered. But the fifties were not a time of "total desperation — it depended on who you are or where you are."

To Ginsberg, the events of the forties were all reasons to rebel against the establishment in the fifties. "In the forties, the bomb dropped," Ginsberg said. "In the forties, the entire planet was threatened biologically. . . . There was a . . . total breakdown of all morality in the concentration camps. For homosexuals there was a sudden realization: 'why are we being intimidated by a bunch of jerks who don't know anything about life? Who are they to tell us what we feel and how we're supposed to behave? And why take all that bullshit?' Why not 'sort of dish it back and start talking openly?'"

During the fifties, "We thought that we were in a decade of such towering dullness and stupidity," said Jay Presson Allen.

"There was a series of trials that liberated the word," Ginsberg recalled, including an unsuccessful attempt to suppress his epic poem *Howl.* "So they lost. So we got a lot of publicity. So the book sold like hotcakes and the censors acted as publicists for a new sensibility." *Howl* became a best-selling book of poetry. And in 1958, *One,* the magazine published by the Mattachine Society, won a case against the United States Post Office, which guaranteed other gay publications access to the mail.

NEW YORK UNDERWENT great physical changes in the fifties. Except for a couple of brief stretches of the Broadway line in Harlem, all the remaining elevated trains were torn down in Manhattan, most of the north-south avenues became broad, one-way thoroughfares below Central Park, and the manufacturers that had made New York City the industrial capital of the East Coast ever since the opening of the Erie Canal were beginning their decades-long exodus.

Heavy industry began to leave in search of lower taxes and wide-open spaces. Following these factories as they moved into the suburbs and beyond were the returning veterans who formed the nucleus of the quickly growing Jewish, Irish and Italian middle classes. Eager to raise their young families far from the soot of the city, they snatched up seventeen thousand houses (reserved for whites only) in Levittown on Long Island and filled new communities in the nearby counties of New York, New Jersey, and Connecticut, creating a vast suburban belt. The new immigrants who the public noticed replacing them in the city were Puerto Ricans, and poor blacks fleeing the rigid segregation that remained intact almost everywhere — above and below the Mason-Dixon Line.

New York at night looked much more forbidding than it does today. Before high-intensity streetlights were installed as an anticrime measure during John Lindsay's administration at the end of the sixties, side streets were often steeped in shadows. The air was dirtier too, in an era when cars lacked catalytic converters and most apartment houses still belched heavy black smoke from their incinerators. To many New Yorkers in the fifties, the city seemed more ominous — and its future more uncertain — than it ever had before.

But nothing would deter a new wave of mostly invisible immigrants, whose arrival was almost never mentioned in the pages of the daily papers. These were the lesbian and gay veterans and recent college graduates who had tasted a different life in Manhattan during the war. Here, many of them had discovered for the first time that they were not alone; and they came back by the thousands to fill up the apartments in Greenwich Village, the East Fifties, and the Upper West Side. The revitalizing effect of these invisible immigrants — invisible in the same sense as Ralph Ellison's *Invisible Man* — would go unreported for twenty-five years. But they played a vital role in New York's postwar renaissance.

And unlike many of the city's more established white residents, many of these lesbians and gay men welcomed the influx of poorer immigrants. "I loved the Puerto Ricans coming to New York," said Franklin Macfie. "It really gave energy to a dying city. My oldest sister married a Puerto Rican, a sensationally wonderful guy."

MURRAY GITLIN was the West Hartford boy who got posted to the Brooklyn Navy Yard and found his first pickup in the orchestra seats of Radio City Music Hall. He had black hair and a long, attractive Semitic face. His low, warm, carefully modulated voice and precise diction made him sound almost British. His close friend Leo Aultman remarked that Gitlin was so charming that he could convert anyone he met into a friend.

In 1949 Gitlin moved back to New York. His first temporary residence was the elegant apartment belonging to his uncle Aaron and aunt Helen on the Grand Concourse, still a magnificent Bronx boulevard right after the war.

He didn't have time to look for his own place because he "just had to become a dancer," Gitlin explained. "I was a late starter, and I didn't have time to waste. I was twenty-two." His aunt Helen was a "very powerful woman" who was seeing a psychiatrist because she was having terrible abdominal pain that her doctor thought was psychosomatic. One night after dinner, she said, "'You know, Murray, Aaron and I know that among male dancers, there are many who are homosexual.' She was suspicious of me. 'And we wonder, since you're a dancer now, what your relationship is to those men.'

"I thought she had balls. You know: 1950. And I said, 'Well, Helen, I am." And Aaron was there. She said, 'Oh.' I said, 'Oh yes.' And I said, 'I've accepted it, and I think I understand it.' And she said, 'Well!'

"She insisted I go to her psychiatrist and have a preliminary consultation with him. And then we'd see."

Gitlin went to the psychiatrist, but it had no effect. "I think there was never any choice for me, which is, you know, par for the course. And as far as I know, as far as I can remember, there was never another way for me. I felt confident because I'd thought it through."

Soon he found a magnificent cold-water flat at 426 West 56th Street with a bathtub in the kitchen and the bathroom in the hall. The rent was $16 a month. During the next forty-four years, Gitlin would never leave the neighborhood, although he did move once to another apartment six blocks away.

He was very good-looking, but too chubby to think of himself as really attractive. His first job was in the chorus of *The King and I.* "I was very happy to be in that show — it was a very glamorous thing to be in. It was just beautiful. I've directed it since and played roles in it since, but that was the most important." In the chorus line, Gitlin replaced Otis Bigelow — the best-looking man in Manhattan in 1940, the one who had chosen a beautiful sailor over a suntanned millionaire.

A year earlier at Martha Graham's dancing school in Vermont, Gitlin spotted a "tall beautiful young man, who looked like a swimmer — which he was. I'll never forget my first impression of him. After class, I asked Martha if she would introduce me to him, and she did. He was very shy. And I said I was living in New York. I said when you come to New York — and I knew he would — look me up if you want to. I'd be very happy to see you."

One day Gitlin was leaving the St. James Theatre, where *The King and I* was playing, and he recognized the same young man. "He was sitting out there just waiting for me. And he said, 'Hi. Remember me?' In a small voice. I said, 'Yes, I do remember you.' And that's when our friendship really began."

The young man was Paul Taylor, who became one of Manhattan's most famous modern dancers and choreographers, as well as the founder of his own dance company, which is still flourishing. Gitlin found him an apartment in his building, and soon Taylor was bringing over a painter friend named Bob Rauschenberg. "Rauschenberg used to come over and he would go to the bathroom," Gitlin remembered. "And I would keep painting that bathroom — to cheer it up a little bit. And I painted it red and orange and it would peel almost immediately. And one day, I'll never forget, Rauschenberg went to the bathroom, and he came in, and said, 'When I become famous' — not *if*, but '*when* I become famous' — *that* bathroom is going to be part of the exhibit I have. Because I think it's *so* beautiful the way the paint's peeling off so delicately.'"

Another frequent visitor was Jerome Robbins, who Gitlin knew slightly because Robbins had choreographed *The King and I.* A couple of years later, Robbins would choose a photograph of Larry Kert and Carol Lawrence standing in front of Gitlin's West Side apartment building to illustrate the cast album of his most spectacular musical.

"Jerry used to come over and visit and we'd laugh," said Gitlin. "But he was always weird. We always got along in those days. I don't know; something happened. He does this to people. He turns people off. Something snaps. Somewhere along the line, something must have happened between him and me. I mean we really liked one another. And in some of my early days on Fire Island, he was out there. He loved the island as much as I did. He loved games and I loved games. And we played with some of the ballet people who were out there. And it was so much fun. He loved to have fun."

EVEN FOR THOSE who weren't mingling with the famous or soon-to-be-famous, Manhattan could be full of exhilarating new experiences. For young lesbians and gay men exploring their sexuality for the first time, a certain amount of danger was often quite exciting. For some there was even an occasional epiphany.

It was the summer of 1955 when Roy Aarons found his very first gay bar. "I was twenty-one, going on twenty-two," and he was handsome. "I walked down an alley and opened a door. There must have been 160 men in the bar. It was all jammed around the bar, with a piano on a pedestal in the middle of the bar. It felt to me like *The Wizard of Oz,* when the house lands, and she opens the door, and the black and white turns to Techni-color — the whole fucking world has suddenly gone to Technicolor. That was exactly how I felt — the power and the impact. That was my initia-tion. And from then on you couldn't stop me: I was crazed."

Growing up in the Bronx, Aarons had been "totally unaware of the gay scene in New York. There was nothing to read, nothing in the newspapers, nothing in the magazines. The only gay references I got were snide jokes about fags in my family."

He discovered his second gay bar one night just after leaving a Passover seder at his aunt's house on West 73d Street. "It was this little bar called the Cork Club on the south side of 72d Street which I'd seen a million times before. There was something about it which just drew me there. And I walked down, and sure enough, all guys. I can remember there was a Sam Cooke song playing on the jukebox — 'You Send Me.' Every time I hear Sam Cooke do that it brings it all back. Of course I asked people if they knew anywhere else to go. And they told me a great spot down on 45th Street called Artie's. That was heaven. Interestingly enough, it was a store-front, brightly lit, right on 45th Street between Sixth and Broadway. In fact it was about five or six doors down from the Peppermint Lounge, which later became famous for the Twist. So you would approach Artie's, and here was this total picture window and it was jammed in there. There was no attempt to darken it.

"You could see right through the window from the street — at a time when one wondered how that was allowed. I assume there were big payoffs going on. It was all men but nobody could come in and say there was any lewd behavior going on. Rep sweaters and jackets, it was all kind of dressy. It had not gotten to the era of the funky look. It was totally, blatantly open, and it was jammed from stem to stern with gorgeous young college-age men. It was at once the most exciting and frustrating place — because I wanted to start at the front and work my way through to the rear. That became my hangout.

"Forty-fifth Street was very lively at that time. . . . Toward Sixth Avenue was another so-called straight bar where people would go do the Twist, but where I would very frequently run into other gays. I remember once I picked up — oh, God, *romance* — a soldier, and we had a little fling. It was wonderful. I am still in the navy. At this point, I'm living off the ship in Brooklyn Navy Yard. So I couldn't bring anybody back. I would have to go to their place. Never with another sailor. I was too scared. I knew it was considered sodomy and I could go to jail.

"You're living a totally secret life. You're showing one face to the world, and you've got this whole other thing happening. There *was* a risk factor, but there was also a certain excitement about that, an illicit excitement. The next thing I heard about were two dancing bars in the Seventies. One was called the Mais Oui and one was called the Bali. Probably 70th Street for the Mais Oui, between Broadway and Amsterdam. The basement of an apartment house. You had to walk down, and they had this secret lighting system. At the Mais Oui, there was always a bouncer to screen you as you came in. A $1.50 cover charge or something like that. They screened you not just for your ID, but they checked you to see if you looked like an undercover cop. And in fact a couple of times I was taken for that and the lights went on and I was very proud of that.

"So whenever it looked like an undercover cop was coming in, the lights would suddenly go on and you had to push your partner away and pretend you were sort of standing around. Rock and roll was just coming in — the Mashed Potato and all of that stuff. So you could meet somebody right away and immediately start grinding away without a lot of ceremony.

"I found it to be very unsatisfying in the long run. There was a kind of ambivalence because it was exciting. There was the promise of sexuality; there was the physical contact; but there was also a lot of rejection. There *was* attitude. You'd ask somebody you thought was absolutely dandy to dance, and they'd say, 'No, thank you very much.' Or you'd get out on the dance floor and the person's just not responding, just kind of going through the motions. And I was kind of shy to start with. And you begin to get into a pattern: Should I ask this guy? I don't want to get rebuffed. So there was all that stuff that still exists today.

"At that point I wasn't conscious of coupling being a manifestation of the gay existence. What I was doing then was trying to figure out how I was going to work out a normal life — how to be straight. I knew that I had the capacity." The year after Aarons entered his first gay bar, he met a girl in Washington and had his first sexual experience with a woman. "So I knew I was capable. My essential flaming passion was not there, but I knew I could accomplish and enjoy it. I was trying to convince myself [to be straight] for the next fifteen years."

There was another famous cluster of gay bars near Third Avenue in the East Fifties known as the Bird Circuit: the Blue Parrot on 53d, the Golden Pheasant on 48th, the Swan and the 316 — at 316 East 54th Street. The Thalia movie theater on West 95th Street was active because it featured foreign films, which attracted an arty crowd. There was also a great deal of outdoor cruising: on Third Avenue between 50th and 57th streets, in Washington Square in the Village, on Central Park West in the Seventies, and around the skating rink in Rockefeller Center.

"Gay life was secretive," Jack Dowling remembered. "It was furtive — *furtive* is a good word to describe the fifties. There were a lot of parties given by people, particularly on the Upper West Side. This was when I first came to New York, and the Upper West Side was the first place I lived. That's all I knew. We met people with very elegant apartments. West End Avenue was filled with gay guys sharing apartments. I knew a lot of kids who didn't live in New York. So we would explore gay New York. I don't think we thought about being gay as something that would eventually become a lifestyle, you know? There wasn't any example of it. Occasionally we would meet older men who would say that they had been together for a long time, and it seemed peculiar that two men had set up life together, and were living together and had been for thirty-some years. We had a certain admiration for them. But it seemed very odd."

Despite the frequent raids on the bars and the possibility of entrapment, Dowling recalled that the streets still had "an outrageous variety of queens parading down them." In 1993, he said, "There's a certain behavior that black queens do today, sort of like 'Look at me, I demand that you see who I am.' You don't see as many white people doing that as you did. At that time, it was all white kids doing that."

The Bird Circuit was conveniently connected to the gay bars in the Village by the E train, and Frank O'Hara and his friends used to jump on the subway to visit both neighborhoods in one night. At the San Remo on

Bleecker Street, the customers ranged from Leonard Bernstein to James Baldwin. "It was a wonderful bar," said Jack Dowling. "It was all glass, a big long rectangular room and one whole wall of windows looking out on Bleecker Street. It was not the kind of bar you went into to hide because you were open to the world. It was wonderful in the winter watching the snow come down. Inside, it was a brownish room with octagon-shaped orangey lights. But just an Italian neighborhood bar during the daytime. There were a lot of writers and painters who dropped in at night and it would get cruisy, but not like a gay bar; it was more incidental. The activity was probably more like a heterosexual bar than a gay bar, where people are more direct. In the San Remo it was more conversational. Introductions were made and you could talk to people."

In the Village, the more conventional gay bars included Mary's, Main Street, the Eighth Street Bar, and the Old Colony. O'Hara celebrated the nighttime scene in a poem called "Homosexuality":

> 14th Street is drunken and credulous
> 53rd tries to tremble but is too at rest. The good
> love a park and the inept a railway station.

AFTER HIS ADVENTURES in the American Field Service in Egypt, France, Italy, and Germany, Stephen Reynolds moved to New York with "George" (a pseudonym), a man he had met in Boston during the war. Both of them were extremely wealthy. They remained together for thirty-two years, until George died of cancer in 1976. During most of these years, they lived in a "great big formal house" on East 73d Street where they were constantly entertaining.

In 1992, Reynolds remembered, "We used to have a man who came in and sort of did butler work when we were giving a party. I went to some hateful charity party a couple of years ago, and he saw me, and said, 'Mr. Reynolds, I've kept a record of all the work I've ever done. Do you know how much you entertained? In a month, you did at least two and sometimes three dinners for thirty-five or forty. At least once or twice a week you would have at least twelve or fourteen people.'"

The house had a huge dining room, and the dinner parties always included plenty of women — except when the English actor John Gielgud was their houseguest. "John used to spend a lot of time at our house, and John can't *stand* women. So we would ask ten or twelve boys and someone would play the piano."

At seventy-five, Reynolds still cut an elegant figure in Manhattan. He spoke in a gravelly tobacco voice with a patrician accent and chain-smoked the cigarettes that his doctor insisted would be his downfall. "The doctor has told me it's just a question of time. When he says that, I blow a huge cloud of smoke in his face. Drives him crazy."

The walls of his carefully decorated East Side apartment were covered with autographed photographs of the Broadway stars and British royals who had been his close friends. Reynolds described the general decline of New York society disdainfully: "It seems to me that twenty years ago, there was an entirely different social setup than there is today. I mean, I don't want to name any names, but I don't think the Donald Trumps would've been awfully big."

One thing which hadn't declined at all was Reynolds's interest in sex. He bragged about the twenty-seven-year-old he was dating, who also had a girlfriend. Once, he reported, the three of them even had lunch together.

"I think that the main thing is that there was no militancy in the fifties," Reynolds recalled. "As a result, I think probably we had more fun. . . . Every generation thinks that their generation had a better time than the one that comes after it. But I do think, in the sense that if we found a place where we could go and relax, it was more of an adventure. I remember George and I went down to a place in the Village. We had to go upstairs, and there we saw [a famous male decorator] dancing with a man. I nearly fainted; we had never seen such a thing as that. We used to call him the Tainted Woman. He's a charming old friend of mine, and I love and adore him. I thought, Well, this is living! There are two men dancing together! Whereas, now you go down to the Village and they dress like nuns. But it seems to me that when we found a place in New York where we could go, and there would be chums there, it wasn't daring exactly, it was just an additional little dessert."

After his stint in the war, Reynolds's family wealth meant that he never had to work again. Neither did his lover. "In our youth, we never heard about job discrimination. I was not aware of it because it was a problem I never encountered. I'm sure it existed. I think that people that I knew were either theatrical people, in which case nobody gave a damn, or they moved in a crowd in which that was talked about but nobody cared very much. I was always painfully aware that if George and I went to the beach club in Southampton, I could see a couple of people murmuring. But what are you going to do?

"I didn't care by then because I was very happy. It did bother me a little, but not a lot. It was muffled; it was unspoken, but it was felt. I think, if I may say so, that George and I sort of had the intelligence to know there were certain things we must not do. I would not propose myself to the Racquet Club. I know many members, but I do not think that I would get into the Racquet Club. Fortunately, I didn't *want* to get into the Racquet Club."

In 1989, militants in ACT UP would cause an uproar by invading a Sunday Mass conducted by John Cardinal O'Connor. The demonstrators infuriated many devout Catholics and caused a sharp split within the gay community over their tactics. Predictably, in the fifties, everything was more ambiguous: Gays favored much more subtle infiltration tactics. At the same time, the private life of the cardinal spawned a steady stream of ribald rumors.

"In those days, St. Patrick's Cathedral was the greatest cruising ground — especially late Mass on Sunday," Reynolds recalled. "People would stumble in and start carrying on right under the eyes of Nellie Spellbound [Francis Cardinal Spellman]. She was very upset when the pope ordered the cardinals to shorten their trains from ten yards to two!"

In 1949 Reynolds visited Cherry Grove, the first postwar gay community on Fire Island. "I'd never seen anything like Cherry Grove. It was very small. There was one bathroom for four of us. Pretty bad: everybody was in drag at cocktail parties. It's not my dish.

"I went out with Eddie Villela* once. We stayed at the Pines. And of course he had the build of the century. And he had his wife with him." Reynolds particularly enjoyed his walks down the beach with Villela. "Honestly, if Jesus had come down, it couldn't have caused more of a flutter. People were coming out of foxholes, they were leaping out of the grass. Eddie was a sensation and he loved it. It's not my dish of tea. I don't like that kind of scene."

Reynolds and his lover made an eccentric choice for summering: they bought a house on Staten Island, with a swimming pool and ten acres. "We gave a huge, great big enormous party for the Royal Ballet. A big bash. We used to give a luncheon for the Royal Ballet every time they came. Margot Fonteyn was our best friend. She was then a dame. We had buses to meet them in Manhattan which we filled with champagne and they all came out to Staten Island. There were huge pink tents. It was a huge thing. Got in all the papers. We had such fun in those days."

They also visited Venice frequently. "George had a great deal of money. We had kind of an unusual life. It was disgusting the way we lived."

*Edward Villela was a (heterosexual) star of the New York City Ballet.

They traveled with two dogs and a valet, and in Venice they always stayed at Cipriani. "In those days there were only twenty people at Cipriani. We gave a big dinner party for Princess Margaret. It was raining, and all the other hotel guests had to eat outside because we took over the whole dining room for dinner. It was only about ten people. It was scandalous.

"I went back to Venice after George died. I was really mortified to go there because we ate at Harry's Bar every day for lunch. The two poodle dogs would go in first. Sit at the table. And we'd come sashaying in, waving. I shudder to think what people said: 'Who are those two outrageous boys!'

"We used to go a lot with Truman Capote when he was young. We were having lunch in Harry's Bar, and Truman was — I believe I can use the word — *extravagant.* He had a long black cape and a big black hat. Of course he was *Maestro* at the time — everybody bowed."

During this same trip to Venice, Capote was thrown into one of the canals by some hustlers. "Because of his attitude, and because of his name," a close friend of the writer explained. In Italian, Capote meant "condom."

Paul Cadmus remembered Capote at an outdoor café in Venice shortly after the war. "Truman lifted his cape up and down, up and down, and said, 'Come to Taormina! Come to Taormina!'" Cadmus recalled. The painter took Capote's advice and met him at the Italian resort. One day Capote returned from the post office with the mail. "I bring tidings of disaster!" he shouted. "Tennessee's play is a great success!"

"I always liked Truman," said Cadmus. "He didn't give a damn what people thought of his voice or anything else. Brave little thing."

"He was so funny in those days," said Reynolds. "He was young and he wasn't on the drugs, he wasn't on the booze. He was a midget with sort of blond hair, kind of a Dutch cut, and he was very thin. Truman worked all summer and played all winter. In those days he was brilliant. He took literature very seriously. All that glamour really went to his head. And then of course he published that *scandalous* thing" — an excerpt from "Answered Prayers," a work in progress. The excerpts that appeared in *Esquire* in 1975 humiliated some of his most famous friends because he named names and repeated, without disguise, many of the most outrageous stories they had told him. Quite a few of his victims never spoke to him again, and his social reputation never recovered. "I was crazy about Truman when he was young," Reynolds continued. "Truman was just outrageous.

He was cute. He was *a*-cute. He always had something funny to say. And the *best* gossip. He was enchanting. I saw him a couple of years before he died in the Madison Avenue Bookshop. And we were walking down the street and he threw his arms around me and kissed me full on the lips — right on the sidewalk. But then he was fat."

FRANKLIN MACFIE was the youngest in a family of ten children who was enamored of all his sisters' soldier-boyfriends during the war. The son of a Scottish Presbyterian merchant seaman and a mother with Portuguese blood, he looked like a Highlander, with vivid green eyes. By his fourteenth birthday in 1951, he had already had sex with several men. But he marks Memorial Day weekend of that year as the moment when he "officially came out."

"I met a man in Rockefeller Center who took me home," Macfie remembered. "The space around the skating rink used to be a big cruising ground. He was an actor. I remember he picked me up — literally — when we got home. He carried me across the threshold like I was Irene Dunne. It was the first time I knew, the minute I started talking to the guy in Rockefeller Center, that I was going to go home with him, and I knew we'd fuck.

"There were plainclothesmen who would cruise. It was entrapment. But entrapment was not something I had to worry about because I was young enough. They would not entrap a kid. The bathrooms on the Seventh Avenue subway, up and down Broadway, were extremely active. Ghastly odor too. And it really was essentially the same six people. A friend of mine from San Francisco wrote me a card not too long ago, when I was still in Portugal, and it said, 'Just been visiting New York. Stopped on 42d Street — and do you know that same black man is still standing there with that same twelve-inch dick, waving it around?' It's been the same for twenty years.

"We used to have something that we called Lucky Pierre. That was a *ménage à trois*. The guy in the middle was Lucky Pierre. And it was rather common; I'm sure it still is. Especially if you're a kid, you know, for lovers to pick up somebody." Macfie started smoking pot as soon as he discovered the San Remo. "The first guy I met was Alvin, who took me to the Henry Hudson Hotel on 57th Street. I was about fifteen. There was a wonderful woman lying in bed who looked like Jan Sterling, who was called the Lady Barbara. She had a make-up case and she rolled joints. And he asked me if I had ever had any. And I said, 'Of course.' But I hadn't. And

I sucked on it and knew what it was and loved it ever since. I just knew this is what I'd been waiting for: the minute it went down my throat, I knew this is love. Even better than dick.

"And the combination was unbeatable. In fact, that's what the doctors would say. They say that it's almost impossible to treat a syndrome where the person is getting pleasure on two levels like that. You got to give up one or the other, or preferably both. Because there was no frustration to work with. You know: you're far too happy to be here.

"In Manhattan, there were straight guys who would be aggressive. And there would be people you would go home with who would be dangerous, who would go a little crazy — who would suddenly turn hostile. Especially if they were on that borderline. Because of the pressure, there wasn't really a gay community. You had your gay friends, of course, but if you had a regular job or a family here, you also had straight friends which somehow were usually kept separate. There was no sense of gay community at all.

"People were far more split about it all, and forced to lead a far more schizo double life. I mean hiding from the parents, hiding from other businesspeople. And having the erotic painting on the bedroom wall to turn around. I saw more than ten of those. You know, so you could just switch it around in case mother came. It sounds funny, but what the few big gay people thought didn't matter, in relation to the enormous, huge society around you — theater, movies, literature. Everything was antigay, in the sense of not admitting it existed. And the boredom of having to laugh at gay jokes. Ones that were tasteless and offensive. That was all tiresome. So it did make you very unhappy. You felt excluded. You also felt like, Oh, it's going to mean misery and unhappiness. You would meet so many men who would be working in offices, who were really striving to create a straight image — going out with women and pretending. In the fifties acting straight was very important. I don't know how many dates I had in that period with guys older than me — working age when I was in school — where they would say, 'I'll meet you Friday at 11:30 'cause I'm taking this girl out after office hours. The date will be over by 11:00. I'll meet you at 11:30 in the Village.' That was really a standard operating procedure on a Friday night.

"One thing I've always liked about being gay is that you used to be able to go into a bar and you would meet anybody from Leonard Bernstein on, up, down, and sideways. A completely democratic society. I came from a very humble family, and I would never have learned a lot of the things I learned if I weren't gay. I simply wouldn't have been exposed to the variety of people. That was a great blessing, actually."*

"Sunday brunch was at home. Generally if they thought you were really a hot trick, they would have a few friends over to show you off. 'Come on over! I have a friend here.' And then, 'I can't wait till he comes and sees you! Oh, no, don't put your shirt on!' Or 'Why don't you take a shower now. He'll be here in two minutes.' And then you come out and meet the friend. 'Oh, new friend! You sly thing.' Being young and a trick — probably most of the people I went home with didn't have lovers. There were a few who lived together and were lovers obviously. But most of them were lonely men, I suppose. It just didn't seem that men lived together as openly as they do now."

Macfie vividly remembered a terrifying party in a private home in Forest Hills, Queens, in 1953. "There were a couple of kids my age and we had dates with older guys, and it was at the house of one of the older guys. I think probably the guy who had the house had had a few pieces of neighborhood trade or something. Somebody obviously knew he lived there and they saw a party going on, and they rang the bell. It was three local toughs. And they came in and started terrorizing the twelve of us.

"It was very, very scary. I mean like wielding knives that they had picked up. It got very frightening. I was really ready to run. I really felt like this is going to be one of those murder scenes — you're going to see twelve bloody queens on the floor.

"And then the most outrageous queen there turned around and said to everybody, 'Get 'em, girls! GET 'EM!' And somehow absolutely galvanized everything. Suddenly we realized, Well, there are twelve of us and there are three of them, you know. GET 'EM! And we got 'em. We just all jumped them and threw them out of the house. Everybody was petrified, to be honest. And afterward we were, like, 'Weren't we brave?' Twelve men of various ages attacking three teenage boys! But it *was* scary. You did feel like you were being terrorized. And queens were not known to carry guns in those days."

Then Macfie went to see Montgomery Clift in *A Place in the Sun*. It was love at first sight, and he began to stalk the actor: he found out where he lived and followed him around for several years. They were in the lobby of a theater when Macfie first approached him. The crazed fan said, "This is

*This democratic aspect was already part of gay life in nineteenth-century England. The testimony at the trials of Oscar Wilde contains many of the prosecutor's sarcastic references to Wilde's habit of dining with a groom and a valet. (Donald Webster Cory, *The Homosexual in America*, 152)

who I am and you're going to see this face a lot. Get used to seeing this face following you!

"I could read the New York paper and tell you where he was going to be in three nights," Macfie remembered. "I knew that much about him and his life at this point." Eventually Macfie got Clift's telephone number from a newspaper columnist and he called him at home. "I said that I was United Parcel Service and I had a package that came from Mr. Brooks Clift, which was his [older] brother — and I knew wherever he lived at the time, in Nebraska or someplace. I said we have the name, but the address is not clear. Do you want us to send it back or send it on to you? He was a little bit cautious, and he said, 'OK.' And I got the address." Clift lived on the second and third floors of a brownstone on East 63d Street.

"It was during the World Series, and I went and rang the bell. The maid let me in, and he was up on the third floor in the bedroom, and in the living room the television was on. He was a big baseball fan, strangely enough. He was one of those kind of straight types. And he came downstairs. I was adjusting the television set, which was flickering, and he was wearing gray khaki pants and a white shirt. He looked quizzically at me, and he said, 'What are you doing here?' And I said, 'Oh, I'm fixing the television, as you can see.' And he smiled and we started talking. Nothing happened that time. Eventually he had something to do and I left. I used to patrol the house quite frequently and see Liz [Taylor] and Deborah Kerr and everybody going in."

When Macfie began his pursuit, he wasn't sure whether Clift was gay or not. "I don't think we actually knew 'Monty is gay.' Not in the fifties. I think people learned when they realized that Liz was madly in love with him and he wasn't responding. There was something wrong with anybody who didn't respond to Elizabeth Taylor if she was in love with you. Mainly you always felt like he was watching you and making all these kinds of judgments that you would never know. He'd look at you and you'd think, Is he thinking that I'm a complete asshole? Is he liking me? Does he want me to leave? Does he want to talk? Does he want me to shut up? You'd get very little response from him. It went on for a period of three years. Whenever he was around New York and I could find him and get in and talk to him."

After many months, they finally had sex together. "I think three times. Once on the staircase. He was not interested in admiration and adoration at all. He was far more interested in a little bit more of an I-don't-give-a-fuck-who-you-are-do-you-want-to-suck-my-dick attitude. A sort of tradey attitude. Which was very stupid of me — I could have done that very easily. But I was madly in love with him. He was the most beautiful creature I ever saw in my life. Monty was for the eyes. It was the eyes and to get a laugh. It was one of those people that if you could get him to laugh, to really, actually laugh at something, you felt that you had achieved some great catharsis for him. I just felt I'd moved a mountain."

WALTER CLEMONS was a brilliant young writer in 1959, full of promise. That year he published a collection of short stories called *The Poison Tree*. Mostly drawn from his Texas childhood, they were written in a spare and elegant style. When they brought him the Prix de Rome, he had established himself as a writer to be reckoned with. Clemons had grown up in Houston, the son of a father who was "sort of a village atheist" and a mother who was a "strict puritan" and a Methodist but who never went to church after she was married. Clemons's early experiences with Catholicism, and his subsequent uprising against it, are typical of the way many rebels embrace, and then replace, early ecstatic experiences. There is a certain kind of iconoclast in whom Catholicism invariably induces a ferocious atheism after an initial period of piety. Clemons was that kind of Catholic.

To placate his paternal grandmother, young Walter was sent to a Catholic elementary school, and his grandmother picked him up every Sunday to take him to Mass. But his parents never went with him. "They were lolling around the house reading the Sunday *Times*. I had to uphold the religious honor of the family."

Clemons's churchgoing created an immediate crisis: "About the first thing you're taught is that if you don't go to Mass on Sunday, you go to hell," Clemons remembered. "I was under the belief that I was going to go to heaven and I was going to be orphaned while my parents burned in hell. So I used to sob in school. I went through the third grade, and the oppression got worse and worse, and I was taken to a Catholic child psychologist who couldn't get my secret out of me — about hell. He was a good Irish Catholic, Dr. Joe Malloy. He said, 'I don't know. Something is scaring the hell out of that little kid in the Catholic school. I think you ought to take him out of the parochial school and let him go to public school.'*

"I went through various religious stages. I was very devout in early elementary school, and I became very, very devout in adolescence. I can

*Clemons wrote a lightly fictionalized account of this experience in his short story "Nana Shellbean."

time it exactly because I can remember the embarrassment of being in Mass on Sunday where you kneel down and stand up and kneel down. It was at that age when you never know when you're going to get a hard-on, and you just don't know what to do about it. I think I was afflicted by some sort of religious grief that has to do with a hard-on, of being in a Catholic Mass and being deeply depressed by the music, and getting teary. So I was very religious during my initial erection stage, when I was ten or eleven. It was very much connected with sexuality. Of course, if I become very devout at the moment I'm having erections in Mass, there will be some guilt.

"I remember that as soon as I became active sexually I totally lost interest in Catholicism because I found that I could not go to confession and say I was sorry. I became a hardened sinner." He also became an atheist. "I think the religiosity was a substitute for sex. It's a fervent emotional experience, and then I didn't need that anymore."

In high school, Clemons read Freud. He had the classic experience of young gay people all over America from the fifties through the eighties. "I read that it was an immature phase in sexual development, so I thought if I could just hang on, the grown-up stuff would start. I knew it was a bad thing.

"My picture was in the Houston paper because I won some kind of an essay contest when I was in high school and I got an anonymous telephone call from a guy who'd seen my picture in the paper and had read about the award. We chatted for a while, and then he asked, 'Are you gay?' I don't even think I was aware of the term *gay* until some years after that. He must have thought that since I was an essay writer, I must have been an incipient fag. I sensed what he was talking about, but I said, 'I don't know what that is.' But I did know. I told people at school that I'd had this peculiar phone call, and that he said, 'Are you gay?' I told them I didn't know what to say, so I said, 'Oh yeah, I have a good time.' And made a schoolyard anecdote out of it. I should have kept my mouth shut."

Until he read James M. Cain's *Serenade* as a teenager, Clemons encountered nothing gay in the culture, although he was aware that he was attracted to male movie stars, like Dana Andrews and Errol Flynn.

"I also had a very vivid childhood nightmare that I blush to even remember. It was a dream about nighttime at a deserted circus ring, and there's a group of elephants, one of whom filled his trunk with water and stuck it in my behind. If that's not a sexual dream, I don't know."

A student two classes ahead of him at Lamar High School was thrown out after the rumor went around that he'd been caught doing something

Christopher Isherwood and W. H. Auden left London at the beginning of 1938 for China. The two were pillars of a gay intellectual community which also included E. M. Forster, the art patron Lincoln Kirstein, the painter Paul Cadmus, the architect Philip Johnson, and the photographer George Platt Lynes. *Courtesy of UPI/Corbis-Bettmann.*

A Paul Cadmus sketch of his lover
Jon Andersson (below) and a Cadmus
self-portrait (right). The two met
on a pier on Nantucket in 1964,
when Andersson was twenty-seven
and Cadmus was fifty-nine. "I never
wanted to be with anyone else,"
Cadmus remarked. Thirty-two years
later, at fifty-nine and ninety-one,
they are still together. *Courtesy
of Paul Cadmus.*

A Cadmus portrait of José Martinez, the man Lincoln Kirstein was dating when he married Cadmus's sister, Fidelma. Kirstein had fallen in love with Paul Cadmus before he met Fidelma, and the painter was surprised by his patron's choice of a spouse. "You hardly know her," Cadmus told Kirstein, "and she's not like me." But Kirstein was insistent: "I know what I want, I want to marry Fidelma." *Courtesy of Paul Cadmus.*

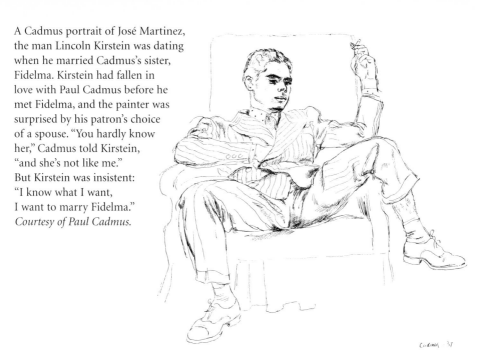

Male nudes by George Platt Lynes. Lynes's photographs were a secret pleasure of wealthy gay collectors in the forties and fifties. Lincoln Kirstein commissioned him to photograph members of the New York City Ballet. *Courtesy of George Platt Lynes.*

Top, left: Sandy Kern was a lookout for the boys from Murder, Incorporated, when they played craps on the Brooklyn block where she grew up. *Courtesy of Sandy Kern.*

Top, right: J. Edgar Hoover in Miami Beach with his top aide and lifelong companion, Clyde Tolson, in 1938. Their relationship appeared "spousal," but whether it was ever consummated remains a mystery. *Courtesy of UPI/Corbis-Bettmann.*

Right: Lincoln Kirstein, a founder of the New York City Ballet and one of the most important art patrons of the twentieth century. *Courtesy of UPI/Corbis-Bettmann.*

Otis Bigelow, the "best-looking man in Manhattan" in 1942. *Courtesy of Otis Bigelow.*

The "portrait painter" William Burton and his daughter, Patricia. Burton became Wayne Lonergan's lover after they met at the World's Fair in 1939. When Burton died, Lonergan transferred his affections to Patricia, whom he married in Las Vegas over her mother's objections. *Courtesy of UPI/Corbis-Bettmann.*

Wayne Lonergan being booked for the murder of Patricia. *Courtesy of UPI/Corbis-Bettmann.*

James Baldwin was open but ambivalent about his homosexuality in *Giovanni's Room*, the novel he published in 1956. *Courtesy of UPI/Corbis-Bettmann.*

This picture of "five boys in trouble" filled four columns on the front page of the *New York Times* one Sunday in the summer of 1954. They were among ninety youths picked up in Times Square as part of a campaign against juvenile delinquents and "generally undesirable characters." *Courtesy of Associated Press.*

Joseph McCarthy, David Schine, and Roy Cohn during the Army-McCarthy hearings, June 1954. Ben Bradlee remembered that "there was a lot of time spent investigating" the possibility that McCarthy was gay, but "nobody ever came close to proving it." *Courtesy of UPI/Corbis-Bettmann.*

Peter Orlovsky and Allen Ginsberg together in Paris in 1957. *Courtesy of H. S. Capman/Corbis-Bettmann.*

in the shower. "He went and finished at San Jacinto High and then came back to receive his diploma at Lamar. He walked out on the stage and was met with thunderous applause — a generous ovation. It was very brave of him to come back, and everyone was sorry it had ever happened. This was in June 1945.

"I remember when I first got laid [with a girl], at sixteen, and somehow the word got around. I remember a football player friend of mine with whom I worked as a lifeguard said something to the effect of, 'Gee, I've always been kind of shy around you because I never knew you would do anything like that. I feel a lot more comfortable with you now.' And I was crazy about him. I just thought, Well, how sweet. I've made the grade! I'm in with the guys now."

Clemons got his first short story published in *Scholastic* magazine while he was still in high school. He chose to go on to Princeton "because of Scott Fitzgerald and Edmund Wilson and wanting to write songs for the Triangle Show." His dream came true: "I was the musical director of the Triangle Show." He was a tall, blond, good-looking Texan, but he went all through college without ever having sex with a man. Then he won a Rhodes Scholarship, and he didn't have sex at Magdalen College in Oxford, either. "There was all sorts of activity at Magdalen. Sort of everywhere but nowhere. I don't know if anybody was actually doing anything, but there was a lot of affection and flirting and all that. I was in no position to know if anybody was getting it on. But surely they were. I would have been so racked with guilt if I'd done anything, and I'm sure they were doing it all without worrying about it. I'm sure many of those people went through what I had read about: they did it and then it was a passing phase. They went on and got married. I have often thought that if I had had a passage of homosexual activity in my teens I might have been much more comfortable. Who knows?"

The Korean War was on and, after Oxford, Clemons would have been vulnerable to the draft. But during his final six months abroad he was diagnosed with diabetes. He took a job as an ordinary seaman on a boat in the Gulf of Mexico which was surveying the gulf's bottom for oil-well drilling.

"I had some very close friends among those men, and a particular friendship with one of the most wonderful guys I ever knew, perfectly straight, very affectionate and physical. His name was L. D. Harris.

"L.D. was my age. He was draped around me at all times, and, to my horror, one of the older guys said, 'There are two guys that ought to just fuck each other and get it over with!'

"I just froze. And my friend hugged me, and said to this guy, 'Oh, toilet-mouth, you'd say anything!' He didn't have the slightest worry about it. That was really one of the happiest moments of my life."

L.D. was a particular kind of male heterosexual cherished by gay men everywhere: someone so confident of his orientation that he never feels threatened by the homosexuality of anyone else. "He was, therefore, very affectionate with me," said Clemons. "He was a terrific fellow. He was tirelessly heterosexual and a very cute country boy."

Arthur Laurents recalled many similar experiences. "I have noticed that straight men who are secure in their sexuality are *very* affectionate, very often physically," said Laurents. "They feel no threat. They are the ones who really hug you. They kiss you. And there's not a slight whiff of sexuality about it. They're not afraid of themselves, is what it is."

Most of the crew on Clemons's boat came from one little Texas town north of Dallas called Quenlin. The total population was six hundred. "They would fix me up with girls, and I would fuck one of the local girls and I was one of the gang," he said.

Finally, on a trip home to Houston, Clemons had his first gay sexual experience. "I was doing some work in the public library, and there was a men's room at the bottom of the public library where I discovered that guys were exhibiting themselves and tempting the passersby, and I simply went down there and picked somebody up and went back with him to his room at the Y, where I fucked him and he fucked me. And I said that I had never done this before, and he didn't believe me. I said, 'No, I'm telling the truth. I've just imagined it.' And he said, 'Well, you've got *some* imagination!' He was a very nice man and I never saw him again, although I often think of him as some sort of lucky first encounter.

"After this first experience, I went over to my girlfriend's house, just dazed. But my thought was, I've done this once and if you don't do it again it will just be an experiment" — another typical reaction to an initial encounter. "I abstained for a solid year after that. I continued with this girl, with whom I became impotent with guilt. I think I was so full of conflict that the relationship began to fall to pieces. And then I didn't want to fuck her anymore.

"It was no longer possible for me to continue the fantasy that I would outgrow this. It didn't seem possible for me to continue a relationship with a woman with whom I would probably be unfaithful. And so I gradually just withdrew from it."

After a year at sea, Clemons had accumulated enough money to go to Europe, so he lived in London and Paris for a couple of years before moving to New York in 1958. In London, he was cruised on the streets of Chelsea. He began to think "that queers had funny eyes. I was afraid that I would get to look like that. And I only gradually worked out what it was. It's the cautious homosexuals that looked at you without moving their face. In order not to be caught looking, you're suddenly aware that you're being looked at by a face that's frankly not looking at you at all. So the eyes look very peculiar. It's a kind of snake-eyed look."

His short stories were published in *Harper's Bazaar* and *Ladies' Home Journal,* among other periodicals. There was nothing gay about any of Clemons's fiction, and many of his straight friends were unaware of his orientation. He was an elegant man, with the understated air of a patrician from Texas. He had great confidence in his own intelligence, but he was never boastful. After he moved to New York in the sixties, he escorted many of the city's most elegant women. He did have one long-term relationship with a man he adored, but many of his closest friends never met his companion: like so many members of his generation, Clemons would always lead a compartmentalized life. But while he remained very discreet, by the time he was thirty, all of his inhibitions about having sex with men had disappeared.

FOR MORE THAN thirty years after World War II, beginning with the widespread availability of penicillin and other antibiotics, sexually active Americans enjoyed a kind of liberty that was without precedent in modern times: an almost total freedom from fear of sexually transmitted diseases. For the first time in many centuries, syphilis and gonorrhea became inconveniences instead of catastrophes. Eventually, medical advances would contribute to a dramatic change in the way Americans of all persuasions thought about sex. But because of the sexual taboos of the fifties, many heterosexual New Yorkers had to wait for the arrival of the Pill — and a whole new set of sixties attitudes — before *their* sexual revolution began.

Gay New Yorkers did not have to wait. "It was vividly exciting to sneak around and be in a black tie at a party and make connection with somebody's eye across the room and meet later after we dumped our dates," said Clemons. And although the scene was much more furtive than it would be two decades later, on any given night in the fifties it could be just as wild as it would be seven nights a week in the seventies.

Clemons was never concerned about catching anything. "Nobody worried about it a bit. You never had a tremor: if you saw somebody you wanted, you went for it. I went to the baths. I went to the Everhard. It cost something like six dollars. I always went at night, and I often stayed all night.*

"If you got a locker, you put your clothes in the locker. If you took a cubicle, you hung your clothes up in your cubicle. Then you had a little knee-length white gown to wrap yourself in, which you usually wore loose with your cock hanging out. The stomach-downs wanted to be fucked. I guess you could have sex with as many as a dozen people. There were group scenes. There was a very impressive steam-bath room down in the lower level, as well as a swimming pool and a big sort of cathedral-like sauna room. It was very steamy and you could hardly see. You could stumble into multiple combinations."

Once he picked up a man at the baths who was "just hot as a firecracker but clearly under pressure. I went off to the bathroom and came back to the cubicle and he had dressed and vanished. I was quite hurt. Then I saw his picture in the paper the next day." He had been arrested for hit-and-run driving.

Clemons also went to a bathhouse on West 58th Street near Columbus Circle. "Once in the afternoon, Truman Capote entered and I quickly left. I didn't know Truman Capote, but I didn't want to be in the same baths with him. Nureyev used to hang out there, and so did Lincoln Kirstein, but I never saw either of them. But the word was around. There was a rather friendly guy at the front desk who I was sort of chatty with, and he would say, 'You don't have any luck. Nureyev was here last night and you missed him again. The best legs I've ever seen!'"

The Penn Post baths across the street from Penn Station were popular at lunchtime and with the commuter crowd in the late afternoon. Murray Gitlin remembered "a room with a lot of double bunks and a steam room slippery with slime. I was lying on the upper bunk at the end of Penn Post, and I heard this very erudite conversation, and I looked down and it was Lincoln Kirstein."

After Clemons's collection of short stories was published in 1959, he made extra money playing the piano in Manhattan nightclubs like the RSVP, where Mabel Mercer was a regular performer. Downtown on West 9th Street, Clemons frequented a popular gay restaurant called the Lion, where he first heard an unseasoned woman singer from Brooklyn.

"It was before I went off to Rome. When her first record came out and we began to hear about her in Rome, somebody brought me the record

---

*Gore Vidal published a paperback original under the pen name Katharine Everhard. "It's a straight romantic novel," said Clemons. "[The pseudonym] was just an inside joke."

and I looked at that face and realized it was a much-glamorized photo of this awful girl that I had heard in the Lion [in 1960]. She was hostile and terribly nervous. She had no contact with the audience and was hunched over the microphone and made something that was supposed to be patter, but was so convoluted and interior that all you felt was this hostility and terrible resentment from this ugly girl. I remember her singing 'Cry Me a River.' It was a very muffled act. It must have been one of her very first appearances because she was so tense. It was memorable not because we saw a great star, but because we saw this awful girl." Despite the way Clemons remembered her, Barbra Streisand won the amateur talent competition at the Lion four weekends in a row.

Streisand was "discovered" three years later by Arthur Laurents, when he directed her in *I Can Get It for You Wholesale* on Broadway in 1962. "One day this girl came in [wearing] these bizarre thrift-shop clothes," Laurents recalled. "She was nineteen. She started to sing, and I thought, *My God, I've never heard anything like this.*" But the show's producer, David Merrick, agreed with Walter Clemons. Merrick kept saying, "She's so unattractive," and he tried to get Laurents to fire her "every night of rehearsal and out of town." But Streisand "knew she was going to be a star right then and there," said Laurents. "And she made sure you knew."

JACK DOWLING first reached Manhattan by bicycle when he was thirteen, in 1945, right after the war ended. He pedaled there from Sewaren, thirty miles away, near the Jersey Shore. "It took me all day to get here and then all day to get home, which left about a half an hour to explore the city. I remember leaving in the morning on a Sunday and getting here late afternoon, passing through Staten Island and taking the ferry.

"When I started to come by bus I was fourteen or fifteen. I wasn't quite sure of what I was looking for. It would have been something that wasn't happening where I was living, something that wasn't happening at home. The beat of the city fascinated me. I needed to see whatever city life might eventually hold."

By the mid-fifties he had a pretty good idea of gay life's parameters. He recalled one night in Manhattan in 1951: "You go to a bar like New Verdi on Verdi Square on the east side of Amsterdam. There's not even a bar there now. Hang out drinking beer with a lot of other people that you know. Then you all get in a cab and race down the West Side Highway and go to Mary's on 8th Street. Go down the street to Main Street and the Old Colony, and then decide the Village is dead — mostly because nobody has cruised you. So you get back in another cab, with another group, and go back to the West Side. There was another bar on 72d Street, the Cork Club, and we would hit that. By now it's getting close to closing and somebody suggests an after-hours party. There was a church a few blocks from the bar, and somebody knows the guy who is the rector. The rector is gay. So this whole gang pours into the rectory — this is after four in the morning — and then somebody discovers the unlocked door from the rectory into the church, so then everybody pours into the church. There wasn't sexual carrying on, but there was a lot of camping. Music was being played on the organ. By now it's past five o'clock in the morning. People are drunk, taking down drapes and wearing them. And then it suddenly dawned on everybody that the church was going to be used pretty soon. We were smoking in there, and people had beer. The place was a mess. So we rushed around and tried to make it all right. It was not exactly a wild night as far as sex goes, but there was always that edge, much more so than now — running on danger — since it was dangerous everywhere. You were always playing and teasing with that aspect of life in the city.

"We also used to go to Lucky's in Harlem. It was a big bar where the waiters and waitresses would sing, and the patrons would sing, and people would come and listen to jazz. It was a straight bar, but there were a lot of gay people from downtown, and there were a lot of gay black guys there.

"Nights went on forever in New York. It was hot. You could take the subways and in minutes be in other gay places. It was dark and shadowy because the streetlights were not as bright as they are now.

"It was a very casual time. I used to leave the San Remo when it closed in my Packard convertible. With a friend, I would take the car off the road in Central Park and drive across the meadow. We would cruise the park, then pick cherry blossoms from behind the Metropolitan Museum, filling up the rumble seat. On the way home, we would drop the boughs off at sleeping friends' apartments before going home to bed ourselves. Although there was police repression against gays, the police were really quite naive. You could go cruising across the lawns of Central Park in an old car, and if they saw you, they probably wouldn't believe it."

FOR LESBIANS AND GAY MEN coming of age in this period, the Kinsey Report made an enormous difference. Despite all the emphasis on conformity, for the first time in the country's history, there was at least a muted minority point of view about what it meant to be a homosexual.

Three other events of the fifties were crucial to the birth of the gay liberation movement at the end of the following decade, and two of them occurred in 1951. The first was the founding of the Mattachine Society in

Los Angeles by Harry Hay, whose political awakening had started when he joined the Communist party and participated in a general strike in San Francisco in 1934. Mattachine took its name from the court jesters of the Middle Ages who were permitted to speak brutal social truths from behind their masks. In the summer of 1950, Hay tried to accumulate names for a gay rights organization by circulating a petition against the Korean War on gay beaches in Los Angeles. But when he raised the subject of growing federal harassment of homosexuals, the petition signers were far too fearful to join an avowedly gay organization. "We didn't know at that point that there had ever been a gay organization of any sort, anywhere in the world before," said Hay. "Absolutely no knowledge of that. So we thought that we had to be very, very careful" because "if we made a mistake, and got into the papers the wrong way, we could hurt the idea of a movement for years to come. And we were terrified of doing that."

After months of discussion with four cofounders, in the winter of 1951 Hay decided to model the society's organization on the structure of the Communist party, with strict secrecy and a carefully defined hierarchy. The first goal would be to change the self-image of gay people to produce a "new pride — a pride in belonging, a pride in participating in the cultural growth and the social achievements of . . . the homosexual minority." A New York chapter soon followed, but it would take another twenty years before that pride became the common goal of thousands of gay Americans.

After the founding of the Mattachine Society, for the first time sophisticated heterosexuals had somewhere to go when they wanted to find gay American men who considered themselves well-adjusted. The first person to take significant advantage of this opportunity was Dr. Evelyn Hooker, an iconoclastic psychologist at the University of California Los Angeles. Dr. Hooker had plenty of gay friends, including W. H. Auden, Christopher Isherwood, and his lover, Don Bachardy. Isherwood described her in the same way that many people had described Kinsey, which may explain why she and Kinsey reached such dramatically different conclusions from other scientists of this period. "She never treated us like some strange tribe," said Isherwood, "so we told her things we never told anyone before."

Hooker had been invited to attend some of the first public meetings of the Mattachine Society, and some of her gay friends urged her to analyze their behavior. She decided to apply for a grant from the National Institute of Mental Health to study homosexual men. To her astonishment, despite the wave of McCarthyite attacks coming out of Washington, her grant

application was accepted. But she always denied that her action had required any courage: "Curiosity and empathy were what compelled me to
do my study," she said.

The Mattachine Society helped her to recruit thirty gay men; then she
found another thirty heterosexual men to act as her control group, including policemen and firemen. The two groups were matched in IQ, age, and
education levels. All of the men were given three standard personality
tests, including the Rorschach inkblot test. Because nearly all psychologists and psychiatrists in this period believed that homosexuality was a
symptom of mental illness, "Every clinical psychologist . . . would tell you
that if he gave those projective tests he could tell whether a person was gay
or not," Dr. Hooker said. "I showed that they couldn't do it. I was very
pleased with that."

The psychologist presented her findings to a meeting of the American
Psychological Association in 1956 and published them the following year
in "The Adjustment of the Male Overt Homosexual" in *The Journal of
Projective Techniques.* The conservative psychoanalytic establishment immediately attacked her and tried to prove that she was "crazy." But her gay
friends were thrilled: "This is great," they said. "We knew it all the time!"
Using widely accepted standardized tests, she had proven for the first time
that "gay men can be as well adjusted as straight men and some are even
better adjusted than some straight men."

Although it would be years before she convinced many of her colleagues of the accuracy of her findings, Dr. Hooker's work provided the
framework that made it possible for the American Psychiatric Association
to rethink its position on this subject seventeen years later. It also gave gay
men hope, when they needed it most, that the psychiatric establishment
might some day change its attitude toward their orientation. Dr. Hooker's
work made her one of the earliest and most important heterosexual allies
of lesbians and gay men in America. In the seventies, eighties, and nineties, she would be the star of many gay-pride events. She died at her home
in Santa Monica in 1996, at the age of eighty-nine.

THE THIRD CRITICAL intellectual event for homosexuals in the 1950s
was the publication of a book that would become the bible of the early gay
movement. William Wynkoop was a college English professor when he
walked into a Doubleday bookstore in Detroit in 1951 and learned about it.
He was talking to the store's gay manager about "how *terrible*" conditions
were for gay people at the time.

"We were old enough then to really see the horror that was being perpetrated on us," Wynkoop recalled four decades later. "And the manager said, 'Well, something is happening! It's the beginning of a change! We've got to organize.'" He had just received a review copy of this new book: "'It lays it on the line! And it's a very *fearless* book.'"

The book was called *The Homosexual in America,* and it was the first essential document of gay liberation in the United States. It was published under the pseudonym Donald Webster Cory. The author was a man with a wife and son, whose family knew nothing about his secret life as a gay oracle. His real name was Edward Sagarin, and he lived in Brooklyn. Sagarin was the friend of a printer who did work for Greenberg, which had published a few gay novels. The printer introduced Sagarin to a Greenberg editor named Brandt Aymar. After the war, Aymar and Jae Greenberg had been indicted on a federal charge of sending obscene materials through the mail.

The offending books were three volumes of gay fiction — *Quatrefoil,* a fine wartime novel by James Fugate; *The Divided Path;* and *The Invisible Glass.* Vociferous complaints from the mother of one of their mail-order customers resulted in the indictment. After the charges had dragged on for five years, they were settled for a fine of $3,500 — and a promise to keep the three novels out of print.

But no official ever challenged the right to publish *The Homosexual in America.* "It was well accepted all over the country," Aymar remembered forty-four years after he published it. There were seven printings of the book between 1951 and 1957. For the thousands of gay readers who discovered it at stores across the country, it was a revelation. Sagarin had participated in "American life as a homosexual" since the 1920s, and he provided the most comprehensive description of gay male life in America ever written. He also sketched a broad plan to revolutionize American attitudes on the subject. Two appendices referred the reader to 59 nonfiction works and 213 novels and dramas with a gay theme or character.

William Wynkoop was overwhelmed when he read it. "I said, '*This* is amazing! This is a breakthrough that has never occurred in history before!'" His lover Roy Strickland agreed: "This was a *revolutionary* book."

Sagarin's preface recorded the author's typical, tortured journey, which made it clear that like nearly all lesbians and gay men, he did not feel that he was a victim of recruitment. He recounted his first attraction to another man, his complete ignorance of "any facts about homosexuality," and his "deep shock" when a teacher in high school took him aside and explained to him that there were people "called inverts." After that Sagarin read every book he could find on the subject, and "sought to understand why I could not be like others."

He felt "deeply ashamed of being abnormal and was aware of the heavy price that must be paid if anyone were to discover my secret. . . . I struggled against my homosexuality, sought to discipline myself to overcome it, punished myself for failures to resist sinful temptations. But the struggles did nothing to diminish the needs within me." And like many of the men studied by the army during World War II, he alternately felt "trapped by a human tragedy to which I could never adjust, or blessed as one of the élite of the world."

But Sagarin's experiences with men discouraged him from believing in the possibility of a long-term homosexual relationship: "Passionate infatuations that seemed permanent were torn asunder after only a short period of time. . . . It appeared to me that I faced a life of dissipation, a hopeless dead-end." So when he discovered at twenty-five that he was "capable of consummating a marriage," he married his childhood sweetheart. His final solution was typical of his generation — a marriage that lasted until the end of his life, and a simultaneous love affair with a black boyfriend.

The Homosexual in America was a call to arms, an attack on every antihomosexual prejudice. As the historian John D'Emilio pointed out, it "not only provided gay men and women with a tool for reinterpreting their lives; it also implied that the conditions of life had changed sufficiently so that the book's message might find a receptive audience."

Sagarin declared that being homosexual "is as involuntary as if it were inborn," and he decried the fact that homosexuals were the only significant minority without "a spokesman, a leader, a publication, an organization, a philosophy of life," or even "an accepted justification" for their own existence. "There is surely no group of such size, and yet with so few who acknowledge that they belong."

To make money and to educate the faithful, Sagarin joined forces with his editor, Brandt Aymar, and opened a gay bookstore called the Book Seller, on Second Avenue near 49th Street. Gore Vidal was among the many gay authors who did signings there. Sagarin and Aymar also started a gay book club called the Cory Book Service (after Sagarin's pseudonym). The club flourished for about a year, until it ran out of new titles to offer.

Sagarin said his "friends" attacked the homosexual for lying to everyone, including himself. Then he identified the dilemma confronting almost every gay person in the fifties: If he were honest about who he was, he faced "discrimination and social ostracism." But if he disguised his true nature to protect himself, he was denounced for "living a life that is a lie." And he wrote, "In this situation, the dominant heterosexual group is without an answer."

Dozens of his declarations foreshadowed themes that would dominate gay political debates for the rest of the twentieth century. For example, he attributed the promiscuity of many gay men to the lack of any "social, legal or ecclesiastical pressure to bind together the homosexual union," a precursor of subsequent arguments in favor of gay marriages. He also believed that heterosexual men would be just as promiscuous as homosexuals if they had the chance: "The fact is that every male who is not woefully undersexed is essentially an undiscriminating satyr. Most men want women. They want many females, and any females. They will whistle after every girl on the street, unless restrained by social convention; they will visit the prostitute without knowing in advance what that partner will look like. . . . The woman on the other hand is restrained. . . . The key to the puzzle . . . of homosexual promiscuity is . . . quite simple: the promiscuous (heterosexual) male meets the discriminating (heterosexual) female" who acts as a restraint, while "the promiscuous (homosexual) male meets the promiscuous (homosexual) male, and the restraints are entirely removed."

Other students of this question argue that the absence of a normal adolescence leads many gay men to be promiscuous young adults. "One of the reasons gay men deal badly with dating and relationships is that they're not trained in the same way as heterosexuals," said Tom Stoddard, one of the most effective gay activists of the eighties and nineties. "They lose that experience in adolescence and have to make up for it in some fashion. I think of all the experiences I missed when I was in high school and college because I was not a sexual person, when all of my peers, except for the gay ones, were experimenting and learning and having a good time. It's one of the reasons that many gay men in their twenties and thirties, perhaps even later, act like adolescents. First of all, it's a lot of fun, at least for a while. And, secondly, they never had an opportunity to progress or to learn. You had no examples — nothing even to read about the subject, other than hostile stuff. In the good world of the future, I think that won't happen. They will be adolescents at an appropriate time in their lives."

Sagarin's original radicalism was suggested by his attack on those who advocated "tolerance" for homosexuals. "Tolerance is the ugliest word in our language," he wrote. "We appeal to people to be tolerant of others —

in other words to be willing to stand them . . . I can't see why anyone should be struggling to be tolerated. If people are not good, they should not be tolerated, and if they are good, they should be *accepted*." This attitude would also become a leitmotif of the gay movement three decades later.

Sagarin was also one of the first to describe what would later be widely labeled as internalized homophobia:

> The prejudice of the dominant group, seen everywhere . . . is most demoralizing when we homosexuals realize to what extent we have accepted hostile attitudes as representing an approximation of the truth. . . . A person cannot live in an atmosphere of universal rejection . . . without a fundamental influence on his personality. . . . There is no Negro problem except that created by whites; no Jewish problem except that created by gentiles . . . and no homosexual problem except that created by the heterosexual society. . . . The very impact of the words I am a homosexual . . . forced me at . . . all moments of the day to convince myself that I was as good as the next person; in fact better.

Sagarin believed the main problem for the homosexual was the hypocrisy of the antisexual society he lived in. He wrote that "Sexual freedom is actually being practiced on a very wide scale in modern life," despite its condemnation "by school, church, newspapers and government. . . . In modern anti-sexual society, [even] the heterosexual is tolerated only because he is necessary for the propagation of the species," while "the virgin and the chaste are glorified as pristine purity."

He called for the abolition of all laws regulating sex.* "All sexual activity [should be] accepted as equally correct," Sagarin wrote, "so long as it is entered into voluntarily by the parties involved, they are perfectly sane and above a reasonable age of consent, free of communicable disease, and no duress or misrepresentation is employed."

And he identified the essential fact about all lesbians and gay men, the element that paradoxically undermined their confidence and simultaneously imbued them with a sense of superiority: "the dominant factor in my life, towering in importance above all others, is a consciousness that I am different. In one all-important respect, I am unlike the great mass of

---

*The book included an appendix that reprinted every state law forbidding sodomy. Oklahoma had a typical statute: "every person who is guilty of the detestable and abominable crime against nature, committed with mankind or with a beast, is punishable by imprisonment in the penitentiary not exceeding ten years. . . . Any sexual penetration, however slight, is sufficient to complete the crime against nature." In 1995, twenty states still carried anti-sodomy laws on their books. (*New York Times,* March 24, 1995)

people always around me, and the knowledge of this fact is with me at all times, influencing profoundly my every thought. . . . To my heterosexual friends and readers" who are baffled by "the desire that I always carry within me, I can only state that I find their own sexual personality just as much an enigma."

Most importantly, he framed what would become a four-decade-long debate about the tyranny of the closet — and accurately predicted the impact of its destruction. "Many homosexuals consider that their greatest fortune, their one saving grace, has been the invisibility of the cross which they have had to bear," Sagarin wrote toward the end of his book. "Actually, the inherent tragedy — not the saving grace — of homosexuality is found in the ease of concealment. If the homosexual were as readily recognizable as . . . members of . . . other minority groups, the social condemnation could not possibly exist. Stereotype thinking on the part of the majority would . . . collapse of its own absurdity if all of us who are gay were known for what we are. . . . If only all of the inverts, the millions in all lands, could simultaneously rise up in our full strength!"

Sadly, Sagarin never took his own advice on this subject, a failure that contributed to his eventual estrangement from the vanguard of the movement he did so much to create.

WILLIAM WYNKOOP was thirty-three in 1949 when he met the thirty-one-year-old Roy Strickland on a park bench in Washington Square in Greenwich Village. It was an unusually mild evening in December. Strickland was the young man from Long Island who had suffered through unsuccessful male hormone treatments paid for by his sister. Now he was working in window display at a department store. Wynkoop was a Dartmouth graduate who had become a college English professor. As a gay man in 1949, his thinking was decades ahead of its time.

Until he met Strickland, Wynkoop remembered, "There wasn't one homosexual that I had talked to — or gone to bed with — who shared *my* view that we were *not* abnormal and sick." His contemporaries told him they had never heard anything like his philosophy before. "I said, we are not inferior in any sense," Wynkoop recalled. "We don't produce babies, thank heavens, because there are too many being born as it is. But so far as our own pleasure in sex is concerned, I'm convinced the pleasure of most homosexuals in sexual activities is *equal* in *passion* and enjoyment to that which the majority of heterosexuals experience. The choice we made was to be true to ourselves.

"The world regarded us as flibbertigibbets. That was the general view of homosexual men, that they were childish, depraved, and *degenerate*. That was the favorite word of heterosexual society in referring to us. Degenerate people who are incapable of any lasting relationship — they are too unstable, too childish, and too vicious." This aspect of the psychiatric profession's formal judgment was its most damaging: the notion that all homosexuals were the victims of some kind of arrested development, coupled with the idea that nearly all of them could change, if only they exerted the will to do so. "I knew from the depths of my *soul* that this was not true. And yet I would get no support from fellow male homosexuals." When Wynkoop made his speech about the health of the average gay man in front of Strickland's roommate on West 9th Street, the roommate told Strickland, "This one's crazy. You've got to turn him in for another one." Strickland ignored the advice. In 1996, he and Wynkoop celebrated their forty-seventh anniversary together.

Two years after Wynkoop met Strickland, *The Homosexual in America* was published. "Before this came out the majority of people that I remember hearing talk about gays — 'faggots,' as they would call us — were convinced that we *chose* this lifestyle," said Wynkoop. The book attracted a devoted following, even though, as Strickland remembered, "You would never see anybody reading it on the subway or a bus because of the title." And although it was stocked by many stores, "People were afraid to go in and ask."

Wynkoop and Strickland wrote to the author in care of his publisher, and Sagarin soon wrote back to invite Wynkoop to meet him for a drink at a hotel on Madison Avenue, right next to St. Patrick's Cathedral. When Wynkoop arrived at the appointed hour, he saw a single man at the bar — very short and hunched. "I do remember the shock that I got when he moved off that stool at the bar," said Wynkoop, who remembered Sagarin being severely crippled and stooped.

Later Sagarin invited Wynkoop and Strickland out to Brooklyn to meet his family. "My wife and child don't know *anything* about this," Sagarin told Wynkoop a few weeks after their first meeting. "He said, 'I would like very much for you to come out there, to meet them, and for them to meet you. But if you do, don't say *anything* that would reveal what I am,'" Wynkoop declined the offer. "That sort of turned me off. I greatly admired his ability, but I didn't feel much rapport with him. He was such an entirely different type of man than I was."

However, in 1952, Wynkoop and Strickland did accompany Sagarin to a meeting of the Veterans Benevolent Association, one of the first gay groups in New York City, founded in 1945. Under discussion that evening was a motion to admit a new member. "Two or three of the members got up and in pretty strong terms opposed his being taken in," William Wynkoop recalled. "And I remember wondering, What in the world are they opposing him for? The guy is gay, he's apparently a veteran, and he wants to be a member. And he's a man. Then it came out after some discussion. He was an effeminate man, and they didn't want to have anything to do with effeminate male homosexuals. This made me boil." Wynkoop put his hand up during the meeting, but he was never allowed to speak. "When we went out, I said I thought that was absolutely *infuriating*. This is not what we're *fighting* for" — yet another form of discrimination. And Sagarin said, "Well, they were in the army and so they're very macho, and they don't want to be identified. They felt that it was just too risky to accept a member who was effeminate."

This debate within the movement continues four decades later between those who believe that lesbians and gay men should strive to look and act as much as possible like their heterosexual counterparts, to hasten their acceptance by the larger community, and those who argue that any movement whose essential purpose is to celebrate diversity must be as flexible and inclusive as possible.

The publication of *The Homosexual in America,* the founding of the Mattachine Society, the pioneering work of Evelyn Hooker and the first tentative moves toward public lives by a handful of lesbian and gay artists all moved the gay cause cautiously forward. Although Sagarin would gradually be left behind by his more militant followers, he had been among the very first to identify the potential for a movement that would finally burst into the streets in the coming decade.

"Millions cannot be excluded from government and private employment," he wrote. "In the millions who are silent and submerged," he saw "a reservoir of protest, a hope for a portion of mankind. And in my knowledge that our number is legion, I raise my head high and proclaim that we, the voiceless millions, are human beings, entitled to breathe the fresh air and enjoy with all humanity, the pleasures of life and love on God's green earth." If an appeal were made "to the American traditions of fair play and equality of opportunity, I am personally convinced that American attitudes will change." In this "anti-sexual culture it is entirely possible that there is no such thing as a persecution of homosexuality; there may be only a persecution of sexuality." And once again echoing the sentiments of Isherwood to Vidal, he concluded, "In arousing the population to the need for such a change, there is a revival of a spirit of humanitarian sympathies" that "will be beneficial to all men and women."

III

The Sixties

"It was a marvelous time. In the sixties you were knocked in the eyeballs."

— DIANA VREELAND

"The thing that most people don't realize is that it's *warmer* to have long hair. . . . People with short hair freeze easily. They try to hide their coldness and they get jealous of everybody that's warm. Then they become either barbers or congressmen."

— BOB DYLAN, 1966

"You do what's appropriate for the time. That's it."

— STORMÉ DELARVERIE

"Queen power exploded with all the fury of a gay atomic bomb. Queens, princesses and ladies-in-waiting began hurling anything they could lay their polished, manicured finger nails on. . . . The lilies of the valley had become carnivorous jungle plants."

— *New York Daily News,* July 6, 1969

"Do you think homosexuals are revolting?"
"You bet your sweet ass we are."

— Headline on the first leaflet distributed by the
Gay Liberation Front, July 1969

ALL THE CROSSCURRENTS flowing beneath the prevailing calm of the fifties — the black civil rights movement in the south; the books and poems of the Beats; the satire of Tom Lehrer, Mort Sahl and Lenny Bruce; the subversive rhythms of Chuck Berry and Buddy Holly; the explicit sexuality of Marlon Brando, Paul Newman, and Elvis Presley; even the outrageous looks of Liberace and Little Richard — all these converged to create the necessary prologue for the sixties, a ten-year-long convulsion that would electrify the connections between culture and politics in America. For a fleeting moment, millions of members of a new generation would sense synergy between artists and politicians — between Bob Dylan and John Kennedy, rock and roll and the antiwar movement, Aretha Franklin and Martin Luther King, even Janis Joplin and the women's movement.

As the new decade began, John Kennedy was the first person to shatter a significant American taboo when he became the only Catholic ever to capture the presidency. Although he won with a tiny plurality of the vote, his victory signaled that the levers of authority might some day become accessible to all kinds of Americans who had been excluded for centuries from real positions of power.

The triumphs of the black civil rights movement in the first half of the decade — especially the March on Washington in 1963 and the passage of the Civil Rights Act in 1964 — provided the blueprints for a much broader national liberation, first for women, then for gays and eventually for practically every other oppressed group in America. As Audre Lorde has pointed out, the civil rights movement was "the prototype of every single liberation movement in this country that we are still dealing with." (As early as 1966, a popular black-and-white civil rights lapel button bearing an equals sign had been reproduced by gay activists with a lavender background.)

"I think the connections between black liberation and women's liberation and gay liberation are very deep," said Grant Gallup, a priest who was active in the civil rights movement. "Many of us who went south to work with Dr. King in the sixties were gay. I remember a plane going down from Chicago. There were six priests, and three of us were gay. A lot of gay people who could not come out for their own liberation could invest the same energies in the liberation of black people."

"America changed because of working black southerners who decided they were going to take on America's apartheid," said the historian Joan Nestle. "I did voter registration work in Alabama and I saw a working-class black family take on history. But at night, when we would gather and everybody told stories, I couldn't tell my story. And at that moment, keeping the secret of my queerness did not seem the biggest thing to me. . . . In fact, I came home with a man, a wonderful man, who . . . said to me, 'The one group of people I hate are homosexuals.'"

The civil rights movement also provided the impetus for the radical student movement, which first got national attention in Berkeley in 1964, exploded at Columbia in 1968, and transformed hundreds of other once somnolent campuses in between and thereafter. Thomas Powers, a fine historian of the period, identified two styles that began to appear among northern white students in the early 1960s: the Student Nonviolent Coordinating Committee vogue "of Levis, denim jackets, dark glasses, and work boots;* and the beat style of army fatigue jackets, long hair, beards, mattresses on the floor and marijuana. The cultural alienation of the beats complemented the inevitable political alienation of the civil rights groups." Both styles "had a vitality lacking in the conservative political groups." Student communities in Greenwich Village, Cambridge, Massachusetts, and San Francisco "provided a concrete image of a way of life which touched the imagination of students throughout the country." In Cambridge, a Harvard undergraduate who was a freshman in 1965 remembered a floormate who was openly gay, "and no one ever bothered him a bit." To his heterosexual classmates, the young man was just another zany sixties character.

A broadly based prosperity gave many members of this new generation the luxury of not worrying too much about what they were going to do after college. Instead they spent long periods thinking about how they might reinvent themselves — politically *and* spiritually.

Vietnam was the corrosive that dissolved America's confidence in every kind of conventional wisdom. The student movement was galvanized by the growth of the antiwar movement in 1967 and 1968. The fight to end the war in Vietnam introduced millions of Americans of all ages to the concept of mass political action — and the kind of power that could be wielded in the streets, especially when the national press became mesmerized by such actions. In New York City, political activity of every kind had exploded. By 1968 you could literally "Dial-a-Demonstration." After the Tet Offensive at the beginning of that year, when the North Vietnamese and the Vietcong simultaneously attacked all the major population centers in South Vietnam, the antiwar movement convinced even the editorial writers of *The Wall Street Journal* that the national establishment could be disastrously mistaken about a crucial matter of public policy.

THE PACE of social change during this decade was unprecedented in modern American life, and nearly all the social, political and spiritual movements of the sixties contributed to the gestation of gay liberation. In

*A style quite similar to the look adopted by ACT UP in the late eighties

the fifties, the silent generation had venerated conformity; in the sixties, the Vietnam generation celebrated diversity: every type of experimentation, every kind of adventure.

That was the crucial difference. Because everything was being questioned, for a moment anything could be imagined — even a world in which homosexuals would finally win a measure of equality.

The two men most responsible for infusing the gay movement with the spirit of the sixties were Franklin Kameny and Jack Nichols, two activists from different generations, with little in common apart from a determination to ignore convention.

Kameny was a man of absolute convictions and unrelenting intensity. Born to Jewish parents in New York City in 1925, he entered Queens College when he was sixteen. Kameny joined the army in 1943 and saw combat in Holland and Germany. "I fought my way virtually slit trench by slit trench through the Rhineland in the Ninth Army under Simpson, halfway across Germany," Kameny remembered. "I was in the army of liberation for three months in Czechoslovakia. We knew with absolute certainty we were all going over to the Pacific. And then they dropped the atom bomb and we got ready to go home." Kameny was convinced that President Truman had done the right thing: "I've had no qualms about that at all."

He was not sexually active during his army service, so he "missed out on all sorts of endless opportunities." Kameny said, "I think my army career would have been utterly different if I had just picked up on the right vibrations at the right time. All kinds of passes were made at me, and I was too naive to know anything." He finally had sex with another man on his twenty-ninth birthday. "Psychologically and emotionally I was *quite* prepared fifteen years earlier, if only somebody had seduced me." He laughed at the memory. "I just wish somebody had!"

Kameny earned his Ph.D. in astronomy from Harvard in 1956 and went to work for the U.S. Army Map Service in July 1957. He was fired five months later when the government learned of a previous arrest for "lewd conduct." He filed one of the first lawsuits challenging the exclusion of gay people from federal employment, but all of his efforts ended in failure when the United States Supreme Court refused to hear his case four years later. During this period he was unemployed, and nearly destitute: "For about eight months in 1959 I was living on twenty cents' worth of food a day. Which even by 1959 prices was not that much. A big day was when I could afford twenty-five cents and put a pat of margarine on my frankfurters and potatoes. I lost so much weight that I couldn't sleep soundly lying on my side because my knees were too bony to rest comfortably on each other. It was difficult. After that I got a series of jobs as a physicist." However, without a security clearance, the only companies he could work for were those without any government contracts, so they were "not financially stable," and they often folded while Kameny was working for them.

In 1960, the same year that John Kennedy was elected president, Kameny met Jack Nichols, a Washington native who had come out to himself and his FBI-agent father when he was still in high school. Nichols had been radicalized by reading *The Homosexual in America* when he was fifteen. Four decades later, he still remembered which lines affected him the most. Sagarin had borrowed them from W.E.B. Du Bois: "The worst effect of slavery was to make the Negroes doubt themselves and share in the general contempt for black folk." Sagarin suggested that the same was true of lesbians and gay men. In November 1961, Nichols and Kameny founded an independent chapter of the Mattachine Society in Washington.* The two men had a completely different attitude from the quiet dissidents who had preceded them.

"As we got into things it became very very clear that one of the major stumbling blocks to any progress was going to be this attribution of sickness," Kameny remembered. "An attribution of mental illness in our culture is devastating, and it's something which is virtually impossible to get beyond. So the first thing was to find out if this was factually based or not. I had no idea what I was going to find. So I looked and I was absolutely appalled." Everything Kameny encountered was "sloppy, slovenly, slipshod, sleazy science — social and cultural and theological value judgments, cloaked and camouflaged in the language of science, without any of the substance of science. There was just nothing there. . . . All psychiatry *assumed* that homosexuality is psychopathological. It was garbage in, garbage out."

In New York in 1964, Kameny declared, "Our opponents will do a fully adequate job of presenting their views, and will not return us the favor of presenting ours; we gain nothing in virtue by presenting theirs, and only provide the enemy . . . with ammunition to be used against us." Kameny was speaking in a period when gay publications like *Mattachine Review* and *One* still routinely printed psychiatric opinions describing homosexuality as an illness — and that particular practice became the

*Although it took the name of the older organization, it had no connection to the national, which had dissolved itself the previous spring. (Letter from Frank Kameny to the author, December 19, 1995)

focus of Kameny's most important philosophical campaign. "I do not see the NAACP . . . worrying about which chromosome and gene produced a black skin, or about the possibility of bleaching the Negro," Kameny explained. "I do not see any great interest on the part of the B'nai B'rith Anti-Defamation League in the possibility of solving problems of anti-Semitism by converting Jews to Christians. . . . We are interested in obtaining rights for our respective minorities as Negroes, as Jews, and as Homosexuals." Then he added words that echoed those of Christopher Isherwood, who had argued in his letter to Gore Vidal in 1948 that success-ful, committed relationships between two members of the same sex were actually beneficial to society as a whole.

"I take the stand that not only is homosexuality . . . not immoral," said Kameny, "but that homosexual acts engaged in by consenting adults are moral, in a positive and real sense, and are right, good and desirable, both for the individual participants and for the society in which they live."

Kameny and his Washington cohorts forced federal officials to meet with them to discuss their exclusionary policies as early as October 1962, the same month as the Cuban Missile Crisis. They didn't change any minds, but they made the bureaucrats aware of their existence. In the summer of 1963, Kameny, Nichols and five others formed their own (un-identified) gay contingent in Martin Luther King, Jr.'s, March on Wash-ington. A few months later, Kameny recruited his first significant ally from the liberal heterosexual community. In March 1964, he persuaded the local chapter of the American Civil Liberties Union to challenge the Civil Serv-ice Commission's regulations excluding gays from federal employment. Five months later, the D.C. ACLU condemned the government's exclusion of homosexuals as "discriminatory" and urged an end to the policy of "rejection of homosexuals." Then the ACLU took the case of Bruce Scott, who had been rejected for a federal job because of "convincing evidence" of gay conduct. At its convention in 1964, the national ACLU adopted the position of its Washington chapter, a major victory for the gay movement. (Since 1957, the ACLU had explicitly supported the constitutionality of sodomy laws and federal regulations denying employment to gay men and lesbians.) In July 1965, the United States Court of Appeals in Washington ruled that the charges against Bruce Scott were too vague to disqualify him for federal employment.

The previous fall, Washington had been rocked by a "homosexual scan-dal" when Walter Jenkins, a top aide in Lyndon Johnson's White House, was arrested for lewd conduct in the basement men's room of a YMCA —

just weeks before a presidential election. Johnson immediately demanded Jenkins's resignation, and the Republican presidential candidate, Barry Goldwater, decided not to make the incident a major issue in the campaign. However, in a speech for Goldwater, Richard Nixon asserted that Americans would "not stand for immorality in the White House" and called on Johnson to tell the nation everything he knew about this "sick man." *The New York Times* declared that "the public can easily understand that men at the summit of government are subject to human frailty," but added, "there can be no place on the White House staff . . . for a person of markedly deviant behavior."

In the scandal's most surprising episode, J. Edgar Hoover inadvertently redirected attacks on the White House to himself when the press reported that he had sent flowers to Jenkins with a card inscribed "J. Edgar Hoover and Associates." The *Times* wrote that right-wing critics had reacted to the gesture with "shock, disbelief, and even outrage." Former Congressman Walter Judd of Minnesota demanded to know whether the FBI or its director "was involved in such a way that it fears being hurt by some revelation Jenkins could make." The congressman said the FBI had been "compromised" by Hoover's bouquet. A bureau spokesman confirmed that Jenkins and Hoover were good friends, but declined further comment. As usual, Washington's underlying fear of Hoover made him immune to all criticism.

JACK NICHOLS CONTINUED to articulate the need to reject the medical establishment's view of homosexuality: "The mental attitude of our own people toward themselves, that they are not well — that they are not whole, that they are less than completely healthy — is responsible for untold numbers of personal tragedies and warped lives. By failing to take a definitive stand . . . I believe that you will not only weaken the movement ten-fold, but that you will fail in your duty to homosexuals who need more than anything else to see themselves in a better light."

This was the fundamental philosophical insight that was necessary to the formation of an effective fighting force among gay men and women. Edward Sagarin had hinted at this idea in *The Homosexual in America* when he wrote that there was "no homosexual problem except that created by the heterosexual society." He had also written, "It remains to be proved that there is anything neurotic about the preference for one's own sex," but during the thirteen years since his landmark volume had been published, he had become increasingly reactionary. Now he led the fight against the new young militants. "He could get very nasty when he chose to be," Kameny said about Sagarin.

Kameny echoed Nichols in his speech to the New York Mattachine Society in July 1964. "The entire homophile movement is going to stand or fall upon the question of whether homosexuality is a sickness, and upon our taking a firm stand on it," he declared. And he was right. The following spring, the Washington chapter overwhelmingly adopted this revolutionary statement: "The Mattachine Society of Washington takes the position that in the absence of valid evidence to the contrary, homosexuality is not a sickness, disturbance or other pathology in any sense, but is merely a preference, orientation, or propensity, on par with, and not different in kind from heterosexuality."

Sagarin vowed to quit the New York chapter if it adopted such a statement, and he ran as part of a slate determined to hold on to the notion that homosexuality *was* an illness. Kameny wrote to him: "You have fallen by the wayside. . . . You have become no longer the rigorous Father of the Homophile Movement, to be revered, respected and listened to, but the senile Grandfather of the Homophile Movement, to be humored and tolerated at best; to be ignored and disregarded usually; and to be ridiculed, at worst."

In May 1965, the New York chapter elected the militant slate with two thirds of the vote. "It is very much a victory for all of us who are working hard and who don't want to see the clock turned backwards by the stick-in-the-muds and the 'sickniks,'" Nichols enthused. Using his real name for the first time, instead of a pseudonym, Sagarin wrote a doctoral dissertation about the New York Mattachine Society in which he made scathing criticisms of the organization and dismissed the possibility that serious philosophical differences were at the heart of the dispute.

On July 4, 1965, Kameny and Nichols organized the first of a series of annual pickets outside Independence Hall in Philadelphia, a tradition that continued through 1969. Kameny believed the sight of people identifying themselves as homosexuals in public had a decisive impact on the movement: "These demonstrations created the necessary mindset for gays demonstrating in public." Without them, he thought the crucial Greenwich Village explosion at the end of the decade might never have occurred.

"IS GOD DEAD?" *Time* magazine asked on its Easter cover in 1966. A sharp drop in religious faith during the sixties helped to put all the old puritan taboos in jeopardy. Because so much antigay prejudice was grounded in religion, the challenges to religious orthodoxy were a necessary prerequisite for a general reconsideration of the subject.

There was tremendous ferment within the Christian denominations surrounding the subject of homosexuality. As early as 1964, the Episcopal Diocese of New York supported the decriminalization of homosexual acts between consenting adults. An Episcopal spokesman said that his church's position was part of its acceptance of "God's continuing and progressive revelation about man's nature" — the very reason why so many people would eventually reject the Bible's injunctions against homosexuality. The following year, even *The New York Times* editorial page quietly endorsed the repeal of the law forbidding homosexual acts in private. But the Catholic Archdiocese mounted a fierce and successful battle to retain statutes making both adultery and homosexuality criminal acts in New York State. On July 22, 1965, Governor Rockefeller signed two special bills to please the Catholics on these issues, after the legislature had passed a complete revision of the state's eighty-four-year-old penal code.

In 1967, ninety Episcopalian priests met at the Cathedral of St. John the Divine in Manhattan, and a large majority declared that homosexuality should no longer be dismissed as wrong "per se." The Reverand Walter D. Dennis, canon of the cathedral and organizer of the conference, said, "A homosexual relationship between two consenting adults should be judged by the same criteria as a heterosexual marriage. That is, whether it is intended to foster a permanent relationship of love." The keynote speaker at the conference was Dr. Wardell Pomeroy, who had coauthored *Sexual Behavior in the Human Male* with Kinsey. Pomeroy attacked the "myths" that homosexuals were more likely than others to be child molesters, and that they were "effeminate and identifiable." The event was front-page news in the *Times*.

In October 1968, twelve gay worshippers met at the home of the Reverand Troy D. Perry in Los Angeles. Sixteen months later the tiny group had become the Metropolitan Community Church with 348 members, the first congregation in the country to identify itself publicly as a gay church. As Edward Sagarin had written seventeen years earlier, "Homosexuality is not an anti-religious force, although religion is anti-homosexual." The truth of that statement would become clear as hundreds of gay churches and synagogues of every denomination were founded throughout the seventies, eighties and nineties.

At the same time, the church had lost its direct power over Hollywood after the film censorship office was finally abolished in 1968. It was replaced by the G, R, and X ratings system, which is still administered by the Motion Picture Association of America.*

DRUGS WERE CHAMPIONED by some as an important complement — if not an outright replacement — for religion. In a speech to Boston's Arlington Street Church in 1966, Allen Ginsberg proposed "that everybody, including the President and his . . . vast hordes of generals, executives, judges and legislators . . . go to nature, find a kindly teacher . . . and assay their consciousness with LSD. Then, I prophesy, we will all have seen some ray of glory of vastness beyond our conditioned social selves, beyond our government, beyond America even, that will unite us into a peaceable community." LSD's strongest proponent, Timothy Leary, pushed the idea that the hallucinogenic had redemptive properties. Inside the sixty-room mansion Leary occupied in Millbrook, New York, the drug was treated with "a studied and religious air, as if one took LSD in the spirit of a communicant," Thomas Powers reported.

In the spring of 1967, *The New York Times Magazine* displayed an unusual willingness to embrace a prophet of the counterculture by publishing Hunter Thompson's report from Haight-Ashbury. A few years later, Thompson would become famous for his "gonzo journalism" from Las Vegas and the presidential campaign trail, as well as his legendary drug consumption. But in 1967 he was still a little-known free-lance writer. "Who needs jazz, or even beer," he asked in the *Times,*

> when you can sit down on a public curbstone, drop a pill in your mouth, and hear fantastic music for hours at a time in your own head? A cap of good acid costs $5, and for that you can hear the Universal Symphony, with God singing solo and the Holy Ghost on drums. . . . There is no shortage of documentation for the thesis that the current Haight-Ashbury scene is only the orgiastic tip of a great psychedelic iceberg that is already drifting in the sea lanes of the Great Society. Submerged and uncountable is the mass of intelligent, capable hands who want nothing so much as peaceful anonymity. In a nervous society where a man's image is frequently more important than his reality, the only people who can afford to advertise their drug menus are those with nothing to lose.

Two other contradictory strains nurtured the atmosphere which gave birth to the modern gay liberation movement. One was the sentimental

---

*The same year, the publishing business was shocked when Harper and Row announced the publication of a children's book that included a homosexual episode in the lives of two thirteen-year-old boys. Written by John Donovan, it was called *I'll Get There. It Better Be Worth the Trip.* (*New York Times,* April 3, 1968)

embrace of peace and love, which began to attract national attention on January 14, 1967, when twenty thousand celebrants joined Ginsberg, the antiwar activist Jerry Rubin and Timothy Leary for a Gathering of the Tribes in San Francisco's Golden Gate Park. A press release explained that political activists would join forces with "the love generation" to "pow-wow, celebrate, and prophesy the epoch of liberation, love, peace, compassion and the unity of mankind." In Manhattan, Roy Aarons remembered the "coming of the psychedelic era, and being flooded with a bunch of runaway kids, and the whole introduction of grass and psychedelics. It became a much looser scene where there was a lot of experimentation by these guys."

The other leitmotif of the sixties was a feverish violence, which peaked in April 1968 after Martin Luther King, Jr., was assassinated in Memphis. The assassinations of John and Robert Kennedy bracketed King's. After Bobby's killing, John Updike wondered if God had withdrawn his blessing on America. William Styron remembered this decade as an era when "one of those liberal well-intentioned people would say, 'You don't mean, do you' — and James Baldwin would interrupt and say, 'Yes, baby, they're going to burn your house down.'"

After King was killed, 65,000 troops were needed to quell riots in 130 cities across the country. The fires that swept through Washington were the worst since the British had burned the White House in 1814, and machine-gun nests sprouted on the steps of the Capitol. The Johnson administration worried that it might actually run out of troops to calm the uprisings. Thirty-nine people were killed and nearly twenty thousand were arrested across the country. The riots extinguished white America's waning interest in the plight of poor blacks inside teeming ghettos.

But these disturbances had a very different effect on another group of disenfranchised Americans. They planted seeds of disobedience inside the hearts of millions who were finally about to assert *their* rights to life, liberty and the pursuit of happiness.

UNDER PRESSURE from the Mattachine Society, the New York City Police Department announced in 1966 that it would stop using undercover cops to entrap homosexuals. Harold Bramson, a thirty-three-year-old schoolteacher, believed that he was the last person to be entrapped by a rookie undercover cop inside a gay bar before the policy was changed. Criminal Court Judge Arthur Braun dismissed the case because of "reasonable doubt," and Bramson kept his job in the public school system.

In 1967, the State Supreme Court of New Jersey threw out a regulation that permitted the state to close any bar that allowed "apparent homosexuals to congregate at their licensed premises." An investigator for the State Division of Alcoholic Beverage Control had complained that gay patrons had "looked into each other's eyes when they conversed" and "swished and swayed down to the other end of the bar." But the Supreme Court justices ruled unanimously that "so long as their public behavior violates no legal proscriptions, [homosexuals] have the undoubted right to congregate in public."

On the other hand, the blackmail that Max Lerner had been unable to confirm in Washington during the 1950s emerged as a serious problem for famous homosexuals in the 1960s. Federal and state law enforcement officials announced in 1966 that they had broken up a national extortion ring with seventy members who had bilked more than a thousand victims of millions of dollars, including an East Coast congressman who paid more than $40,000 to thieves posing as policemen. At least thirteen people were indicted for extortion, and several were sentenced to prison terms of up to ten years. Officials said the ring was headed by a former detective from the Chicago police force.

In one case, two gang members posing as New York City detectives marched into the Pentagon, and marched out with a senior officer. After they shook him down for several thousand dollars, the officer killed himself — the night before he was scheduled to testify before a Manhattan grand jury.

Other victims included "a general and an admiral," "a British producer," "two deans of East Coast colleges," "a musician who has made numerous appearances on television," "a partner in a well-known nightspot," "a leading motion picture actor," "a nuclear scientist," "a number of professors," and "a much-admired television personality."

COLUMBIA UNIVERSITY made national headlines in 1967 when it became one of the first colleges to give formal recognition to a gay students organization. The Student Homophile League claimed a dozen members and issued a thirteen-point declaration of principles which asserted "the fundamental human right" of every homosexual "to develop and achieve his full potential and dignity as a human being." It said that gay people should have the right to declare themselves without risking ostracism from school or loss of employment, as well as living "free from unwelcomed pressures to conform to the prevailing heterosexuality."

"At first the students seemed to think it was some sort of April Fool hoax," said Charles Skoro, who wrote about the organization in The

Spectator, the student newspaper. "But now they realize it is for real." In an editorial, *The Spectator* praised the creation of the organization.

Gay sex was still a mostly furtive thing in Manhattan in the mid-sixties. Nearly all the gay bars had been closed in another "cleanup" campaign just before the 1964 World's Fair. But there were the glimmerings of a new kind of community.

John Koch was an Iowa farmboy who had moved to New York in 1964, thinking he would return home after a single summer. But he never left. In 1965, he moved up to 74th Street and Central Park West from the Village, and he discovered the Ramble. This heavily wooded area in the middle of Central Park had been an active gay meeting ground (and bird-watching area) at least since the forties, but now the men who went there were using a new system to protect one another. "If someone saw the cops coming, they'd take a stick and start beating it," Koch recalled. "And all of a sudden you'd hear these clothes being put on and rustle, rustle, rustle. It was a good system. It really was. And the cops would come and we'd just be standing there because in those days it wasn't illegal to be in the park or anything, so they couldn't do anything to you. I felt totally safe there. Central Park West was a place to pick people up and take them home. Central Park was where you did it."

IN THE SUMMER of 1968, Frank Kameny explicitly emulated the example of radical blacks after he saw Stokely Carmichael on television leading a group of protesters in a chant of "Black is beautiful!" Kameny said, "I understood the psychodynamic at work here in a context in which *black* is universally equated with everything that is bad." He realized at once the need to do something similar for gays.

In July 1968, Kameny coined the slogan "Gay is good." He said, "If I had to specify the one thing in my life of which I am most proud, it is that." He described the phrase as a direct response to the "unrelieved, relentless barrage of negativism coming to us from every source."*

Later in 1968, the violent confrontations between Chicago policemen

---

*While gays explicitly emulated black radicals, collaboration between them was rare, and some blacks resented any comparison of the two movements. However, in an unusual expression of solidarity, Huey Newton wrote in *The Black Panther* on August 21, 1970, "Whatever your personal opinions and your insecurities about homosexuality and the various liberation movements among homosexuals and women . . . we should try to unite with them in a revolutionary fashion . . . I know through reading and through my life experience . . . that homosexuals are not given freedom and liberty by anyone in the society. Maybe they might be the most oppressed people in the society. A person should have freedom to use his body in whatever way he wants to. That's not endorsing things in homosexuality that we wouldn't view as revolutionary. But there's nothing to

and antiwar protesters during the Democratic National Convention briefly fostered the impression of a society on the brink of anarchy. These scenes on national television created a political reaction that resulted in the election (by a tiny margin) of Richard Milhous Nixon, the quintessential white man of the fifties. Paradoxically, on a social level, these paroxysms of violence also contributed to a steady loosening of the puritan bonds that had kept the lid on American attitudes and activities throughout the previous decade.

ABC News hired Gore Vidal and the conservative columnist William F. Buckley, Jr., to provide commentary for the convention. During a debate over one of the police riots in Chicago, Vidal called Buckley a "crypto-Nazi." Buckley shouted back, "Now listen, you queer . . . I'll sock you in the goddamn face and you'll stay plastered." The bickering continued in *Esquire* the following year, when the magazine published a telegram that it said Buckley had intended to send to Vidal: "Please inform Gore Vidal neither I nor my family is disposed to receive lessons in morality from a pink queer." Vidal replied in the following issue: "I am not an evangelist of anything in sexual matters except a decent withdrawal of the state from the bedroom. There will always be morbid twisted men like Buckley, sniggering and giggling and speculating on the sexual lives of others."

The North American Conference of Homophile Organizations also met in Chicago that summer and sent questionnaires to all the candidates' headquarters, requesting their views on a "homosexual bill of rights" that would decriminalize sexual acts between consenting adults and remove all government strictures on the employment of gay people. At Kameny's urging, NACHO also adopted "Gay is good" as its official slogan. But even the liberal *New Republic* seemed skeptical about the whole undertaking: "History indicates that politicians generally prefer to leave such embarrassments in obscurity," the magazine observed, "but the homosexuals profess determination to make an issue of this serious problem for society."

THE LOUDEST REVERBERATION from the collapse of the old order was a revolution in the way Americans thought about sex. The widespread use

---

say that a homosexual cannot be a revolutionary. . . . Quite the contrary, maybe a homosexual could be the most revolutionary. . . . When we have revolutionary conferences, rallies and demonstrations there should be full participation of the gay liberation movement and the women's liberation movement. . . . The terms 'faggot' and 'punk' should be deleted from our vocabulary." (Quoted in David Deitcher, ed., *The Question of Equality*, 33.) More typically, Eldridge Cleaver wrote in *Soul on Ice*, "Homosexuality is a sickness, just as are baby-rape or wanting to become head of General Motors." (Quoted in *New York Times*, January 17, 1971)

of the Pill at the beginning of the sixties made sex simpler, more accessible and seemingly less consequential. It also encouraged public acceptance of a truly radical notion for a prudish nation: the idea that sex might actually be valuable for its own sake. That idea represented a sea change in the way millions of Americans of all orientations thought about copulation; in fact, it was *the* fundamental philosophical leap, *the* indispensable step before homosexual sex could gain any legitimacy within the larger society. By definition, until sex was given a value unconnected to procreation, sex between two people of the same gender could only be worthless and "unnatural." As one Episcopalian opponent of reform put it in 1967, homosexual acts "must always be regarded as perversions because they are not part of the natural process of rearing children." But as John D'Emilio has pointed out, once the Pill gained widespread acceptance, the defense of heterosexual intercourse as the only "natural" act became increasingly difficult because "modern technology was obstructing the 'natural' outcome" of that act.

"The difference was, for the first time, *everybody* at the grassroots level found all these taboos wanting and unpersuasive and irrational," said Frank Kameny. "And *that's* what changed." In April 1969, *Playboy* published an interview with Allen Ginsberg in which the poet even made positive comments about being gay.

In 1967, Rita Hauser, a prominent Republican lawyer from New York City, made a speech that was remarkably radical for its time. In a forum of the American Bar Association on "Women's Liberation and the Constitution," she declared that laws banning marriages between people of the same sex were unconstitutional. Mrs. Hauser said such laws were based on an antiquated notion that reproduction is the purpose of marriage. Because of overpopulation, she called that rationale outmoded. Limiting reproduction was the new social goal, "And I know no better way of accomplishing this than marriage between the same sexes."*

Dan Stewart, a landscape architect, made his first visit to Cherry Grove on Fire Island in 1967, when he was thirty-seven. "I was scared to death to go because I thought everybody was totally sexually *crazed* out there. And I didn't know how to deal with that at the time. If I knew somebody — knew who they were and liked them — I'd do anything, OK. But to do anything with someone I didn't know was very frightening to me. And

---

*In 1969, the Internal Revenue Service told the *Advocate* that it had never ruled on whether the government would accept a joint tax return from a gay couple. But the following year, White House Press Secretary Ron Ziegler told the magazine that President Nixon "doesn't think that people of the same sex should marry." (Mark Thompson, ed., *The Long Road to Freedom*, 20, 37)

that's what Fire Island represented. I will never forget that first weekend in the Grove. We stayed at the Belvedere, a guest house place that looks like an Italian palazzo. It's still there: it's unreal. It was one of those nights when the sunset was pink, and it lasted for three hours. So you had all this pink light, and here were all these muscle builders and all this stuff going on. It was Fellini for days." But no one asked Stewart to participate. "I was also miserable about that. You know, my fear must have shown."

As early as 1964, the New York Academy of Medicine provided hard evidence of the arrival of the sexual revolution: a surge in reported cases of venereal disease. The incidence of syphilis in New York City increased almost seven-fold, from seven new cases per one hundred thousand reported in 1955 to forty-five new cases in 1963. The academy cited these reasons for the change: a "releasing of moral and cultural values in present-day society, [the elevation of sex] to a status of glamour, success and happiness, salacious literature directed at youth, a breakdown in the home and family life, the automobile, and the feminist movement." It also noted the "organized and aggressive action" by homosexuals to "gain at least tolerance, hopefully to achieve" acceptance, "and most ambitiously to have it recognized as a noble way of life."

THE INTENSE CROSS-CULTURAL exchange between America and Britain produced additional fuel for what gradually became a general cultural and political conflagration — the necessary preamble for a fundamental revolution in the way Americans thought about sex. One reason the country changed so rapidly in the sixties was a colossal infusion of energy from the largest generation of adolescents America had ever produced.

"It's at that age when you really feel you can make things happen," Bob Dylan explained. "Things matter."

By the middle of 1967, the Beatles had become much more than Britain's most successful cultural export since Shakespeare. By synthesizing the best of American rock and roll from the fifties (Elvis, Buddy Holly, Little Richard, and the Everly Brothers, among others) into their own spellbinding soundtrack for the sixties, they managed to embody the entire British-American fifties-into-sixties cultural transformation. Their beguiling public persona was shaped by Brian Epstein, their closeted gay manager, who fell in love with all of them as soon as he laid eyes on them. According to Paul McCartney, the Beatles were more baffled than upset by their new manager's sexual orientation. "We were more confused by it than turned off," said McCartney. "We really didn't know what it meant to be gay at the time."

George Martin, who signed them to their first record contract, described a similarly intense (though nonsexual) reaction to the Merseyside quartet. While Martin wasn't particularly impressed when he first heard their music, as soon as he met them he was entranced. "They exuded exuberance," said Martin. "Sparks flew off them."

Their magic combination of charm and cheerfulness was first displayed in theaters everywhere in 1964 when Richard Lester directed their smash black-and-white film debut, *A Hard Day's Night*. This was the first film to capture the emerging countercultural spirit for the masses. "While I was watching that movie my hair started to grow," the film critic Roger Ebert remembered.

Although it was aimed at kids, almost everyone adored it. "You didn't take your eyes off them because you never knew at what moment they would do something unexpected," said Lester, while Andrew Sarris considered the film "the *Citizen Kane* of jukebox musicals." For millions of rockers of all ages, the impishness of these sexy performers transformed ancient notions of how macho a "real" man had to act and look. Suddenly humor was hipper than brawn. The gay activist Jack Nichols considered the Beatles the "undisputed troubadours of the revolution I represented" because "they showed true care for one another," which was "unheard of by 1950s standards."

By becoming the most celebrated artists on the planet, the Beatles pushed postadolescent male sexuality to the center of Western culture. Their triumph completed a twenty-year process that began when Marlon Brando starred on Broadway in a torn T-shirt, gained momentum with Elvis Presley,* and reached its first plateau when John Kennedy entered the White House. "In the age of Calvin Klein's steaming hunks, it must be hard for those under 40 to realize that there was ever a time when a man was nothing but a suit of clothes, a shirt and tie, shined leather shoes, and a gray, felt hat," Gore Vidal wrote. "If he was thought attractive, it was because he had a nice smile and a twinkle in his eye."

In a subtle way, the national veneration of the long-haired Kennedy and the longer-haired Beatles may even have contributed to a painfully slow acceptance by gay men of their own desires. With the "male as sex object" at our "culture's center stage," as Vidal put it, one man's obsession with another stopped seeming quite so unnatural as it had been before. Or, to

---

*Margo Jefferson pointed out that "Little Richard was an advance man for mass culture's acceptance of camp," and from what we can now call the "gay theatrics" of Liberace, Little Richard, and Jackie Wilson, Elvis Presley "got glamour and self-parody." (*New York Times,* March 5, 1995, and October 26, 1994)

put it more concretely, it no longer felt so odd to a fourteen-year-old boy who discovered that he worshipped George Harrison, when so many of his male classmates seemed to feel just as strongly about John Lennon, Paul McCartney, and Ringo Starr (and strove to look exactly like them). Allen Ginsberg thought, "The Beatles provided an example to youth around the world: that guys could be friends." Ringo explained, "It was four guys who really loved each other" — and everyone else noticed.

Janis Joplin accomplished a different kind of gender-bending feat for women. As the critic Ellen Willis pointed out, Joplin's "metamorphosis from the ugly duckling of Port Arthur to the peacock of Haight-Ashbury" meant that "a woman who was not conventionally pretty, who had acne and an intermittent weight problem and hair that stuck out" could "invent her own beauty out of sheer energy, soul, sweetness, arrogance and a sense of humor" — and thereby alter our very "notions of attractiveness."

The sixties celebration of diversity was most apparent in the world of music. At no other moment in American history have so many different musical styles been promoted on commercial radio stations — everyone from the Beatles and Bob Dylan to the Supremes and Jefferson Airplane.

Dylan was a direct descendant of the Beats. "It was Ginsberg and Jack Kerouac who inspired me at first," he explained — and Ginsberg was in the studio with him when he first recorded "The Chimes of Freedom" for *Another Side of Bob Dylan* in 1964. "Listen," exulted Ginsberg, quoting a lyric, "he's singing for 'every hung-up person in the whole wide universe!'" Dylan paid homage to his friend by giving the poet a cameo in the opening scene of the brilliant documentary of Dylan's 1965 tour of Britain, *Don't Look Back.*

The celebrity of Dylan, the Beatles, Janis Joplin and dozens of other iconoclasts sent another important subliminal message to an emerging generation of lesbians and gay men: these role models proved that outsiders — even outlaws — could become heroes in an age like this.

For almost a decade, cultural and political ferment in England had provided much more explicit encouragement to the nascent gay liberation movement in America. Ever since the Wolfenden Report had recommended the decriminalization of homosexual acts between adults in 1957, a spirited debate in Great Britain about whether the law should regulate sexual activity between consenting adults had received considerable attention in the American news magazines and *The New York Times.*

This controversy stimulated the production of *Victim,* a landmark British film about the routine blackmail of homosexuals. The film in turn intensified the political debate, leading to a dramatic legal reform. But at the end of 1960, the man who would direct *Victim*, Basil Dearden, had almost given up on getting it made. Just before Christmas, Dearden sent the script to Dirk Bogarde, a fine British actor who was discovered by Hollywood at end of the fifties, but now hungered to do something that would have real meaning. Before the script arrived at the actor's country home in Beaconsfield, a few miles west of London, Dearden telephoned Bogarde to warn him that every other actor he had approached had rejected it.

"Thanks," said Bogarde. "What's it about, paedophilia?"

"No," said Dearden. "Homosexuality, actually. Middle-aged married man with a yen for a bloke on a building site. . . . If it's any comfort we don't call anyone a queer, homo, pouf, nancy or faggot." (*Invert* was the word that the screenwriter had selected.)

Bogarde seized the chance to play the leading role: a London barrister whose ex-boyfriend kills himself rather than disclose the barrister's identity to a blackmail ring or to the police. The barrister jettisons his career in order to crush the blackmailers. Bogarde wrote in his autobiography,

> It was the wisest decision I ever made in my cinematic life. It is extraordinary in this over-permissive age, to believe that this modest film could ever have been considered courageous, daring or dangerous to make. [But] it was, in its time, all three. . . . Some critics complained that it was only a thriller with a message tacked on rather loosely. But the best way to persuade a patient to take his medicine is by sugaring the pill — and this was the only possible way the film could have been approached in those early days. Whatever else, it was a tremendous success, pleasing us and confounding our detractors. The countless letters of gratitude which flooded in were proof enough of that . . . I had achieved what I had longed to do for so long, to be in a film which disturbed, educated and illuminated.

"It was the first film in which a man said 'I love you' to another man," said Bogarde. "I wrote that scene in. I said, 'There's no point in half-measures. We either make a film about queers or we don't.'"

The film was propaganda: it was explicit and effective. This exchange took place between the two policemen in charge of the investigation:

Senior Detective:	If only these unfortunate devils had come to us in the first place.
Junior Detective:	If only they led normal lives they wouldn't need to come at all.

Senior Detective: If the law punished every abnormality we'd be kept
                     pretty busy, son.
Junior Detective: Even so, sir, this law was made for a very good reason.
                     If it were changed, other weaknesses would follow.
Senior Detective: I can see you're a true puritan, Bridy.
Junior Detective: Well, there's nothing wrong with that, sir.
Senior Detective: Of course not. There was a time when *that* was against
                     the law, you know.

In the film, a barber who is being blackmailed tells Bogarde, "I can't
help the way I am, but the law says I'm a criminal. I've been to prison four
times. Couldn't go through that again. Not at my age. I'm going to Canada. I've made up my mind to be 'sensible,' as the prison doctor used to
say. Don't care how lonely, but sensible. Can't stand any more trouble. . . .
Nature played me a dirty trick. I'm going to see I get a few years peace and
quiet in return." Another blackmail victim asks, "Do you ever wonder
about the law that makes us all victims of any cheap thug who finds out
about our natural instincts?" The movie was also careful to address the
most common objection to the reform of laws regulating homosexual
behavior. "Of course youth must be protected," said one of the gay characters. "We all agree about that. But that doesn't mean that consenting males
in private should be pilloried by an antiquated law."

The film was a critical and financial success in Great Britain, and it had
a dramatic effect on the political debate about homosexuality. Just four
years after it was released, the twelfth marquess of Queensberry — the
great grandson of the man who accused Oscar Wilde of having an affair
with his son — rose in the House of Lords to support a bill that would
decriminalize homosexual acts between adults. "I do not believe that our
laws on this subject are a solution," the thirty-five-year-old marquess
declared in his maiden speech to his fellow lords. "They have, if anything,
helped to produce a nasty, furtive underworld which is bad for society and
bad for the homosexual" — the very world depicted in *Victim*. Dr. Arthur
M. Ramsay, the archbishop of Canterbury, also endorsed the recommendations of the Wolfenden Report. Two years later, in 1967 — with the
support of the Church of England, the Methodists, and even the Roman
Catholics — the bill received final approval from the House of Commons,
a milestone recorded in a page-one story by Anthony Lewis in *The New
York Times*.

Victim might have ignited a similar debate in America, but it never got
into general release here. Always alert to the dangerous connections be-

tween culture and politics, the Catholic-dominated censorship office in Hollywood refused to give *Victim* its seal of approval. According to the film historian Vito Russo, the first objection was to the use of the words *homosexual* and *homosexuality,* "which had never before been uttered on screen." A spokesman for the Production Code Administration explained that the film was unacceptable because of its "candid and clinical discussion of homosexuality" and its "overtly expressed plea for social acceptance of the homosexual, to the extent that he be made socially tolerable." A handful of art houses in big cities did exhibit *Victim,* despite the absence of censorship office endorsement. Murray Gitlin went to see the film in Chicago with an actor friend. "We came out, and Woody said to me, 'Well, our secret is out!'" Gitlin remembered. "This is, like, sixty-two. And that may have been the beginning of an awareness that had not been around before. A very important moment."

Ironically, the censorship office acted to keep *Victim* out of general release just five weeks after Arthur Krim, the president of United Artists, had petitioned the Motion Picture Association of America to loosen the code to permit *some* references to homosexuality. Krim was concerned because his company was in the process of producing *The Children's Hour,* inspired by the Lillian Hellman play in which an evil child's accusation of lesbianism destroys the lives of two teachers, and *Advise and Consent,* the film based on the Allen Drury novel in which a senator commits suicide because of the revelation of a homosexual incident in his past. Because neither film "promoted" homosexuality, the MPAA granted Krim's request. But the fact that *Victim* advocated reform of the law was more than the censorship office could stomach.

In 1961 a virulent homophobia remained routine for many of America's most influential film critics. *Time* magazine called *Victim* "a coyly sensational exploitation of homosexuality as a theme — and what's more offensive — an implicit approval of homosexuality as a practice. . . . Nowhere does the film suggest that homosexuality is a serious but often curable neurosis that attacks the biological basis of life itself." Another British offering that year, *A Taste of Honey,* included an affectionate portrayal of an effeminate gay character named Geoff, played by Murray Melvin. After the film received a favorable review in *The New York Times* from Abe Weiler, a junior critic on the paper, his superior, Bosley Crowther, immediately objected. "Certainly you'd think the grubby people who swarm through [the film] might shake out one disagreeable individual whose meanness we might despise," wrote Crowther, who was chief film critic for the *Times* for three decades. "The homosexual could do with some sharp and dirty digs. No one is more easily rendered odious than an obvious homosexual." Five years later, Crowther wrote that "too many people who should know better in the steamy front offices of Hollywood" used "adult theme" as a synonym for "abnormal sex."

IN 1963 *The New York Times* published a landmark piece about homosexuals on its front page. The article was inspired by the convictions of the man who would dominate the news department for more than twenty years. His opinions would often have a decisive effect on the way gay employees were treated and gay issues were covered by the *Times*.

A. M. Rosenthal was a brilliant, ambitious, volatile and fiercely opinionated newsman. The son of Russian Jews who first settled in Canada before moving to the Bronx, he started his career at the *Times* while still an undergraduate at City College. In 1963 he had returned from Japan, the last of four foreign postings, to become the paper's metropolitan editor. Six years later, he would be named managing editor and, in 1977, executive editor, a job that gave him control of the entire news department. He held that position until 1986.

One of the first things Rosenthal noticed after he returned to New York after a long absence was how obvious homosexuals had become on the city's streets. To explain this phenomenon, he assigned the kind of story he would become famous for: a huge attention-getting account that purported to tell the reader everything he needed to know about a particular subject.

In the early 1960s, *The New York Times* was much more than the newspaper of record. It was the bible of the eastern liberal establishment, the media outlet that set the tone for the coverage of every important story in America. Its news judgment was considered unimpeachable by all other serious newspapers and every network news broadcast. In this period before Watergate and Ben Bradlee made the *Washington Post* a significant competitor, the *Times* was the newspaper almost every ambitious print reporter dreamed of working for. Its long page-one stories on sociological subjects were studied by the intelligentsia as if they were the secular equivalent of papal encyclicals.

This was the headline at the bottom of the front page on December 17, 1963:

**GROWTH OF HOMOSEXUALITY
IN CITY PROVOKES WIDE CONCERN**

The story was written by Robert Doty, who had recently returned from a foreign assignment. It began with a routine report about the closings of two more "homosexual haunts," but quickly declared its main purpose: "The city's most sensitive open secret — the presence of what is probably the greatest homosexual population in the world and its increasing openness — has become the subject of growing concern of psychiatrists, religious leaders and the police."

The article was a breakthrough simply because of the amount of attention it devoted to a sexual subject, since any explicit discussion of sex was generally discouraged in the gray pages of the *Times*.* It was most startling because of its length: five thousand words on the growing angst of the city's fathers over this disturbing phenomenon. Homosexual bars, it explained "are only a small part of the homosexual problem in New York. . . . Sexual inverts have colonized three areas of the city. The city's homosexual community acts as a lodestar, attracting others from all over the country." It was the kind of derisive treatment from which Jews, blacks, and Puerto Ricans were protected in the pages of the *Times*. But none of the reporters in the newsroom challenged its appropriateness for homosexuals. Unlike these other minorities, gay people were a "curable" problem, as the story made clear right from the start:

> The old idea, assiduously propagated by homosexuals, that homosexuality is an inborn, incurable disease, has been exploded by modern psychiatry, in the opinion of many experts. It can be both prevented and cured, these experts say.
>
> It is a problem that has grown in the shadows, protected by taboos on open discussion that have only recently begun to be breached.
>
> The overt homosexual — and those who are identifiable probably represent no more than half the total — has become such an obtrusive part of the New York scene that the phenomenon needs public discussion, in the opinion of a number of legal and medical experts.

The story acknowledged that a "minority of militant homosexuals" were "agitating for removal of legal, social and cultural discriminations against sexual inverts" and "fundamental to this aim is the concept that homosexuality is an incurable, congenital disorder." But it immediately

---

*Iphigene Sulzberger, who was the daughter, wife, mother, and grandmother of publishers of *The New York Times*, was particularly squeamish about the coverage of sex. When she thought it was getting too much space in the paper in 1968, she wrote a note to her son Arthur Ochs Sulzberger. "Why not put sex in perspective?" she asked. "It went on in my day too." (Gay Talese, *The Kingdom and the Power*, 517)

added that this idea was "disputed by the bulk of scientific evidence." Psychiatrists

> have what they consider to be overwhelming evidence that homosexuals are created — generally by ill-adjusted parents — not born.
>
> They assert that homosexuality can be cured by sophisticated analytical and therapeutic techniques.
>
> More significantly, the weight of the most recent findings suggests that public discussion of the nature of those parental misdeeds and attitudes that tend to foster homosexual development of children could improve family environments and reduce the incidence of sexual inversion.

Therefore, the story was nothing more than simple public service because "Leaving the subject exclusively to barroom jesters, policemen concerned with public aspects of the problem and the homosexuals themselves can only perpetuate the mystery and misconceptions that have grown in the dark, according to expert opinion."

Other choice observations included the following:

> The homosexual has a range of gay periodicals that is a kind of distorted mirror image of the straight publishing world . . .
>
> The tendency of homosexuals to be promiscuous and seek pick-ups — a tendency recognized even by the gay writer, Donald Webster Cory, in his book, "The Homosexual in America" — makes them particularly vulnerable to police entrapment . . .
>
> A homosexual who had achieved good progress toward cure under psychoanalysis recently told his analyst that at certain hours on certain evenings he could identify as homosexual approximately one man out of three along Third Avenue in the fifties and sixties. This was probably an exaggeration . . .
>
> Homosexuals are traditionally willing to spend all they have on a gay night. They will pay admission fees and outrageous prices for drinks in order to be left alone with their own kind to chatter and dance together without pretense or constraint . . .
>
> There is a cliquishness about gay individuals that often leads one who achieves an influential position in the theater — as many of them do — to choose for employment another homosexual candidate over a straight applicant, unless the latter had an indisputable edge of talent that would bear on the artistic success of the venture . . .
>
> "The increase in homosexuality is only one aspect of the general atmosphere of moral breakdown that has been going on around us," says

Monsignor Robert Gallagher of the Youth Counseling Service of the
Roman Catholic Archdiocese . . .

[Ten psychoanalysts] reported that 27 percent of the homosexuals
under treatment by the group achieved a heterosexual orientation.

Obviously, this meant that 73 *percent* of their patients remained homosexual. But no one editing the story noticed the contradiction between
that fact and the statement immediately following it: "Our findings are
optimistic guideposts not only for the homosexuals but for the psychoanalysts who treat them. . . . We are firmly convinced that psychoanalysts
may well orient themselves to a heterosexual objective in treating homosexual patients rather than 'adjust' even the more recalcitrant patient to a
homosexual destiny."

The story appeared exactly twenty years after the *Journal-American's*
explanation of this orientation following Wayne Lonergan's arrest; and
though couched in more polite language, it was brimming with exactly the
same kind of virulent prejudice published by the Hearst tabloid during
World War II. But because it appeared under the imprimatur of the *Times,*
the story had a much more serious and lasting effect. This was the worst
kind of *Times* article, pretending to offer scientific certainty where there
was none, and repeatedly citing anonymous "expert opinion" to justify the
prejudices of its invisible editors.

Unlike the earlier wartime piece, the *Times* article at least pretended
to give "the other side" of the story, although even these attempts at
balance could be quite misleading. For example, the statement that "truly
psychotic inverts who prey upon pre-adolescent boys are no more common than molesters of girl juveniles," might have suggested fairness —
except for the fact crime statistics reveal that heterosexual child molestation is much more common that homosexual molestation. In any case, the
article was strongly tilted toward the opinion of homophobic psychiatrists
like Charles W. Socarides, and the story made it clear that its progenitors
believed the only good homosexual was one who was determined to
become a heterosexual. Considering the vehemence with which this opinion was expressed in the newspaper of record, the ability of Kameny and
Nichols to overturn the traditional positions inside the Mattachine Society barely two years later is all the more impressive.*

*

*On the other hand, in 1969, when Gay Talese published *The Kingdom and the Power*, his history
of the *Times,* he referred to the page-one piece as a "superb article." (Gay Talese, *The Kingdom
and the Power,* 373)

TWO YEARS AFTER the *Times* article appeared, "CBS Reports" began researching its own documentary about male homosexuals. The principal interviewer on the program was Mike Wallace. The CBS veteran was already well known as a network reporter, but not nearly as famous as he would become after "60 Minutes" began its marathon run in 1968.

It took two years of filming, editing, and fierce internal debate before "The Homosexuals" was finally broadcast on March 7, 1967. "No sponsor wanted *anything* to do with it," Wallace recalled, and the breaks were filled by public service spots provided by the Peace Corps and the Internal Revenue Service. "This was 1967. People weren't talking openly about homosexuality," Wallace said. There were two documentaries from "CBS Reports" during this period that were about "verboten" subjects, the reporter remembered; the other was about the growing popularity of marijuana in America.

The first version of "The Homosexuals" was made by "CBS Reports" producer William Peters under the supervision of Fred Friendly, who was president of CBS News from 1964 to 1966. According to Wallace, after Friendly viewed an early version of the documentary, he praised it, but asked for one addition. "Fred said, 'We don't have in what homosexuals *do* [in bed]. For pure reportage, we have to put that on the air.' I said, 'Fred, do you know what it is that homosexuals do?' He said, 'No, that's the point, I don't.' I said, 'Here's what they do.' And his face blanched. And he said, 'Well, maybe we don't have to put it on the air.' *Many* people didn't have a *clue!*"

But after Friendly had viewed the documentary and before it was broadcast, he resigned as CBS News president because the network refused to provide live coverage of congressional hearings about the Vietnam War. Friendly was replaced by Richard Salant, who found the original version of "The Homosexuals" objectionable. According to a contemporary account in *Variety,* Salant assigned the producer Harry Morgan to recut the program, partly because he was unhappy with footage dealing "directly with homosexual activities in the U.S. environment," including "footage from a homosexual tavern and the street pickup scenes." The show was "gutted and virtually remade," *Variety* reported. According to C. A. Tripp, a psychologist whose patient had appeared on the program, the first version was discarded because it might have been interpreted as "for" homosexuality. Wallace told the producer of the original version that Salant thought it smacked of sensationalism.

Although the one-hour broadcast repeated many of the prejudices, quoted several of the same psychiatrists, and even used some of the same words as the article in the *Times* ("there is a growing concern about homosexuals in society — about their increasing visibility"), the making of the CBS documentary was an extraordinary development for a medium that had generally avoided any discussion of homosexuality. It was also a crucial event for gay people: by reaching forty million prime-time viewers, it probably gave more Americans more information about homosexuals than any journalistic effort (or artistic endeavor) had ever provided before.*

The documentary was heavily weighted toward the traditional view of homosexuality as a debilitating and curable illness; it also repeated the myth that the typical homosexual is "not interested in, nor capable of, a lasting relationship, like that of a heterosexual marriage." But the specific impact of Kameny and his cohorts and the general effects of the sixties were evident throughout. Not only did CBS acknowledge the existence of more than one point of view about homosexuals; it also opened the program with a strikingly handsome, happily adjusted, twenty-eight-year-old blond homosexual. For millions of viewers, this young man was probably the first they ever had heard declare, "I am a homosexual."

The attractive interviewee was identified as Lars Larson. Watching Larson again thirty years after he interviewed him, Wallace remarked, "He's nervous." The correspondent didn't notice that he himself also looks uncharacteristically anxious, kneading his hands throughout the conversation. Larson acknowledged that when he first realized that he was homosexual, he was "terribly frightened" because he didn't want to be different. "I wanted to have everything that everybody else had. . . . And the cost was really quite terrific in human terms." Then he spoke with the honesty made possible by all the swift changes of this decade: "I could be a nice little robot and go through the motions of life for some sixty, seventy, eighty, years. . . . But it wouldn't be right, not for me. And I couldn't sit back and take that."

Larson had first seen gay life up close in New Orleans, and after seven

---

*"The Homosexuals" was not, however, the first television documentary on this subject. "The Rejected," produced by John Reavis, was broadcast by affiliates of the Educational Televison Network in September 1961. Originally entitled "The Gay Ones," it was filmed mostly in the studio. Its only location shots were inside the Black Cat, one of San Francisco's most famous gay bars (author's interview with Edward Alwood, November 6, 1995). In New York City, Channel 13's "Intertel" series had also broadcast a one-hour documentary about gay men and lesbians produced by Associated Rediffusion in England.

days "without experience," he decided that homosexuality was "furtive" and "ugly," and he wanted no part of it. But then he met another young man in the service, and they spent the weekend together. For nearly everyone who tuned in to CBS at 10:00 P.M. that evening, Larson described his initial encounter with an attitude that must have sounded revolutionary. "It was just a grand, grand experience. It was the first moment in my life where I was open, where I didn't have to hide, where I could lower all my barriers, where I could be absolutely me — without worrying about it. I had all the freedom in the world to be Lars Larson."*

Wallace explained that Larson was a member of "the most despised minority in the United States" and "not typical" because of his willingness to appear on television. The reporter gave the results of a newly commissioned CBS poll: "Americans consider homosexuality more harmful to society than adultery, abortion, or prostitution . . . two out of three Americans look upon homosexuals with 'disgust, discomfort, or fear.' One out of ten says 'hatred.' A vast majority believe that homosexuality is an illness; only ten percent say it is a crime; and yet — here is the paradox — the majority of Americans favor legal punishment, even for homosexual acts performed in private between consenting adults. The homosexual responds by going underground."

After Larson, the show's second subject was interviewed on his psychiatrist's couch, with one hand on his forehead and the other one covering his mouth. When he came out to his parents, "They were sorry for me as if I were some kind of wounded animal they were going to send to the vet," the patient confided. "I think I always had the feeling that I couldn't do anything to please my father." But he was followed by another attractive young man, shown full face, and identified as Warren Adkins of the Washington chapter of the Mattachine Society.

Adkins was really Frank Kameny's ally Jack Nichols. Adkins was the name of one of Nichols's former boyfriends. Years later Nichols explained that because he was a "Jr." he had made a deal with his FBI agent–father not to use his real name in public until after his father had retired from the bureau. "I can't imagine myself giving this up," Nichols said on the program. "And I don't think most other people who are sure of their sexuality, whether they're homosexuals or heterosexuals, could imagine giving that up either." Already, the Mattachine militants seemed to understand the

*Larson was furious after the program aired because he had been led to believe that it would provide a much more positive picture of gay life in America. (Author's interview with Edward Alwood, November 6, 1995)

political advantages of emphasizing the possibility that homosexuality had a genetic origin. Asked by Wallace what had made him gay, Nichols replied, "It really doesn't concern me very much. I never would imagine that if I had blond hair that I would worry what genes or what chromosomes caused my blond hair. My homosexuality to me is very much in the same category. I feel no more guilt about my homosexuality . . . than a person with blond hair or dark skin or with light skin would feel about what they had."* Nichols said he had told his parents he was gay when he was just fourteen, and "they have accepted me as a person. They don't think of me as some kind of creature." He felt "very lucky to have such a warm and understanding family."

After the camera had been turned off, "Mike said I had answered his questions to his satisfaction," Nichols recalled. "But," said Wallace, "I really don't think you truly believe in your heart what you're saying to me. I think you know it's wrong."

"I think *you* think it's wrong," Nichols replied. "I remember after that being kind of pissed off." Asked about this exchange thirty years later, Wallace said, "It seems perfectly possible because my eyes were being opened at the time."

The day after the program was aired, Nichols was fired from his job as a sales manager for a Washington hotel.

Charles Socarides was one of a number of psychiatrists who gained notoriety in the fifties and sixties entirely because of his views about homosexuality, and he remains one of the most virulent opponents of the gay liberation movement, right up to the present day. For CBS, he provided his standard diagnosis: "The fact that someone is homosexual, a true obligatory homosexual, automatically rules out the possibility that he will remain happy for long . . . The stresses and strains the psychic apparatus is subjected to" will cause him "to have increasing difficulties. I think the whole idea of the happy homosexual is to create a mythology about the nature of homosexuality." But in another concession to the budding gay movement, Wallace noted that "Dr. Socarides's views are not universally held. There is a smaller group who do not consider homosexuality an illness at all. Instead they regard it as a deviation within the range of normalcy."

---

*Thirty years later, Nichols said that he didn't realize he was making an "inborn" argument. "I've never really thought heterosexuality or homosexuality to be inborn states," Nichols wrote. "In my more experimental days when I was about twenty, I saw that I could easily seduce hosts of 'straight' guys and that they'd do *everything* sexually except kiss — or talk about it in the morning." (Letter from Jack Nichols to the author, December 12, 1995)

Almost two decades after the broadcast, Socarides's son publicly declared his homosexuality. "I don't think it's easy for anybody to grow up gay," Richard Socarides told David Dunlap of *The New York Times* in 1995. "But given [my father] Charles's outspokenness on the subject of a so-called cure for homosexuality, it sure wasn't any easier." In 1996, Richard Socarides went to work in the White House as Bill Clinton's liaison to the gay community.

Wallace reported that "homosexual acts are not considered a crime in most of Western Europe," and he pointed out that the British were about to legalize homosexual behavior between consenting adults in private. In America in 1967, Illinois was the only state where such acts had become legal. Then the program featured this enlightened statement from James Braxton Craven, a federal district court judge in Charlotte, North Carolina:

Is there any public purpose served by a possible sixty-year-maximum or even five-year-minimum imprisonment of the occasional or one-time homosexual without treatment, and if so, what is it? Are homosexuals twice as dangerous to society as second-degree murderers? Is there any good reason why a person convicted of a single homosexual act with another adult may be imprisoned six times as long as an abortionist? Twice as long as an armed bank robber? And seven hundred and thirty times as long as the public drunk?

In 1964, Judge Craven had thrown out a state conviction of a man who had been sentenced to a minimum of twenty years in prison for engaging in a homosexual act. "Is it not time to redraft a criminal statute first enacted in 1533?" the judge asked.

The CBS program showed footage of Nichols's and Kameny's pickets in front of Independence Hall in Philadelphia and the State Department and the White House in Washington. Kameny appeared using his real name and offered this sound bite about security clearances: "Every American citizen has the right to be considered by his government on the basis of his own personal character, as an individual. Certainly some homosexuals are poor risks. This is no possible excuse for penalizing all homosexuals." In front of the White House, there was also this baffled reaction to twelve gay pickets* from a self-described "country boy" from West Virginia: "I just

---

*Actually, a UPI dispatch identified two of the pickets as married women. A Mattachine spokesman explained that the organization accepted members "without regard to race, religion, sex, or 'sexual orientation.'" In the UPI photograph of the event, Jack Nichols was the first person visible in the picket line, holding a sign that read, "Fifteen million U.S. Homosexuals *Protest* Federal

don't understand it. They're weird! You people are getting much more cosmopolitan than I thought you were!"

Finally, Wallace reported "talk of a homosexual mafia in the arts." The *Times* had repeatedly printed pieces on the corrupting influence of homosexual playwrights in the theater. In 1961 Howard Taubman complained, "Writers feel they must state a homosexual theme in heterosexual situations. . . . Dissembling is unhealthy. . . . The audience senses rot at the drama's core." Five years later, the headline at the top of the "Arts and Leisure" section read "Homosexual Drama and Its Disguises." Stanley Kauffmann argued in this famous article that because "three of the most successful playwrights of the last twenty years are (reputed) homosexuals . . . postwar American drama presents a badly distorted picture of American women, marriage and society." Knowledgeable theatergoers deduced that Kauffmann was referring to Tennessee Williams, Edward Albee, and William Inge.

At the heart of Kauffmann's criticism was the implicit assumption that only a heterosexual man who was *having sex* with a woman could possibly write a realistic woman character. This argument grew out of a quintessentially fifties attitude: the idea that a woman's only value to a man was as a sex object, or as the mother of his children. Turning reality on its head, Kauffmann implied that all gay men were misogynistic; therefore, their portraits of women were always malicious. The fact that gay men frequently have much closer friendships with women than heterosexual men do — or that a gay playwright who had learned to appreciate both the masculine *and* the feminine within him might be adequately equipped to create convincing women characters — never occurred to these critics. They also ignored another fundamental truth: that the similarities between long-term homosexual and heterosexual relationships tend to be much greater than the differences.

The *Newsweek* theater critic Jack Kroll remembered sitting on a peer review board of the National Endowment for the Arts with Kauffmann. "Stanley had this absolutely gut reaction if a gay group came up — it was just 'no way,'" said Kroll. "It was amazing to me that a man of that intelligence could not get beyond that reaction. Maybe it was some sort of Jewish morality. What I think was bad about Stanley's piece was not the

---

Treatment." Kameny was right behind him. The lesbian activist Lilli Vincenz is third. Kameny said, "There were always women on our picket lines, including at least one, and more usually two, of the nongay ones, in our Washington pickets." (*New York Times*, May 30, 1965; UPI–Bettmann; and letters from Jack Nichols, December 12, 1995, and Frank Kameny, December 19, 1995, to the author)

fact that he detected signs of a gay sensibility. It was his attitude; it was a prosecutorial thing: 'You're under arrest!'"*

The debate about the competence of the homosexual playwright had intensified after the huge success of *Who's Afraid of Virginia Woolf?* Edward Albee's scalding portrait of two married couples took Broadway by storm in 1962. In its honesty and its intensity, Albee's was the first important play to reflect the sensibility of the new decade. But because the playwright was gay, the rumor was rampant that his characters were really male homosexuals in disguise. Twenty-five years later, Albee remembered Kauffmann's "disgusting article," and the "absolutely preposterous" notion that

> gays were writing about gays, but disguising them as straights, and writing about men, but disguising them as women . . . Tennessee Williams knew the difference between men and women as well as I do. If you're writing about men, you're writing about men, and if you're writing about women, you're writing about women. But then the rumor began that *Who's Afraid of Virginia Woolf?* was really about four men, which led to attempts at all-male productions of the play, which led to me closing them down . . . because they're incorrect. But somehow that sniping has never gone away.

"People make the mistake of thinking gay playwrights can't write women characters," said Arthur Laurents. "They think the women are really gays in disguise. The truth is that gays write women very well, and they are apt to have trouble writing men. What many write instead are studs and hunks. Look at Williams and Inge. There aren't men; there are these hustlers in one guise or another — or dream bodies without much mind."

On the CBS documentary, a year after Kauffmann's article had appeared, Gore Vidal noted the "theory which one reads all the time about how a certain successful playwright in a very successful play describes married people, heterosexuals, as being wicked and vicious and clawing at each other." He continued,

> This is supposed to be really a story about two homosexual couples. Well . . . there are wicked homosexuals and there are wicked heterosexuals and this is a playwright who deals in savage and extreme situations. And

*Kauffmann said that he could not recall "a single instance" in which he "voted against a gay group because it was gay." He added that to have done so "would have been inconsistent" with the views he expressed in his *Times* article. (Letter from Stanley Kauffmann to the author, April 16, 1997)

I don't see any of it as being translatable particularly as a homosexual situation posing as a heterosexual. And furthermore, if it were, then why is it popular? Obviously it's popular because what he has to say about married couples speaks to everybody. As a matter of fact, there's a certain homosexual who has written the only really good women characters in the American theater. So the idea that the homosexual in some way is a seditious person trying to absolutely destroy the family structure of the United States is *nonsense*.

The "certain homosexual who has written the only really good women characters" was Tennessee Williams. Watching his own program almost three decades later, Mike Wallace was astonished: "He won't even mention his name! I can't believe it. Do you believe this? 1967? In the middle of the sexual revolution, the black revolution, Vietnam!"

Vidal wrote later, "It is now widely believed that since Tennessee Williams liked to have sex with men (true), he hated women (untrue). As a result, his women characters are thought to be malicious caricatures, designed to subvert and destroy godly straightness. But there is no actress on earth who will not testify that Williams created the best women characters in the modern theater." Stephen Sondheim agreed: "It seems to me that Blanche DuBois alone refutes it all."

"Somebody would become successful, then the word would spread he was a fairy," said Vidal. "That meant that all the women were really men in disguise and the relationships were all degenerate ones. And this was a plot — by the fifties it was all a 'homintern plot' — to overthrow heterosexuality."

Vidal wrote that

faced with the contrary evidence, the anti-fag brigade promptly switch to their fallback position. All right, so [Williams] didn't hate women (as real guys do — the ball breakers!) but, worse, far worse, *he thought he was a woman*. Needless to say, a biblical hatred of women intertwines with the good team's hatred of fags. But Williams never thought of himself as anything but a man who could, as an artist, inhabit any gender; on the other hand, his sympathies were always with those defeated by "the squares"; or by time, once the sweet bird of youth is flown. Or by death, "which has never been much in the way of completion." Williams had a great deal of creative and sexual energy; and he used both. Why not? And so what?

Arthur Laurents remembered all his friends reacting with "horror at the fact that the *Times* didn't fire Kauffmann right then and there" after his article was published. "There is no excuse for it. They let him stay in business for a year, to their discredit." A few years later, Laurents wrote the screenplay for *The Way We Were,* the hugely successful Barbra Streisand–Robert Redford vehicle about Hollywood during the witch-hunts of the fifties. It was directed by Sydney Pollack, and Laurents had gotten Pollack the job. One day Pollack told Laurents, "You know, everybody in Hollywood is just so surprised."

"Why?" said Laurents.

"This is the best love story anybody has written in years. And you wrote it."

"Why are they surprised?"

"You're a homosexual."

Laurents said nothing. "Because I thought, *You're such an asshole, what can I say?*"

The year before the CBS broadcast, *Time* referred gravely to the "homintern" that Vidal had ridiculed, and offered this pithy observation from the Broadway producer David Merrick about gays in the movie business: "In Hollywood, you have to scrape them off the ceiling." Laurents had gotten his first job as a stage director when Merrick hired him for *I Can Get It for You Wholesale.* When Laurents asked Merrick to stop attacking homosexuals, the producer replied, "Oh, I don't mean it — it's just for publicity." Laurents also noticed that nearly everyone who worked for Merrick was gay. "That's because they don't have anyone to go home to, so they can work all night," the producer explained.

The *Time* essayist opined that "even in ordinary conversation, most homosexuals will sooner or later attack the things that normal men take seriously. . . . [Homosexuality is] essentially a case of arrested development, a failure of learning, a refusal to accept the full responsibilities of life. This is nowhere more apparent than in the pathetic pseudo marriages in which many homosexuals act out conventional roles — wearing wedding rings, calling themselves 'he' and 'she.'" The essay described pop art as part of a "vengeful, derisive counterattack" by "homosexual ethics and esthetics" on "the 'straight world.'" Pop "insists on reducing art to the trivial."* *Time's* conclusion: homosexuality "deserves fairness, compas-

---

*Not every gay artist was aware of the pop art conspiracy. When Paul Cadmus ran into Andy Warhol in the sixties, Cadmus asked him what he was up to. Warhol said, "Now I'm into pop art." And Cadmus replied, "Pop Hart, why should anyone be interested in Pop Hart?" The older artist thought Warhol was referring to George Overbury "Pop" Hart, who was born in Cairo, Illinois, in 1866 and reared in Rochester, New York.

sion, understanding and, when possible, treatment. But it deserves no encouragement, no glamorization, no rationalization, no fake status as minority martyrdom, no sophistry about simple differences in taste — and, above all, no pretense that it is anything but a pernicious sickness." Vidal noted the "anti-homintern hysteria was absolutely out of control — and *Time* was one of the centers."

The CBS documentary concluded with a debate between Vidal and Albert Goldman, an adjunct assistant professor of English at Columbia, who later gained minor fame as the author of tabloid biographies of Elvis Presley and John Lennon. Goldman was among the first to sound the refrain that would become so popular among conservatives three decades later:

> It seems to me that there are a lot of features of ordinary life which are enormously exaggerated in homosexual life. I mean the kind of jealousy and rage and promiscuity that is just inherent in the homosexual life. . . . We're in the course of gradually rolling back from our former cultural values or cultural identifications to a more narcissistic, more self-indulgent, to a more self-centered and essentially adolescent lifestyle. The homosexual thing cannot really be separated from a lot of other parallel phenomena in our society today. I mean we see this on every hand; forty percent of modern marriages end in divorce; we have a very widespread tendency to live lives of nonstop promiscuity. This is played out in a kind of playboy philosophy which is celebrated and sugar-coated and offered to the masses and received with pleasure. We have all sorts of fun-and-games approaches to sex. We have rampant exhibitionism today in every conceivable form. We have a sort of masochistic, sadistic vogue. We have a smut industry that grinds out millions of dollars of pornography a year. We have a sort of masturbatory dance style that's embraced as if it were something profoundly sexual, whereas actually, all those dances do is just grind away without any consciousness of other people or their partners. And homosexuality is just one of a number of such things all tending toward the subversion, toward the final erosion, of our traditional cultural values. After all, when you're culturally bankrupt, why you fall into the hands of receivers.

Needless to say, Vidal had a very different point of view: "It is as natural to be a homosexual as it is to be a heterosexual. The difference between a homosexual and a heterosexual is about the difference between somebody who has brown eyes and somebody who has blue eyes."

"Who says so?" Wallace asked.

"I say so," Vidal replied.

It is a completely natural act from the beginning of time. . . . We have a
sexual ethic which is the joke of the world. We are laughed at in every
country of the world for our attitudes toward sex. The United States is
living out some mad Protestant nineteenth-century dream of human
behavior. Instead of saying, Aren't we wicked because we have a high
divorce rate, or aren't we wicked because men like to go to bed with men
and women like to go to bed with women, why not begin by saying that
our basic values are all wrong? The idea of marriage is obsolete in our
society. Everybody knows it. There are natural monogamists, there are
people who indeed enjoy one another's company, but can you imagine a
man and a woman who are told that for sixty years they are going to have
to live together and have sex only with one another. This is nonsense.
Why not begin by accepting the fact of what human beings really are. . . .
We are open, we have something that André Gide referred to as floating
sensuality. We can be aroused by this, by that, not necessarily by men and
not necessarily by women. . . . And I think the so-called breaking of the
moral fiber of this country is one of the healthiest things that's begun to
happen.*

Wallace ended with a "politically correct" conclusion for an era when
nearly everyone considered homosexuals to be sick: an interview with a
gay man with a wife and two children, who explained, "I personally don't
believe in a love relationship with another man. I think this is part of the
gay folklore, something they try to obtain, but never obtain, primarily
because the gay crowd is so narcissistic that they can't establish a love
relationship with another male." Wallace's final words on the program
were: "The dilemma of the homosexual: told by the medical profession he
is sick; by the law that he's a criminal; shunned by employers, rejected by
heterosexual society. Incapable of a fulfilling relationship with a woman,
or for that matter with a man. At the center of his life, he remains anonymous. A displaced person. An outsider."

The program embodied all the prejudices and preconceptions of "respectable" American media outlets in 1967. In determining its point of
view, the swirling changes of the sixties were much less important than the
"objective authority" of psychiatrists. After watching excerpts of the program in 1995, Wallace exclaimed, "Jesus Christ! That was a good piece back

---

*Vidal's growing militancy on this subject had one significant effect on his literary output during
the sixties. When he decided to write a revised version of *The City and the Pillar,* he finally heeded
the advice of Tennessee Williams and Chrisopher Isherwood: he made the ending less cata-
strophic. Instead of Jim murdering the object of his unrequited affection, he merely raped him.

then!" He even endorsed much of what Albert Goldman said about the decline of American society. "Look," he said, "I cannot believe some of the trash I see on television. And the sexual permissiveness with which we live in this country is frequently — to me — sexual ugliness. Grossness."

Wallace conceded that he no longer believed that two homosexuals were incapable of a lasting relationship; in fact, he even knew that wasn't true at the time the program was broadcast.

"It's not a question now," said Wallace. "But what I'm doing [at the end of the program] is, I'm synthesizing what we've just seen. Look: I had a good friend, by the name of James Amster" — a famous decorator, who created Amster Yard, a group of houses surrounding an L-shaped garden on East 48th Street. "He owned all of those little houses there. And he had a man, a companion. And they were a wonderful old married couple. And this was back in the fifties. Both very attractive people. Both people that I admired." But to journalists like Mike Wallace, the fact that homosexuality remained part of the American Psychiatric Association's official catalogue of mental disorders was more important than their own personal experiences.

"Do you think it's curable?" Wallace was asked in 1995.

"I think probably, if you really want to, I suppose," the correspondent said.

"You can replace one desire with another?"

"I don't know. I'm not a scientist. I had a good friend in Detroit, when I was in my twenties still, and working at WXYZ. And there was a guy there — good-lookin' fella — he was one of the sound guys. . . . What he used to do was make the sound of the Lone Ranger's horse, in a big flower box with pebbles. And I thought to myself, Well, I could understand the relationship. I found him a *very, very* attractive man. But to act out in that way . . ." That was something Wallace could never imagine.

The same year that CBS broadcast "The Homosexuals," three Los Angeles men tried to counter some of the impressions of gay life conveyed by the mainstream media. In September 1967, Dick Michaels, Bill Rand and Sam Watson secretly printed the first issue of the *Los Angeles Advocate* in the basement of the Los Angeles headquarters of ABC television. The first five hundred copies of the twelve-page paper were sold for 25 cents each at gay bars throughout the city. Its precursor had been the newsletter of PRIDE, Personal Rights in Defense and Education, a local gay group founded in 1966. Gay activists had been energized by an unusually brutal raid of the Black Cat Bar by the Los Angeles Police Department on New Year's Day in 1967.

Within a year of publishing its first issue, the periodical had a telephone, an IBM electric typewriter, and its first paid employee, and 5,500 copies were in circulation throughout southern California. For many people, the *Advocate* was "the first exposure we'd had to the idea that what we are is not bad," said a longtime reader. By the mid-1970s, 40,000 copies of each issue were being distributed nationally, and the *Advocate* was the most important gay-owned and operated magazine in America, a status it retains today.

TRUMAN CAPOTE'S FLAMBOYANCE made him one of the few famous writers whom the public could recognize as obviously homosexual in the fifties and the sixties. The novella *Breakfast at Tiffany's* and the movie it inspired had made him a sensation within the literary world, and his charm and his intelligence made him a confidant of many of Manhattan's richest and most powerful denizens, particularly the women whom he dined with regularly at Manhattan's most exclusive restaurants.

Katharine Graham, the owner and publisher of the *Washington Post*, was one of the powerful women whom Capote befriended in the 1960s. They were introduced by Babe Paley, a Capote favorite and the wife of the founder of CBS. When Mrs. Paley arranged a lunch for them in her apartment, she warned Graham about what to expect: "Babe had said, 'Truman's voice is high when you start talking to him, but when he relaxes it goes down.'" But Graham "certainly never thought of Truman as dainty." She considered him "very strong — in intelligence and insights and will."

After her husband committed suicide in 1963, Graham came to New York more frequently to participate in editorial meetings at *Newsweek*, which was also owned by her company. Capote told her she should stop staying in a hotel and buy an apartment at the U.N. Plaza, an elegant new apartment house across from the United Nations where he was already living himself. When she resisted the idea because she didn't have time to run another house, "He said in that voice [she imitated his Southern drawl], 'Why if you can't run it, honey, I will.'

"And I didn't for a moment think he would run it, but it did sort of push me into thinking, Well, maybe it's not that hard. Maybe I should look. And then I did. I looked at one and bought it and we still have it."

In 1965, Capote reached the height of his fame with the publication of *In Cold Blood*, his classic account of the brutal murder of a Kansas farm family and the capture, trial, and execution of their killers. He had given the book to Graham to read in sections, and she loved it. At the end of 1966, he decided to celebrate his new celebrity by inviting 540 of his closest friends to a "Black and White Dance" at the Plaza. "In honor of Mrs. Katharine Graham" was handwritten across the top of the printed invitation.

Graham had become publisher of the *Washington Post* only three years earlier, after the death of her husband, and she was not yet well known in New York society. Why did he choose her as his guest of honor?

"God knows," said Graham. "Because I was certainly an unlikely subject. . . . We were fond of each other . . . I think if you eliminated all the worldly friends, which I guess he couldn't choose one of, I was somebody people didn't really know. And I obviously had just come into this position. . . . I suppose it was an act of imagination. Obviously, I had a great time with Truman."

But Graham was allowed to add only twenty couples to Capote's list. She said that was easy — she just chose her closest Washington friends.

There was tremendous anticipation, and almost continuous coverage of the party in the New York social pages for weeks before it took place. "The publicity had bounded and bounded and bounded," said Graham. "The *World Telegram* had whole *pages* of what people were going to wear. It was unbelievable."

When it finally occurred, the *Times* reporter Charlotte Curtis called the guests "as spectacular a group as has ever been assembled for a private party in New York" — and her newspaper printed the entire list on its society page. (Its publisher, Arthur Ochs Sulzberger, was one of the guests invited by Graham.)

It *was* an amazing list. Among those honored with an invitation were Harry Belafonte; Tallulah Bankhead; James Baldwin; Brooke Astor; McGeorge Bundy; Ralph Ellison; Cecil Beaton; Jacqueline, Rose, Bobby, and Teddy Kennedy; Lionel and Diana Trilling; Robert McNamara; Arthur Miller; Robert Penn Warren; Andy Warhol; Ashton Hawkins; Edmund Wilson; Frank Sinatra and Mia Farrow; Douglas Fairbanks, Jr.; Sammy Davis, Jr.; Blair Clark; Christopher Isherwood; and the duke and duchess of Windsor.

If he hadn't actually gathered together everyone who mattered in the Western world, Capote had come closer to accomplishing that feat than anyone in America ever had before. "I'd never seen anything like the [number of] photographers," said Graham. "Never!"

Russell Baker thought writers would "experience an instant inflation of self-esteem from the knowledge that one of their colleagues has seized Mrs. Astor's former role as social arbiter."

Nevertheless, not everyone was amused. Stephen Reynolds thought it was "a boring party." He said, "I really did. But we were *thrilled* to be invited. We couldn't *wait* to tell our enemies. A lot of people were mad because they weren't invited. They made up all kinds of excuses — their mother was dying, the doctor said they had cancer. I mean *anything* to excuse them from not going."

Herb Caen, the doyen of San Francisco journalists, compared it to the Super Bowl: "There was such a buildup that by the time the game was played, it didn't amount to much."

Lauren Bacall and Jerome Robbins dominated the dance floor. Bacall was horrified when Arthur Schlesinger, Jr., tried to cut in on them. "Don't you see whom I'm dancing with?" she demanded. The historian retired, "crestfallen."

An actress's complaint to Capote the next day suggested a possible difference between gay and straight — or male and female — sensibilities. She had left the party with an attractive stranger whom she had assumed was a guest, only to discover to her horror the next morning that he was just one of the detectives in black tie.

"So," Capote asked, "what's wrong with that? You had a good time with him, didn't you?"

"I did," she conceded.

"Well then, what are you complaining about?"

Three decades later, Graham said that she "loved" her party. What she remembered most clearly about the evening was her first meeting with Jack Dunphy, Capote's longtime companion. "I'd never met Jack because Jack never appeared. You never saw Jack. When he came through the line, Truman said, 'Now *here's Jack.*'"

Paul Cadmus was one of a handful of gay men invited to the ball by Jack Dunphy. "Truman said he didn't want to ask 'a bunch of fags' to his party," said Cadmus. The painter was not allowed to bring another man, and his lover, Jon Andersson, was furious.

For decades Capote had kept his sex life completely separate from his elegant social life. "*Completely,*" said Graham. "And that indeed was the difference when it started down the sad and awful path later. And then *those* people started appearing."

"Those people" included an air-conditioning repairman whom Capote started dating, and to whom Graham was also introduced: "He wasn't a social asset, I would say" — particularly after he proved incapable of repairing a broken air conditioner belonging to one of Capote's fancy friends.

The Washington newspaper publisher was one of the very few women companions Capote spared when he published "Answered Prayers" in *Esquire* nine years later. But as he became progressively more addicted to drugs and drink, Graham spent less and less time with him: "It just became harder and harder to see him. Because of his condition. He'd be drunk. I remember once I went out to dinner with him and he ended up in tears."

At the beginning, "The relationship was a very easy one. The only strains were that he absolutely *demanded* to know everything you knew. And if he found out that you'd withheld something, he'd get very angry."

Graham thought "the decline" began because of "middle age" or "writer's block" or a combination of the two. "You know, he had his face done," she said. "It made him look very young, in a weird way. He once took me to his face person and tried to get me to do it. And I said, 'No thank you,' and left. And he said, 'You'll be back.'"

But, she said, "I never was."

DURING A. M. ROSENTHAL'S tenure, gay employees were treated just as capriciously as gay issues at *The New York Times*.

After his first collection of short stories was published to general acclaim, Walter Clemons stopped writing fiction. Three decades later, he said he had been concerned that if he continued, he might reveal his sexual orientation. "That's really why I gave up writing fiction: In explaining things, I thought it would show. It sort of dried me up as a fiction writer because I exhausted my safely writable experiences." Whether that was the real reason for his writing block is probably less important than the fact that Clemons *believed* it was real. Until the 1980s, most gay writers assumed that public identification as a homosexual could quickly end their careers. "Any writer suspected of being homosexual would be immediately attacked by . . . something like ninety percent of the press," said Vidal. "And the other ten percent would be very edgy in praise, for fear that the writer might be thought to be sexually degenerate."

This fear may have been why playwrights like Albee and Williams focused on heterosexual subjects. Not everyone saw that as a disadvantage. "I always thought those guys were lucky," Jack Kroll said about Albee and Williams, "because later on they would have had to write about gay things."

After he had stopped writing fiction, Clemons became an editor at McGraw-Hill in Manhattan. One day in 1968 he received a call from a friend at *The New York Times Book Review*, offering him an editorship.

After he had accepted, but before he had started the new job, Clemons went home to Houston to visit his parents.

"My mother was planning to have a party the night before I flew back to New York, and the morning of the party I was up very early with my father. He went into the bedroom and came out sort of white, and said, 'I think she's gone.' My mother had simply died in her sleep. So after the funeral and all the production, I went back to New York and I had bitten the hell out of my fingernails. I had to go for a physical at the *Times,* and the doctor looked at my hands and asked if I had been under some sort of nervous strain. I explained that my mother had just died and it was a shock. He asked, 'Were you very close to your mother?' And I said, 'Not especially.' Then he asked if I had had any homosexual experiences, and I said, 'Well, yes.' It never occurred to me to lie. Ask me a simple question and I'll give you a straightforward answer. So he said that I'd better see the psychiatrist. They sent me off to a doctor. I wish I could remember his name because he was absolutely angelic.

"He asked me about my homosexual experience and when I came out and this and that. Then he asked if I was promiscuous, and I said, 'No, I'm not now. But I have been. When I first came to New York I was on the streets and in the bars at every opportunity. But I lead a quieter life now.' At the end of the interview, he said, 'I'm going to recommend that they hire you because you had several chances to lie and you didn't. I think you have good values and you're a good person.'"

Clemons was baffled: "Well, what did I do right?" he asked. The doctor replied, "When I asked you if you were promiscuous, you could have easily said, 'Oh no, never.' It's perfectly natural that coming from Texas to New York you would have had sort of a wild first few years here, and you were perfectly frank about that. I like the way you talked to me." Clemons continued, "That's why I wish I could remember his name. Who could be nicer?"

Clemons's first years at the *Times* were pleasant ones. "I was sort of unconscious of homophobia at the *Times* because I did what I think a lot of sort of polite, button-down homosexuals did in those days: I thought I was invisible." Leo Aultman, who began his ascent through the corporate ranks at Time Inc. in the fifties, agreed: "I think our aspirations were limited. We were content to rise as far as we could, and conceal our gayness in doing it. I think we had to be. You did not wear it on your sleeve. You just didn't."

At the *Times,* Clemons "didn't really think so much about whether people were thinking about me because I thought, Nobody can see me." But he turned out to be mistaken.

Two years after he arrived on West 43d Street, Clemons was asked to apply for the prestigious position of daily book reviewer. He was widely regarded as the most qualified candidate for the job, but it went to Anatole Broyard instead. Clemons was horrified when he learned from his colleague, John Leonard, that top editors at the paper had launched an investigation of Clemons's sexual orientation during his tryout. And Clemons was furious when he learned that three of his colleagues — including Christopher Lehmann-Haupt, already a daily book critic — had told his bosses that he was gay. "I was outraged and hurt, and thought, What has this got to do with anything?" Clemons remembered.

Shortly after Clemons had been passed over for the job as daily reviewer, Jack Kroll lured him over to *Newsweek,* where he had a distinguished career as one of the magazine's senior book critics. "Writing for Walter was definitely a moral act," said Kroll. "He was my favorite among the *Times* critics. He was too good a man to fall in love with himself. It's so wonderful to deal with talent and sensibility." The admiration was entirely mutual: "Jack's the best editor imaginable," Clemons said.

Kroll had no suspicion that Clemons was homosexual. "I always assumed that he and [arts patron] Mimi Kilgore had some sort of thing. I used to think, That lucky fuck, he even got Mimi. I remember a dinner he had with me and a couple of other people at which it soon became clear that he wanted to tell us this. It was very straight and very sweet. The details have been overwhelmed by my failure to spot this — straight guys like to think they can spot this. The word I always used to describe his writing was *masculine.* And maybe I liked him too much. If you like a guy too much and you're straight, there's something that prevents you from making that connection."

Clemons confirmed the identity of one of his accusers at the *Times* several years later, after another *Times* editor, Charles Simmons, wrote a novel in which he recounted the incident. When the novel was published, Christopher Lehmann-Haupt telephoned Clemons to arrange a meeting over drinks at the Four Seasons restaurant.

"I had never gotten over this even five years later, and I was foolish enough to think they had finally caught on about needing to get rid of Anatole Broyard and they wanted to sound me out about coming back as daily book reviewer," Clemons recalled. His fleeting optimism was understandable because nearly everyone in the world of books considered

Clemons's criticism far superior to the work of Broyard or Lehmann-Haupt.

Clemons's failure to become the daily critic at the *Times* had "made a grievous imprint" on him. "It was the first rejection I had ever had. I had never even asked for a job before. People came to me, and asked, Would you like to do this, would you like to do that? So when I really wanted that job and didn't get it, I was deeply crushed. So I met Chris and we made chitchat for a while, and he finally said, 'I'll tell you the reason I called. I wanted to talk to you about Charlie Simmons's book.'

"I hadn't even seen it. So I said that I wished he had told me because I thought he was looking for someone to review it. But he said, 'Let me read you a passage':

> The first person he knew with a hyphenated name, a young attractive bachelor, took him up as a confidant and reported regularly on progress in finding a suitable girlfriend. He was unhappily married at the time and envied the bachelor's single life until one day the bachelor said, 'I haven't had sex in two years, not since I broke up with the dancer friend.' 'What happened to her?' he asked the bachelor. 'Him,' the bachelor said, and he realized sexual confessions contain propositions. The second man he knew with a hyphenated name, who affected intricate designs with facial hair, who was both boyish and avuncular and who was liked by everyone for a while, prevented a colleague from getting an influential job by telling the employer that the colleague was homosexual. The colleague, over drinks in a bar one evening, said to him, 'He didn't even ask me if I was.' And then after a pause, 'You know what's the matter with him? He wants to be a good guy but just can't.'

"So Chris read me this passage, and I said, 'Yes, I did say something like that.' And he said, 'Since Charlie has published this, I have always wanted a chance to explain to you. I was too shy to open up the subject and this gives me an opportunity. I have always felt bad about this. You see, the reason I did that was that it's a very demanding job, and writing reviews can be very personal and under the pressure of the job, I thought that it'" — Clemons's homosexuality — "'might come out in your reviews.'

"He thought it was better to prevent this disaster. I thought the explanation was worse than the original events."

Clemons was too stunned to reply.

"Yes. I just had a friendly drink with Chris and we went on to other subjects. I went home and told my friend, and he said, 'What! Weren't you furious? Didn't you say anything?' And I said, 'No. I couldn't think of anything much to say.' I was seeing a psychiatrist at the time, and I brought this up the following week, and he said, 'You sat still for that?' So we had a discussion about not being able to express anger."

Lehmann-Haupt's recollection of this conversation does not differ markedly from Clemons's account. Although Lehmann-Haupt denied that his motivation was to prevent Clemons from being hired as his fellow critic, he called Clemons's description of their drink at the Four Seasons "certainly a way of putting it . . . I mean that's the way he saw it." He also confirmed that after "four, or five, or six hours" of drinking Scotch with Rosenthal in the managing editor's private office, he told Rosenthal that Clemons was gay.

Lehmann-Haupt said he confided to Rosenthal "personally and privately" that he thought Clemons was blocked as a fiction writer "because he doesn't accept his sexual orientation."

"And Abe nodded, and said, 'Well, that's very interesting.' And that was, again I say, we took a number of people over similar indiscreet . . ." the critic's voice trailed off.

A quarter century after the event, Lehmann-Haupt admitted that it had been a mistake to confirm to Rosenthal that Clemons was a homosexual. Lehmann-Haupt also agreed that Clemons was "absolutely" a better critic than Anatole Broyard.* Rosenthal said he had "absolutely no recollection either that Walter Clemons was gay or that I ever discussed it" with Lehmann-Haupt. He also denied that he had ever discriminated against any employee because he was gay.

Lehmann-Haupt recalled that during their drink at the Four Seasons, "Walter was not giving me an inch. The more I went, the more he sort of looked at me. He wouldn't even nod. He wouldn't say, 'Look, I understand this was tough for you' — or anything that would have given me any kind of relief. And I was stumbling around trying to explain what had happened. I probably didn't perform very well. I mean, it was certainly one of the most unpleasant experiences I've ever been through, and it got worse by the minute."

While Clemons had been working at the *Book Review,* its editor, Francis Brown, had put him up for membership in the Century Club, a Manhattan institution housed in a Stanford White palace, which counts many of the city's most accomplished writers and artists among its members. "I

---

*Lehmann-Haupt didn't want Rosenthal to hire Broyard, either. Lehmann-Haupt told Henry Louis Gates, Jr., that when Rosenthal asked him for "five reasons" why Broyard shouldn't get the job, the critic "thoughtlessly blurted out, 'Well, first of all, he is the biggest ass man in town.' And Rosenthal rose up from his desk and said, 'If that were a disqualification for working at *The New York Times*' — and he waved — 'this place would be empty!'" (*The New Yorker,* June 17, 1996)

had gone to *Newsweek* in 1971, and at the fall dinner with the new members I ran into Abe Rosenthal — who I had beat in by a couple of years — in his little tux. We found ourselves drinks, and he was very flustered, and said, 'You've gone somewhere, haven't you?' And I said, 'Yes, I'm the book reviewer for *Newsweek* now.' And he said, 'I didn't mean to say that! I didn't mean to say that!' It was the weirdest thing. He was deeply embarrassed and flustered. All I can think is that he was so flustered by running into this fag that he had denied a job to, on the august occasion of his induction, he just lost his head."

HOWARD ROSENMAN was a very good-looking twenty-two-year-old medical student in 1967, the son of an Orthodox Jewish family on Long Island. He was living a "very religious life," wearing a yarmulke and eating kosher. He already knew that he was gay, but he had gone only so far as to look surreptitiously at a few gay magazines. Every weekend he visited his family for the Sabbath. After going to synagogue with his father on Saturday night, he would pick up his girlfriend and drive into Manhattan. "She was also very religious. In the trunk of the car, I had bell-bottom pants and a Nehru jacket, and she had a miniskirt. We would change into our uniform and we would go to Arthur, the club that Sybil Burton owned, and pretend that we were hip." Sybil Burton was Richard Burton's ex-wife, and in 1967, Arthur was internationally famous as the chicest nightclub in Manhattan, one of the very first places in America to be called a discotheque.

Arthur, named for George Harrison's haircut,* was also one of the first places where would-be patrons were forced to line up in front of a "velvet truncheon" — a nocturnal rite later made famous by Studio 54. Mickey Deans was the man who made the selections from behind Arthur's cordon. "That was the first time I experienced it," said Rosenman. "Because we were young and I guess fairly cute, they let us in, and we danced all night long to Otis Redding — 'Sitting on the Dock at the Bay' — and Aretha Franklin — 'Respect.' R and B heaven. It was so hip it was beyond hip. Two little rooms, one room over here and the disco was in the back and then another room with a bar and the celebrity table.

"It was the most glamorous place I had ever been to in my entire life up to then. I saw Leonard Bernstein and I saw Nureyev and I saw Liza Minnelli and I saw Peter Allen. Beautiful black women, beautiful black

---

*"What would you call that hairstyle you're wearing?" a reporter asked Harrison in *A Hard Day's Night.* "Arthur," he replied.

men. It was also hustlers and hookers and celebrities and intellectuals. It was that democratic thing that, later, Studio 54 picked up on. I had gotten friendly with Sybil by that point, and she loved the fact that I was a medical student and that I was so articulate, and I came to her, and I said, 'Do you think I could be a waiter here?' At that time you had to be very good-looking: it was like a prestige thing, being a waiter at Arthur. So I became a waiter at Arthur, and Sybil let me serve the celebrity table. And every night my pockets would be filled with numbers from men and women. Liza Minnelli and Peter Allen once broke a popper under my nose. And I saw Mrs. Kennedy there. And Margot Fonteyn. Sybil had a real connection to the ballet world, so she mixed that whole ballet world and the English world and English actors and actresses and socialites and Didi Ryan and Mrs. Vreeland, and it was like that. To me, it was like, Whoa!"

Then, in June 1967, the Six Day War broke out in Israel, and Rosenman decided he should go there as a medical volunteer. "My parents are Israeli, and I had been to Israel a lot. My parents were born in the Old City of Jerusalem — my mother is fifth-generation, my father is fourth-genera-tion. Their great-grandparents came to Palestine in the 1870s. So I had traveled to Israel my whole life growing up. My relatives had houses and villas overlooking the Old City. My family was forced to move out of the Old City in 1947. My father was born ten yards from the Wailing Wall. They were in the New City overlooking the Old City.

"On the evening of June 4 of 1967 I was at my cousin's apartment studying for my med boards. My cousin Aryeh Maidenbaum calls me up, and I say that there are reports on the radio that the refineries in Haifa were blown up and burning, which was a disinformation report that the Israelis had put out. But we didn't know that here in the States. All I have is my medical bag with me and my Levis. At that time, the Rothschilds were gutting Air France jets and filling them with spare parts and war materiel and shipping them to Israel, and we got on one of these jets. I got a lift through a cousin. By the time we landed, for all intents and purposes the war was over. The Israelis hadn't attacked Jerusalem yet, but they had reached Suez and they were also pushing toward the north, to the Golan. When we landed, I was immediately taken from the Tel Aviv airport straight to the Gaza Strip to a medical field hospital in a town called Rafah. I was put into a medical field hospital as a medical volunteer."

The war had lasted only six days — an astonishing victory over incred-ible odds. No one doubted that these Jews could have kept going all the way to Cairo — and Damascus — if they had chosen to.

The war transformed the way millions of Jews thought about themselves. Twenty-two years after the end of World War II, the most viciously oppressed victim of the twentieth century was suddenly its most extraordinary warrior. Jews around the world who had forgotten, or even obliterated, their origins were suddenly celebrating them. In 1969, a dramatically different kind of David and Goliath event in Greenwich Village would have a strikingly similar effect on the self-image of gay people in America, providing them for the first time with the courage to be proud.

"I remember my commanding officer came to me," said Rosenman. "My family was known as the Vatikay Yerushalayim, which means the Ancients of Jerusalem, the equivalent to the Mayflower generation. And so my commander came to me, and said, 'Because you come from the Vatikay Yerushalayim, you can have the privilege of escorting the troops into the Old City.' Which I did. And I saw Rabbi Goren* blowing the shofar at the Wailing Wall, and I saw these young Israeli soldiers crying at the wall.

"It was the most unreal, momentous event that I ever participated in. And the sense of *euphoria:* the sense that the new Jew is no longer a ghetto Jew, the Jew is now cast in the mold of King David. In the Bible, King David is described as beautiful of appearance, he sings poetry, he knows how to play a harp, and he's a warrior! In other words, he's the warrior prince, the philosopher prince. And I remember I wrapped myself in the mantle of that romanticism. I said to myself, I don't have to be religious anymore because I was here when Jerusalem was unified after two thousand years. I had the honor of being here. And I remember throwing away my tallis and my yarmulke." This reaction was the exact opposite of what most Jews experienced after this conquest.

After the cease-fire, Rosenman was transferred to Hadassah Hospital in Jerusalem. As a waiter at Arthur, he had flirted with Leonard Bernstein. On July 1, Bernstein arrived in Israel to participate in the victory celebrations. He was going to conduct Mahler's Resurrection Symphony on the newly reconquered Mount Scopus.

Beginning with the Jewish state's War of Independence, Bernstein had a blazing, lifelong love affair with Israel. "How to begin?" he had written to Serge Koussevitzky during the war in 1947. "Which of all the glorious facts,

---

*Rabbi Shlomo Goren was the chief military chaplain in 1967 and the first person to lead a prayer service at the Western Wall after Israeli soldiers captured the Old City. Between 1972 and 1983, he served as Israel's Ashkenazic chief rabbi. In December 1993, he enraged the Israeli government by asserting that the Law of Moses overshadowed government policies and that Israeli soldiers must disobey any order to evacuate Jewish settlements in the West Bank and Gaza Strip. He died of a heart attack in 1994 at the age of seventy-seven. (*New York Times,* October 30, 1994)

faces, actions, ideals, beauties of scenery, nobilities of purpose shall I report? I am simply overcome with this land and its people. I have never so gloried in an army, in simple farmers, in a concert public." During the same trip, he disclosed to Aaron Copland that he had fallen in love with Azariah Rapoport, a handsome young Israeli army officer who was his guide. Bernstein was thirty, and the year before he had broken off his engagement to be married. "It's the works," he wrote of his new affair, "and I can't quite believe that I should have found *all* the things I've wanted rolled into one. It's a hell of an experience — nervewracking and guts-tearing and wonderful. It's changed everything." (By the following year, his romantic interest in Rapoport had ended.)

Rosenman thought Bernstein was "fabulous . . . Leonard is an iconic figure in Israel," the younger man recalled. "He spoke Hebrew. And he had many lovers there. Many. I was totally obsessed with him. The whole concept of meeting any one of the creators of *West Side Story* became my focus. Hal and Stephen and Jerry and all of them." Then Bernstein arrived to visit the medical volunteers in Jerusalem. "And there I was with Levis, white buck shoes, white jacket, my stethoscope hanging out of my pocket, wearing glasses. And Leonard Bernstein comes along, says hello to everybody, and sees me, and says, 'I know a boy just like you. He's a waiter at a discotheque in New York. He has the same cleft in his chin that you have.' And I say to him, in perfect Hebrew, taking off my glasses: 'I *am* your waiter at Arthur.' Whereupon he kisses me on the lips and invites me to this concert where Americans are flying in and ready to contribute $25,000 a ticket — in 1967. And I march into the King David Hotel, and I say to my aunts and uncles, 'Got two tickets!' and I brought one of my cousins."

In the fall of 1948, the Israeli army captured Beersheba, an important crossroads with biblical importance. Bernstein played three piano concertos in a row for the first time in his career: the Mozart in B-flat, K. 450, Beethoven's First Piano Concerto, and *Rhapsody in Blue*, which he offered as an encore.

In 1967, the concert on Mount Scopus was the climax of Bernstein's trip. Before he conducted Mahler's Resurrection Symphony, Bernstein recalled the concerts he had given in 1948. "The idea of resurrection at that time was momentous," he remembered. "After all this land had just been re-born. But still the ancient cycle of threat, destruction and re-birth goes on; and it is all mirrored in Mahler's music — above all the expression of simple faith — of belief that good must triumph."

Rosenman was seated next to Felicia: "Mrs. Leonard Bernstein, Felicia

Montealegre Cohn Bernstein — with her and the kids. And this was so
emotional because he was celebrating the hegemony of the Jews over the
divided city of Jerusalem after two thousand years of a diaspora. It was
very heavy. And on the downbeat of the Resurrection, on Mount Scopus,
with the Old City in front of us and the New City behind us, on the
downbeat of the Resurrection, the wildest feeling of exhilaration and
elation swept over me. The celebration of Jewish hegemony over the holy
city of Jerusalem after two thousand years. I couldn't believe that I was
there. With Leonard fucking Bernstein." The songwriter Adolph Green
remarked that Bernstein had "a look of almost angelic peace on his face."

Up to this point, Rosenman had never slept with a man. But he made
love with Bernstein immediately after the concert on Mount Scopus.

"He was incredible," said Rosenman. "All that passionate energy, right
there. He had the most wide-ranging knowledge of anybody that I ever
met until then, about everything. Whether it was musical philosophy or
the theater or opera or history or geography. It bowled me over. I was
dazzled. I had never, ever seen an intelligence like this. He was also revered,
you know. And he was unsure of himself. As much as he was confident, he
was equally insecure. He was extremely humble. And sweet and teaching,
much like a pedant, but not in a bad way, in a good way — the way
Sondheim is like a don. It was very exhilarating. And very hip and wildly
sophisticated because there I was being very, very friendly with Felicia."

Rosenman thought Mrs. Bernstein was probably aware of their affair:
"She treated me like a real star. She had unmatched social grace, manners,
and poise. She was very cool that way, whether she knew or not."

Mike Mindlin and Frank Yablans were making a documentary about
the conductor's trip called *Journey to Jerusalem,* and Bernstein got Rosenman a job on the movie as a gofer. Altogether, his liaison with the maestro
lasted three weeks.

Rosenman had chosen an incredible moment to come out, and he
stayed in Israel for the rest of the summer after Bernstein left. "The first
communities that actually got together in Jerusalem after the war were the
gay Arab and gay Jewish communities," he said. "There was a park called
the Independence Garden in Jerusalem where the Arabs and the Jews
would meet. And I brought an Arab home to the King David Hotel, which
I thought was both very glamorous and very audacious. The whole summer was exciting that way because anybody who was worth his salt, who
was a Jew, who had any Zionist connection, came that summer. I was
flipped out about it. Number one, it was like F.A.O. Schwarz: being gay
was like a new toy. And there were many Israeli Defense Forces personnel.

And the atmosphere was so euphoric and so free, it was surreal. It was delicious. The country was partying all summer. And every Jew from every country in the world seemed to be there. It was unbelievable. Action central."

In the fall, Rosenman returned to America. He took a leave of absence from medical school and never returned. "I went home and told my family that I was no longer religious, that I was leaving medical school, and that I was experimenting with alternative lifestyles. I remember once having a fight with my father. I had the album of *West Side Story* under my arm, and I said, 'See this? I'm going to sleep with every one of the principals involved with this show.' And my father said, 'You'll never make it in the world of the goyim.' Rosenman's boast nearly came true: eventually he would have affairs with most of *West Side Story*'s progenitors. "It wasn't just that I was a star fucker," said Rosenman. "I was a talent fucker. If someone had a real talent, or genius, no matter what it was, I was turned on to it."

PART OF STANLEY KAUFFMANN's proposed solution to the "problem" of the homosexual playwright was to provide him with the freedom "to write truthfully of what he knows, rather than try to transform it to a life he does not know, to the detriment of others." When Mart Crowley read those words one Sunday in Los Angeles, he decided to accept Kauffmann's challenge.

Crowley was a thirty-year-old Mississippian "with a sugarcane accent" whose ascent out of obscurity began after he learned that Elia Kazan was shooting a movie in a cotton patch near his hometown of Vicksburg. Crowley went over to schmooze with Kazan, and the director told Crowley to look him up if he ever came to New York. So he did, which led to "a rather glamorous production-assistant period: *Butterfield 8, The Fugitive Kind*" — and, eventually, close friendships with Natalie Wood and Dominick Dunne.

When Kauffmann's piece appeared, Natalie Wood was paying for Crowley's analysis as a Christmas present. The unemployed scriptwriter was house-sitting for a friend in Hollywood and feeling alternately "ambitious, disappointed, down, out [and] enraged." He figured he had nothing to lose because no one he knew of had "really written this 'uncloseted' play. Some people wouldn't speak to me anymore. . . . And most would think I was nuts. But I was broke and depressed."

The Boys in the Band was the first "uncloseted" look at gay life inside a New York closet — with all the brittle intelligence, bitter humor and exaggerated pathos on which white, male, middle-class gay life thrived in this era. Crowley took his title from *A Star Is Born,* in which James Mason tells Judy Garland, "Relax, it's three A.M. at the Downbeat Club, and you're singing for yourself and the boys in the band."

The title worked. The action takes place in a single evening, at a birthday party hosted by Michael, a profligate writer who is briefly on the wagon. Leonard Frey gave a brilliant performance as Harold, the guest of honor whose introduction of himself at the beginning of the second act immediately became famous: "What I *am,* Michael, is a thirty-two-year-old, ugly, pock-marked Jew fairy — and if it takes me a while to pull myself together and if I smoke a little grass before I can get up the nerve to show my face to the world, it's nobody's goddamn business but my own. . . . And how are *you* this evening?"

When Crowley first showed the script to his agent, she was so embarrassed that she couldn't even look him in the eye. She whispered, "I can't send this out with my name on it. Why, it's like a weekend on Fire Island!" But the agent hadn't absorbed the changes already wrought by an amazing decade, while Crowley had perfect timing and perfect pitch. Twenty-four hours after leaving his agent's office he was in Richard Barr's apartment; Barr and Charles Woodward, Jr., agreed to produce his new play on the spot.* Then Crowley sat down with the director Bob Moore, whom he had known at Catholic University in Washington, and together they cut the script in half. "It worked as a play when Bob and Mart together trimmed it down to a workable size," said Murray Gitlin, the former Broadway chorus boy who stage-managed the first workshop production of *Boys* on Vandam Street.

The word of mouth was extraordinary — even before the first public performance in 1968. At least eight of the nine characters were gay men, while the uninvited guest at the birthday party insisted that he really was in love with his wife, despite the steady taunts of his host. Crowley told colleagues that the married character was based on his friend Dominick Dunne. The gay characters ranged from the passing-for-straight formerly married Hank, who hadn't come out until he was thirty-two, to the flam-

*Barr and Woodward were involved in a workshop with Edward Albee, but according to Murray Gitlin, Albee refused to be associated with their new project. "From the word go, Edward did not want *anything* to do with it. He hated that play, hated everything about it, didn't want to be associated with it *at all.*" That may have been because many people felt that Crowley had borrowed the form (and some of the substance) of Albee's smash hit, *Who's Afraid of Virginia Woolf?* The repartee between Michael and Harold was particularly reminiscent of the clash between Albee's George and Martha — but Michael had eight guests to attack at his party, instead of just two.

ingly gay Emory, who called everyone Mary. Gitlin had recruited Cliff Gorman for the role of Emory, and Gitlin said it was a "transforming" moment when Gorman first read for the part. After the opening, Gorman gave frequent interviews to make sure that everyone knew that he really was a happily married, beer-swigging heterosexual ("You Don't Have To Be One To Play One," a *Times* headline explained).

On opening night, Crowley was jittery. "You think they'll laugh?" Crowley asked Bob Moore.

"Mart, they've been laughing at fags since Aristophanes. They're not going to stop tonight."

Moore was right. Along with the musical *Hair,* which was shocking Broadway audiences that year with its own explicit language ("sodomy, fellatio, cunnilingus, pederasty") and a cast who stripped down to their birthday suits, *Boys* became the sensation of the 1968 season. Crowley immersed himself in every detail of the production, spending $20 from his own pocket for just the right "green Rhine wine glass" for one of the boys to drink from and shopping with the actors to find the perfect clothes — a trip that got featured in *Women's Wear Daily* ("The Clothes The Boys Wear On Stage Are Woven Into The Fabric Of The Play"). Seven months into the production, the play had already earned its backers a $70,000 profit, and $5.95 seats were being scalped for $25. A Presbyterian minister even brought the cast across the river to address his Brooklyn congregation. "As Christians," he explained, "we must look at one another with love and compassion."

Although widely seen as self-loathing by subsequent generations of gay men, the play was revolutionary because of its honesty and its openness. "The thing I always hated about homosexual plays was that the homosexuality was always the big surprise in the third act," Crowley said shortly after *Boys* opened. "Well, life is not like that. Not all faggots bump themselves off at the end of the play." Gitlin was impressed because "these were people who were queer who could think, who could talk, who could read. I thought, It's outrageous, and terribly courageous. It was about many aspects of my life — not exactly, but the situation." The actors were also good-looking, which was another advance, especially for teenaged theatergoers, most of whom had never seen an attractive person identified as a homosexual. In the *Times,* the theater critic Clive Barnes called it "by far the frankest treatment of homosexuality I have ever seen." He also thought it made *Who's Afraid of Virginia Woolf?* look like "a vicarage tea party." Barnes felt that the relentlessly camp humor of *Boys* was a little much, but he acknowledged how thoroughly it had been absorbed into the culture: "the New York wit, famous the world over, is little more than a mixture of Jewish humor and homosexual humor seen through the bottom of a dry martini glass." And Barnes called the play an explicit answer to Kauffmann's plea for "a more honest homosexual drama. . . . It is quite an achievement."

Stephen Sondheim saw the play during its first week of performances and considered it "the shot heard round the world." Sondheim said, "I thought the play would be genuinely important, if it got made into a movie. I thought, boy, if this could only become popular, it will do so much to educate people who have no idea about homosexuality, gay life, gay subculture. And in fact it did." Howard Rosenman went with Leonard Bernstein early in the run. "I thought it was the most incredible play I had ever seen," said Rosenman. "And I'll never forget it: at the end of the play, Leonard jumped up and screamed 'Bravo!' *He* thought it was the most incredible thing he'd ever seen." Neil Simon said he had never witnessed such honesty on the stage before. He told the writer Richard Kramer that *Boys* "did for plays what *Oklahoma!* did for musicals."

The play achieved for the theater what the decade accomplished for the country: it made people think differently by puncturing hypocrisy. It also demonstrated the value of all kinds of people who did not fit into the neat little boxes of the fifties, and made a plea for their acceptance, neuroses and all. Writing in the "Arts and Leisure" section of the *Times* a couple of months after it opened, Rex Reed called *Boys* a breakthrough because the characters are human beings who "have fun. . . . They don't kill themselves or want to get married or spend the rest of their lives tortured by conscience. The only way they 'pay' is to know who they are."

As Michael gets drunker and drunker during the second half of the play, the party gets progressively nastier, with the host aiming nearly as many darts at himself as he does at everyone else. Gradually, it builds into a volcanic portrait of stylish self-hatred. Michael describes the boredom he felt from compulsive coupling, in words that shocked Off-Broadway audiences in 1968: "Bored with Scandinavia, try Greece. Fed up with dark meat, try light. Hate tequila, what about Slivovitz? Tired of boys, what about girls — or how about boys and girls mixed, and in what combination? And if you're sick of people, what about poppers? Or pot or pills or the hard stuff?"*

---

*In his autobiography, *Young Man from the Provinces: A Gay Life before Stonewall*, the actor Alan Helms offered this description of his drug consumption in the era when *Boys* was playing Off-Broadway. "We bought by the pound — eighty to one hundred dollars for superb grass with

"Michael doesn't have charm," Harold explains. "Michael has counter-charm."

"I knew a lot of people like those people, and I would say that probably all nine of them are split-up pieces of myself," said Crowley. "It was definitely a reflection of what was wrong in my head; but that's the way that I saw things then."

Harold appears to be at his most vicious when he fires this parting shot at his host: "You are a sad and pathetic man. You're a homosexual and you don't want to be. But there is nothing you can do to change it — not all your prayers to your God, not all the analysis you can buy in all the years you've got left to live. You may very well one day be able to know a heterosexual life if you want it desperately enough — if you pursue it with the fervor with which you annihilate — but you will always be homosex-ual as well. Always, Michael. Always. Until the day you die."

On the surface, this speech is an assault on Michael's malignant self-ha-tred. But hidden in the subtext is a surprisingly liberating message. Harold is proclaiming the immutability of homosexuality — and the appalling complicity of psychiatry and religion in gay self-hatred. Thousands of psychiatrists had committed unprosecutable malpractice by nurturing the myth that homosexuality could be — and *should* be — "cured," instead of encouraging gay people to value themselves for who they were. And al-though there were no sixties militants among Crowley's characters on stage, there were plenty of them every night sitting in the audience — and these were the offenses they were about to avenge.

In the final scene, Michael pleads, "If we could just learn not to hate ourselves so much." To which his friend Donald replies, "Inconceivable as it may be, you used to be worse than you are now. Maybe with a lot more work you can help yourself some more — if you try." These lines sug-gested how far gay men had come by 1968 — and just how far they still

---

odd names and accompanying myths: 'Ice Pack' was grown on top of a sacred mountain in Mexico that was under ice half the year. . . . Hash followed soon after, then seco synatan (a 'set-up,' part upper and part downer, speed without the jagged edges) which we called the 'love pill' since it allowed us to have marathon sex. Then acid and mescaline and cocaine occurred somewhere in there, along with kef and occasionally opium and always Tuinals and Valiums and Percocets and Placidils (all sleeping pills or pain killers) and once we encountered it MDA whenever we could get it. And of course Methedrine, the Dom Perignon of speed. The pop-pers had been there from the beginning; then Ben, my barber, began shooting me up. . . . Was there anyone in the late sixties who didn't take drugs except Nixon and Kissinger?" The original working title of Helms's book was *Damaged Goods*. (Alan Helms, *Young Man from the Provinces*, p. 130)

had to travel. The play provided a precise diagram of the place that they needed to get beyond. Part of its importance would be as a benchmark: a permanent reminder of how not to behave toward friends.

The play was a hit all around the world, with productions in London, Los Angeles, Paris, Melbourne, Tokyo,* Tel Aviv, Las Vegas, Amsterdam — even Philadelphia. Crowley pulled off the rare feat of keeping both the script and the original cast intact for the movie. But gay life would change dramatically between 1968 and 1970, and many of his words seemed dated almost as soon as they were spoken.† Just a year after it opened, six different Off-Broadway shows featured gay themes, including *Fortune and Men's Eyes,* a prison drama starring the newcomer Don Johnson in what *Time* described as a "grimly visible" onstage rape scene.

When the film of *Boys* opened in 1970, a twenty-three-year-old Harvard graduate took a nineteen-year-old girl whom he had just met as his date. She was "very pretty, obviously bright, obviously a little shy." He considered the choice of the movie "a bit of a gamble with someone I didn't know at all, but what the hell." He discovered it was "a challenge to the established order from the word go. I enjoyed the intensity of it. What was interesting was that my date obviously did too. She immediately began laughing at all the jokes, including, or even especially, the raunchiest ones. I was very much intrigued. It turned out to be an example of how liberation works across the spectrum. I suppose it was liberating for everyone to see those guys articulating those forbidden impulses so frankly." Their first date was "quite chaste," but three years later they were married — and they've been married ever since.

In 1970, the film was still startling in the heartland, but in Manhattan it lacked the shock value (and the live power) of the original. Jack Nichols and his lover Lige Clarke dismissed it in a joint review as "Bores in the Band." Frank Kameny hated the play *and* the movie. He said his slogan "Gay is good" was intended as a "direct antidote to the mindset among gays epitomized by that abomination, *Boys in the Band.*" However, the play continued to have a trickle-down effect: in 1972 a group of suburban

---

*Murray Gitlin directed one of the Tokyo productions: "Some of it was easily translatable, but some of it wasn't. For example, there was no word that had the pejorative connotation of *cunt*. There was a word that's used in physiology, but that wasn't right. If you said 'vagina,' that certainly doesn't have the impact. So we had to give it up."

†In *The Season,* William Goldman reported that of the fifty-eight Broadway shows presented during the 1967–1968 season, 31 percent were produced by gays, and at least 38 percent were directed by them. *The New York Times* reported that a Cinema Center Films advertisement for the movie version of *Boys* was the first film ad to contain the word *homosexual.* (*New York Times,* June 5, 1969, quoted by John Reid in *New York,* September 24, 1973)

fathers starred in a community production in Westchester. The *Times* reported that all of the amateur thespians — including two IBM men and an insurance salesman — "have learned to hug and kiss each other 'without wanting to die inside,' as one of them expressed it." Tony Comitto, an IBM budgets manager, put it this way: "It boils down to recognition and escape. . . . In order for a guy to get up onstage and do it, he has to be secure in his own masculinity. If every person in the room thinks I'm queer for the two and a half hours I'm onstage, that's great. But I'm not sure I want them to go out of the theater thinking that."

Twenty-five years after the play first opened, Richard Kramer prepared himself for an anniversary interview with Crowley by screening the movie version of *Boys* for gay men in their forties, thirties, and twenties. Those in their forties told Kramer, "We're not like that anymore." The thirty-year-olds said, "We're more like that than we'd like to admit." And the twenty-year-olds said, "We're just like that."

Kramer's survey suggests that despite all the changes of the last thirty years, most gay people still start out with tremendous self-hatred. Most of them go through a twenty-year process of self-acceptance. The big change after the last three decades is that genuine progress is no longer so unusual.

Harold's birthday present in the play is a laconic $20-a-night hustler whom Harold immediately nicknames Tex. Murray Gitlin had asked Robert La Tourneaux to audition for the part after he met him at the Westside YMCA. "He was one of the most beautiful young men," Gitlin recalled. La Tourneaux hesitated at first because he thought it was demeaning to play a hustler. But after the play became a hit, he repeated the role in London and Los Angeles, and again for the film.

La Tourneaux complained during the seventies that he never got any more good roles because he "was typecast as a gay hustler, and it was an image I couldn't shake." By 1978, he was working in a male porno theater in Manhattan, doing a one-man cabaret act.

Then life imitated art altogether: La Tourneaux *became* a hustler.

"He tried to extort money from someone who was supposedly a friend — probably a john," said Gitlin. La Tourneaux was arrested and sent to the New York City prison on Rikers Island. There he tried to kill himself. Finally he was hospitalized at Bellevue where Gitlin went to visit him: "He was in a private room with leg shackles. And the guard guarding twenty-four hours a day, wearing a gown and mask. It was just awful. And Bob just kept getting sicker and sicker. It was just such a waste: he was so sweet and so beautiful and had so much going for him. I saw him a couple of weeks before he died. He was in Metropolitan Hospital, he was out of prison. And the nurse who was assigned to him had seen *The Boys in the Band* on television the night before. And he died in her arms. And to her, he was a star."

THE BOYS IN THE BAND marked the beginning of the end of an era personified by gay men who adored Judy Garland (and carried a poodle as their "insignia," as one character puts it in the play). Garland was an icon of a camp culture in which a group of people had a special devotion to otherwise enormously popular stars. Like so many other camp figures, Garland was an extremist, constantly alternating between exuberance and depression. At times her behavior looked like a parody of the dark side of gay life — the corrosive repetition of sex, drugs, and pathos which Michael had described in *Boys*. ("What's more boring than a queen doing a Judy Garland imitation?" Michael asked at the beginning of the play. "A queen doing a Bette Davis imitation," Donald replied.) When she was thirty-eight, Garland called her life "a combination of absolute chaos and absolute solitude."

"I believe in doing what I can, crying when I must, laughing when I choose." That was the most apt Noel Coward lyric she ever sang. When she chose to, this one-hundred-pound, five-foot-tall dynamo could charm anyone. Dirk Bogarde thought she was "without doubt . . . the funniest woman I have ever met." She could also display a brutal self-regard: "I have a voice that hurts people when they think they want to be hurt. That's all," she told Bogarde. After Peter Lawford had introduced her to his brother-in-law Jack Kennedy, she campaigned for the future president among American troops in Germany in 1960; afterward, the president took her calls in the White House whenever she needed cheering up. To cheer *him* up, at the end of every conversation, JFK always asked her to sing the last eight bars of "Over the Rainbow." Her daughter Liza Minnelli listened with astonishment whenever that happened.

Kennedy and Garland had both lived like figures from the sixties long before the decade began. "All my life I've done everything to excess:" that was her motto, and her method. It was also one reason why so many gay men identified with her. "There was a vulnerability there that anyone could appreciate," said Minnelli. "If you were going through any kind of pain, you had company when you watched my mother."

Garland loved men — and women — of all persuasions. She had five husbands, three children, and frequent lesbian affairs; she also got a special kick out of seducing gay and bisexual men. One of those was Tyrone

Power, with whom she had a torrid affair during World War II. Her androgynous looks made her look like the "girl and boy next door," Margo Jefferson observed. "She is at bottom a sort of early-twentieth-century kid," said the critic Harold Clurman. "But the marks of the big city wounds are on her."

Like many of her most devoted fans, Garland was a beguiling outlaw, someone who broke all the rules but still managed to make almost everyone love her. She was born Frances Ethel Gumm on June 10, 1922, in Grand Rapids, Minnesota. Gumm made her debut two and a half years later singing a chorus of "Jingle Bells" on the stage of New Grand Theatre in her hometown. From that moment on, her fierce stage mother was certain that she would be a star. Twelve years later, daughter's talent and mother's determination merged to land her a contract at Metro-Goldwyn-Mayer. For the next seventeen years, she "worked, slept, ate, appeared in public, dated, married and divorced" at Louis B. Mayer's command, according to her biographer Anne Edwards. But she always denied a persistent rumor that she had been a victim of Mayer's weakness for very young girls before she reached her fifteenth birthday.

In 1939 she tapped her ruby slippers together and planted herself inside the hearts of millions of Americans of all ages. "I sort of grew up with Judy Garland," said Walter Clemons, who saw *The Wizard of Oz* when he was ten. "Judy Garland was a very big deal for my generation." Garland thought, "The American people put their arms around me when I was a child performer, and they've kept them there — even when I was in trouble." It was during the making of *Oz* that her lifelong addiction to uppers and downers began; the studio had provided her with them. "I don't seem to either get up or go to sleep without them anymore," she explained to Margaret Hamilton (the Wicked Witch of the West), who had inquired about the source of the seventeen-year-old girl's limitless energy. For the rest of her life, her prodigious ingestion of these insidious pills fueled the psychodrama in which she was the permanent star.

Garland made a halfhearted attempt at suicide in 1947, slitting her wrist with a broken tumbler, but her mother was able to stem the bleeding with a Band-Aid. Even so, the actress was bundled off to her first sanitarium. Two years later she was given shock treatments to cure her addiction. Their effects wore off quickly. Then there was another suicide attempt, and she was fired from the movie set of *Annie Get Your Gun*. In 1950 and 1952, she tried to cut her throat; in 1957, it was her wrist again. Each time a new incident was reported by the tabloids, fanatical gay fans wore Band-Aids on their own wrists in solidarity. At the end of 1959, her drinking and drug taking forced her into Doctor's Hospital in Manhattan with a bloated liver four times its normal size. She was also fifty pounds overweight — 150 percent of her usual self. Seven weeks later, she had lost thirty pounds, but she left the hospital in a wheelchair and was told that she would always be a semi-invalid. As usual, her doctors had underestimated her.

"I think she beat on life," said Arthur Laurents. "Like most of those divas, she was both sides of the coin. They cling to you and they suck the blood out of you. She was a tough customer."

What redeemed Garland was her gigantic talent: a huge voice out of a wee body — and the ability to make every note sound effortless, just when everyone was certain the game was over. "She ate up music like a vacuum cleaner," said the songwriter and producer Saul Chaplin. The director Stanley Kramer believed that with every performance, she declared, "Here is my heart, break it."

Laurents found Garland much more exciting to watch than Barbra Streisand "because with Streisand you know nothing will go wrong. She may be in the flesh, but you're seeing film — and literally, too: everybody is looking back over their shoulders at the TelePrompters. Judy Garland was always naked: 'Here I am. Throw me your slings and arrows or give me your hearts!'"

To Judy Barnett, a singer-songwriter who came of age just as Garland's career was ending, "the range of her talent was extraordinary — she could act, she could dance, she could sing. The gay community was just one facet of a much broader audience. After all, this woman was a star from the time she was fourteen until she died."

By the winter of 1961, the wheelchair had long since been thrown away and Garland had begun her umpteenth comeback — a fourteen-city tour that opened in Dallas. Stanley Kramer was considering casting her in a small part in *Judgment at Nuremberg,* so he traveled to Texas to see her perform. There he discovered that her legendary connection to her audience remained entirely intact. "I saw staid citizens acting like bobby-soxers at an Elvis Presley show," said Kramer. "There's nobody in the entertainment world today, actor or singer, who can run the complete range of emotions, from utter pathos to power . . . the way she can." Garland's cameo was a triumph. "I could never cheat on a performance, or coast through," Garland explained, because "my emotions are involved." In April 1961, she performed at Constitution Hall in Washington, and the president invited her for a quick visit to the White House.

The tour reached its climax in Manhattan on April 23. She arrived at her Carnegie Hall dressing room at 5:00 P.M. For the next three and a half hours, she suffered from a paralyzing stage fright, insisting that she could not possibly perform that evening. One reason for her nervousness was the addition of a new number, the song "San Francisco," which she had never sung in public before. By 8:30, Lauren Bacall, Jason Robards, Henry Fonda, Rock Hudson, Betty Comden, Adolph Green, Tony Perkins, Hedda Hopper, Richard Burton, Carol Channing, Spencer Tracy, Arthur Schwartz, Myrna Loy, Mike Nichols, Harold Arlen, Rex Reed, and 3,149 other fans were all waiting inside the auditorium, wondering whether she would ever appear at all. Outside, scalpers were offering tickets for an astonishing $500 apiece.

Garland finally opened the show with "When You're Smiling (the Whole World Smiles with You)," another one of her ironic trademarks. Then she proceeded to give a performance that many witnesses still describe as the most electrifying night in the history of show business.

Rex Reed had just arrived in New York City. He was only an "office boy in some publicity office," but he still managed to wangle a ticket. Seeing Judy Garland was "the thing I wanted to do all my life." He had a great seat: right next to Eli Wallach and Anne Jackson. "I think it was probably the greatest experience I've ever had in the theater," said Reed. "I had never seen that much love given to a performer." Jackson and Wallach didn't know Reed, but they grabbed him anyway: "They were holding on to each other, and Tony Perkins was right in front of me; and Bernstein. . . . It wasn't just the cult who supported her. This was . . . really an audience of hard-nosed professional critics."

A lilting "San Francisco" came out as if it had always been part of her repertoire. But after forty minutes she was drenched. "I don't know why it is that I can't perspire," she complained from the stage. "I just sweat. It's so unladylike." But after the intermission she was changed, blow-dried, and ready to go all over again. "Well, you know, I'm like [the prize fighter] Rocky Graziano," she explained backstage.

A joyous "Zing! Went the Strings of My Heart" brought her another ovation. Then she performed her trademark, which was also her covenant. This time "Over the Rainbow" was sung with an eerie combination of mother and child. She followed with an effortless "Swanee" and a glittering "After You've Gone."

It was past 10:30, and Garland had already sung twenty-seven songs. "You really want more?" she asked. "Aren't you tired?"

"NOOOOOOOO!" the audience roared back, and she finally ended with "Chicago."

Judith Crist saw tears running down Leonard Bernstein's face, and a usually impassive Henry Fonda was shouting "Bravo!" Garland said, "I love you very much! Good night! God Bless!" But nobody wanted to leave.

"It was absolute pandemonium," Crist reported. "The entire audience ran to the footlights with their hands in the air, screaming 'Judy! Judy!' And she touched all the hands she could. Then Rock Hudson lifted [Garland's children] Lorna and little Joey on the stage, and she hugged them and leaned down to kiss Liza, who was in the front row, and the audience screamed for more. . . . The children were touching people's hands and it was like a sea." Rex Reed thought, "It was the greatest triumph in anyone's life." It was also the elegy for an era.

SEVEN YEARS LATER, America had become a different country altogether. John and Robert Kennedy and Malcolm X and Martin Luther King had all been murdered, and the kind of music that Judy Garland was famous for had been pushed off center stage by the Beatles, the Rolling Stones, Janis Joplin, Aretha Franklin, the Supremes — and scores of other artists embraced by a new generation of music lovers.

In 1968, a dazzling twenty-year-old New Yorker named Laura Nyro proved just how much the world had changed when she released *Eli and the Thirteenth Confession,* a brilliant concept album of "bright gospel rock," in which all the songs fit together to tell a story. None of them sounded anything like any pop record of the past. Nyro's fans included gay men, lesbians, and (in 1968) a much larger group of the young and the hip. Her compositions celebrated everything that was different and original about the new decade. And they explicitly celebrated the joys of cocaine and bisexuality — the guilty pleasures that performers from Garland's generation had only been able to enjoy secret.

By the end of 1968, Garland had entered her final decline. At a Christmas party at Arthur, Garland started a long conversation with the night manager, Mickey Deans, who was already an acquaintance. On an impulse, Garland and Deans told the gossip columnist Earl Wilson that evening that they were getting married. Three months later, the wedding actually occurred at the Chelsea registry office in London. Three months after that, in London, on June 21, 1969, Garland took yet another overdose of barbiturates. But this time she never woke up. She was forty-seven. She was also $4 million in debt.

"The greatest shock about her death was that there was no shock," Vincent Canby wrote in the *Times.* Her body was flown back to New York City. Liza Minnelli remembered that her mother had told her to get Gene

Hibbs, a famous makeup man, to do her face for her funeral, but Hibbs was unavailable, so Minnelli got Charles Schram instead, the man who had done her mother's face for *The Wizard of Oz*. Frank Sinatra wanted to pay for the funeral but Minnelli declined his offer. When she viewed the coffin, she was sure she could hear her mother's voice. "Don't I look just beautiful?" Garland seemed to ask. "Goddamn you do!" Minnelli answered back out loud. For a day and a night, more than twenty thousand fans waited in the fierce summer heat to pay their last respects to Garland in a white, glass-covered coffin in the Frank Campbell funeral chapel on the East Side. Manhattan had seen nothing like it since 1926, when Valentino's death sparked riots, and his lying-in-state attracted a crowd eleven blocks long.

Minnelli requested that no one wear black to the funeral. James Mason began his eulogy at one o'clock on Friday, June 27, and it was broadcast into the street by loudspeakers for the thousands who were lined up outside 1076 Madison Avenue. When Mason was finished, the mourners sang "The Battle Hymn of the Republic," the same song that Garland had insisted on singing on her CBS television program as a tribute to John Kennedy after his murder.*

NO ONE WILL ever know for sure which was the most important reason for what happened next: the freshness in their minds of Judy Garland's funeral, or the example of all the previous rebellions of the sixties — the civil rights revolution, the sexual revolution and the psychedelic revolution, each of which had punctured gaping holes in crumbling traditions of passivity, puritanism and bigotry. All that is certain is that twelve hours after Garland's funeral, a handful of New York City policemen began a routine raid of a gay Greenwich Village nightspot, and the drag queens, teenagers, lesbians, hippies — even the gay men in suits — behaved unlike any homosexual patrons had ever behaved before. Deputy Police Inspector Seymour Pine, who led the raiding party, would never forget it. "I had been in combat situations," he said, but "there was never any time that I felt more scared than then. . . . You have no idea how close we came to killing somebody."

The Stonewall Inn at 53 Christopher Street was not an elegant establishment; it didn't even have running water behind the bar. But the crowd was unusually eclectic for a gay place in this era, and sixties types like

---

*Seven weeks after Kennedy's assassination, the television audience had risen "in a body and gave her the most genuine standing ovation I have ever witnessed," Mel Tormé remembered. (Shipman, *Judy Garland*, 463)

Jack Nichols enjoyed the feeling of "free-wheeling anarchy" inside. Like nearly all gay bars in 1969, its existence depended on two groups that younger gay people despised: the Mob, which owned it, and the local police, who took weekly payoffs from it. Because the "inn" was without a liquor license, it pretended to be a "bottle club," which meant that everyone had to sign in at the door. "Judy Garland" and "Elizabeth Taylor" were two of the most popular pseudonyms. On the weekends, admission cost $3, in return for which one got two tickets, good for two drinks. According to the historian Martin Duberman, this obscure venue was an unlikely gold mine: the weekend take often approached $12,000, the weekly payoff to the precinct was always $2,000 and the rent was just $300 a month.

The bar had often been raided before, but this raid was different because it occurred without a prior warning to the owners.* Shortly after midnight, about a dozen policemen arrived at the front door.

Inside, the fifties tradition of flashing white lights to warn of incoming undercover men had been maintained, and the dancing stopped before the raiding party entered. After checking for attire "appropriate" to gender — a requirement of New York state law — the police released most of the two hundred patrons. Only a couple of employees and some of the most outrageous drag queens were arrested. Outdoors in the summer heat, the mood was festive, but many eyewitnesses also remember a febrile feeling in the air. Several spectators agreed that it was the action of a cross-dressing lesbian — possibly Stormé DeLarverie — which would change everyone's attitude forever. DeLarverie denied that she was the catalyst, but her own recollection matched others' descriptions of the defining moment. "The cop hit me, and I hit him back," DeLarverie explained.

For the first time in history, "The cops got what they gave."

This had never happened before.

There was instant pandemonium. The police were pelted with pennies, dimes, and insults, as shouts of "Pigs," "Faggot cops," and "This is your payoff!" filled the night. Morty Manford remembered a rock shattering a second-floor window above the bar's entrance, which produced a collective "Ooh!" from the crowd. The raiders quickly retreated inside and bolted the heavy door behind them. But one of the demonstrators had pulled a loose parking meter out of the ground and started to use it as a

*One theory was that the Federal Bureau of Alcohol, Tobacco and Firearms had discovered that the bottles at the Stonewall didn't have any federal stamps; then the Feds had discovered the payoffs to the local precinct and pressured police headquarters to carry out the raid with men who were not on the take from the bar. (Martin Duberman, *Stonewall*, 194)

battering ram. Jeremiah Newton saw inmates of the Women's House of Detention throwing flaming pieces of toilet paper out their cells. "They fell down very delicately, very gracefully, extinguishing before they hit the bottom," he said. Sheridan Square Park was directly across the street, and it provided excellent ammunition: "It was full of bottles and bricks," said Newton. "It just happened to be the right place at the right time. If the Stonewall had been further down the block, where nobody could stand across from it, perhaps nothing would have happened."

Believing he could intimidate the crowd, Inspector Pine raced outside and grabbed one of the demonstrators around the waist. When Pine pulled him back in, Howard Smith, a *Village Voice* reporter who had accompanied the raiding party, quickly recognized the policeman's quarry: it was Dave Van Ronk, a well-known *heterosexual* folksinger who had wandered over from the Lion's Head next door to investigate the disturbance. Once inside, Van Ronk was badly beaten by the furious policemen. Then the cops grabbed a fire hose to try to keep the screaming demonstrators away, but it produced only a feeble spray — and more ridicule from their attackers. "Grab it, grab his cock!" someone yelled from the crowd, and Craig Rodwell shouted, "Gay Power!"

Now one of the attackers was spraying lighter fluid through the Stonewall's shattered windows and throwing in matches to try to ignite it. Suddenly there was a whoosh of flame inside the bar. The cops pulled their guns from their holsters and trained them on the entrance. Inspector Pine was afraid: he thought he might have to kill some of the kids, and he really didn't want to.

"The homosexuals were usually very docile, quiet people," said the policeman.

"But this night was different."

At the very moment that the cops were preparing to shoot the next demonstrator who came through the door, they finally heard the distant sirens of the Tactical Patrol Force, the helmeted veterans of countless antiwar demonstrations who had finally arrived to rescue them.

"It was that close," the witness from the *Voice* reported.

"We were completely relieved," said Pine.

As the TPF waded into the crowd of protesters in the street, the cops inside put their guns away. But the newly formed lavender brigade continued to confound them: instead of running from the TPF, they kept on throwing bricks and bottles and setting fires in trash cans. Randy Wicker remembered bonfires in the street and barrels going through windows: "All I could think was, Oh my God, they're going to burn up a little old

Italian lady or some child is going to be killed and we're going to be the bogey-man of the seventies."

Randy Bourscheidt saw a "black guy, a queen, running in a mincing way up Christopher Street, screaming in falsetto, *'Let my people go!'* — as gay people were being shoved in paddy-wagons."

"This was in the time of Martin Luther King. It was both funny and touching."

Stormé DeLarverie thought, "Stonewall was just the flip side of the black revolt when Rosa Parks took a stand. Finally, the kids down there took a stand. But it was peaceful. I mean, they said it was a riot; it was more like a civil disobedience. Noses got broken, there were bruises and banged-up knuckles and things like that, but no one was seriously injured. The police got the shock of their lives when those queens came out of that bar and pulled off their wigs and went after them. I knew sooner or later people were going to get the same attitude that I had. They had just pushed once too often."

William Wynkoop, who had first been radicalized a quarter century earlier, was awakened by the noise: "I got up and I looked out the window and really, it was amazing. They were coming from east of here, from Sixth Avenue. In *droves!* Not only on the sidewalk, but on the street. They were coming down Gay Street — large numbers of people — some running. They were coming down Waverly Place. I stuck my head out and I saw a *big* crowd over on Christopher Street. It was two o'clock in the morning. I had to get out and see what was going on. They were all ages, and I was overjoyed. The more I heard about this, the more *exalted* I felt. I remember walking over to Sheridan Square, and everybody was talking about what had happened. It was amazing! And I think it's wonderful that the ones who started it were drag queens. Young, young, tender drag queens. Flaming faggot types. They were the ones who started the rebellion. And I think maybe this is ordained because those who had been most oppressed were they.

"No doubt: Oppressed, despised, laughed at, scorned."

But suddenly, the scorn and contempt were all flowing in the opposite direction. When the TPF challenged the protesters from behind their shielded helmets and bulletproof vests, they were greeted by an astonishing, impromptu performance. The drag queens kicked up their heels and sang at the top of their lungs:

> We are the Stonewall girls
> We wear our hair in curls

We wear no underwear
We show our pubic hair
We wear our dungarees
Above our nelly knees!

It was "totally spontaneous" theater, the underground paper *Rat* reported.

Lucien Truscott IV wrote in the *Voice* that "the generation gap existed even here. Older boys had strained looks on their faces and talked in concerned whispers as they watched the up-and-coming generation take being gay and flaunt it before the masses."

By four A.M., the first night's riot was finally over, with four policemen injured and thirteen demonstrators under arrest. But twenty-four hours later, both sides were back in the streets, and Allen Ginsberg had arrived to investigate. "Gay Power! Isn't that great!" he exclaimed. He was delighted by the scene inside the Stonewall, which had already reopened. "The guys there were so beautiful. They've lost that wounded look that fags all had ten years ago."

When the *Voice* hit the street three days later, some people thought the tone of Truscott's story sparked the riots all over again. "Sheridan Square this weekend looked like something from a William Burroughs novel as the sudden specter of 'gay power' erected its brazen head and spat out a fairy tale the likes of which the area has never seen," Truscott wrote. Once again, a crowd of at least five hundred roamed the streets, and another four demonstrators were arrested.

The *Daily News* returned to the scene to investigate the following week. On July 6, the largest-selling newspaper in the country proclaimed to its millions of readers, "Homo Nest Raided, Queen Bees Are Stinging Mad." *News* reporter Jerry Lisker wrote, "The whole proceedings took on the aura of a homosexual Academy Awards Night. The Queens pranced out to the street blowing kisses and waving to the crowd. . . . The War of the Roses lasted about two hours from about midnight to 2 A.M."

The very first gay-authored account of the uprising appeared in *Screw* magazine, the almost entirely heterosexual pornographic tabloid founded by Al Goldstein. Within it, there was a regular column cowritten by Lige Clarke and his lover Jack Nichols, who was now *Screw*'s managing editor. The column reported Ginsberg's visit to the Stonewall, as well as a peace offering from the Electric Circus, a famously hip nightclub on St. Marks Place, which had taken the unprecedented step of inviting openly gay people to mingle with heterosexuals on the dance floor. "If you are tired of raids, Mafia control, and checks at the door," said the Circus, "join us for a beautiful evening on Sunday night, July 6th." Clarke and Nichols reported that "for the first time in New York's history, a huge club was experimenting with social integration between heterosexuals and homosexuals." The evening was a huge success, except for a single "uncool creep" who suddenly started shouting "Goddamn faggots!" He was quickly hustled out of the premises.

The columnists concluded their report with a rousing call to arms:

> The revolution in Sheridan Square must step beyond its present boundaries. The homosexual revolution is only a part of a larger revolution sweeping through all segments of society. We hope that 'Gay Power' will not become a call for separation, but for sexual integration, and that the young activists will read, study, and make themselves acquainted with all of the facts that will help them carry the sexual revolt triumphantly into the councils of the U.S. Government, into the anti-homosexual churches, into the offices of anti-homosexual psychiatrists, into the city government, and into the state legislatures which make our manner of love-making a crime. It is time to push the homosexual revolution to its logical conclusion. We must crush tyranny wherever it exists and join forces with those who would assist in the utter destruction of the puritanical, repressive, anti-sexual Establishment.

All their dreams were about to come true.

IV

The Seventies

"The 'homosexual problem' . . . is the problem of condemning *variety* in human existence."

— DR. GEORGE W. WEINBERG, 1971

"It is one thing to confess to political unorthodoxy but quite another to admit to sexual unorthodoxy."

— MERLE MILLER, 1971

"This was a very idealistic era, when young people felt they could change the world. We truly felt we were part of history. We were doing something new. We were doing something righteous. We were part of the generation of committed youths."

— MORTY MANFORD, gay activist

"To Victory!"

— CHRISTOPHER ISHERWOOD, 1974

N O OTHER CIVIL RIGHTS movement in America ever had such an improbable unveiling: an urban riot sparked by drag queens. But while many gay people remained ignorant of Stonewall and others reacted to it with discomfort, this 1960s version of the Boston Tea Party would do more than any other event to transform gay life in America. The thick bottle that had contained an entire culture was uncorked in 1969; within a few years it would be shattered into a thousand pieces.

Stonewall's impact on gay men and lesbians would eventually be comparable to the effect of the Six Day War on Jews around the world: for the first time, thousands of members of each tribe finally thought of themselves as warriors. But because gay people started with so much less self-esteem in 1969 than most Jews had before 1967, the consequences of Stonewall were even more dramatic. Although millions would remain in the closet, within a year after Stonewall, thousands of men and women would find the courage to declare themselves for the first time: to march and lobby and "zap"* — and even to be identified as gay in their local newspapers.

Never again would American children baffled by this mystery within themselves grow up without seeing any manifestation of it in the world around them. The ancient conspiracy of cultural invisibility was finally over.

In 1969, the only gay organizations with any significant public identity were the Mattachine Society and the Daughters of Bilitis. Just four years later, one could join a radical Gay Liberation Front, Radicalesbians, a more mainstream Gay Activists Alliance, the National Gay Task Force,† the Lambda Legal Defense and Education Fund, and hundreds of other groups in New York, across the country, and around the world. "It was like fire, you know," said Jim Fouratt, a founder of the Gay Liberation Front in New York. "Like a prairie fire: let it roar. . . . People were ready." Fouratt joined a group that traveled around the country to create other GLFs. "I think we set up about forty chapters, most of them on university campuses," he recalled. Even at Catholic Notre Dame in South Bend, Indiana, gay students decided in 1971 to start their own organization. "I am a great believer in nonviolence," one of them wrote, "but if any of the football jocks or whoever starts to give me a hard time . . . well, I don't like to brag about my karate, but . . ."

"It's amazing when you suddenly find pride," said Arthur Laurents. "When you suddenly stand up."

By 1973, the Gay Activists Alliance's National Gay Movement Committee in Manhattan carried the names of 1,100 gay groups all over America in its records. According to the historian Toby Marotta, "Gay and lesbian liberationists in New York City elaborated and publicized the ideologies, set the examples and offered the help that encouraged" gay people everywhere to organize.

THE PERSON WHO played the largest role in ending the invisibility of gay life in America was an Irish-Catholic heterosexual, a television interviewer who never hesitated to take positions that enraged his church. His name

---

*To demonstrate disruptively
†Later the National Lesbian and Gay Task Force

was Phil Donahue, and on scores of shows during his marathon run on network television, he explored every facet of the gay experience. For millions of Americans, he provided their first window into this mysterious world. By the end of his twenty-nine years on the tube, he had done more than anyone else to turn the exotic into the commonplace.

In 1996, Donahue vividly recalled his first show with a gay man, Clark Polak, a prominent gay leader from Philadelphia and a close ally of Frank Kameny. "I do remember featuring the first out of the closet: 'right here, right now, yes, here he is, folks — Clark Polak.'" It was the year before Stonewall: "the first gay Donahue show out of Dayton.

"There was the phone number and here was this gay guy — you could actually call up a gay guy! It really was a *sensation*." Donahue readily admitted his original motivation for exploring this subject: "People didn't leave the barber shop — even when their haircut was over!" Although he felt uncomfortable the first time he interviewed a gay man, he was also extremely curious. "And I *know* they're going to watch this program. And, remember, that's what I'm paid to do: I'm paid to draw a crowd."

Gradually, Donahue began to understand "that gayness was not a moral issue." Over the next three decades, he made an enormous contribution to America's enlightenment by regularly sharing that commonsense idea with a gigantic audience.

"This was a very big nirvana," he said. "This was truly a big, big moment of awareness for me: that there were homosexual jerks, but that had to do not with their gayness, but with their humanness. And that jerks do not abound in any greater numbers in the gay community than in the so-called straight community."

His Catholic upbringing never prevented him from having an open mind. "I looked up after sixteen years of Catholic education to realize Catholics were supporting the Vietnam War, voting for Nixon. I was starting to realize first of all that the church is not divinely inspired in all matters. It is as corrupt as any large institution, including General Motors and the United States government.

"I was never going to let an institution or another person tell me what was a mortal or a venial sin. . . . And then as the years went on, I began to realize that one of the biggest closets of all was the one that was occupied by so many thousands of priests of the Roman Catholic Church.

"Then we did programs that showed that most children are abused by straight people — and that gay people are not in the bushes waiting to grab your child. I began to see the tremendous mountain that had to be climbed on the matter of gay rights. I began to explore the fascinating legal issues that obtained to gayness: guys getting thrown out of their apartment; guys not getting promoted; guys losing their jobs; usually guys, not always. We did shows with guys who took their lover to the senior prom in high school. And the sheriff who wouldn't let them on the dance floor. We had some *fabulous* shows — I mean truly riveting personal accounts of bizarre behavior.

"We did *many* shows on gay bashing. I think that homophobia is most virulently expressed in male adolescence and also in the twenties. I'm not prepared to say that all gay bashers are gay. But I am prepared to say that a significant percentage of gay bashers probably are, and they're in deep, deep denial.

"When you see what organized religion does to legitimize homophobia, you begin to appreciate the enormously complicated issue of attacking this fear. If the church says gay bashing is all right, then people can say, 'Why the hell isn't it?'

"That is to me the biggest sin of all."

IN 1972, Hal Holbrook and Martin Sheen starred in the first made-for-TV gay movie. The following year, public television provided America with its most prolonged prime-time exposure to a gay character to date in its twelve-hour multipart documentary, *An American Family*. The parents, Bill and Pat Loud, actually decided to divorce during this cinéma vérité exercise, but the character who captured most people's attention was their gay son, Lance — "the California suburban kid who really had become what Bette Midler called everything you were afraid your little boy would grow up to be," as Frank Rich put it in a landmark piece about gay culture in *Esquire*. Lance was an "Andy Warhol camp follower who had dyed his hair silver at age fourteen, later painted his lips David Bowie blue, and now lived in New York's Chelsea hotel," Rich wrote. "Yet Lance was too witty and attractive to be repellent: he epitomized the young homosexuals now beginning to come out of the closet — the wisecracking, benign, artistic types that men and women of my generation sought out, especially for party invitation lists . . . Lance was not a fake like David Bowie but an accessible, ingratiating prime-time boy next door — Billy Gray or Jerry Mathers or David Cassidy." But to someone a little older like the novelist Anne Roiphe, Lance was "the evil flower of the Loud family" with a "campy wit and all the warmth of an iguana." Getting a little carried away, Margaret Mead called the series "as important a moment in the history of human thought as the invention of the novel." *Time* called it "the ultimate soap opera." What it really amounted to was a model for the incessant confessional television of Sally Jessy Raphael and countless rivals — and later, MTV's "The Real World."

THE SPIRIT of the sixties was born in the big cities on both coasts, and peaked on the East Coast in 1969 — just two months after Stonewall — when three hundred thousand kids gathered to celebrate the magic of peace, love, music, marijuana and mud at Woodstock in Bethel, New York. In the following decade, the ethos of the sixties gradually spread through the American heartland. Members of the Vietnam generation consumed vast amounts of grass, cocaine, mescaline, LSD, and other stimulants that fueled the most unbridled sexual freedom ever seen in a modern Western society. Writing in *Esquire* at the end of 1969, Tom Burke described the new homosexual as "an unfettered, guiltless male child of the new morality in a Zapata moustache and an outlaw hat, who couldn't care less for Establishment approval, would as soon sleep with boys as girls, and thinks that 'Over the Rainbow' is a place to fly on 200 micrograms of Lysergic Acid Diethylamide." Without the constraints of religion, the fear of contagion, or (in most cases) the slightest desire to seek the counsel of psychiatrists, promiscuity replaced puritanism with a vengeance. And no one was more promiscuous than the gay men of New York City.

Bisexuality was suddenly fashionable within the cosmopolitan vanguard of a new generation, and it was depicted in two fine movies that violated all the rules of the now defunct censorship office. *Sunday, Bloody Sunday* was written by Penelope Gilliatt and directed by John Schlesinger, a gay man who was still in the closet in 1971. In it, a young Glenda Jackson and a middle-aged Peter Finch compete for the affections of Murray Head, a pretty boy who enjoys a guiltless pleasure playing the two of them off each other. Most of the film was marvelously understated, but one shot made cinematic history, producing gasps from part of the audience — and silent smiles from the rest: a full-on-the-lips kiss between Peter Finch and Murray Head. For millions of gay moviegoers who had long been accustomed to gruesome fates for any gay character who managed a brief on-screen appearance, a close-up of the first really sexy kiss between two attractive men was a moment of rare fulfillment.*

The following year, Bob Fosse directed *Cabaret*, perhaps the best film musical-drama ever. Inspired by Christopher Isherwood's *Berlin Stories*,

---

*It was also a big step forward from Schlesinger's first American film, *Midnight Cowboy*, released in 1969. Jon Voight played a male hustler who hated "faggots," and beat up one of his johns. "I deserve this," moaned his victim, played by Barnard Hughes. "I brought this about myself, I know I did."

Cabaret had been produced on Broadway in 1966, but even at that late date all of the gay elements had been expunged.* The screenwriter Jay Presson Allen restored them, and the result was a film set in Weimar Berlin in the thirties which also captured the sexual milieu of hip young America in the seventies. *Cabaret* reminded the gay novelist Armistead Maupin of his own life in San Francisco, and he remembered it as the first movie that "really celebrated homosexuality." The seventies were an era when activists like Jack Nichols were hoping for the "final crumbling of gay/straight divisions and the creation of a sexually integrated society in which everybody would be free to love and make love" — without labeling himself.

Cabaret depicted all of the permissiveness that drew gay Americans like Philip Johnson and Paul Cadmus and Englishmen like Isherwood and Auden to Berlin in the twenties and thirties. Sixty years later, Johnson still remembered buses adorned by with advertisements for bars reading "Come to Us Because We Do Gay Things," and an atmosphere that was "much more decadent" than France under Louis XVI. Every summer, for several years, Johnson would travel to Berlin to select a new boy from the streets to live with him for a month or two. "It was a very open town because they'd lost the war," Johnson remembered. "And that still rankled, of course. The defeated parties have to be sort of, 'Well, I'm being fucked. I'm fucked. So I better make money doing it.' And I enjoyed the payment part of it. They were Germans. They were boys. Very nice. Every summer I had a different friend. I stayed with a family, who were obviously tolerant." When Paul Cadmus visited Germany in 1932, he purchased his first male photographs, which he spotted in shop windows.

In *Cabaret*, Liza Minnelli seized her mother's mantle as a gay icon and gave the greatest performance of her career, winning one of the eight Oscars awarded to the film. Borrowing from her mother's life for her own art, Minnelli's character seduced the gay English (Isherwood) character played by Michael York.† Then Minnelli and York shared the affections of a wealthy German count, who introduced himself to Minnelli this way: "You are like me adrift in Berlin. I think it's my duty to corrupt you."

Fosse encouraged improvisation on the set, which made everyone feel as if he was part of the "creative process," Michael York remembered. The director badly needed a hit after *Sweet Charity*, and he worked feverishly on his new project. Musical collaborators John Kander and Fred Ebb

---

*Its nonmusical precursor, *I Am a Camera*, starring Julie Harris, won the New York Drama Critics' Circle Award for best American play in 1952.

†York asked Isherwood if he had ever gone to bed with the real Sally Bowles. "Once," Isherwood replied, when the flat had been "overfilled with friends." (Michael York, *Travelling Player*, 220.)

added several showstopping songs, including "Maybe This Time" and "Money, Money." Because nearly all the songs were performed inside a club, this movie musical was unusually seamless. York thought it was "one of the best-edited films" he had ever seen. Fosse's "angular sexy choreography matched the Brechtian mood of the cabaret, a perfect expression of a disjointed time," York wrote. "Fosse's achievement was to make the sleaziness of the cabaret believable while at the same time showcasing the improbable brilliance of the performers in it."

During a "long, extraordinary day" of shooting and improvisation inside a German castle in Schleswig-Holstein, York marveled when a whole sequence was invented that "culminated in the three principals' faces interlocking in a revolving triangle, with looks speaking more poignantly than any improvised words."

Soon after their romp in the castle, Minnelli and York confronted each other over their mutual involvement with the count.

"Screw Maximilian!" York shouted at her.*

"I do," Minnelli replied.

"So do I!" said York. Minnelli cringed, York grinned, and gay audience members around the world reacted with a roar.

"You two bastards!" said Minnelli.

"Two?" said York. "*Two?* Shouldn't that be *three?*"

The film was brimming with menace, with the sexual antics of Minnelli and York set against the steady penetration of German society by the Nazis. This juxtaposition reinforced the old American notion that loose German morals between the wars contributed to the rise of Hitler. Isherwood was disgusted by this point of view. "People take this attitude that Germany went to pieces between the wars because of its 'decadence,'" he said in 1975. "By which they always mean homosexuality. . . . It's such rubbish, sheer Nazi propaganda. Germany went to pieces because of a war started by greedy old men who sent out all the best young people of a generation to die."

THE BIG NEWS in the British literary world at the beginning of the seventies was the imminent publication of *Maurice*, the gay novel that E. M. Forster had completed sixty years earlier. Forster had read *Maurice* aloud to some of his gay friends, including Paul Cadmus, but he chose not to publish it during his own lifetime, partly because he was worried about the impact it might have had on his (married) policeman-lover. In the fall

*In the British version of the film, the line is "Fuck Maximilian!"

of 1970 *New York Times* London bureau chief Anthony Lewis wrote that
the novel would surprise many of Forster's readers because "his sensitively
drawn women are widely regarded as his outstanding fictional creations
and the sorrow and the joy of marriage are portrayed with convincing
emotion." Despite the persistence of these Stanley Kauffmannesque prejudices, the changing climate had finally made it possible to acknowledge
Forster's sexuality in public. Lord Annan, an intellectual historian, told the
BBC in 1970, "Of course Forster was a homosexual, there's no question
about this. He wouldn't want to have denied it." Forster had watched
"public opinion change very gradually from the hysterical outburst of the
trial of Oscar Wilde in 1895 to the recent repeal of laws against adult
homosexual relations."

THE SEXUAL FREEDOM of the seventies and the political awareness that
flowed from Stonewall exerted two different influences on gay people
coming of age in this era. The essential messages of the sexual revolution
were about freedom and experimentation, and they encouraged men and
women to sample every kind of erotic experience. Stonewall's lessons were
less about sex and more about politics.

Among many lesbians, the sexual revolution diminished the impulse
toward role-playing that had been so strong in previous decades. The
singer Judy Barnett, who was nineteen in 1970, felt that "through the sixties, before the love revolution, the role-playing thing was much stronger.
In the forties and fifties, the butch and femme thing was very distinct.
By the time it got to our generation, we had the 'love is all you need'
thing, where it didn't matter who it was or how androgynous or what it
was, and that helped break down some of the role-playing — at least
the stereotypic manifestation of the role-playing."

The opposite trend was apparent within part of the gay male population in the seventies. Perhaps because of a new impulse to define themselves as "masculine" in traditional heterosexual terms, there was now a
vogue for male role-playing, with more men insisting on defining themselves as "tops" who assumed the (theoretically) dominant position over
"bottoms."* "In the fifties I never knew what a top or bottom was," said
Dan Stewart, a landscape architect who came out at the end of that
mellower decade. "People were versatile. If you were attracted to somebody, you just did whatever. There was no left earring, or red handker-

*While Gore Vidal has always dismissed the categories of "hetero" and "homo," he strongly
believes in "tops" and "bottoms" — placing himself firmly in the former category.

chief. You just made love to men, usually playing both roles. So when that happened during the seventies, that was very extraordinary to me — the fact that somebody's going to play a role, and you're going to play another role."

While the sexual revolution encouraged all kinds of experimentation, Stonewall produced a different imperative for an emerging generation of gay people — the pressure to become politically involved, and to declare themselves as exclusively gay. Self-identified *bi*sexuals were dismissed by radical activists as being too cowardly to call themselves gay. In some cases, this political imperative merely prevented honest self-description.

Although millions of lesbians and gay men were relishing the fruits of an unprecedented sexual freedom, most of them remained firmly inside the closet — and only a tiny proportion were becoming politically active. During most of the seventies, there wasn't a single gay reporter out of the closet at any daily newspaper in Manhattan. The *Washington Post* reporter Roy Aarons remembered recoiling when he ran into a *Post* colleague, Herb Denton, at a gay bar. "We both turned around and barely acknowledged each other," said Aarons. Even at an "alternative" weekly like the *Village Voice,* a demonstration had been necessary shortly after Stonewall to force the newspaper to permit the use of the word *gay* in an advertisement.

When Calvin Tomkins profiled Philip Johnson in *The New Yorker* in 1977, the architect pleaded with the author not to identify him as a gay man. Johnson was negotiating with AT&T executives for the commission to design the company's new headquarters on Madison Avenue in Manhattan, and he thought the disclosure might jeopardize his employment. "This was in the early stages, when I wasn't sure I had the job," Johnson said. Tomkins was "furious," but he complied with Johnson's request. The architect's lover, David Whitney, was discreetly identified in the article as "his friend."

Johnson was of a class and a generation who were routinely invited to the fanciest dinner parties, but who never brought along a male companion. On the other hand, single gay men were most welcome: "Mrs. [Vincent] Astor said she always had a homosexual to dinner" because they were "the only people who could talk," the architect remembered.

After Johnson had been living with David Whitney for more than fifteen years (they first met in 1960), Barbara Walters interrogated Johnson during a dinner party at the home of Kitty Carlisle Hart. "Why don't you ever bring your boyfriend to these events?" Walters demanded.

"I said, 'By God, you're right, Barbara.' Got up from the table and went home," Johnson recalled. "She was a very great help. I was so mean and selfish: 'I'll be home late tonight,' that kind of thing."

Leonard Bernstein had been conflicted about his sexuality all his life. In 1976 he shocked his friends when he separated from his wife, Felicia, to live with a male lover, Tom Cothran. It was actually Mrs. Bernstein who had precipitated the split by telling her husband that if he continued to spend time alone with Cothran, she did not want him back. The press reported the breakup in October, and in December Bernstein hinted at his reasons in public. Before conducting the New York Philharmonic in performances of Shostakovich's Fourteenth Symphony, he startled the audience with a fifteen-minute confession.

He said that after studying Shostakovich's life and work, "I came to realize that as death approaches, an artist must cast off everything that may be restraining him and create in complete freedom. I decided that I had to do this for myself, to live the rest of my life as I want." But by the following summer Bernstein was back with his wife.

THE SEVENTIES were a challenging decade for New York City. The flight of the middle class which had started after World War II was continuing, reducing its tax base and straining its finances. John Lindsay had brought glamour, style and excitement to city hall after he was elected mayor in 1965. He had reclaimed the verdant center of Manhattan for all kinds of recreation with a single, uncomplicated act: the exclusion of the automobile from Central Park on weekends. The park came alive, and the mayor rechristened New York, with tongue in cheek, as "Fun City." But Lindsay had also spent much more money than the city was actually taking in, and a year after he left office in 1973, New York was slouching toward bankruptcy. By 1975 new construction of all kinds was at a standstill, all kinds of buildings were defaulting on their mortgages, and the assessed value of the city's real estate was suddenly declining.

Much of the rest of the nation considered Manhattan's misfortune wholly appropriate for what they thought of as America's version of Sodom on the Hudson. This anti–New York sentiment was embraced by President Gerald Ford, whose resistance to federal loan guarantees to rescue the city from default was summarized in another pithy *Daily News* headline: "Ford to City: Drop Dead." The vibrancy of the growing gay movement was in vivid contrast to the dreary predictions of obsolescence for the city that was nurturing it. At the very moment gay people were exulting in their newfound urban freedom, pundits were prophesying the imminent death of the greatest of all American metropolises.

The bold new activists in the streets of Manhattan were dramatically increasing the public profile of gay people in America. "When we first started out, we were all focused on taking the spirit of Stonewall into the streets," said Michela Griffo. "Just making ourselves more visible as a political organization. Trying to get more and more men and women to join us."

The young militants set an intoxicating pace.

Nine months after Stonewall, another police raid led by Deputy Inspector Seymour Pine brought instant notoriety to the Snake Pit, an after-hours club in Greenwich Village. The raid became controversial after the police arrested 167 patrons, one of whom was a twenty-three-year-old Argentinean named Diego Vinales who jumped from the second-floor window of the Sixth Precinct house and impaled himself on the spike of a steel fence. After several major operations, Vinales survived.

John Koch, the manager of the Ninth Circle Steakhouse, remembered when two of the policemen who had participated in the raid came in for dinner the following evening. "This cop is the nicest guy you'd ever want to meet," said Koch, "and he was there with his partner, and he was so distraught. He was a young kid then, and he said, 'I can't believe they won't leave these people alone.' He was really upset that this had happened."

After the raid, a freshman congressman named Edward I. Koch became one of the first elected officials to publicly lobby on behalf of the homosexuals of Greenwich Village. Koch wrote to Police Commissioner Howard Leary to point out that the raid violated a previous promise from the commissioner to end entrapment and harassment of homosexuals. "I would like to know, Commissioner, whether there has been a change in policy. I cannot understand arresting 167 people in a bar for disorderly conduct. . . . It is not a violation of the law to be homosexual or heterosexual, and the law should never be used to harass either." In their column in *Gay,* Jack Nichols and Lige Clarke expressed their delight: "It takes real balls for a politician to stand up for the civil rights and liberties of homosexual citizens," they wrote. "Congressman Koch has earned the distinction of being the first to do so."

Up on First Avenue in the Nineties at the Charade, black and white men celebrated two civil rights revolutions at once. Mingling happily around a small horseshoe bar in the front, and dancing to the Supremes and Aretha Franklin in the back, no one ever felt the slightest racial animosity. "Everybody was very interested in everybody else," remembered "Edward Stone" (a pseudonym), a thirty-two-year-old white free-lance writer who dated only black men at the time. "There were students and hairdressers and accountants," said Stone, and there was "no element of danger even im-plicit in all of this." Stone remembered boisterous parties in Harlem and the Village, where almost every guest was part of an interracial couple. "People were interested in music and pot; they were not political at all. They seemed very much at ease. I had very good relations with blacks back then." (Twenty-five years later, Stone said he hardly had any black friends at all.)

In 1970, Arthur Goldberg was the Democratic candidate for governor. As a former secretary of labor, United States Supreme Court justice, and ambassador to the United Nations, Goldberg was one of the most famous liberals of his era. During a campaign swing on the Upper West Side of Manhattan in June, Goldberg was accosted by three dozen members of the Gay Activists Alliance. First they asked him politely whether he favored fair employment laws for homosexuals and the repeal of the sodomy law. Goldberg replied, "I think there are more important things to think about." That provoked cries of "Answer homosexuals!" and "Gay power!" and finally — after he retreated into his white limousine — shouts of "Crime of silence!"

That same month, during Gay Pride Week — newly invented to mark the first anniversary of Stonewall — GAA staged a sit-in at the Manhattan office of the Republican State Committee, demanding to learn Governor Nelson Rockefeller's views on homosexuality. A small group of demon-strators were arrested and immediately dubbed the "Rockefeller Five."[*]

On June 28, between five and fifteen thousand newly minted gay activ-ists marched up Sixth Avenue from Sheridan Square in Greenwich Village to the Sheep Meadow in Central Park for a "Gay-In" to celebrate the Stonewall anniversary. This gathering was by far the largest public display of homosexuality Manhattan had ever seen, and it made the front page of the *Times*. Even notoriously blasé New Yorkers reacted with silent astonishment. The marchers carried bright red, green, purple, and yellow silk banners, and shouted "Say it loud, gay is proud!" and "Join us!" at the curious; occasionally a passerby filed into the parade. A tall attractive girl carried a sign reading "I am a lesbian" to the applause of some of the bystanders. "Not long ago the scene would have been unthinkable," Lacey Fosburgh wrote in the *Times*, "but the spirit of militancy and determina-tion is growing so rapidly among the legions of young homosexuals that last weekend thousands of them came from all over the Northeast."

---

[*]Arthur Bell wrote about the "Rockefeller Five" in his first article for the *Village Voice*. He later became the weekly's first openly gay columnist. (Toby Marotta, *The Politics of Homosexuality*, 159)

"The main thing we have to understand," said Michael Kotis, the president of the Mattachine Society, "is that we're different, but we're not inferior."

Similar festivities were held in San Francisco, Los Angeles, and Chicago.

Less than four months later, Goldberg and both of the major party candidates for United States senator — the Republican incumbent, Charles Goodell, and the Democratic challenger, Richard Ottinger — became three of the first statewide candidates in New York to endorse GAA's civil rights platform. "Today we know not only that gay is good, gay is angry," the activist Arthur Evans later told the *Times*. "We are telling all the politicians . . . that they are going to become responsible to the people. We will make them responsible to us, or we will stop the conduct of the business of government." The following year, Mayor John Lindsay quietly endorsed the gay civil rights law, which was stalled in the city council. "The idea of a 'homosexual vote' is slowly gaining ground," *Times* reporter (and future executive editor) Joseph Lelyveld wrote in the summer of 1971, in one of the paper's first serious assessments of the budding gay movement.

ETHAN GETO was twenty-six in 1970, a Bronx native who had grown up on the Grand Concourse near 163d Street, listening at night to the roar of the crowd floating through his window from nearby Yankee Stadium. In the seventies, he would discover that he was completely bisexual — "right in the middle" of the Kinsey scale.

It had not been an easy childhood: "I was an only child doted on by an obsessive mother and a hyper borscht-belt comedian father and this is what produced me." His father started out with the Mercury Theatre, where Orson Welles also starred. "My father was a very talented guy in the theater but, unlike many of his friends and contemporaries, he never achieved significant commercial success."

In 1949, the family had moved to Paris so that Geto's father could study literature at the Sorbonne on the GI Bill. At the end of the year, his parents split up, and the six-year-old Geto returned home alone with his mother. "When I was a little kid, I was emotionally disturbed, in no small part because of my mother's near clinical hysteria. And I was put away for four years from age ten through thirteen in an institution for emotionally disturbed children. I first went to Bellevue, and I was locked up for four months in the psychiatric ward instead of the standard two-week observation period because they couldn't figure out what to do with me. So I spent four months with every psychopathic kid in New York, mostly from tough neighborhoods. I was this scared, Jewish, middle-class kid in the violent psycho ward. My mother called the police department, and said, 'My son is poisoning me.' I was not. The truth is that I was an extremely fragile and withdrawn kid who stayed in my room all day long and played alone with my collection of one thousand toy soldiers.

"In Bellevue they tested me and said I had a genius IQ." Geto was eventually sent to the Pleasantville Cottage School in Westchester, which was run by the Federation of Jewish Philanthropies. Most of the counselors and teachers were highly educated Jewish refugees from Hitler's Germany.

"It was a nice place. I was very sexually active there. We lived in cottages with twenty other boys. There was a house mother and a house father who lived downstairs. And we boys upstairs. The boys in my cottage were ten, eleven, twelve. And we had sex every night. It was heaven. We used to say to each other, 'Pretend you're the girl!' And the other one would say, 'No, pretend *you're* the girl!' And the 'girl' would lie down on her tummy and the other boy would get on top of 'her,' insert his penis between her thighs or against her buttocks and have an orgasm. We were too young to ejaculate, but we had intense orgasms. I had crushes on a couple of boys. And I was really hot to get them in bed and sometimes I did, and sometimes I didn't."

After four years Geto moved back into his mother's house in the Bronx. "When I was thirteen years old and I went home, all of a sudden I realized that there's something called a homosexual. When I entered puberty, I keyed into the fact that there were queers, fags, homosexuals. This is 1956. And my mother's attitude and my whole family, who were intellectual, liberal Jews, was that gay people were, at best, marginal characters in society. Not respectable people. And so I panicked. My experience all along, after that, was that the liberal Jews were always the most terrified and the most disdainful. Surprisingly, a lot of the working-class Italians and Irish were more accepting of gay people in New York.

"I remember my grandmother walking down the street with me when I was five or six years old, and saying, 'Look! Look, sweetheart! There's one of those powder puffs!' And I said, 'What is that, Grandma?' 'Oh, you know, a cream puff — those men who think they're ladies.' So for six years, from the ages of thirteen to nineteen years old, which is 1956 to 1962, I am totally in the closet. I didn't want to think about it. I didn't do anything. I didn't seek it out.

"My mother was a Freudian. And if you were homosexual, you were sick! Freud was God to Jewish intellectuals of my mother's generation. For my family, it was Stalin and Freud. Those were the Gods. They could do no wrong. My father was a passionate idealist, dedicated to improving the lot of workers, fighting for civil rights, and he believed that American capitalism was the root of all evil. Like many young idealists of his generation, when he was in his twenties — during the 1930s — he joined the Communist party.

"This is my family background."

When Geto turned twenty in 1963, he was a junior at Columbia College, living near the campus on 113th Street and hanging out at the West End, then and now the principal Columbia saloon. There, he spotted a "total, flitting queen — that's how I noticed him because I wouldn't know how to figure out another gay person. And I kept staring at him." After gazing at his intended every night for three weeks, Geto finally got up the nerve to speak to him. "They're closing the bar, and I say, 'Hey, how would you like to come up to my apartment for a drink?' So he says, 'Oh, OK, but what else do you have in mind?' I said, 'Well, I don't know. You seem like a nice person. I want to get to know you.' He says, 'Oh, really. Oh, all right. Let's go!'

"So, I take this guy up. We have sex. I have a big crush on him. For three months, I didn't do any work. I almost dropped out of Columbia. I just hung out with him. He lived in a penthouse on 72d Street and West End Ave. And he was not rich. He was a librarian who worked for the federal government. He was very proper: he wore very conservative Brooks Brothers clothes to work. And I waited for him to come home every night. He gave me the keys to his apartment. He used to call up all his friends, and say, 'Darling, guess what's doing me now! Cora, girl of twenty!' That was me. And I'd say, 'Don't call me girls' names! What do you mean, Cora?! What does that mean?!' The first time I had sex with this guy, he said to me, 'You might not want to do that tonight because I was just with someone else a couple of days ago and he called me up, and he says, 'Sarah, I have the clap.' And I said, 'I don't know what that is.'

"And I had sex with him and I got the clap for the first time. I'm twenty years old. I was terrified. He took me to a gay dermatologist doctor who was his buddy. And Gerald took care of all the boys when they got the clap or anything else. Everyone would go to Gerald. He was the 'in' doctor for the gay set. So I'm twenty years old. I'm quaking in fear. My penis pouring this horrible, burning discharge. He shot me up with something, and then he gave me pills, and then he did a smear on a slide, and he says, 'Oh, you got it, darling!' He says, 'Mary, you've got *it!* What were you doing with Rodney?!' I was with him every day. Every day! He couldn't get rid of me. I slept there. I ate there. Every day, we had sex all day. He was great. And he was in heaven. He was a riot. Anyway, he was in big trouble because he owed Macy's $600 that he couldn't pay on his Macy's credit card because he'd bought so much yarn to knit with. All he did was knit."

After three months of this experiment, Geto decided that he was gay, which caused even more anxiety. Frightened, he chose what was still a common solution for this kind of "homosexual panic" in the early sixties: at the age of twenty-one, he decided to marry his childhood sweetheart, whom he had been dating since he was fifteen.

Geto's wife came from a "very refined Northern Italian family," but Geto's mother was horrified because her new daughter-in-law wasn't Jewish. "The thing is," Geto explained, "I've been bisexual my whole life. I strongly identify as gay, culturally, aesthetically, and politically, but sexually it's pretty much right in the middle. Maybe I'm one of the few people that say that and mean it. So we had a real sex life that I enjoyed, and everything else." They had two children, and Geto would stay married for eight years, until he was twenty-nine.

Geto had spent his youth working in reform Democratic politics, and in 1964 he worked to elect Jonathan Bingham and James Scheuer, two distinguished liberal reformers who vanquished the ancient Bronx Democratic machine controlled by Charlie Buckley. In 1969, Robert Abrams became the second nonmachine Democrat in modern times to be elected Bronx borough president, and Geto became his press secretary and political adviser. In 1971, barely two years after the Stonewall riot, Geto was visited for the first time by a young man named Hal Offen.

"I demand to see Bob Abrams!" said Offen.

"Well, OK, what's the issue?" Geto asked.

"I represent BUG! Bronx United Gays! And we demand that Bob Abrams, who says he's a liberal, support gay people! We want Bob Abrams to support the gay rights bill that's being introduced for the first time next month in the city council."

"So I'm sitting in my chair, and I'm saying, 'Well, listen. I'm very sympathetic to your point of view and I, I, I, I — Bob Abrams is a great guy. I'm sure he'd be sympathetic.' So he gives me this whole militant thing about 'supporting gays is civil rights!' And I'm saying, 'Well, no one's ever really thought of it that way. You may have some problems with that approach.' So he says, 'Well it *is* civil rights! Think about it! It's the same as everybody else!'"

Offen was a member of the Gay Activists Alliance, which was founded in 1970 when it broke away from the more radical Gay Liberation Front.

One of the first things that GAA decided to do was to reach out beyond Manhattan to the other four boroughs of New York City, and Offen was in charge of the Bronx. "He had a couple of lesbians and himself — that was Bronx United Gays," said Geto. "But he had a lot of guts."

When Geto first went to see Abrams, he had the same experience that Mike Wallace had with Fred Friendly five years earlier. "Abrams wasn't quite sure what the entire definition of a homosexual was." After Geto explained the orientation, Abrams was inclined to support the bill, but he wanted to check with his other advisers first. "Abrams, by instinct, was always an extraordinarily decent and progressive person," said Geto.

But the rest of Abrams's advisers — all longtime liberal activists — were appalled at the idea. "Are you crazy?" they asked. "It's the most radical fringe thing. Your problem already is that people think you're too left-wing. And you're a thirty-three-year-old bachelor!"

For the "first and last time" in his life, Geto began to cry during a meeting with his boss. "I was so overcome with emotion because I was in the closet, and it was so personal, and I was tormented by my own conflicts. And I'm saying to Bob, 'These are people that need your help. You've got to do this! You've got to go to city hall! No one else will stand up for these people.' And I started to cry."

Geto's appeal was successful: Bob Abrams became one of the first elected officials in New York to support the gay rights bill in New York City. "He went to city hall, and people were flabbergasted."

Abrams himself remembered "catcalls from the balcony of city hall. People said, 'How could you do this?' There was fingerpointing and screaming and then I came back to my office, and my secretary said, 'What did you do today? The phones have not stopped ringing.' But I did it because I thought it was the right thing to do."

"We were flooded with phone calls," said Geto. "You couldn't make a phone call because the lines were flooded, people protesting. Jewish people, Catholic people. Supporting homosexuals was disgusting! They'd never vote for Abrams again! How dare he! It was the absolute beginning of the end of New York."

Abrams rode out the huge reaction, and during the next twenty-five years, he would always be a fervent supporter of gay rights.

JUST AS STONEWALL was energizing gay activists across America, it was also having an equal — and opposite — effect on many traditional liberals. Although the American Civil Liberties Union and a handful of politicians like Ed Koch, Bella Abzug, Arthur Goldberg, and Bob Abrams had acknowledged the need to protect the basic rights of gay Americans, many opinion makers were encouraging a backlash. The *Washington Post* columnist and "60 Minutes" commentator Nicholas von Hoffman attacked Jack Paar for inviting members of the Gay Activists Alliance on his late-night talk show and permitting their opinions to go unchallenged. Five years later, von Hoffman complained bitterly about the proliferation of attractive gay characters on network television. "The old-style Chinese have the Year of the Tiger and the Year of the Pig," he wrote. "The new-style Americans are having the Year of the Fag. Is a new stereotype being born? Is network television about to kill off the bitchy, old-time, courageous fruit and replace him with a new-type homo? . . . *The Nancy Walker Show* has a continuing major fag character whose representation is monitored by representatives of the Gay Task Force on the set. . . ." Eighteen years later, von Hoffman said he could no longer remember any of the programs he had written about. "While I am pleased with the vigor of my prose, on further cogitation after twenty years, I am slightly aghast," said von Hoffman. "I guess I went over the top."

As late as 1978, Bobby Kennedy's former speechwriter Jeff Greenfield argued vehemently against legislation to protect gays from discrimination in housing and employment. In a front-page article in the *Village Voice* entitled "Why Is Gay Rights Different from All Other Rights?" Greenfield asserted that "the cultural majority always sets the rules, and minorities have the choice of conforming, defying those rules, or finding a community where *they* are the cultural majority." He implied that gays had to remain inside the closet to avoid discrimination because "it is not a denial of a fundamental right to be refused promotion because of your companions." He also described the fight for an antibias law for gay people as "a diversion from the business of working for political and social justice." In the 1980s, Greenfield campaigned in his newspaper column for the expulsion of Gerry Studds from Congress, after the Massachusetts representative acknowledged that he was gay and admitted having had sex with a seventeen-year-old congressional page. (Greenfield's effort was a failure; Studds was reelected.) And in 1996, when Greenfield was making $1 million a year as an ABC correspondent, his colleagues reported he was still cracking gay "jokes" at the office — even when he knew gay people were present. "Jeff is one of those people who is so wrapped up in himself, the idea of giving offense to anyone else is always a second thought," said one ABC newsman. "He's convinced that he's a classic liberal — but he's not."

But the article that drew by far the most attention was published in *Harper's* just fifteen months after Stonewall. Written by the Chicago academic (and future neoconservative) Joseph Epstein, the story offered vivid confirmation of Ethan Geto's observation that liberal Jews were often "the most terrified and the most disdainful" whenever the "homosexual question" was discussed.

Many journalists still remember 1970 as a "hot" year for *Harper's,* when it was edited by Willie Morris, a Mississippian who was the youngest editor in the magazine's history. Morris showcased the work of some of the era's most acclaimed journalists, including Seymour Hersh and David Halberstam, and he was lionized by the younger liberal establishment.

Naturally not everything Morris published was brilliant; but the ignorance, virulence, and occasional incoherence of Epstein's ten-thousand-word diatribe distinguished it from everything else *Harper's* published during Morris's regime.

The magazine's cover advertised the piece with a picture of a muscular torso clothed in a tight red blouse. Inside, it was illustrated with pictures of a fey young man. Epstein saw evidence everywhere that "homosexuality is spreading" because the zeitgeist was encouraging "hedonism in all its forms" and homosexuality was suddenly "where the action is."

He described his fury at being "victimized" by a handsome, masculine army buddy named Richard. Had Epstein been the victim of an unwelcome advance from his colleague? Not at all. His friend Richard's crime was his determination to be *discreet* about his sexual orientation. Epstein conceded that this discretion was "necessary," but the writer was still furious after he learned the truth. Epstein felt "victimized by [Richard's] duplicity . . . I never felt quite right about [him] again." But honesty wouldn't have helped Richard either. A few pages later Epstein wrote, "Men who are defiant about their homosexuality, or claim to have found happiness in it, will . . . require neither my admiration nor sympathy."

Elsewhere in the piece, the writer hinted at why it had been so terrifying to discover that he had unwittingly shared an office with a good-looking gay man. "Heterosexuality has not been without its special horrors," Epstein wrote; his own "once marvelous" marriage had ended in divorce. And on the subject of his fears about the possible homosexuality of one of his four sons, Epstein asked, "Uptight? You're damn right! . . . My ignorance makes me frightened. . . . Read enough case histories and you soon begin to wonder how anyone has achieved heterosexuality."

Picking up larger stones as he rolled along, Epstein described homosexuality as "anathema" and homosexuals as "cursed . . . quite literally, in the medieval sense of having been struck by an unexplained injury, an extreme piece of evil luck." Consulting a hairdresser who was his personal expert on the subject, Epstein explained that he did not want to sleep with a man because he didn't feel any desire to do so, and he didn't place "that high a premium on experience for its own sake." He told the hairdresser that "a whole cluster of interesting emotions go along with murdering a man, but I was not ready to murder to experience them."

Incoherence began to overtake the writer when he asked, "Who's repressing? Oppressing? No one I know, and certainly not most of the writers I read. . . . The truth is, when it comes to repression, why bother? Especially when so many voices are shouting to go the other way." But then, just four sentences later, he cited Dr. David Reuben, the author of *Everything You Always Wanted to Know About Sex . . . But Were Afraid to Ask,* then a mammoth best-seller in the how-to category. And how did Dr. Reuben fit into this campaign to encourage a deviant hedonism? According to Epstein, even though Dr. Reuben made it perfectly clear that he hated homosexuality, gay people were just as likely as anyone else to use his book to try to make their sex lives more interesting.*

Because "private acceptance of homosexuality" did not exist in Epstein's experience, even among "the most liberal-minded, sophisticated and liberated people," he had a simple solution for the gay "problem":

"If I had the power to do so, I would wish homosexuality off the face of the earth" because it caused "infinitely more pain than pleasure to those who are forced to live with it; because I think there is no resolution for this pain in our lifetime . . . and because, wholly selfishly," he was "completely incapable of coming to terms with it."

Epstein preceded this statement with the boast that he had "never done anything to harm any single homosexual," and he hoped he never would. Obviously, wishing for the obliteration of such an unhappy group of people could not possibly harm them.

Finally, Epstein concluded that there were many things that his four sons could do that might cause him "anguish" or "outrage" but "nothing they could ever do would make me sadder than if any of them were to become homosexual. For then I should know them condemned to a state of permanent niggerdom among men, their lives . . . to be lived out as part of the pain of the earth."

The article caused an uproar in the gay community. Some people defended Epstein because of his "honesty" and considered the piece a fine example of the new journalism pioneered by Tom Wolfe. But the gay

---

*In 1974, ten gay activists disrupted a lecture by Reuben and accused him of being a "criminal" because of his views on homosexuality. (*New York Times,* June 19, 1974)

activist Arthur Evans pointed out that what Epstein had done was actually the equivalent of someone writing, "'I look into myself and I discover that I really hate blacks — boy, do I hate blacks! I think they're stupid, they're too sensual and they eat watermelon.' That's the level of the Epstein article." Nevertheless, Morris refused to print any of the rebuttals prepared by GAA members; he maintained that the publication of twenty letters about the Epstein piece was an adequate response.

Pete Fisher was selected to organize GAA's protest, and he understood the importance of striking the right tone. He would stage a sit-in, but it would be "civilized, intelligent, educational, consciousness-raising, hospitable — no demands, no threats, no damages to office or files." After they had invaded the *Harper's* office, the demonstrators set up a table in the reception area with coffee and doughnuts; then they placed leaflets on every desk. As each *Harper's* employee arrived for work, a protester greeted him: "Good morning, I'm a homosexual. Would you like some coffee?" Downstairs, other demonstrators handed out flyers urging passersby to "join us in our Surprise Visit to *Harper's*. . . . Bring a sandwich on your lunch hour — have lunch with a homosexual."

Harper's executive editor Midge Decter defended Epstein's piece as "serious and honest and misread," but Arthur Evans was unmoved. "You knew that his article would contribute to the suffering of homosexuals," he told Decter. "And if you didn't know that, you're inexcusably naive." By the end of the afternoon, three local television stations had turned up to cover the demonstration.

"That was a *dreadful* article," Frank Kameny remembered.

The activist Eric Thorndale concluded that the "chronic affliction of *Harper's* is cultural lag." Thorndale had discovered that exactly one hundred years earlier the magazine had published an eight-page tirade against female suffrage. "The natural position of woman is clearly . . . a subservient one," *Harper's* stated. If women gained the right to vote, they would sell it "any day for a yard of ribbon or a tinsel brooch." Thorndale concluded that if this cultural lag wasn't "willfully vicious," it was "at least — like the Epstein article of a century later — cheap, canting, pretentious and wrong."

THE MOST WIDELY read reply to Epstein's article appeared four months later in an unlikely venue: *The New York Times Magazine.* Abe Rosenthal, who had commissioned the big front-page piece on the "growth" of homosexuality in 1963, had continued to consolidate his power over the daily news department: by now he was managing editor. But in 1971, there were

still two separate *New York Times*es — the daily paper, which reported to
Rosenthal, and the Sunday sections, whose editors reported to Sunday
editor Daniel Schwarz. Because of this division, there was real diversity
within the news pages, and the Sunday paper often expressed distinctly
different points of view from the daily — especially on the subject of
homosexuality. (Rosenthal gained control of both the Sunday and daily
news departments in 1977.)

The editorial page remained independent of Rosenthal, and from the
mid-sixties onward, under John B. Oakes, Max Frankel, Jack Rosenthal,
and Howell Raines, it consistently supported the repeal of sodomy laws
and the enactment of basic civil rights protection for gay citizens. As early
as November 1967, the Sunday *Magazine* had run a long piece advocating
the repeal of sodomy laws and "civil rights for homosexuals," although it
also described homosexuality as "theoretically destructive of the species."

The lead article in *The New York Times Magazine* on January 17, 1971,
was entitled "What It Means to Be a Homosexual." This was a landmark
event because the author, Merle Miller, was a well-known and well-liked
novelist, and *The New York Times* had given its imprimatur to his confession. At this early stage of the movement, Miller was by far the most
famous writer ever to "come out" in the pages of the *Times*. The vehemence of the *Harper's* piece made it perfectly clear how much courage that
required.

Miller revealed many years later that Epstein's piece had directly inspired his assignment from the *Times*. Soon after the *Harper's* article was
published, Miller had had lunch with two "liberal" *Times* editors, both of
whom expressed their admiration for Epstein's opinions. For the first time
in his life, Miller finally spoke up. "Damn it," he said, "I'm a homosexual!"
The editors responded by commissioning Miller's response.

The implication of Epstein's piece was that homosexuals had no right to
exist — and that society certainly had no obligation to temper its prejudices against them. Miller quoted part of what Epstein had written right at
the start of his own article: "Nobody says, or at least I have never heard
anyone say, 'Some of my best friends are homosexual,'" Epstein had written. "People do say — I say — 'fag' and 'queer' without hesitation — and
these words, no matter who is uttering them, are put-down words, in
intent every bit as vicious as 'kike' or 'nigger.'"

"Is it true?" Miller asked.

Is that the way it is? Have my heterosexual friends . . . been going
through an elaborate charade all these years? I would like to think they

agree with George Weinberg,* a therapist . . . who says, "I would never consider a person healthy unless he had overcome his prejudice against homosexuality." But even Mr. Weinberg assumes that there is a prejudice, apparently built-in, a natural part of the human psyche. . . . The late Otto Kahn, I think it was, said, "A kike is a Jewish gentleman who has just left the room." Is a fag a homosexual gentleman who has just stepped out? Me?

I can never be sure, of course, will never be sure. I know it shouldn't bother me. That's what everybody says, but it does bother me . . . every time I enter a room in which there is anyone else. Friend or foe? Is there a difference?

Miller's piece had all of the knowledge, nuance and humanity that Epstein's lacked. The only things the two men agreed about were that "nobody seems to know why homosexuality happens" and "the great fear is that a son will turn out to be homosexual," as Miller put it. But the gay writer added, "Not all mothers are afraid that their sons will be homosexuals. Everywhere among us are those dominant ladies who welcome homosexuality in their sons. That way the mothers know they won't lose them to another woman."

Miller described himself as a bookish youth who "read about sensitive boys, odd boys, boys who were lonely and misunderstood, boys who really didn't care all that much for baseball, boys who were teased by their classmates . . . but for years nobody in any of the books I read was ever tortured by the strange fantasies that tore at me." As an adult, he was a closeted liberal who belonged to twenty-two organizations devoted to improving the lot of the world's outcasts; homosexuals were the only group he "never spoke up for." He recalled the silence of the ACLU in the fifties when gay people were being fired from "all kinds of government posts. . . . And the most silent of all was a closet queen who was a member of the board of directors, myself."

He displeased some young activists by saying he would have preferred to have been straight. But the piece still represented a tremendous leap forward, simply because it did so much to humanize the homosexual's predicament. During the next ten months Miller received more than two thousand letters, including one from an American army installation in Germany: "I was on leave in Paris and a French boy gave [your article] to me . . . I read it, after which I burned it. . . . Thank you, though, just seeing something like that in print has meant more to me than you can rightly imagine."

*A heterosexual therapist who coined the word *homophobia* in 1970.

Miller said the most common themes from his correspondents were "nothing I have ever read has helped as much to restore my own self-respect" and "so much of what you have to say I have experienced myself and have rarely been able to trust anyone to 'let go.'"

A "great many" straight readers realized for the first time "that homosexuals were people, too, with feelings, just like anybody else." Most telling was the reader who suddenly felt all the guilt that Epstein had specifically disavowed: "I've always reacted with horror and indignation at words like 'Kike, Dago, Spic, Nigger, Pollack,' and yet for every time I've said homosexual, I've said 'fag' a thousand times. You've made me wonder how I could have believed that I had modeled my life on the dignity of man while being so cruel, so thoughtless to so many."

To placate the young activists who were upset because he had said that he would have preferred to be straight, Miller explained in his follow-up article: "The assumption seems to have been that I consider straightness more virtuous, somehow superior. That is not what I meant. I meant that in this place and time, indeed in most others since the Hellenic Age . . . being straight is easier." But even that sentiment was one that very few of the new young activists agreed with.

Although Miller's roommate at their house in the country had purchased a shotgun for protection the day before the original piece had appeared, like virtually everyone else who finally comes out of the closet, Miller was buoyed by the whole experience. He said that he had received "more than 2,000 pieces of evidence" that "most people are basically decent."

FIFTEEN YEARS AFTER he had written that "nothing [my sons] could ever do would make me sadder than if any of them were to become homosexual," Epstein chose to cloud the record. By now he was a prominent neoconservative, and the art critic Hilton Kramer's closest friend. In an article called "True Virtue" in *The New York Times Magazine,* Epstein described his "rage" after a student reporter called to ask whether he had ever said that he would prefer that his sons "be murderers or dope addicts than homosexuals."

"I could not, after 15 years, recall all that I had written in that essay," Epstein wrote. Apparently, he didn't save his clips, either. "I was, nonetheless, quite certain that I could not have said that I would rather have my sons be murderers or dope addicts than homosexuals, and this for a simple reason: I believe no such thing, nor have I ever believed it."

When Willie Morris published his memoirs in 1993, the former *Harper's* editor offered no apology for Epstein's invective. And his description of the controversy was completely disingenuous: "several dozen homosexuals arrived en masse . . . to demand redress for *a paragraph* [emphasis supplied] in an article by Joseph Epstein which they considered unsympathetic to homosexuality."

THE MONTH AFTER Merle Miller's article appeared, the conservative psychiatric establishment aired its point of view in two stories in the *Times* by Jane Brody, the paper's "personal health" expert. The first one, on the "Women's Page," carried the headline "Homosexuality: Parents Aren't Always to Blame." It quoted Dr. Lawrence J. Hatterer of New York Hospital's Payne Whitney Clinic, who "believes that environmental and cultural factors are becoming increasingly important contributors to the development of homosexuality." Among the influences the doctor cited were the "$1 billion hard core homosexual pornography industry," "the growing public tolerance of homosexuality, which may make some men feel, 'Maybe it's easier, and why not?'" and "the blending of traditional male and female roles that can lead to confusion in a boy's mind as to what is male and what is female." Nowhere in Brody's article did anyone suggest a parent's proper role might be to accept a child's sexual orientation.

The mother of a gay son who wrote to Merle Miller put it best a few months later: "Being a nice human being, people everywhere accept [my son]. Above all, as he grows older he knows his family loves him always. . . . Families of gay young men should not treat them as 'sick.' Different, yes, but not sick. I think we'd have less suicides and better adjusted 'different males' if the family unit stayed close to these boys. . . . The whole problem in our generation is that we worry so much about what our neighbors think. Thank God this young generation doesn't give a damn."

Brody's editors put her second article on the front page eighteen days after her previous story about homosexuality had appeared. The headline read "More Homosexuals Aided to Become Heterosexual." It reported the work of three therapists treating those "strongly motivated" to become heterosexual, although Brody conceded at the beginning of her story that "the vast majority of homosexuals are not interested in psychiatric treatment" and "most of those who do enter therapy do not want to become heterosexual."

The article began with the crucial moment in *The Boys in the Band*, when Harold tells Michael, "You are a sad and pathetic man. . . . You're a homosexual and you don't want to be. But there is nothing you can do to change it." Recognizing the revolutionary implications of that statement,

Brody's expert psychiatrists denied that inevitability; but their prescriptions made them sound naive. Once again, Dr. Hatterer was one of Brody's principal sources. Among the latest "techniques" he cited for successful conversions included telling patients to "stop frequenting 'gay' bars and go to 'straight' ones instead" and asking them to "substitute *Playboy* magazine and images of women for homosexual pornography and images of men." A medical team used a more extreme technique, giving patients "mild electric shocks when shown pictures of naked men." A doctor using the electric shock method admitted that he didn't have enough data to evaluate its effectiveness, but that didn't stop him from offering his "impression" anyway: "'about 75 percent' of patients become heterosexually oriented after about six months of therapy."

Gay people who had begun to accept who they were read a clear subtext from Brody's omission of any description of homosexuals who were comfortable with their orientation: the only worthy homosexual was the one who was determined to transform himself into a heterosexual. The reporter ended the article with a psychiatrist's prediction that some day there might be a "Homosexuals Anonymous," to "do for homosexuals what Alcoholics Anonymous has done for many alcoholics."

A much shorter accompanying article without a byline was the only place any doctor was quoted as suggesting that homosexuality might be normal. Dr. Evelyn Hooker, whose landmark study had been so important in the fifties, said her work had revealed no "'demonstrable pathology' that would differentiate" homosexuals "in any way from a group of relatively normal heterosexuals."

A colleague remarked to Brody that she was the first *Times* reporter to "turn the penis into a beat."

"I try to get it in whenever I can," Brody replied.

Twenty-five years later, after Brody was asked to reread her articles, she said she had no idea that they had been offensive to gay readers when they appeared. "I love my stories actually," Brody said in an interview in 1996. "You have to remember this was 1970 or so. . . . They were really ahead of their time." Brody acknowledged in 1996 that it was "much easier" to use psychoanalysis to become comfortable with one's sexuality than it was to change it — but she never made that point in either of her stories in 1971 because "that was not what the pieces were intended to do."

Despite their one-sidedness, Brody denied that the articles expressed her own opinions; that would have made them editorials instead of news articles, she explained. She said the second story was for those people who were homosexual because of "reasons such as having been seduced as young adolescents." Most researchers now believe that homosexuality is caused by a genetic predisposition, very early childhood experiences (before the age of three) — or a combination of the two.

But in 1996 Brody still believed that adolescent seduction was a cause. She said, "I know it is a cause because I know people this has happened to, and who subsequently, when they got over their fear and became informed that there were options" realized that "just because they had had sex with a man when they were thirteen didn't mean that that was the only type of sexuality that they were ever capable of expressing."

Brody said she had "a minimum of a dozen homosexual friends in 1971. . . . To suggest that I was writing these pieces as a homophobic person is absurd because it was quite the opposite. I was very empathetic. I knew people who were very content with their homosexuality and lived happily that way and had stable relationships." But like Mike Wallace in the previous decade, Brody did not discuss those happy homosexuals in these two stories. "I also knew people who were very unhappy," she said.

"SARAH WATERS" (a pseudonym) was a product of the migration that brought thousands of African Americans from the south to New York in the fifties and the sixties. She turned fourteen in 1970, and she benefited from the generosity of the Lindsay administration because "there was a lot of art money then," and she became a member of the New York City Theater Workshop.

It was as a teenager in the theater group that she first witnessed gay lovemaking. "The cast was made up of folk from nine to twenty-five years old. I was the youngest member in the company, and so I was babied by all of these other ninety-nine actors. I saw a lot: I saw two women making love, 'cause I just happened to wander in their room one day. I saw two men making love in the company. I saw two women and one man making love. And I saw it was OK. 'Cause it wasn't a big thing, it wasn't a discussion. It was just people loving each other. I never told anybody about the things that happened there. Because, God, my mother'd probably make me come back home."

Although she did not act on it until she was twenty-one, Sarah had first recognized her attraction to women in the second grade. "I knew that I wanted to touch the girls, that I didn't want to touch the boys." She remembered a lesbian who lived in her neighborhood when she was a child, who was called a "bull dagger."

"My mom told us, 'Never let that woman touch you. Because if she ever touches, you'll never want a man.' So the kids, whenever they saw her, they would run from her. But my mom let her in our house. We just couldn't let her touch us. And then there was a drag queen who lived in our neighborhood. And we used to all run down the block to see him when he went to a ball. He was a fabulous queen.

"Sexuality, period, was a secret. And it was reserved to be discussed with somebody who was your life partner. And not before. And that was it."

Waters's mother had come from South Carolina in 1947, and Sarah was the sixth of seven children. Her Alabama-born father was a window dresser for stores like Bergdorf Goodman, but he left the house when Sarah was only nine months old. After her father disappeared, the family was evicted during a snowstorm, and her mother came home to find all her children in the street with their babysitter. Sarah's mother went to the local police precinct and pleaded for a chance to keep her children. For once, New York's labyrinthine system of social services worked, and the family was given an apartment in the Soundview section of the Bronx so they could stay together. They lived in a former army officers barracks, "so they had backyards and front yards and upstairs and downstairs." It was "a real integrated neighborhood," with Irish and Italians and Jews.

Waters's mother arranged for each of her children to have godparents in the neighborhood. Sarah's godmother was a runway model, and her godfather was an engineer. "Each set of godparents were either working-class or had pretty good jobs and came from pretty good families," Waters remembered. Her mother had "five different jobs" and worked for "wealthy Jewish families," including a couple who were both psychiatrists. "My aunt was their full-time maid. And my mom believed that we had to work. And so we always worked." Besides holding down five different jobs, her mother was also going to school, "so when we sat at the table and did our homework, she sat at the table and did her homework. And so she had godparents and other primary people in our lives to make sure that we had gotten everything that we needed. It was good." All seven of the children attended college.

As a child, Sarah had a lot of boyfriends, "only because when you're a southern girl child, from the day you're born, you're trained how to have a husband."

When she was twenty-one in 1977, she had a fling with a married man, but "none of these things satisfied me or made me happy. Because I felt like I could always kind of predict what they were going to do. And it was too simple for me. It wasn't complex enough." But rebelliousness had nothing to do with her being a lesbian:

"No way!

"I think that the appeal for me, in being gay and loving women, is the gentleness of it. The relationships that I enjoy most with men are not ones of intimacy, but are ones of battles and ones of admiration. And also ones of protection. I like the way that men protect women when they do. But I don't like the dues you have to pay for the protection. So I like the protection of males in *friendships*. And I also like the bonding of men with women in secrets. I like the secrets that they share. I would never want to be a man because I wouldn't want the responsibility that our society places on you when you are a man."

Waters never saw herself as a feminist, partly because she never hated men. "I wasn't angry at men. I didn't become a lesbian because I hated men. I loved men! I still love men! I don't love men intimately. I love men as comrades. I love men as friends."

She met her first female lover in an acting company of thirty-five women which she had organized herself. "There was a great love between us. And we had decided that, one day, that we were going to rent a hotel room for a weekend. And it was like one of those Holiday Inn kind of rooms, on Ninth Avenue at 40-something. And we stayed in the hotel for the weekend. And we only went out at night. We didn't sleep together, actually, until our last night there. Because we were acting like silly girls. And we had made up all the excuses in the world why we were at this hotel. It's very complicated, the mechanics of it all. 'Cause we didn't know what to do!

"And we bought all this junk. Our first lovemaking came out of a food fight. 'Cause we were throwing food across the room. And some food landed on her face, or something like that. And she says, 'Now you have to lick it off.' And I said, 'Ooooohhh shit!' 'Cause I didn't know what to do. And the rest was history."

They were together for five years, and they rented a house near River-dale in the Bronx. "We created our own world. Because the black lesbian community was very specific, in a way. It had two worlds to it. You were either very Afrocentric and you had to play instruments and be real grassroots and wear African garments. Or you had to be this other group of well-known, upper-middle-class, fancy. The Audre Lorde kind, you know. I didn't like any of them."

Then Waters and her lover started a daycare center for working, single women in Waters's mother's Baptist church. "We pretty much gave up our lives and our real jobs and we went into this little church and we renovated it with our own hands. They really weren't payin' no more than like $10 a week. And we took their children, some of the most difficult children that nobody else would take because they hadn't been toilet-trained and all these different things.

"The minister of the church saw this as this money-making opportunity, and he wanted it back. And after we had renovated the space, he suddenly decided he needed to use this space all the time now."

At the time, Waters and her lover knew two women who fascinated them because "they were a couple and they were out and it scared us. They didn't flaunt it, it was that they had no problems loving women. And they were beautiful black, black, black women, and they would wear all of the African garments and large jewelry and big things on their heads. And they came to visit us at the daycare center one day to do an art project with the kids. They were artists. And the minister saw them.

"He felt who they were. He felt their energy. He felt the difference in their womanness. And he went back in the church and he told the congregation that we were all lesbians and he knew it. And he wanted the daycare center closed. And that Sunday he stood up and he put me out of the church, in my mother's church, in front of that congregation. And my mother fought for me in that church. She said, 'I know my daughter. My daughter's not a lesbian. As God is my witness and my judge.' And she said, 'If you can't have my daughter here you can't have me 'cause she worked hard to build the daycare center.' And he threw me out of the church in front of the congregation."

Waters never did come out to her mother, partly because she thought she would be "letting down her race. You know, you're taught everything is connected to race. Can't let down your people. Just being black is enough. Because if you do something wrong, you've embarrassed the race and, 'Oh, we've been through so much.' And, 'Oh Lord, help the people. If we do anything we're gonna bring the whole race down and we all work so hard.' And it's such a responsibility. All the time. It never stops. The expectation is that you're always gonna uphold the race.

"Because within the black community, it's believed that gay and lesbianism is a white people's curse. That white people made this thing up and it has nothing to do with black people. It's one more of those things that white folks came up with so that they could keep us down." Waters thinks that's one reason for the virulence of the homophobia in so much of the black community — "because it's a white folks' thing.

"This has never been about us. This is destroying the family. They would rather you could be pregnant! You could have fifty-five children. Anything but this. Incest is more tolerable. Anything but this! But they're still a part of the community. That's the confusion. More the gay men than the lesbian.

"It's so funny: in that very same damn church that that minister threw me out of, the church treasurer was a lesbian. And my mother found out later on, after she left the church, that the church treasurer and the church secretary were having an affair."

Waters's first lover married a Senegalese man and moved to Dakar. But Waters doesn't believe that people become straight: "I think that they want something different. I had another lover for seven years. Then one day, in our seventh year of relationship, she got up, and she said, 'I don't want to be gay anymore.' And I said, 'Well, what does that mean?' And she says, 'I don't want to be gay anymore. I want to be a mother of children. I want to raise children and I want to do all those kinds of things.'

"And I said, 'Well, why can't you do that and have a lover?' And she said, 'Because it's going to be hard enough for my children being black. And for them to have two black mothers, you know, I can't live like this. So I'm outta here.'"

MERLE MILLER WROTE that the psychiatric establishment had come out "in full force" against his article. One Park Avenue therapist even offered to treat him for free, for a time — "because it is clear from your tone that you are in desperate, even frantic need of help" — even though nothing in the article suggested desperation.

Given the vehemence with which antigay psychiatrists continued to express themselves, it's easy to understand why Miller predicted that "most of the psychiatric establishment will continue to insist that homosexuality is a disease." But the writer had underestimated the pace of social change in the new decade. The gay movement's most important victory was now less than four years away.

Frank Kameny had been among the first to point out in the early sixties that "an attribution of mental illness in our culture is devastating" and that this accusation of sickness was going to be "one of the major stumbling blocks" to real progress. He recognized that this battle would be more important than any single election or the passage of any piece of legislation. Most importantly, it turned out to be a battle that could be won.

In 1970 Kameny overcame the initial resistance of the Gay Activists Alliance in New York and convinced them they needed to persuade the American Psychiatric Association to reverse its position on homosexuality. For nearly a century, the APA had listed homosexuality as an illness and Kameny and his cohorts were determined to change that.

As usual, there was a two-prong strategy. Privately, Dr. Charles Silverstein, a GAA activist, met with Dr. Robert Spitzer, a psychiatrist at the Columbia College of Physicians and Surgeons who was in charge of the APA's *Diagnostic and Statistical Manual of Mental Disorders.* Publicly, the activists invaded the APA's annual convention at the Shoreham Hotel in Washington in 1971 and demanded the right to challenge the association's position on homosexuality. The following year a panel discussion included Barbara Gittings, a veteran lesbian activist from Philadelphia; Frank Kameny; and a psychiatrist from Philadelphia who wore a mask and used a microphone that disguised his voice. "It was a very dramatic session with this fellow speaking with a grotesque mask on," a conference participant recalled.

At this point Kameny did not know any openly gay psychiatrists within the organization: "In those days gay psychiatrists were not out. Period. End. That's why the one gay psychiatrist wore a mask." But the gay activists did have many important heterosexual allies. Probably most important were Evelyn Hooker, the researcher who had done groundbreaking work confirming the sanity of gay men, and Dr. Judd Marmor, who was an officer of the APA. Each of them played a heroic role in changing the official psychiatric orthodoxy on homosexuality.

In 1969, Hooker was part of a panel of the National Institute of Mental Health which recommended the repeal of all laws prohibiting sex in private between consenting adults, and Marmor had always been open-minded on the subject of homosexuality.

Thirty years earlier, Marmor was a young Hollywood analyst, and in 1947 Arthur Laurents was one of his patients. Laurents remembered that Marmor had greeted him with the usual question: "Why are you here?"

"I'm afraid I'm homosexual."

"So?"

"What do you mean 'So?' You know it's dirty and disgusting."

"I don't know anything about it."

Then Marmor said something that would change Laurents's life forever: "All I know is whoever or whatever you are, if you lead your life with pride and dignity, that's all that matters."*

Marmor had always been an iconoclast: he once presented a paper on

---

*In 1955 Allen Ginsberg had a similar experience with a psychoanalyst in Berkeley. "Shouldn't I be a heterosexual?" Ginsberg asked.

"Why don't you do what you want?" the doctor replied.

infidelity which suggested that coveting your neighbor's wife might be healthy. Right from the start Marmor was "appalled by the stereotypic generalizations being made about homosexuals" by the psychiatrists he knew. "I was still a young analyst, but . . . I'd hear about the homosexual personality and about the fact that homosexuals were vindictive and aggressive, couldn't have decent relationships, and were not to be trusted — all terribly nasty, negative disparaging things. I knew gay men and women. This view just didn't make sense to me. I felt we were making generalizations about people who were really very different from one another, just as heterosexuals are." To correct some of these misconceptions, in 1965 he published *Sexual Inversion: The Multiple Roots of Homosexuality*. In it he argued that "our attitudes toward homosexuality were culturally determined and influenced." At the time, that statement was considered "relatively revolutionary," from a member of the American Psychoanalytic Association.

In the third year of the activists' campaign, the APA met in Hawaii. A formal debate about the *Diagnostic and Statistical Manual's* listing for homosexuality was scheduled. The participants included Richard Green, Robert Stoller, Charles Socarides, Irving Bieber, and Judd Marmor. "It was a very, very dramatic debate," said Marmor, and one of the association's largest meetings ever, with "several thousand psychiatrists" in the audience. Marmor argued eloquently that it was time for the organization to end a policy that misused psychiatry and had detrimental "social and legal consequences" for gay people. He said the association categorized homosexuality as a sickness mostly because "society disapproves of this behavior." Psychiatrists who labeled it an illness were merely acting as agents of a cultural value system. And he reminded the audience that only one hundred years earlier, medical authorities were certain that a dependency on masturbation was evidence of a serious mental disturbance.

Behind the scenes at the same convention, Frank Kameny was meeting in a gay bar on Waikiki Beach with Ron Gold of GAA and Robert Spitzer, who was still in charge of the APA diagnostic manual. "Right there we wrote the resolutions," said Kameny. "There were two resolutions: one had to do with security clearances, and the other was the sickness one." The GAYPA, an informal and very closeted gay caucus of the association, was also meeting in the same bar that evening. "They were very, very, very shocked when we came in and sat down in the bar," said Kameny. "They

---

"So," said Ginsberg, "in a sense he gave me permission to be free, not to worry about consequences." (Allen Young, *Gay Sunshine Interview* with Allen Ginsberg, 22)

felt their cover was being blown. But there was no malice aforethought on our part."

Marmor thought his side had won the debate, and the activists left Hawaii filled with optimism. But they would not know the final outcome until the APA's Board of Trustees met in Washington seven months later. On December 15, 1973, an enormous burden was lifted from every gay American: the board announced its 13–0 vote to remove homosexuality from its list of psychiatric disorders. The news was reported on front pages all over the country.

Across America there was exhilaration within the community — and gigantic relief. A single action had removed the official psychiatric curse hanging over every homosexual. Robert Spitzer said the APA had acted because homosexuality did not "regularly cause emotional distress" or generally create "impairment of social functioning." In New York, Ron Gold was ecstatic: "We have won the ball game," he declared. Then he added, a little too optimistically, "No longer can gay people grow up thinking they're sick."

Marmor considered it a crucial step because those who wanted to discriminate against gay people could no longer say "psychiatrists call it an illness" and consider it "a sexual perversion."

Psychiatrists like Charles Socarides and Irving Bieber had not only based their professional lives on the doctrine that all homosexuals required treatment; that idea had also been their ticket to celebrity. When the Board of Trustees repudiated them, they were apoplectic. These men had prospered in the fifties by promoting conformity and intolerance. Now their very livelihood was at stake. They might become irrelevant in an era that deplored prejudice and celebrated diversity.

For the first time in the history of the APA, Socarides demanded a referendum of the membership to overturn the trustees' action because he was certain that most psychiatrists would be "aghast" at the decision.

Socarides had been tangling with Kameny since 1965, when the psychiatrist had testified as a hostile witness in one of Kameny's security cases before the Pentagon. "His rhetoric has not changed by a syllable in thirty years," Kameny said. And when Socarides began to describe himself as a "civil libertarian" in 1973, Kameny circulated his remarks at the 1965 hearing to discredit him.

The referendum was held simultaneously with the election for a new president of the APA, and Marmor was one of the candidates. Both of his opponents — Herbert Modlin and Louis West — were also strong supporters of gay rights, and all three of them signed a letter urging APA members to confirm the action of the trustees.* The letter noted that the decision to remove homosexuality *per se* from the *Diagnostic and Statistical Manual* had been approved unanimously by the Council on Research and Development and the Reference Committee as well as the trustees. It had also been ratified by the Assembly of District Branches. The National Gay Task Force raised $3,000 to pay for a mailing of this letter to all eighteen thousand members of the association. The authors warned that "it would be a serious and potentially embarrassing step for our profession to vote down a decision which was taken after serious and extended consideration."

On April 9, 1974, Frank Kameny and Bruce Voeller, executive director of the National Gay Task Force, were present in the APA boardroom in Washington to hear the outcome of the vote. The result of the referendum was the last item on the agenda. Nervousness turned into optimism after the announcement that Marmor had become the APA's new president. Then the crucial news was finally announced: 58 percent had voted to remove homosexuality from the list of illnesses, and 37.8 percent had voted against.

"We were ecstatic," Kameny recalled.

Still Socarides refused to give up. He described the letter financed by the task force as an unfair campaign practice — because it hadn't mentioned who had paid for it. The psychiatrist demanded a new election, but this time the association rejected his protest. The men who had dominated the public debate about homosexuality for thirty years were now officially outsiders in their own profession.

The losers considered the result illegitimate because they thought the APA had been manipulated by gay activists. "They claimed the whole thing was handled within the APA on a political basis," said Kameny. "It was not. It was a mixture of efforts from the inside and the outside. Those were times of rapid cultural change. Things were being looked at that hadn't been looked at before. I think our effort precipitated the internal action. I don't think it would have happened for a very, very long time, if ever, otherwise. As often happens in a culture that was pervaded by democratic principles, it was a good, sound, scientific decision, *administered* by a political process. But there's a very real difference between that and saying that the whole thing was political, which it was not."

Marmor agreed: "I don't in any way want to minimize the importance

*The letter was also signed by APA vice presidents Harold M. Visotsky and Mildred Mitchell-Bateman. (*New York Times,* May 26, 1974, and letter in author's collection)

of the gay liberation movement," he told the historian Eric Marcus. "But there were people like myself and Evelyn Hooker . . . who were independently developing their views about the wrongness of our attitudes toward homosexuality."

For Frank Kameny and the rest of the movement, the action of the APA was a stunning achievement. It came just nine years after Kameny and Jack Nichols had been forced to wage a battle *within* the movement to convince gay people to think of themselves as healthy human beings. The psychiatric establishment had been one of the biggest roadblocks to that early victory. Now, in less than a decade, Kameny and his friends had converted the movement's most potent enemy into an important ally.

"We stated that there was no reason why . . . a gay man or woman could not be just as healthy, just as effective, just as law abiding and just as capable of functioning as any heterosexual," said Marmor. "Furthermore, we asserted that laws that discriminated against them in housing or in employment were unjustified. So it was a total statement, and I think it was a very significant move."

The Stonewall riot had served as the movement's de facto Declaration of Independence. Just four years later, psychiatrists had become the wildly unlikely ratifiers of its Constitution.

ONE BENEFIT of the sexual revolution, combined with the action of the APA, was the obliteration of the doubts that haunted so many gay men in the fifties — even radicals like William Wynkoop — who had to convince themselves that "the pleasure of most homosexuals in sexual activities is *equal* in *passion* and enjoyment to that which the majority of heterosexuals experience." In the seventies, gay New Yorkers never doubted their ability to have as much fun as anyone else.

Some Greenwich Village saloon owners decided to catch the wave of the new revolution by changing the nature of their businesses. The Ninth Circle, which occupied the bottom two floors of a row house at 139 West 10th Street, had been a very successful steak house in the sixties with a slightly bohemian and overwhelmingly heterosexual clientele. In its heyday, waiters there made as much as $150 a night, a huge sum in that period. It was just a couple of blocks north of the Stonewall Inn, but the Circle was "totally straight" and "totally antigay." John Koch started there as a dishwasher but quickly worked his way up to bar manager. "They used to get on the microphone, and say, 'If you're gay go away,'" Koch recalled. "Everybody would laugh. I don't know if it was meant seriously or what."

The rent was a bargain: the restaurant owner, Bobby Krivit, who was a veteran of the carnival business on the Jersey Shore, leased the entire building for $600 a month. But by the end of 1971, business had dropped off sharply, and Krivit decided to go in a new direction. His partner had already left him to found Max's Kansas City, a famous East Village watering hole.

In January 1972 Krivit told Koch he wanted the Ninth Circle to become a gay bar. At the time, Koch wasn't sure whether Krivit, who was straight, knew that Koch was gay. The owner asked Koch if he could hire a whole new staff within two weeks, and his manager told him he thought he could. Koch believed this was the first straight establishment in Greenwich Village to "go gay" overnight in the seventies.

The old staff was fired, and the bar bought an ad in *Michael's Thing*, a guide to New York nightlife, to announce the makeover. The response was instantaneous — and "overwhelming." The owner hedged his bets a bit by keeping the restaurant going for a while on the lower floor after he converted the upstairs into a gay bar. This transition caused a certain amount of amusement because the men's room was downstairs, forcing gay bargoers to walk through the straight restaurant to relieve themselves. But within a few weeks the gay part of the business had taken over the whole place. However, the big black and white sign outside announcing the "Ninth Circle Steakhouse" remained unaltered; no one saw any need to change it. Within a month, it was the hottest gay bar in Manhattan, a distinction it retained for most of the decade. Practically every night of the week, both floors were jammed from wall to wall with beautiful young men, eager to sample the spoils of the Stonewall revolution.

"It was like a victory for gay people or something," said Koch. "They conquered this straight bastion. We really weren't ready for it. And it just went up and up and up from that."

There were two separate bars, a long one upstairs with a row of low tables in front of it, and a smaller one below, with a dance floor and a pool table. Everyone from Andy Warhol to Harvey Fierstein was an occasional customer. An autographed poster of Janis Joplin next to the front door nurtured the myth that the singer had once been a customer. The garden in the back provided a third place to sit on languid summer evenings, and patrons lined up at the same table every night to purchase their drug of choice. Nearly everyone smoked joints outdoors, and no one bothered to be discreet about it. When Koch suggested to the owner that such flagrant commerce in illicit substances might be imprudent, Krivit was always dismissive. "You don't understand this younger generation," the owner would say. "It's good for business."

Koch never witnessed any payoffs, but he was certain there were "Christmas gifts" for the local precinct, and he believed the owner had "big dealings" with police headquarters. "That cost him some money. He'd make a pretty big contribution there, which protected him all the way down."

Everyone remembered Stormy the bartender, whose real name was Norman Sabine. He had walked into the bar for an interview in 1974, and Koch was immediately beguiled by him; he started work that same night. Eventually, Koch broke his own rule against sleeping with a staff member and became Stormy's lover after the bartender seduced him on Fire Island.

Stormy was the fastest bartender most customers had ever seen, serving drinks with amazing speed — and making matches among his customers between almost every pour. From where the customer stood, Stormy always looked utterly smooth. But he benefited from the camouflage provided by a dark bar, which hid his shortcuts; after washing a glass, he never bothered to dry his hands. As a result, "When we'd take his drawer out at the end of the night it would be half full of water," said Koch. "All the money was soaking wet. And when he came home from the bar, he was literally soaked from the waist down. He was the messiest bartender I ever knew in my life. But he got it done."

Eventually Stormy and Koch worked behind the bar together on Wednesdays and Thursdays. "We made so much. We used to take the money home and we would just throw it in a dresser drawer. And it used to be such a pain in the ass, like once a month, to count that damned money. We hated counting that damned money! We'd always argue about it: 'It's your turn to count the money. I'm not counting it!'"

Naturally the owner was delighted with his booming new business, but success was not without its consequences. "He ended up going to a psychiatrist over this," said Koch. "Bobby was so freaked out that his friends were going to think that he had turned gay." According to others, Krivit also spent *all* of his profits on drugs, gambling and girlfriends. Krivit died in 1990, and the bar finally closed in 1993.

PHILIP GEFTER was twenty-five in the fall of 1976, a beautiful young man in New York City, where young men and women come to be beautiful. Gefter had graduated from the Pratt Institute in Brooklyn. In college, he was a fixture at demonstrations against the war in Vietnam, and he had been tear-gassed during the March on Washington in 1970. "My view of the world was shaped by the utopian values of the sixties," Gefter said.

"My attentions were always divided between art and politics, and my life quest was to find a way to integrate the two." He was involved in GAA activities at the Wooster Street firehouse, and he had joined the Gay Academic Union. He worked as a picture researcher at Time-Life, but there was no question about his favorite activity.

"I was a slut," Gefter remembered, laughing out loud. "And proud of it. I mean that in the highest sense of the word, you know. An ironic locution that signifies my reckless abandon to the pleasure, joy and celebration of sex." In 1976 he left his "respectable career path" at Time-Life and took a job as a waiter at Berry's in Soho.

"This period was really fun for me," Gefter said. "Almost every afternoon I would go down to the Christopher Street pier, where there were always people hanging out. I would inevitably meet some cute guy. We'd talk for a while, smoke a joint, then end up at his apartment or mine, and have sex. My daily recreational activity.

"Sex was like a handshake at that point in time. It was so accessible and easy, and there were always attractive people on the street. So many beautiful men parading around in T-shirts and cutoffs, and sex was on everybody's mind. The streets were so fertile then."

Like many of his contemporaries, Gefter thought the constant pursuit of sex certified him as a liberated gay man. "I recorded every sexual encounter in my journal as if they were running tallies of my gay identity, as if they were proof of my defiance of convention, as if the highest number of sexual encounters meant that I would win in the Olympic sport of 'being gay.'

"At one point during this period, I had accrued enough fuck buddies so that I didn't even have to leave my apartment. For several months, a different fuck buddy would come over each day of the week. There was Nick on Monday. Rodney on Tuesday. Tucker on Wednesday. David on Thursday. Michael on Friday. I had them on a schedule. These are their real names; I don't remember now if those were their days of the week. I met Nick while riding my bike through the Ramble in Central Park. He was Italian, he was great. I met Rodney at the gym, in the showers. He was a tall, blond baritone who went on to sing with the New York City Opera. I met Tucker in the back room at the International Stud. Michael I met at the pier. Nick was a school bus driver, and came over in the afternoon because he had a lover. Tucker was in graduate school at NYU, and came over at night. Rodney came over in the daytime, after his voice lessons. We'd talk for a while, smoke a joint, fuck, and shower. Or shower and fuck. They were all such lovely interludes. Such easy relationships."

But none of this activity prevented Gefter from going out at night.

"As a waiter at Berry's, I'd work from five to midnight. After my shift, I'd have several drinks at the bar, usually with Chuck, the chef, who became my cruising buddy. Chuck and I would go off into the night, often smoking a joint along the way, sometimes after taking drugs of every variety: cocaine, MDA, Quaaludes, and angel dust — which I rarely did because it numbed me, made me feel stupid, half-conscious, subhuman, unlike MDA, or THC, which made me feel alive, made everything seem to glisten, as if everything were outlined in electric pastels. I hated angel dust, but a lot of people used it. Chuck and I would begin our rounds at various bars. We'd arrive at the Ninth Circle to see who was there. We'd walk down Christopher Street, which was still lively at one o'clock in the morning. We'd hang out for a while at Keller's across the street from the Trucks, or the Cock Ring, where people would dance with handkerchiefs doused with ethyl chloride clenched between their teeth. Eventually, we'd wend our way up West Street to the Stud and to our inevitable destination, the Anvil."

The Anvil was an extraordinary establishment in the meatpacking district of the West Village, located on the two lower floors of a building at the corner of 14th Street and Eleventh Avenue. Tom Stoddard remembered its special "Weimar Germany" quality, which meant it sometimes felt a little bit like the cabaret in *Cabaret*. Upstairs, after 4:00 A.M., the closing time for regular bars, hundreds of gay men would move in waves around a bar decorated with go-go dancers, one of whom later became the Indian in the Village People. Downstairs customers checked their shirts, watched grainy porno movies, and had sex in a pitch-black back room. Pickpockets were a permanent fixture, prompting the shouted warning constantly repeated by one of the bouncers: "Gentlemen: watch your wallets!"

"I remember long lines to get in on Friday and Saturday nights," said Gefter, "and, sometimes, you'd see women on line masquerading as men. Women were not allowed inside, and there were always rumors that Bianca Jagger or Diane Von Furstenberg or Susan Sontag had been spotted there in disguise.

"The Anvil was my favorite bar in the entire world. It was what I imagined Weimar culture to be like — on acid. It seemed more like a club with a kind of festive, ersatz honky-tonk atmosphere than the dingy, seedy dive it appeared to be from the outside. Not that it wasn't seedy. It was. Dark, dank, dirty. Thank God the lights were out in the back room. I can't imagine what really lived and crawled on those floors in the vague light of day.

"When you entered the Anvil, you walked down a flight of stairs to the first level. What was so great was so much was going on at once. It was such a carnival — dancing men were parading around on top of the horseshoe bar, little red lights were strewn across the ceiling, as if it were always Christmas. There was always a pathetic little parody of a drag show on the little stage in the corner. And hundreds of men. It was always packed. The crowd ran the gamut from the most illustrious names in the press to the sleaziest people you would never want to meet. Of course, sometimes they're one and the same, but never mind. It was truly the most fabulous place.

"Sometimes I had sex in the back room at the Anvil, on the level below the first floor. I remember one evening which characterized a deep dark level of my sexual activity, the ninth circle of my sexual experience. Looking back at my twenties, after all that has since transpired, I'm grateful that I experienced that sexual freedom." Gefter felt he was representative of a time, "the beginning of homosexual identity in America," and "all of this made sense then.

"Anyway, Chuck and I had been making our usual rounds. Our drink of choice then was the Wild Turkey Manhattan, and we must have had more than a few of those that night. I'm sure we had smoked a few joints, and, maybe, popped a Quaalude, and ended up at the Anvil at four or five in the morning. Not unusual. I was in the back room having a grand old time. There was a ledge that ran the length of the back room, which I never actually saw, but people would lie on the ledge and get fucked. I remember this particular night, there I was lying on the ledge, my underpants and my jeans cradled in my armpit beside me, being fucked randomly by several different men. I could feel them one at a time inside me, even though I never saw them. Either I was truly liberated or truly psychotic. Who knows? But you know what William Blake said: 'The road of excess leads to the palace of wisdom.' All I know is, I was in heaven, and I learned a few things while I was there.

"That may have been the darkest moment of my sexual experience, but I had experienced pure animal pleasure. I was having the time of my life."

However, the Anvil was not the darkest meeting place in Manhattan in the period. Howard Rosenman thought, "The Anvil was like a bunch of fairies and a bunch of preppy boys having wild sex." The Mineshaft, also in the Manhattan meat district, was the most notorious meeting place of all. "The Mineshaft was a much more advanced thing," said Rosenman.

"Much darker. The visuals were darker. The music was darker. I went with Tony Perkins there. I took a lot of people there. It was great. It was the first place that I knew that you had to be dressed in a certain way. You had to be in dungarees. If you had anything else on, they wouldn't let you in. And it was really wanton, wild sex. It was really, really free. A lot of fist-fucking. And a lot of S and M. And a lot of just wild threesomes, foursomes, you know — untrammeled, psychopathia sexualis on Saturday night."

For most people, the Mineshaft went far beyond the boundaries they were willing to cross. "The people seemed crazy," said Tom Stoddard. "They all seemed like lapsed Catholics who were working out some deep personal issues, which most of them were — except for the Mormons and Orthodox Jews."

Rosenman also remembered "huge orgies" that would begin promptly at 6:00 P.M. in a loft on 14th Street:

"You would check your clothes in a bag. And you would wear boots and you'd put the little check in your boot and you would walk around naked. And there were like four hundred guys in a loft. This happened a lot. Marijuana, poppers, wine, and I think the beginning of cocaine and the beginning of those exotic drugs, MDMA and MDMMA and all. It later became much more ritualized, you know, in the midseventies. All of it. The powders and the pills. You had dealers all over the city and you got a form where you would check off your powders and pills, and everybody would have to come at a certain time on Friday. And they would walk into a room and there would be pills on this side and powders over there, and they would fill their order. A lot of that. That was fun. It was all fun. Then it stopped being fun. It became a job. It was too much work keeping up. How do you get high? How do you get that original high? But the scene was changing.

"The downtown thing was the new world. The Cockettes were the apotheosis of the downtown thing. Ahmet Ertegün had an evening where he invited all the uptown folk to go downtown to the Second Avenue theater. These San Francisco queens would have beards and long eyelashes and dress like fantastical women, with motorcycle jackets, and motorcycle boots on motorcycles. They were unbelievable. That's where Sister Mary Indulgence came from. She was in the Cockettes. And they had this moment, that was 1972, I think that was, the most glamorous thing that I had ever seen in my entire life: that particular evening when the Cockettes were performing downtown, and uptown came to downtown, and it was the mixture of Andy's world and the social world and the art world and the music world and the fashion world and the film world. And it was very very electrifying for me."

THE EFFECTS of the sexual revolution were hardly confined to the homosexual community in Manhattan. In the seventies, there was an explosion of massage parlors, thinly disguised brothels where scantily clad women satisfied their male customers. The going rate was $15 for half an hour. Gay Talese, who was already famous for his books about *The New York Times* (*The Kingdom and the Power*) and the Mafia (*Honor Thy Father*) decided that his next volume should be about sex, and he became the manager of two different massage parlors to research his subject.

The attitude of hip heterosexuals was suggested by Talese's willingness to let Aaron Latham accompany him to a massage parlor and chronicle his exploits in a lengthy feature in *New York* magazine. The story included the reactions of Talese's very understanding wife, Nan, a prominent New York book editor. Mrs. Talese explained that "she did not want to take a lover for every lover Gay had because to her sex was 'terribly private.'" But her husband had a very different point of view: "I want to get into my subject and I did," he said. "Getting head from an NYU student is not going to threaten a marriage of fourteen years."

Latham recorded this nude scene during his visit with Mr. Talese to the Fifth Season massage parlor on West 57th Street:

Amy reached out and took hold of Gay's penis as calmly as if it had been a pool cue. She was ready to play a new game.

"I'm going to tear it off," she said.

"I love it. I love it," he said. "Do it. I have dreams about it. I have fantasies about it."

Amy continued to tug gently at Gay as if his appendage were the knob of some reluctant bureau drawer.

Gay kidded, "Next time I work there [at another massage parlor] you can chain me and then whip me."

. . . Gay lounged beside the Fifth Season's pool like some decadent John the Baptist waiting for new believers to baptize. He welled with the fervor of someone new to the faith. He seemed to want everyone to dive head first into the wet, warm sexual revolution.

The frankness of Latham's account caused a sensation in the summer of 1973, but it was only one of the earliest indications of the similarities between the appetites of all kinds of sex-crazed New Yorkers. Five years

later, what had been the Continental Baths, a gay sex club where Bette
Midler made her debut entertaining comely men clad in towels,* meta-
morphosed into Plato's Retreat, exactly the same kind of establishment,
only this time for a heterosexual clientele. On December 26, 1978, the
club's owner, Larry Levenson, threw a Christmas party for the children of
club members and their friends. The *Times* reported that the children
(mostly in their late teens) did not look askance at their parents' behavior.

TOM STODDARD had grown up in upper-middle-class white suburbs all
over the Midwest, "very much a repressive culture." In 1970, he had graduated from Georgetown University in Washington. During college, he "felt
lonely and confused" and he knew he "wanted to meet men, but I would
have rejected them if I had met them." But he did meet an important role
model, a straight student who contributed to Stoddard's decision to get
involved in politics. Eventually, Stoddard would become one of the gay
movement's most thoughtful and effective activists, writing the gay civil
rights law for New York City, running the Lambda Legal Defense and
Education Fund for six years beginning in 1986, and serving as an adjunct
professor at the New York University School of Law from 1981 to 1997.

One of Stoddard's earliest role models was two years ahead of him at
Georgetown. He was "very cute," and Stoddard had a crush on him.

His name was Bill Clinton. "That's one of the reasons I've remembered
him for twenty years," Stoddard recalled. "He was also an appropriate role
model for me because he was smart, he was political and he was very well
known. He ran for office at Georgetown, and he made a friend of everybody he met, a quality he's kept. I knew him not only because he went to
Georgetown. We were both in the School of Foreign Service and he also
worked on Capitol Hill, on the Senate side, which I did. He worked for
[William] Fulbright, his U.S. senator, and I worked for Chuck Percy, my
U.S. senator. So we met through the Capitol Hill connection as much as
anything else. Particularly when he won the Rhodes Scholarship, I was in
awe.

"He was handsome, he was very well liked, he was political. And, I
thought, here is the person I would like to be. When he got the Rhodes
Scholarship, I thought, Well, he can get anything he wants. What's remarkable about him is that he's not a bad person. Most people who are that
ambitious really are bad people."

Stoddard thought that working for Bill Fulbright, the Arkansas senator

*Barry Manilow backed her up on piano.

who was one of the earliest and most vocal opponents of the war in Vietnam, was an especially important experience for Clinton. "That was very good for him because Fulbright was a principled, very smart politician who did what he did because of certain principles. And he wrote about them. He was a scholar as well. The Vietnam War in a sense produced a healthy Bill Clinton because he was forced very early, as I was, to confront the issue."

Stoddard was also smart, political, and very good looking, although he considered himself "very shy and very fearful," shortcomings he overcame by thrusting himself into hostile environments.

In the winter of 1970, he moved to New York, at the age of twenty-two. He had worried that he might be gay since he had been a high school student outside Chicago in 1965, and he had gone to the biggest bookstore he could find to look for an appropriate volume in the psychology section. The two books he found were by Charles Socarides and Irving Bieber, two of the most homophobic psychiatrists in America. "Both of them took the position that not only was homosexuality wrong, but that 'single status' was wrong. Bieber's belief was that bachelors were inherently disturbed people, regardless of their sexual orientation. I read these books, they sounded plausible to me, I believed them, and then I hid them in the house." And during college, he never had sex with a man.

When he moved to New York, he lived in an apartment a half a block from one of the main gay cruising areas of that era — Central Park West and 72d Street. "It was dangerously close." So the first time Stoddard's roommate went away for the weekend, he picked someone up and brought him back to his apartment. "That was my first sexual experience. And it was extremely unpleasant and painful, as most of these stories run. He fucked me. I had never imagined that people did such things, yet was too young and too fearful to say no. I just found it painful as well as bizarre. I decided that if that was what gay men did, then I wasn't gay. I remember how old he was because he seemed so old to me. In 1970 I was twenty-two and he was thirty."

Stoddard waited a year before he repeated the experience, and the second time was a little better. But then he decided to retreat from Manhattan temporarily, and he moved to Minneapolis, where he worked for the American Field Service, a student exchange program.

"Minneapolis is much colder than anyone can possibly imagine. I would occasionally give myself frostbite because I didn't know how to behave in that cold weather. But one of the consequences of that cold weather was to accentuate my sense of loneliness. I would sit in my apartment by myself, feeling very cold. I was quirky then in some ways similar to the way I'm quirky now: I didn't turn the radiators on enough in the apartment. I believed it was a waste of energy and the building was overheated anyway. I thought I would just receive the heat from the other apartments. I did this the entire winter. What I was doing was driving myself into a gay bar. I'm quite serious. At some point I wanted to make myself so uncomfortable that I had to make a change and do something that was otherwise frightening."

He had noticed a lot of men going into a downtown bar called Sutton Place, so he drove there and sat in his car for an hour until he got up the courage to go in. "It was probably the most important event of my life. I got out of the car, I locked it, and I walked into the bar. I'm *sure* that I had my head down because that's what I do when I'm really frightened. I walked in and I heard this extraordinary music. That was the first thing I remember. It was the beginning of disco. I remember hearing Barry White's "Love Unlimited." That is my coming-out song. I opened the door, and all of a sudden here was all this activity, this bizarre music that I would not have heard on the radio or anywhere else, and I thought that I had entered another universe. I sidled up to the bar, ordered a beer, with my head down, drank the beer, and the bartender would occasionally say things to me, which frightened me, and went back home. The next night, I went back and met a man who became my first boyfriend. I also met, through him, his roommate and a whole host of people who became my first community of gay friends. Within about a week, I had joined the Minnesota Committee for Gay Rights. It was easy for me at that point because I was more of a human being, apart from my sexuality, than most other people at that level because I had done a lot and knew who I was. So it was fairly easy once I figured out my sexuality."

In Minneapolis, he met his second role model, a man named Howard Brown, who had served in New York City as Mayor John Lindsay's first health services administrator. In 1973, he caused a sensation when he announced that he was gay, and that he intended to become a "militant homosexual" who would march and lobby for the gay civil rights bill, which remained bottled up in the New York City Council.*

Just after Brown's disclosure had made the front page of *The New York Times*, he came to Minneapolis to address the Minnesota Committee for Gay Rights, and Stoddard was immediately "enthralled" by him: "He was

*Four years later, in 1977, Robert L. Livingston became the first gay activist appointed to the New York City Human Rights Commission by Mayor Abraham Beame.

a wonderful speaker. A stirring speaker. Funny, expansive, inspirational, and he was from 'my city' because I knew at this point I was going back to New York. He was a learned, successful person, and a political person. It's clear to me why he was so attractive to me. Here was someone from my world, from the east, who could be a role model for me, and who was gay. Openly gay! Such a thing never occurred to me, and I was in a trance that entire day. I ended up going to a party held for him, given at the home of Allan Spear, a state senator who was also openly gay. I believe he was the first openly gay legislator in the United States. He's still in the state legislature. He teaches history. He's a wonderful man. At any rate, I went to this party that night and met a whole additional group of people and got to hear Howard Brown tell personal stories of life in New York. It was my first hearing of the term *fist-fucking,* which they all talked about with great energy. At the time, I couldn't understand what was so novel about it because I thought it was simply another word for masturbation. Only later when I moved back to New York did I understand why all the commotion. That party was a very important event for me. In some degree I patterned my own speeches after Brown's."

In 1974, Stoddard moved back to Manhattan to attend New York University Law School. And he did not find gay culture to be merely hedonistic:

"It was in the largest sense exploratory. That's really the key to understanding it. For me it was an exploration of sex, but it was also an exploration of relationships: casual relationships, friendships, and deeply felt romantic relationships. I could only begin to piece together my emotional life through that exploration. Gay men, at that time in particular, had no avenue of self-discovery apart from trial and error. And I made a lot of tries, and a lot of errors."

He rarely went to the baths, partly because he thought men clothed in towels offered too little information about who they were. "Part of the interesting thing about sexual relationships is figuring out who somebody is in the larger sense: what they think, what they do, how they react to the world. Part of that has to do with the clothes that they wear, the class in which they grew up. And those are things that are hard to figure out at the baths. There aren't as many games and there isn't as much complexity to a bathhouse."

At the same time Stoddard was beginning to develop his voice as an activist. When Herbert Hendin wrote about "homosexuality and the family" in *The New York Times* in the summer of 1975, Stoddard fired off a letter to the editor. "A piece as sloppy, ill-reasoned and inhumane as

Herbert Hendin's demands rebuttal," Stoddard wrote. "For Hendin, homosexuals are like alcoholics. They deserve pity and help, but their way of life demands censure. In order to preserve Hendin's notions of what is healthy behavior and what is not, they must continue to live as social misfits."

The following year Stoddard was infuriated when the United States Supreme Court summarily affirmed a lower court ruling that upheld Virginia's sodomy statute. The court acted without hearing arguments or issuing an opinion. Justices William J. Brennan, Jr., Thurgood Marshall and John Paul Stevens dissented from the six-to-three ruling.

Chief Justice Warren Burger was scheduled to visit the NYU Law School right after the decision was announced, and Stoddard joined forces with his friend Peter Kazaras to convince eight professors and seven other students to write Burger a letter of protest about the sodomy case.

The letter was firm but polite. It argued that the Court's latest action was an unwarranted departure from other recent decisions that affirmed privacy rights, including *Roe* v. *Wade,* the landmark abortion case of 1974, in which the Court "recognized the importance of personal privacy and autonomy with regard to sexual matters. We appreciate that a summary affirmance probably does not reflect the Court's considered judgment on this issue; nevertheless, the disposition of [the sodomy case] can be read to indicate that the right of sexual privacy does not extend to homosexuals."

"The case made me really angry," said Stoddard. "By that time, I was quite political, I was very interested in constitutional law. I was very proud of that. It was professional, it was lawyerly, and it was quite stirring. It was a dramatic thing to do, particularly for law students. We had convinced our teachers that they should go along with us."

Stoddard did everything "with the quiet conviction that all he was seeking was what was just and fair," said his close friend Rich Meislin. "When he went into his 'we hold these truths to be self-evident' mode, people listened. Change happened." He was also, in his own way, a subversive "because he looked like what every mother wanted her son to be — and he was unabashedly gay."

The other important event during his law school career was Stoddard's application for a Civil Liberties fellowship at NYU as an openly gay person. He believed he was the first person who had ever done that. And he was accepted. It was a scholarship and an internship, and he ended up at the New York Civil Liberties Union, where he eventually worked for eight years. "I guess I'm still connected because I'm on the Board of ACLU.

"That experience made clear to me that I wanted to be a public interest lawyer. I feel great passion about this program at NYU because of what it did to me." In 1995, the program established a fellowship in Stoddard's name to farm out law students to work for gay organizations.

"Sometimes the things that are best for us are the things that we most avoid. It took me a long time to figure things out, but once I did it was absolutely clear to me. There were certain steps along the way, including activism and law school that moved me in this direction.

"But I'm very grateful for being gay. It's my salvation: it's my escape from an ordinary life that would have made me unhappy. Otherwise I would be living in the suburbs because I am by nature a strange combination of rebel and conservative."

THE FIRST PLACE that hip Manhattan patronized to pay public homage to the glitzy part of the gay world of the seventies was an abandoned television studio that had been built as an opera house a half century earlier. When it opened in 1977, its location was the least fashionable one could imagine: 254 West 54th Street, near Eighth Avenue, on the fringes of the theater district, twelve blocks north of the Port Authority Bus Terminal.

Technically, only Thursdays and Sundays were "gay nights," but the crowd was always very mixed — and progressively gayer every night after 2:00 A.M. The bar stopped serving booze at 4:00, and the club closed at 6:00.

Studio 54 was the brainchild of Steve Rubell, the thirty-three-year-old gay owner of a string of suburban steak houses who survived the demise of his first discotheque in Queens to become the most famous nightspot impresario of his generation.

Rubell had a straight partner, Ian Schrager, but it was the five-foot, six-inch Rubell who was out front every night, deciding who was cool enough to get in, carefully excluding all the men in "double-knit three-piece suits" and favoring "dancers and Broadway actors" because "they're loose and fluid."

"I look at it like casting for a play," Rubell explained. "A year ago, I wouldn't have let myself in," an ironic reference to his own "bridge and tunnel" origins. His goal was to make it not too straight and not too gay: "we want it to be bisexual."

Frank Rich wondered in *Esquire* if the nightclub owner's behavior was "the revenge of the nerd." Watching Rubell in action, "one could imagine that he was getting back at the cool crowd of his own suburban high school — the handholding jocks and cheerleaders who might have tyrannically ruled his senior prom. . . . Whatever their actual sexuality, the stars who passed through Studio 54 achieved the ultimate status: they could emulate the gay night life . . . Rubell hooked his civilian heterosexual admittees by allowing them to become, for a night, vicarious members of a club that did not want them."

Rubell and Schrager had very similar backgrounds. Both of them grew up in East Flatbush, a working-class section of Brooklyn; both of them attended Syracuse University and both of them were fraternity brothers at Sigma Alpha Mu. The first model for their future extravaganza was Le Jardin, a gay disco in the basement of the rundown Diplomat Hotel, which Schrager remembered as "overwhelming . . . like a Sodom and Gomorrah." Schrager saw Bianca Jagger there, and he knew that was the kind of person he wanted at his own club. Later, Rubell dated Studio's takeoff to the night that Bianca rented it for Mick's thirty-fourth birthday.

Depending on which story you read, Rubell and his partners had invested $1.1 million *(New York Times)*, $800,000 *(People)*, or $400,000 *(Money)* to install four hundred separate light programs, long leather couches, a man in the moon with a (coke) spoon who descended from the ceiling, and a constantly changing decor, ranging from a recreation of Peking for restaurateur Michael Chow's birthday party to a farm with pigs, goats and sheep for Dolly Parton — all of which produced an atmosphere that Rubell boasted was "something out of Fellini." The club could handle two thousand revelers at a time.

Howard Rosenman was there the first night the club opened. He thought Rubell "had an impeccable eye about guys and about fame and celebrity and power. And he was able to arbitrate and calibrate levels of power, taste, charisma, glamour, chic, looks, talent, and sexual desirability — in an instant."

Rubell himself attributed his success to two factors: a "need to be liked and accepted," and a lifelong competition with an older brother who had "a higher IQ," had become "a successful gynecologist," and was "even nine inches taller than I am."

Inside the club were Andy Warhol, Bianca Jagger, Halston, Liza Minnelli, Margaux Hemingway, Michael Jackson, Farrah Fawcett, Warren Beatty, O. J. Simpson, Moshe Dayan, Gina Lollabrigida, and Baryshnikov — and anyone close to Roy Cohn, because Cohn was the lawyer for Rubell and Schrager, a fact that fueled never-confirmed rumors that the club was close to the Mob. Titled Europeans did not impress Rubell: "Turn some of these princes and princesses upside down and you'd be lucky if 25 cents dropped out," he said. "They're sort of like loss leaders."

In 1978, Cohn's connection to the discotheque — the "hot spot of the universe" as Ethan Geto remembered it, or "the greatest club of all time," in rock impresario Ahmet Ertegün's estimation — was a crucial element in the lawyer's influence peddling in Manhattan. It was also tremendously ironic: the easiest way to get into the most fashionable gay-run nightspot on the planet was to befriend one of the most self-hating gay men in America. To show their disdain, most of Cohn's legions of enemies never entered Studio 54 at all. A feeling of moral superiority amply compensated them for their absence.

Cohn's law partner, Stanley M. Friedman, remembered the scene this way: "Roy would have an entourage of boys and, quote, legitimate people: clients, friends, political figures. It was Hollywood. Here are people from normal walks of life, going out at midnight. The music was blaring, the lights were blitzing, dozens of beautiful people dancing. Men and women, men and men. Crazy clothes some of them: the tight clothes, the cutoff clothes. The bar: six deep, people getting drinks. I didn't see the coke snorting in the bathrooms. Roy was treated like royalty — Steve and Ian and Andy Warhol and whatever other beautiful people or jet-setters he would be with.

"You know how many phone calls we would get in a week? 'I'm coming into New York, can you get me into Studio 54?' They don't want to go in the front door, so they go in the back door on 53d. Go in there and your name will be on the list. That was a premium. There wasn't a day that went by that we didn't get a call. I mean, if you gave somebody a couple of bars of gold bullion, it wouldn't be as good.

"When they started off, the place was empty, and they had a line two blocks long outside, creating the impression they were full. They wouldn't let anybody in. And then they'd say, 'You, all right *you*, in the back, you can go in.' They knew how to market," said Friedman. *Times* reporter Robert McG. Thomas, Jr., who covered Studio 54's opening, remembered that this tactic of keeping the lines long regardless of how crowded it was inside began on the very first night.

Like many others, Ethan Geto resisted going to Studio 54 because he didn't want to risk being rejected at the front door. And he certainly wasn't going to drop the name of Roy Cohn, the embodiment of evil to anyone with Geto's convictions. But an out-of-town friend finally convinced him to test his luck:

"There's these mobs of people trying to get in, including a lot of the beautiful people: people that are so chic and stylish and gorgeous and models and show business people. And I'm way in the back of the crowd.

And I'm saying to the people I'm with, 'Let's get outta here. Let's go somewhere else.' And all of the sudden, from the door, comes a voice that yells out, 'Let that tall guy in back there! Get the tall guy!' And these monstrous bouncers come, like Paul Bunyan.

"I get up to the door. And there's this guy who was the head doorman named Marc Benecke. And Marc says, 'Are you Ethan Geto?'

"I said, 'Yeah, I am.'

"He says, 'Don't you remember me?'"

Geto did not, but Marc remembered the pol very well because Marc was a political junkie who had known Geto in several Democratic campaigns, including Bella Abzug's run for the Senate in 1976. "Marc had been a political groupie as a kid," said Geto. "And all he ever cared about, before he got to this great elevated stage in life, was politics. Bob Abrams and Bella Abzug were the big people in his life."

So Marc told Geto he could get in for free any night of the week. "From that day on, it was the greatest thing in the world. I went to Studio 54 five hundred times. I didn't have to pay to get in [the cover was $10 on weekends]. Inside it was an enormous amount of drugs. People used to do cocaine openly. They had a lounge upstairs. You walked up a flight of stairs, and there was, like, a plateau before you walked around to the balcony. And all kinds of things went on in the balcony," where the Rubber Bar was located.

"You would sit around in this lounge and people would just put lines of cocaine out. This wasn't the VIP lounge! This was an open, public lounge with a massive amount of pedestrian traffic and people sitting around drinking and talking. And in the middle of this lounge was a big, black, glossy table. And people would put lines of cocaine on the table and take $100 bills, and just lean over the table and start snorting. And one day, a top political consultant was leaning over the table, snorting the cocaine. Gets tapped on the shoulder by a young city councilman. And the council-man says, 'You shouldn't be doin' that in public.'"

Philip Gefter remembered arriving one night in a group of four and immediately giving up on getting in because of the size of the crowd. "We started to lean against a car to decide where to go next, when all of a sudden the ropes parted and the doorman pointed at us and we were in — and it was only because of our insouciance that he noticed us. God knows I did a lot of things there. But I could have been there every Thursday night and I still felt like an outsider: that I was missing out on the epicen-ter of activity."

As well as movie stars on the dance floor, there were future movie stars eager to serve them. Waiters at Studio 54 were beautiful boys of about twenty with prominent muscles, satin gym shorts, tennis shoes — and no shirts. Bartenders were slightly older, in black tank tops and blue jeans. In 1978, Alec Baldwin was a twenty-one-year-old waiter in the balcony at Studio 54.

Was he hit on continuously by members of both sexes?

"Usually men," Baldwin remembered.

"Gay men would go up to the balcony and fondle one another. Usually couples. Very distinguished, wealthy, well-dressed, *well-heeled* gay men would go up to the balcony and 'discuss things.' And they'd ask your boy here to go downstairs and, quote unquote, 'fetch them' a pack of cigarettes. They'd give me $10 and I'd get a pack of cigarettes. Cigarettes at Studio 54 were probably like *eight* dollars. And they'd say, 'Well, keep the change.'

"I was a very popular cigarette snatcher in the balcony," said Baldwin. "I was the Rick Blaine* of well-heeled homosexual balcony dwellers at Studio 54."

Naturally, Howard Rosenman was a frequent customer at the discotheque. "You needed something to get in: You needed either good looks or brilliance or talent or a big dick or big tits or money or social cachet. Or Roy Cohn's friendship. When you walked in, there was that incredible lobby, brightly lit, like a movie theater lobby, ornate and mirrored. Then you walked through those grandiose, glamorous doors, like theater doors, and you came on a space that was dark. The coat check was over on the right, and then there were the steps going up in front of you. Slightly to the left was the bar, the dance floor in front of it, and in back of the dance floor, in the fly and scrim area of the old stage, was a VIP area. It wasn't a room — it was separated by curtains and stanchions and guards. They wouldn't let you in unless you were one of the chosen. On the second-floor balcony there was another VIP area. Finally, there was the sanctum sanctorum, which was downstairs.

"Steve would ask you to go down those stairs. It was a grovelly, horrible little basement, where Liza and Andy and Halston and Calvin and Diane and Barry and David and the chicest women and tricks galore and Elsa Peretti and Marina Schiano would be."

It was also where Rubell handed out drugs to anyone who wanted them.

"Oh yes: Just handed you a bottle of Quaaludes, or handed you a bottle of cut blow. He got those huge shipments of giant Quaaludes. He was always botsy out of his mind on Quaaludes. [But] there was something

---

*The proprietor of Rick's in *Casablanca*.

about him everybody loved. He had that club and he had that power and he had all that connection to Halston. Above all, he was very generous to those he liked."

But the "Roy Cohn thing" was "scary," Rosenman remembered: "I'll never forget. There was a bartender at 54, he was Armenian, and he was preternaturally beautiful. One night he asked me to wait for him. I went to his home in New Jersey and spent the whole night there. We had an incredible time. And the next morning he said, 'Let's fly into Manhattan.' He had a biplane. He flew me down the Hudson, all the way around Manhattan Island, and it was unbelievably romantic. And I was on the moon."

But the next night Calvin Klein took Rosenman aside when he noticed he was about to leave with the bartender again.

"Very gently, Calvin said to me, 'I don't think you should do this again.'"

"Why?" asked Rosenman.

"Because that's Roy Cohn's boyfriend," Klein explained. "And if you want to have cement wedgies on your feet when you wake up in the Hudson tomorrow morning . . ."

"Who knew?" said Rosenman. "The Roy Cohn thing wasn't my scene." Rosenman did not leave with the bartender again that night, nor did he fly down the Hudson the next day.

Everything about the ambience of Studio 54 made it the antithesis of the spirit of the sixties. There was certainly nothing democratic about it. Frank Rich remembered that "to be there as a peon, as I was on a few occasions, was to feel that the Continental Baths crowd had finally turned nasty toward the intruding straights and was determined to make them pay (with overpriced drinks and condescending treatment). Even as everyone was telling you that this was where the action was, you felt that the real action, not all of it appetizing, was somewhere in the dark periphery, out of view — and kept there, to make you feel left out."

The excluded establishment took its revenge on Rubell and Schrager at the end of 1978 when a squad of Internal Revenue agents descended on the club, seized its records, and arrested Schrager for cocaine possession. Federal agents told reporters that they had raided the club because they believed it had been financed by the Mob, an accusation that Cohn heatedly denied. But six months later Rubell and Schrager were indicted on twelve counts of "systematically" skimming $2.5 million — or more than sixty percent of the club's daily receipts during its first two years.

Their first ploy to get the charges dropped against them was to offer up someone more important than themselves to the Feds. The club owners alleged that the presidential aide Hamilton Jordan had used cocaine at Studio 54. Federal officials immediately told reporters that they were dubious about this information, but the accusation still led to the appointment of a special prosecutor, a very lengthy investigation, and Jordan's eventual exoneration. After that strategy had failed, Rubell and Schrager pled guilty to charges of tax evasion. Both men were sentenced to three and a half years in jail after conceding that they had evaded more than $400,000 in taxes.

Ethan Geto was at Studio 54 for the farewell party in February 1980, just before Schrager and Rubell went to jail. Rubell said good-bye from a mechanical platform which held him and Bianca Jagger above the dance floor. "They stopped everything in the place," Geto remembered. "And Steve was coked out of his mind. And Bianca was hugging him, and he was saying, 'I love you people! I love you people! I don't know what I'm gonna do without Studio!' And everyone was crying and weeping." Diana Ross was there, and Liza Minnelli sang "New York, New York."

Later the club owners' sentences were reduced to twenty months after they cooperated with another investigation that revealed widespread fraud among their competitors in the discotheque industry. During their prison visit, the club was sold to the hotel owner Mark Fleischman. It closed in 1983.

FIVE YEARS AFTER young muscle boys had become standard-issue Studio 54 waiters, Calvin Klein brought this aesthetic into the mainstream with his first underwear ads, most of them photographed by Bruce Weber. Then he went further with a huge billboard of a young man who looked to many like a forty-five-by-forty-eight-foot gay pinup in the heart of Times Square. Klein had "consummated the country's previously unheard-of love affair with the male torso," as Frank Rich put it.

It *was* a consummation, but it was hardly "unheard of." It had started with Brando's bare chest on Broadway in 1947, accelerated through Elvis and the Beatles, and reached its first culmination with Mick Jagger's bare-chested (and bisexual) looks and leaps.

"The gay physical ideal, once rigidly enforced by the culture, could be as cruel to those who didn't match it as straight conformity was to gays," Rich wrote. "The Klein style excluded unpretty men, zaftig women, the imperfect, the overweight, the square." What had been a magnificently inclusive culture in the sixties suddenly seemed very exclusive indeed. "As had also been true of the discos that restricted entry to the gay and the pretty, there was a scent of fascistic decadence to the Klein ads," Rich believed. "The least appealing aspect of gay aesthetics, the obsession with a standardized perfection of surface beauty, could be dynamite in the hands of the heterosexual majority. Such a rigidly enforced code of prettiness aroused nightmare visions of a latter-day master race."

Rich's observations, which appeared in *Esquire* at the end of 1987, split the gay community in Manhattan down the middle. Those who had embraced the Calvin Klein–Fire Island aesthetic found them offensive, but those who still clung to the more democratic ideal of the sixties were delighted by his plainspeaking.

AT THE BEGINNING of the seventies, Hal Offen invited Ethan Geto to come visit the Gay Activists Alliance headquarters in the former New York City firehouse at 99 Wooster Street in SoHo, before gentrification had converted the neighborhood into a colony of artists, and later, stockbrokers. Geto was nervous because he was still firmly in the closet. "I said, 'I can't go down there. People'll think I'm, you know, I'm, uh, I'm gay!' And he says, 'Well, aren't you?' And then I said, 'Well, let's talk outside of the office.'"

Geto made an appointment to meet Offen, and the activist picked him up in his Volkswagen after work. Geto decided to tell him the truth, but he didn't get exactly the reaction he was looking for. "I said, 'Well, I think I'm gay.'"

"And he says, 'I knew it! No straight person would ever support us! You were too sympathetic!' He was so disappointed in one way.

"So I came out to Hal. He was the first person I ever came out to in a political context." Offen continued to want Geto to come to GAA headquarters, but Geto was still living with his wife and two children. So he asked Offen to tell all his friends that Geto was really heterosexual: "You have to tell everybody that this is your straight, political friend who's coming down because he's a sympathetic liberal who knows city hall and knows New York politics. He works for the Bronx borough president."

Geto was very assertive in the GAA meetings; he knew he was a political hotshot and never hesitated to act like one. In 1972 he was tapped to help run George McGovern's New York campaign for president, and McGovern swept the New York primary. "I was one of the leading strategists in the whole Democratic reform movement." And he told the gay activists, "No! Ya gotta do this! No! Here's what you tell Mayor Lindsay! No! You go there! I knew what I was talking about. I was in politics."

But GAA president Jim Owles was not amused. He rose at a meeting to declare, "I'm sick and tired of straight people coming down here and telling us what we should do! We shouldn't listen to straight people! Even if they're friends. We should be doing this ourselves! Gay people should be telling gay people what to do!"

When Offen drove Geto home that evening, Geto was crying: "They don't want me. They hate me. They think I'm straight. I'm being disingenuous. I'm in the closet. It's disgusting. I'm not being brave. I'm not coming out. I can't live with myself anymore. So I said, 'OK, Hal. The next time you're down there, just go around quietly, and say, 'He's really gay.' So Hal told everybody that I was gay. And then I came down to the firehouse and came out."

In 1972, Geto came out to his wife. She was devastated, and he agreed to move out. He told McGovern that he needed a place to stay. Fortunately, two of the candidate's supporters were the owners of the Plaza Hotel. "So I go to McGovern and I say, 'Look, I need a place to live and I don't have any money. I'm splitting up with my wife.'" McGovern called his friends at the Plaza and for the next six months Geto was living in a suite: "I'm twenty-nine years old. I've left my wife. I'm going down every night to the trucks down on West Street and picking up guys. Bringing them back to the Plaza Hotel. I was impressing these guys. Everyone's dressed in leather and chains and this is 1972. And I'm marching them into the Plaza. And I'm working for McGovern."

The trucks were parked in Greenwich Village, and the trailers were left open between trips. At night, they were pitch-black inside, and filled with men having sex. "I totally disappeared into the gay subculture, culturally, socially, and sexually," said Geto. "That's it! My straight life is over. I'm totally gay. I'm going to be gay for the rest of my life. I went to all the back room bars, the trucks, the Continental Baths — the whole thing."

He was also extremely active politically. Two of his best friends were Morty Manford, a founder of the gay students organization at Columbia who became president of the Gay Activists Alliance, and Bruce Voeller, who left GAA to help found the National Gay Task Force. "Bruce was in GAA and he thought GAA had become, by 1973, too ideological, dogmatic, left-wing, fringy, too militant, too radical for him. We were never going to change America. We were never going to get legislation in Congress, unless we had a respectable mainstream civil rights organization like the NAACP. So Bruce led a walkout from GAA. He got up on the floor in GAA, and said, 'Anybody that wants to meet with me so that we can have a mainstream NAACP-like civil rights organization. We're having fun here making ourselves feel good with all these zaps and militant actions. But no one recognizes us. No one takes us seriously. We're a fringe group. We have to have professional staff, fund-raising, lobbyists!'"

GAA had no staff, but it had a fine sense of theater and a knack for gaining the attention of the media. "It was really the ACT UP of its time," said Geto. "So Voeller founded the NGTF, and he and Jean O'Leary became the first co–executive directors. It was in New York at 80 Fifth Ave. Morty Manford and my crowd were on the GAA side."

In 1972, Manford asked his mother Jeanne to march in the third annual Gay Pride March in June. She agreed, but only if she could carry a sign. It read "Parents of Gays Unite in Support for Our Children." As she walked along, people on the sidewalk ran up to her, kissed her, and exclaimed, "Will you talk to my mother?" Dr. Benjamin Spock was marching right behind her. "The outpouring of emotion from our community was overwhelming," Manford told Eric Marcus. "No one else got the loud emotional cheers that she did." The following year, Dr. and Mrs. Manford held a meeting with other gay parents at the Metropolitan Duane Methodist Church and founded the organization that became Parents and Friends of Lesbians and Gays, now one of the largest and most effective pro-gay organizations in America.

Jeff Katzoff, who had known Manford at Columbia University as well as through the Gay Activists Alliance, remembered a party at the Manfords' soon after Mrs. Manford publicly embraced her son. "We all trudged out to Queens," Katzoff remembered. "It was a lovely, nice big suburban-type house, and we had a big sort of like graduation. And Morty's aunts were there helping his mother. And she had food for days, and Morty's father was there. It was just wonderful. I remember the overwhelming feeling was, I wish I could have parents like this. I now do, but it took twenty years to get them."

Frank Kameny had not come out to his mother until 1967 — just before he appeared in the CBS documentary "The Homosexuals." Seven years later Kameny was in New York for the annual Gay Pride March and arranged to have his mother come in from Queens to watch the procession from the sidewalk at 50th Street. "She saw for the first time that parents of gays marched — Morty Manford and Jeanne Manford," said Kameny. "I knew Morty very well and I knew Jeanne. And very hesitantly, because she had no idea what my reaction would be, my mother said, 'Would you mind if I contacted them?' And I said 'Fine! Go ahead.'" So Kameny's mother called Jeanne Manford, who became the center of her social life. "She went to meetings," Kameny remembered. "At that time it was Parents of Gays. It ultimately became PFLAG. She was one of their referral people. She used to get calls from people and advise them. And it worked out extremely well. I never had to come to New York anymore. My mother used to march for me in the Gay Pride March. And they always used to put her in a limousine or sometimes they would have a truck. She marched in style, and got all the applause. And I could stay home at the Washington demonstration."

THE WOOSTER STREET FIREHOUSE functioned as the first gay community center in Manhattan. Philip Gefter remembered political meetings "packed to the gills: I remember being *amazed* that there were that many homosexuals." Arthur Laurents was dragged to one by his lover, Tom Hatcher. "I walked in, and I thought, 'Oh my God, I'm back with the lefties.' I mean, there was no difference. The beards and the leather jackets and the point of order and the furious lesbians and parliamentary procedure. And humorless. No theatricality except for a transvestite named Marsha. She was famous. She swam over from Rikers Island. Really. She was a black guy with women's hair, a tunic, blue jeans, and big boots. And he carried on: 'You know what? Neither one of you want any part of us.' He was quite right. Neither the gays nor the lesbians. 'We embarrass you. If you're really for freedom, you've got to include us.' And he was right. But it was tough."

There were also weekly dances that were wonderfully democratic events. Jeff Katzoff remembered that the dances took place on the ground floor with a "very high ceiling because they had space for fire trucks. So it wasn't at all claustrophobic, though it got pretty sweaty in there when it got crowded. I remember the incredible energy on that dance floor. There were hundreds and hundreds of people; at some point you could not move. And I used to go up to the second or third floor just to escape the mob. Then there was a very claustrophobic basement, where you checked your coat and they had sodas. I used to work one of those concessions occasionally. And there was a second floor, above the main floor, that had administration offices. And then there was another floor above that. And that floor had a big lounge, and during the dances, that's where Vito Russo used to show films that he used to make of zaps. I used to watch them to get away from the craziness once in a while, just to chill out."

One Saturday night Ethan Geto was on his way to the firehouse when he got behind a group of people on the street who were looking for a bathroom. "This was before SoHo was SoHo," said Geto. "This was when SoHo was totally an industrial district. And it was gloomy and dark and foreboding. And in this one place, in the middle of this block on Saturday night, all of a sudden you hear this thumping disco music! And you see dozens of people streaming in and they're milling around out on the sidewalk and smoking cigarettes.

"So someone in this group says, 'Oh, there's a place!' And I'm walking in right behind this guy 'cause I'm going to the dance. His friends are a mixed crowd of straight people. They stay outside and he goes up to the door of the firehouse. And I'm right behind him. And he says, 'Hey! Ya got a bathroom in here?' And the guy supervising the door says, 'That'll be two dollars.' And he says, 'Yeah, but I'm not comin' in here to dance. I don't even know what this is. What is this here?' And the guy at the door says, 'This is the headquarters of the Gay Activists Alliance.' And the other guy says, 'Oh. Well, ya got a bathroom?'

"And this voice sounds so familiar to me. So I sort of lean over because he's right in front of me, and it's Bob Dylan. And the guy at the door doesn't recognize Bob Dylan! So Bob Dylan says, 'Hey, listen, man! You're a gay place in here? Aren't you gays supposed to be for the people!' So the guy at the door, some grungy guy, says, 'Hey, listen. Anybody could come in here and say they want to go to the bathroom. We need money to support this organization! Two fucking dollars or beat it!' Bob Dylan says, 'Wait a minute. You say this is the gay activist group here! Aren't you, like, radical people?!' So finally Bob Dylan in total disgust throws his two dollars on the table, and says to him, 'Fuck you!' and heads for the bathroom. And I walk in, and I say, *That's Bob Dylan!*'

"And this guy says, 'I don't care if it's the fucking queen of England!'"

After Geto left his wife, he moved in with Morty Manford on 14th Street. They were very close friends — not lovers — and they were "working day and night on gay rights politics, very militant stuff."

But Geto was still "totally in the closet to the straight world — to my career and in politics. I was totally hiding. And when Abrams would come over to the apartment, which he did often, I would put away anything that was gay, like magazines, or a gay calendar. It was really nerve-racking. And I'd tell my roommate, the famous Manhattan gay leader, Morty Manford, not to be there. It was really very upsetting and you felt sleazy. It was very unpleasant, the closet of that period. Or any period. Or anybody that feels they have to be in one."

In 1973, the Bronx Democratic machine mounted a big effort to get rid of Abrams and recapture the patronage of the borough president's office, and Geto took a leave of absence from his job as Abrams's press secretary to become his campaign manager. In June, they beat the machine and won the primary election. Now Geto was urging Abrams to run for state attorney general in 1974. But he could not go on without telling his boss the whole truth about his life.

"We sat down on a bench in City Hall Park, right outside city hall. He had no idea what I was going to tell him. And I made a big deal of it, like 'it's real serious.' So he says, 'Go ahead, what's on your mind?'

"I'll never forget this as long as I live. I said, 'All right, Bob, here's the story. I'm gay. And not only am I gay, I'm a gay activist. And I've been working with the Gay Activists Alliance, secretly, for the last two years. Now you are about to run for attorney general. You and I have had a terrific professional relationship for these three years. I admire you and I want to continue to work for you and be associated with you and manage your career in politics, but I will resign if you want me to. I don't think someone should resign a job because they're gay. I don't think there's anything bad about being gay.' And I said, 'Look, I'll tell you what I will do and what I won't do. I won't be an open, public spokesperson for the gay rights movement because it's inconsistent with my role as a campaign manager or a governmental employee on your staff at a high level. I won't project myself as a gay leader. But I will have relationships with men. I may walk down the street holding hands with another man.' This is 1973. I said, 'I will not hide my sexuality. And if you feel now, having heard this and, especially, because you're a bachelor' — he was the straightest person I've ever met in my life, believe me — 'but because you're a bachelor and because you're thinking of running for state attorney general, if you think it will be a terrible handicap to have an openly gay person as your chief aide, I will resign quietly and I won't have any hard feelings.'"

There was a long pause, and Geto had no idea what Abrams would say. Finally, his boss spoke: "Ethan, I respect you. You're my friend. I care about you. And I will support you in all of this. And I can accept everything you said. And I need you and want you on my team. And I will back you up. And I will take whatever negatives come along with this, if people try to attack me because you're gay."

For Geto, it was "a wonderful moment." He "felt totally free. To be able to hear this, in those days, that the guy was so supportive and so committed and would let me keep my job. I saw myself attached to him, managing him into big-time politics. It was very important to me in my career. It was just a wonderful thing. And I was very lucky because for years after that, very, very few other people in politics or government came out the way I did."

V

The Eighties

"I don't think people's sex lives are very interesting, unless they destroy the person."

— JOHN FAIRCHILD

"San Francisco is where gay fantasies come true. . . . The problem the city presents is whether, after all, we wanted these particular dreams to be fulfilled — or would we have preferred others? Did we know what price these dreams would exact?"

— EDMUND WHITE, 1980

"What everyone had wanted was bringing them death."

— RANDY SHILTS

"Out of the closets and into the streets!"

— ACT UP CHANT

THE SEVENTIES had been a time of amazing progress and almost nonstop celebration for much of the gay community. By the end of the decade, gay invisibility was just a distant memory, with the proliferation of gay characters on network TV sitcoms and frequent political battles over gay civil rights laws. Even damaging defeats, like Anita Bryant's successful campaign to overturn a gay rights ordinance in Miami, were not without incidental benefits. Such reversals proved once again how much the movement could be strengthened by adversity.

Ethan Geto, who had temporarily decamped from New York to Miami to help fight Bryant's effort, saw the Florida fight as "a watershed." He said, "I thought this was the first great opportunity nationally to mobilize the gay community with a political consciousness. I hoped that gay rights would mature into a major civil rights issue on the national agenda. And it happened. We were on the nightly news a million times. We got letters and notes that came in by the thousands. They were like this: 'I live in rural Indiana. And we can't really say we're gay here, but there is a place where we do hang out once a week on Sunday afternoons. It becomes like a gay bar, but nobody really knows it. There are three women and five men. We didn't have much money, but we said we'll take one week's pay check from everybody and send it to you people in Dade County because you're standing up for homosexuals.'"

By 1980, in response to the growing clamor for equality, 120 of the largest corporations, including AT&T and IBM, had adopted personnel policies prohibiting discrimination on the basis of sexual orientation, and 40 towns and cities had passed similar laws or issued executive orders. (Mostly because of fierce opposition from the Catholic Church — whose lobbyist was Roy Cohn — New York City remained pointedly absent from this list at the beginning of the decade.)

Twenty-two states had ended all restrictions on sexual relations between consenting adults, and on the tenth anniversary of Stonewall, seventeen-year-old Randy Rohl took twenty-year-old Grady Quinn to the senior prom in Sioux Falls, South Dakota. The National Gay Task Force announced that this was the first time two acknowledged homosexuals had attended a high school prom together in America.

But while thousands of lesbians and gay men responded to these changes by publicly declaring who they were, thousands more still assumed that safety, comfort, and prosperity would continue to flow from inside a closet. And most gay people still believed that a public declaration of their homosexuality would mean losing the chance to rise to the pinnacle of their profession. In his first career as a film executive, even a future firebrand like Larry Kramer was careful to bring a woman friend with him to the Monday-night executive screenings. "I was more interested in learning what my professional talents might be and how to get to the next step on the ladder of success," Kramer explained.

Mixed messages from all kinds of American institutions encouraged this timidity. After the tennis star Billie Jean King was publicly identified as a lesbian in 1981, she continued to do commentary for tennis tournaments, but her lucrative product endorsements disappeared. Similarly, while both NBC and CBS prohibited discrimination on the basis of sexual orientation, NBC also had a policy forbidding employees "from getting involved in a public way in controversial subjects." An NBC executive told the *Columbia Journalism Review* in 1982 that this meant that any correspondent who "came out publicly as gay" would automatically be asked to leave the network. "The biggest enemies are the totally closeted people who have real power," the same executive said.

And the silent convictions of the senior executives at CBS News became clear when CBS Reports presented "Gay Power, Gay Politics," in April 1980. Narrated and coproduced by George Crile, this "documentary" about gay political power in San Francisco made Mike Wallace's 1967 effort look like a model of fairness and enlightenment. Crile's work bore little resemblance to objective journalism. This was straightforward, anti-gay propaganda, with a heavy emphasis on drag queens and sado-masochism, including a description of an S and M parlor where the sexual activities were "so dangerous that they have a gynecological table there with a doctor and nurse on hand to sew people up." Crile's source for this particular tidbit was the city coroner, who subsequently admitted that his own information was based on hearsay. Crile's critics also pointed out that the S and M establishment he highlighted in the broadcast was actually patronized almost exclusively by *hetero*sexuals. The program even included Crile's very traditional question to a gay activist about whether the toleration of homosexuality wouldn't automatically lead to disaster, as the producer believed it had in Weimar Germany. "It was a very decadent society, if you remember it," said Crile. "Isn't it a sign of decadence when you have so many gays emerging, breaking apart all the values of a society?"

Crile reported that gay influence over the city's politicians had become so strong that many elected officials felt obliged to bow to even the most exotic gay concerns. The program caused an uproar in San Francisco. "It's shocking that CBS News, home of Walter Cronkite, would partake of such bigotry," Jeff Jarvis wrote in the *San Francisco Examiner,* while in the *Chronicle,* Terrence O'Flaherty called it a "dreadful little program" which "is deadly for everyone it touches."

The only suggestion of social progress occurred during one of the commercial breaks, which was filled by an example of what sociologist Laud Humphreys described as "gay window advertising," which permitted gay and straight consumers to receive different messages from the same advertisement. In the commercial sponsoring the documentary, a man strolled with a woman in one hand and a bottle of Old Spice in the other. But in the final shot, he tossed the Old Spice to another attractive man, making his intentions seem rather ambiguous.

Randy Alfred, a free-lance reporter in San Francisco, spent three hundred hours researching "Gay Power, Gay Politics" after it aired. His friends held a cocktail party to raise money to cover his expenses. Then he filed a formal protest detailing its inaccuracies to the National News Council, a short-lived effort at self-regulation by the news industry which never gained much clout, partly because *The New York Times* refused to cooperate with it.

The council found that "by concentrating on certain flamboyant examples of homosexual behavior," Crile's program "tended to reinforce stereotypes." It also "exaggerated political concessions to gays and made those concessions appear as threats to public morals and decency." In October, CBS reported the council's verdict on the air, and acknowledged that in at least one instance there had been a violation of the network's "own journalistic standards." This was the first time a major news organization had issued a formal apology to gay activists.*

Crile's work resembles a couple of antigay propaganda films produced by the religious right in the nineties, *The Gay Agenda* and *Equal Rights, Special Rights,* which stressed sadomasochism, while also featuring antigay sound bites from Republican custodians of morality like former Secretary of Education William Bennett and Senate Majority Leader Trent Lott of Mississippi. But these programs were never broadcast on a major network. They were shown on Christian cable networks. Copies were also distributed by fundamentalists throughout the country.

TO EVERYONE WHO still cherished the generous spirit of the sixties, two events at the end of 1980 made it feel as though America was entering a bleak new era, while a third incident sent a tremor through the gay community in Manhattan.

The first omen was the landslide victory of Ronald Reagan on November 4, coupled with the arrival of the first Republican majority in the Senate in more than a quarter century. The Republican gains marked a sharp turn to the right, and sparked a new reverence for all kinds of conspicuous consumption. In the age of Reagan, no one would be encour-

---

*Three years later William Westmoreland sued Crile and CBS for libel and asked for $120 million in damages because of a new documentary Crile had produced, "The Uncounted Enemy: A Vietnam Deception." After a five-month trial and millions of dollars in legal fees, Westmoreland dropped his suit in 1985 in return for a statement in which the network said it "never intended to assert, and does not believe, that General Westmoreland was unpatriotic or disloyal in performing his duties as he saw them" during his tour as American commander in Vietnam. (*New York Times,* February 19, 1985)

aged to worry about anyone less fortunate than himself. The new president's sole preoccupations would be lower taxes and a bloated defense budget.

The election also meant a greatly expanded political role for Evangelical Christians. Robert J. Billings, a cofounder of Jerry Falwell's Moral Majority, had served as Reagan's liaison on religious issues during the campaign, and fundamentalist Christians were given major credit for the Republican sweep. Not since the presidential runs of William Jennings Bryan had Protestant fundamentalism played such a large role in a national campaign.

When Massachusetts Senator Edward Kennedy unsuccessfully challenged Jimmy Carter for the presidential nomination in 1980, Kennedy became the first significant major party candidate to actively pursue gay voters. A total of seventy-six gay delegates and alternates attended the Democratic National Convention that year in New York City, and the party's platform acknowledged their growing influence. It said, "We must affirm the dignity of all people and . . . protect all groups from discrimination based on race, color, religion, national origin, sex or sexual orientation." Though almost unnoticed by the national media at the time, this modest statement of nondiscrimination gave the Republicans another opportunity to exploit antigay prejudice in a national campaign — just as they had during the hysteria of the McCarthy period in the 1950s.* Twelve days before the election, Christians for Reagan, a supposedly independent lobby organized to capture the fundamentalist vote for the Republican nominee, announced that it would pay for a barrage of advertisements throughout the south, which attacked President Carter for "catering" to homosexuals. Citing the language of the Democratic party platform, Gary Jarmin, national director of Christians for Reagan, described the purpose of the campaign this way: "If there's any reason at all they should oppose Carter, this is it." On one spot, an announcer intoned, "The gays in San Francisco elected a mayor; now they're going to elect a president." Before the ads began, polls had shown that Carter, a born-again Christian, still had considerable support among the Evangelicals. But the hard-hitting TV spots were extremely effective, and they helped Reagan carry every southern state except Georgia, where Carter had been governor. Partly because the commercials never aired in New York or Washington, most people outside the south were never aware of them.

*See pages 73–74.

The *Times* mentioned them only once — in a single paragraph two weeks before the election.

THE SECOND LACERATING EVENT at the end of 1980 was the murder of John Lennon. New Yorkers had proudly claimed the Liverpudlian as one of their own; but they had also respected his privacy, even when they spotted him cavorting in Central Park with his wife and son. The late-night shooting by a crazed "fan" on December 8, in the doorway of the Dakota apartment building on West 72d Street, was the most depressing murder that Manhattan had endured in decades.

For six days, thousands made a daily pilgrimage past the assassination site, until Yoko Ono specified a moment for mourning and more than one hundred thousand of the faithful gathered in Central Park for what was supposed to be a ten-minute moment of silence. Within the huge throng in front of the Naumberg Bandshell, there was inexpressible sadness — but no silence at all, because a huge flotilla of helicopters hired by the press hovered low during the entire event.

Lennon had believed in brotherhood and peace and creativity, and he had done as much as any artist to shape the sensibility of his genera-tion. The progress of the gay movement in the seventies, and its venera-tion of diversity and iconoclasm, all owed a great deal to that sensibility. The confluence of Lennon's death with the impending inauguration of a deeply reactionary president filled millions of Americans with a feeling of foreboding.

ANOTHER SENSELESS SHOOTING was the third incident to traumatize the gay community in New York City and spark fears of a backlash against its growing visibility. In the middle of November, Ronald Crumpley, a former New York City transit policeman, stole his father's year-old white Cadillac and drove it to Virginia. Outside Richmond, he stole an Uzi submachine gun and three other weapons from a sporting goods store. Then he drove thirty miles away and robbed a bank.

The following evening, Wednesday, November 19, 1980, Crumpley took the car to Greenwich Village and went on a shooting spree at three differ-ent locations, firing forty bullets from three guns. Two men were killed and six were wounded.

Just before 11:00 P.M., Crumpley opened fire on three men near Sim's Deli at the corner of 10th and Washington streets. He fired eight times and wounded two people. Then he drove to the Ramrod Bar at 394 West Street. There he aimed at a group of men standing outside the Ramrod and an adjoining bar, Sneakers. Victims crumpled as he fired twenty-four rounds in a few seconds. Jing Wenz and Vernon Kroenig were both fatally wounded.

Jack Gamrecki was standing inside the Ramrod with about 150 others when he heard something that he thought sounded like firecrackers; then he saw "a lot of people fall down." Bullets rained through the window of the bar, and at least one person inside was wounded.

Then Crumpley drove away again, stopping at 10th and Greenwich streets, where he fired eight more shots into another group of men, but this time all of them missed. As police cars approached, he sped away. After abandoning his car, he hid under a van, clinging to the undercarriage, until he was arrested.

Crumpley immediately admitted to the killings. He told the police he had committed them because he hated homosexuals. "I want to kill them all," he told detectives. "They're no good. They ruin everything."

"It's frightening for everyone to think that there are people sick enough to go around doing this kind of thing," Lee Pietrangelon, manager of the Ramrod, told the *Times*. Most people thought the paper had underplayed the story, putting it on the first page of the second section, instead of the front page.

Although gay men had often been beaten on the streets of Greenwich Village, nothing this violent had occurred within any resident's memory. The night after the shootings, more than four hundred demonstrators gathered in Sheridan Square, wearing black armbands. One carried a sign reading, "There is no justice in America if you are gay." Then they marched down Christopher Street, singing "We Shall Overcome."

The following year, Crumpley went on trial. His lawyer said, "This defendant is crazy, as nuts as they come." A defense psychiatrist testified that Crumpley believed that "demons in the guise of homosexuals" were "stalking him" and that "he was merely protecting the nation and himself by attacking them." Crumpley was found not guilty by reason of insanity. He was committed to a state mental institution, where he remained incarcerated in 1996.

ALTHOUGH RONALD REAGAN was elected president with the explicit support of groups that exploited antigay prejudice, before he entered the White House his positions on gay issues had been somewhat unpredictable. First elected governor of California in 1966, he had originally hoped to run for president in 1968. That effort was derailed after two of his top aides were fired in 1967 — and the syndicated columnist Drew Pearson reported that it was because they were homosexuals. "From this blow, the Reagan campaign never recovered," Theodore White wrote in *The Making of the President, 1968.**

After he became governor, Reagan indicated that he would veto any attempt to repeal the state's antisodomy statute; it was his successor, Jerry Brown, who signed that reform into law. But after Reagan left the governorship, he made a surprising contribution to the gay rights movement.

In 1978, California became the site of the first statewide electoral battle over gay rights when state senator John Briggs introduced Proposition 6, which would have forbidden homosexuals from teaching in any public school. Briggs used inflammatory language. "Homosexuals want your children," he asserted. "They don't have any children of their own. If they don't recruit children or very young people, they'd all die away. They have no means of replenishing. That's why they want to be teachers."

The first statewide poll in September 1978 predicted that the measure would pass by a huge margin — sixty-one to thirty-one percent. Because he was a famous conservative, Reagan's surprise announcement made him a crucial recruit for the Briggs opponents. The former governor explained his opposition to the initiative this way: "Whatever else it is, homosexuality is not a contagious disease like measles." In November, the proposition was defeated by a two-to-one margin.

The Reagans came from a Hollywood milieu that had always embraced discreet homosexuals; that was probably the reason for their occasional displays of enlightenment. Besides Rock Hudson, Nancy Reagan's gay friends included the decorator Ted Graber, who supervised a $1 million renovation of the family quarters at the White House. After Mrs. Reagan's sixtieth birthday celebration, her spokesman confirmed that Graber had spent the night at the White House with his lover, Archie Case. Graber was also a frequent guest at state dinners, as was the ubiquitous Jerry Zipkin, the New York socialite and marathon walker of wealthy women.

By far the most influential gay man in the Reagan inner circle was Robert Gray, an extremely successful Washington public relations man who had been a closeted capital player ever since he had served as Dwight Eisenhower's appointments secretary. In 1980 he was Reagan's deputy campaign director and campaign communications chief; then he became cochairman of the president-elect's inaugural committee. Coded references to Mr. Gray in *The New York Times* included descriptions of him as

---

*The football star and future Republican officeholder Jack Kemp worked for the fired chief aide and invested in a house the aide owned in Lake Tahoe. Kemp has said that he is not a homosexual — and he hadn't known that his boss was either. (*New York Times,* June 28, 1987)

A month after the 1960 presidential election, Gore Vidal greeted John F. Kennedy as Kennedy arrived at the Morosco Theater to see *The Best Man*, Vidal's Broadway hit (and future movie), which had a gay sub-plot. *Courtesy of UPI/Corbis-Bettmann.*

Jack Nichols headed the first gay picket line in front of the White House in 1965. Frank Kameny was right behind him. These two men did more than any-one else to infuse the gay movement with the spirit of the sixties. *Courtesy of UPI/Corbis-Bettmann.*

The Beatles and their gay manager, Brian Epstein, in London, July 1966. When Epstein first saw them perform, it was literally love at first sight. *Courtesy of UPI/Corbis-Bettmann.*

The crowd outside the Frank Campbell chapel during Judy Garland's funeral, a few hours before the Stonewall riot in 1969. *Courtesy of UPI/Corbis-Bettmann.*

Left: Stormé DeLarverie, a cross-dressing lesbian who witnessed the Stonewall riot — and may have helped to precipitate it. "The cop hit me and I hit him back," she remembered. *Courtesy of Stormé DeLarverie.* Below: Jack Nichols (right) and his lover Lige Clarke were the first gay authors to write about Stonewall. Their article appeared in *Screw* magazine. *Courtesy of Eric Stephen Jacobs.*

Left: Howard Rosenman had an affair with Leonard Bernstein in Israel after the Six Day War in 1967. *Courtesy of Kitty Hawks.* Right: Walter Clemons was denied the job of daily book critic at the *New York Times* after the managing editor learned that Clemons was gay. *Courtesy of Frank DiStefano.*

Michael York and Liza Minnelli in *Cabaret* in 1972. "Screw Maximilian!" York shouted at her. "I do," Minnelli replied. "So do I!" said York. *Courtesy of Springer/Corbis-Bettmann.*

Thousands gathered outside San Francisco's city hall for a candlelight vigil after the assassinations of Mayor George Moscone and Supervisor Harvey Milk in November 1978. *Courtesy of UPI/ Corbis-Bettmann.*

Jack Fitzsimmons at Fire Island Pines in 1981. That year the Reagan administration asked him to become an assistant White House counsel, but the offer was rescinded after Fitzsimmons told his boss that he was gay. *Courtesy of Philip Gefter.*

Philip Gefter was Fitzsimmons's lover. Gefter was one of the earliest anti-AIDS activists in Manhattan. *Courtesy of Jonathan Tamarkin.*

Right: Ann Northrop: the memory of her sixties activism attracted her to ACT UP in the eighties. In 1996, Northrop and Tom Stoddard served as the grand marshals of the Gay and Lesbian Pride March in New York City. *Courtesy of Milagros Melendez.*

Below: David Bartolomi (right) in camp in 1983: he learned about AIDS by reading a copy of *Hustler* in his father's smoke shop. *Courtesy of David Bartolomi.*

In 1988, Todd Alexius Long changed his name to "Xax" because "it had no gender connotation, it had no connotation of anything." *XAX, The Kiss,* © *1989 Robert Miller.*

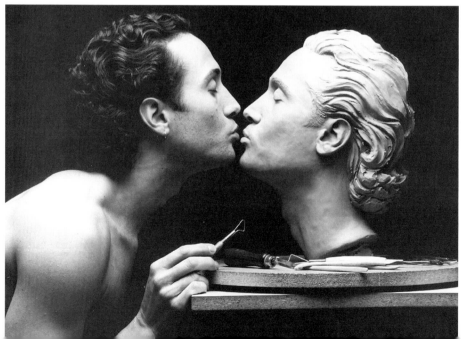

Men who "live together for years and make homes and share their lives and their work," as Christopher Isherwood put it: Walter Rieman and Tom Stoddard (top; © *Annie Liebovitz/Contact Press Images*), Paul Cadmus and Jon Andersson (bottom; *courtesy of Joseph Stouter*), and Tom Hatcher and Arthur Laurents (overleaf; *courtesy of Arthur Laurents*). Rieman and Stoddard had been together more than eight years when Stoddard died of complications from AIDS in 1997. Cadmus and Andersson have been together since 1964, Hatcher and Laurents since 1955.

a "a trim, precisely groomed man" and a "perennial bachelor noted for his charm and connections."

In New York, the gay power broker Roy Cohn boasted of his influence within the Reagan White House, and his law partner, Tom Bolan, became head of the screening committee for federal judgeships in New York State. Six autographed pictures of Reagan decorated Cohn's office, including one inscribed, "With Deepest Appreciation for your Love and Support." On New York op-ed pages, Cohn wrote of Reagan's "generous nature, great warmth and reluctance to inflict personal hurt." In some ways, Cohn was the ideal gay friend for the Reagans because he was not only deeply closeted but also publicly self-hating.

Asked about the persistent rumor that his ballet dancer son, Ron Jr., might be gay, the presidential candidate said in 1980, "He's all man — we made sure of that."

Steve Weisman, who covered Reagan's first term as president for *The New York Times,* thought the "White House wasn't that homophobic because Nancy had friends who were gay. But it was definitely a place where you would hear one staff member call another staff member 'a fag' behind his back."

It was also a place where anyone who *was* gay — and not a decorator — was expected to remain firmly within the closet. As a health catastrophe developed at the beginning of this administration, the lack of any openly gay officials in Reagan's entourage would have terrible consequences. In fact, the presence or absence of openly gay people would determine how almost every major American institution reacted to the greatest medical crisis of the decade.

JACK FITZSIMMONS was a very disciplined, rather laconic, "best-little-boy-in-the-world type," as Philip Gefter remembered him. In 1981 Fitzsimmons was a thirty-one-year-old associate at Willkie Farr and Gallagher, one of Manhattan's most prestigious law firms. He was also Gefter's lover.

At the beginning of the Reagan presidency, Willkie Farr loaned Fitzsimmons to the White House counsel's office for three months. His job was to screen new administration employees for the incoming Reagan administration, and he loved it.

"Jack was gay and a Republican," Gefter remembered. "He was not out. He was in heaven at the White House. This was the pinnacle to him. He had arrived." Because Gefter was "anything but Republican," he constantly argued with his lover about his admiration for the new administration. After three months, Fitzsimmons was bubbling with enthusiasm: he announced that he had accepted a permanent job as an assistant White House counsel. But the next time Fitzsimmons saw Gefter in person, he began to cry.

Through his tears, Fitzsimmons explained that the day after he had accepted the job, he had gone back to White House counsel Fred Fielding to have another discussion with him. "Jack said, in all good conscience, he couldn't take this job without letting Fred Fielding know that he was homosexual," Gefter recalled. "He said that it was bound to show up on the FBI reports. He knew enough to know that. And Fred Fielding immediately rescinded the offer because Jack was gay."

His lover's narrative made Gefter livid. "Didn't you want to blow up the White House?" Gefter asked.

"No," his lover replied softly.

Fitzsimmons thought "they were right to rescind the offer because he was homosexual," Gefter recalled. "He thought he was inferior in some way because he was homosexual. So he bought into their view of the world. Jack was someone who had so much self-hatred for being gay. Here was somebody who was a model human being — the best little boy in the world — a graduate of Dartmouth and Harvard Law School. A couple of years later he became a partner in Willkie Farr. . . . I said, 'Look at you. Look at who you are. Look where you work. Look where you live — 400 East 58th Street. You belong to the New York Athletic Club. Everything about you is unblemished. Even if it *had* shown up on the FBI report, if you had said nothing they would have said nothing.' And he didn't believe that. But there were enough gay people working in the Reagan administration, so if Jack had been complicit in their silence there would not have been a problem."

IT WAS A baffling and virulent new disease that would finally make it impossible for Jack Fitzsimmons, Rock Hudson, Roy Cohn, and hundreds of thousands of other gay men to hide who they really were. Acquired Immune Deficiency Syndrome would have a greater impact on the shape of the gay community than all the other events of the previous forty years put together. At a gigantic cost, it would prove the truth of what Edward Sagarin had written thirty years earlier in *The Homosexual in America:* "The inherent tragedy — not the saving grace — of homosexuality is found in the ease of concealment." It also did more than anything else ever could to further Sagarin's greatest hope for the movement: "If only all of the inverts, the millions in all lands, could simultaneously rise up in our full strength!"

If you are a sexually active gay man in America, being alive at the beginning of this epidemic feels like standing without a helmet at the front line of a shooting war. Friends are falling all around you but no one even knows where the bullets are coming from. There are no weapons to defend yourself, no medicine for the wounded, and if you want to flee, when you start running you won't know whether your own wounds are fatal — or nonexistent. Three years into this war, the battlefield is just as lethal, but now it feels more like a huge tunnel filled with fire, strewn with bodies and booby traps. If you're still standing — one of the "lucky" ones — you keep running faster and faster, but you can never outpace the inferno.

At the beginning, there was nothing but terror and mystery.

No one knew how this illness was transmitted — or even whether it *could be* transmitted — and no one could cure it. Although there had been a handful of stories about a mysterious new disease in the gay press earlier in 1981, most gay men in Manhattan first learned about what would become known as AIDS at the beginning of the July Fourth weekend of that year — less than six months after Ronald Reagan's inauguration. The story that alerted them was written by Lawrence K. Altman, a physician who is the senior medical writer for the *Times*.

RARE CANCER SEEN IN 41 HOMOSEXUALS

Doctors in New York and California have diagnosed among homosexual men 41 cases of a rare and often rapidly fatal form of cancer. Eight of the victims died less than 24 months after the diagnosis was made.

The cause of the outbreak is unknown, and there is as yet no evidence of contagion. But the doctors who have made the diagnoses, mostly in New York City and the San Francisco Bay area, are alerting other physicians who treat large numbers of homosexual men to the problem in an effort to help identify more cases and to reduce the delay in offering chemotherapy treatment.

The sudden appearance of the cancer, called Kaposi's Sarcoma, has prompted a medical investigation that experts say could have as much scientific as public health importance because of what it may teach about determining the causes of more common types of cancer.

Doctors have been taught in the past that the cancer usually appeared first in spots on the legs and that the disease took a slow course of up to 10 years. But these recent cases have shown that it appears in one or more

violet-colored spots anywhere on the body. The spots generally do not
itch or cause other symptoms, often can be mistaken for bruises, sometimes appear as lumps and can turn brown after a period of time. The
cancer often causes swollen lymph glands, and then kills by spreading
throughout the body.

Doctors investigating the outbreak believe that many cases have gone
undetected because of the rarity of the condition and the difficulty even
dermatologists may have in diagnosing it.

In a letter alerting other physicians to the problem, Dr. Alvin E. Friedman-Kien of New York University Medical Center, one of the investigators, described the appearance of the outbreak as "rather devastating."

Dr. Friedman-Kien said in an interview yesterday that he knew of 41
cases collated in the last five weeks, with the cases themselves dating to
the past 30 months. The Federal Centers for Disease Control in Atlanta is
expected to publish the first description of the outbreak in its weekly
report today, according to a spokesman, Dr. James Curran. The report
notes 26 of the cases — 20 in New York and six in California.

There is no national registry of cancer victims, but the nationwide
incidence of Kaposi's Sarcoma in the past had been estimated by the
Centers for Disease Control to be less than six-one-hundredths of a case
per 100,000 people annually, or about two cases in every three million
people. However, the disease accounts for up to 9 percent of all cancers
in a belt across equatorial Africa, where it commonly affects children and
young adults.

In the United States, it has primarily affected men older than 50 years.
But in the recent cases, doctors at nine medical centers in New York and
seven hospitals in California have been diagnosing the condition among
younger men, all of whom said in the course of standard diagnostic
interviews that they were homosexual. Although the ages of the patients
have ranged from 26 to 51 years, many have been under 40, with the
mean at 39.

Nine of the 41 cases known to Dr. Friedman-Kien were diagnosed in
California, and several of those victims reported that they had been in
New York in the period preceding the diagnosis. Dr. Friedman-Kien said
that his colleagues were checking on reports of two victims diagnosed in
Copenhagen, one of whom had visited New York.

No one medical investigator has yet interviewed all the victims, Dr.
Curran said. According to Dr. Friedman-Kien, the reporting doctors said
that most cases had involved homosexual men who have had multiple
and frequent sexual encounters with different partners, as many as 10
sexual encounters each night up to four times a week.

Many of the patients have also been treated for viral infections such as
herpes, cytomegalovirus and hepatitis B as well as parasitic infections

such as amebiasis and giardiasis. Many patients also reported that they had used drugs such as amyl nitrite and LSD to heighten sexual pleasure.

Cancer is not believed to be contagious, but conditions that might precipitate it, such as particular viruses or environmental factors, might account for an outbreak among a single group.

The medical investigators say some indirect evidence actually points away from contagion as a cause. None of the patients knew each other, although the theoretical possibility that some may have had sexual contact with a person with Kaposi's Sarcoma at some point in the past could not be excluded, Dr. Friedman-Kien said.

Dr. Curran said there was no apparent danger to nonhomosexuals from contagion. "The best evidence against contagion," he said, "is that no cases have been reported to date outside the homosexual community or in women."

Dr. Friedman-Kien said he had tested nine of the victims and found severe defects in their immunological systems. The patients had serious malfunctions of two types of cells called T and B cell lymphocytes, which have important roles in fighting infections and cancer.

But Dr. Friedman-Kien emphasized that the researchers did not know whether the immunological defects were the underlying problem or had developed secondarily to the infections or drug use.

The research team is testing various hypotheses, one of which is a possible link between past infection with cytomegalovirus and development of Kaposi's Sarcoma.

Altman did a good job of summarizing the state of scientific knowledge at this moment, including all the hypotheses for the causes for these puzzling events. But like everything else people read during the first stage of the epidemic, Altman's article was filled with conflicting signals — enough to make most gay men careen between confidence that they were safe and a conviction that they were surely infected.

The fear grew from the lack of any reliable diagnostic test, and the vagueness of the indicators of possible infection, such as the "violet-colored spots anywhere on the body" which "often can be mistaken for bruises." For years, this symptom would transform almost every morning for a seemingly healthy gay man into a search for a possible death sentence. Equally alarming were the slightest suggestion of "swollen lymph glands," a bout of diarrhea, an unfamiliar sore in the mouth, a prolonged flu, or even just a patch of unexplained fatigue.

"I was in a state of shock and grief and numbness," said Howard Rosenman, who by now had moved to Hollywood to pursue a film career. "All my friends were dying and I thought *I* was sick because I was so wild in those days. For sure. There was no way of testing and the mode of transmission wasn't as clear as it is now. At the time if you got a cold or sneezed or you saw a pimple, you thought, That's it! I called my skin doctor up in the middle of the night to come to his office because I was so hysterical. And my doctor, my general practitioner, who wasn't gay, looked at it, and said, 'You have AIDS. That's Kaposi's sarcoma.' And I quickly called Arnie Klein at his office. He walked me across the street and ordered the biopsy and two days later the biopsy came back and it was just a hematoma.

"It was only in 1987 that I got tested for the first time and found out I was HIV-negative. I never had anal sex for various reasons. Just a throw of the dice."

The disease itself was as frightening as anything known to twentieth-century man. If it didn't kill you within weeks with a particularly virulent strain of pneumonia, it would cover your entire body with sores, sometimes blind you, addle your brain, and force you into diapers with violent diarrhea.

More optimistic notions flowed from the description of the earliest casualties as gay men who had "as many as 10 sexual encounters each night up to four times a week." A federal study at the beginning of 1982 estimated the lifetime number of sexual partners for early victims of the disease at 1,200; for some, the number approached 20,000. Even in the rollicking seventies, those were figures very few gay men could match. These statistics nurtured the hope that the immune systems of the first men to get sick were being overwhelmed by overexposure to a whole variety of diseases including hepatitis, syphilis, and intestinal parasites, instead of a single new infectious agent.

Anyone who was healthy and had been monogamous at first assumed he was safe. (Although rarely articulated, there was plenty of interior speculation among gay men that this pestilence was some kind of retribution for rampant promiscuity.)* But once the disease began to strike men who had been monogamous while their lovers had been promiscuous, only the celibate could retain any confidence about the future.

Because there are only educated guesses about the number of gay peo-

---

*That view was expressed in the *Southern Medical Journal* by James Fletcher in 1984: "We see homosexual men reaping not only expected consequences of sexual promiscuity, suffering even as promiscuous homosexuals the usual venereal diseases, but other unusual consequences as well. Perhaps, then, homosexuality is not alternative behavior at all, but as the ancient wisdom of the Bible states, most certainly pathologic." (Quoted in Richard A. Isay, *Being Homosexual*, 80, and Dennis Altman, *AIDS in the Mind of America*, 66)

ple in America, no one will ever know precisely what proportion of the gay population has been afflicted by this disease. However, anecdotal evidence from doctors with gay practices suggests that at least half of the gay men in New York and San Francisco born between 1945 and 1960 were probably infected by the AIDS virus between the end of the seventies and the end of the eighties. In the earliest stages of the epidemic, some died within a month after their diagnosis; most were dead less than three years later.

Gay men in Manhattan from the generation born after World War II would suffer at least a fifty percent casualty rate from this scourge. (By comparison, less than three percent of the American soldiers who served in World War II died in or after battle.) Virtually every gay man in every large American city would experience the death of at least ten friends during the epidemic; for some, the number of deceased friends and acquaintances has surpassed three hundred.

At the beginning, in Manhattan, it was known as "Saint's Disease," in honor of the downtown discotheque favored by the most beautiful and sought-after men of all — because so many of the best-looking were among the first to die. The novelist David Leavitt recalled the mid-1980s as "a time when the streets were filled with an almost palpable sense of mourning and panic."

One gay doctor in Greenwich Village concluded that half of his gay male patients had been exposed to the virus. The office nurse said the test results had been "completely unpredictable." Patients he had been certain would be positive because of their medical history were sometimes negative, and others who had barely had any sexually transmitted diseases were sometimes positive.

For more than a year, the doctor pressured his patient "James Blair" (a pseudonym) to get tested. "All your other blood work is fine — why don't you do it?" the doctor asked. But so many of Blair's friends had already tested positive, he was certain he would as well — and like thousands of others, he was concerned that he might literally worry himself to death if his fears became concrete. Finally the doctor said, "What if I tested you without telling you, and I only told you the result if you were negative?"

"Well, obviously that would be ideal," Blair replied.

"Well, I did, and you are," the doctor told him. When he had taken over the practice from another doctor, the new practitioner had apparently tested all of his patients — regardless of whether they had given their consent. The doctor's behavior was illegal, but Blair felt such gigantic relief that he never challenged the physician's ethics.

The AIDS epidemic would cause more pain and loss than anyone within the gay community had hitherto imagined possible. And the deaths among artists would ravage the creativity of American culture for at least a generation. A typical disaster was the decimation of the Violet Quill, a group of seven novelists formed at the end of the 1970s. Its members were Edmund White, then working on *A Boy's Own Story;* Felice Picano; Andrew Holleran; Robert Ferro; George Whitmore; Christopher Cox; and Michael Grumley. Vito Russo, who was writing *The Celluloid Closet,* was also an occasional visitor. By the end of 1991, only White, Holleran, and Picano were still alive.

"For me these losses were definitive," Edmund White wrote. "The witnesses to my life, the people who had shared the same references and sense of humor, were gone. The loss of all the books they might have written remains incalculable."

IN AMERICA SINCE World War II, only life-and-death struggles have been able to inspire mass political action on the left, and that was especially true of gay people and AIDS. The disease would convert a generation of mostly selfish men, consumed by sex, into a highly disciplined army of fearless and selfless street fighters and caregivers. Since lesbians were never at much risk of infection, the depth of their commitment to this battle was even more impressive.

This war transformed the survivors, leaving them alternately awed by their strength and guilt-ridden over the mystery of their survival. Partly because just as many healthy people were forced out of the closet by this battle as sick people, for the first time in its history, the gay movement would begin to have the kind of political clout that was roughly commensurate with its size and talents. Beyond the gay community, ten years of lobbying by gay activists obsessed with survival overturned revered scientific assumptions about how quickly experimental drugs for the terminally ill should be introduced — and whether it can ever be ethical to offer anyone facing death a placebo.

Antibiotics and other so-called miracle drugs had made Americans supremely arrogant about their power over contagion. After polio had been conquered in the fifties, we remained vulnerable to cancer and plenty of other incurable diseases. But the possibility of an incurable disease that was also *infectious* had practically disappeared from the nation's consciousness.

Everything about AIDS — from its long latency period to the groups it first affected and the moment in American history when it was first detected — all these factors conspired against swift and dramatic action to contain it. AIDS was so unlike any other illness that Americans had dealt with in the previous twenty-five years that its behavior and its impact were literally unimaginable to almost everyone, except for a handful of prescient researchers.

The latency period and the initial mystery about its transmissibility led most experts to underestimate the threat AIDS posed to America's health. And because all of the initial cases reported to the Centers for Disease Control were among homosexuals, for many months there was far less response than the government and the media exhibited after outbreaks of Legionnaires' disease, toxic shock syndrome, or even the poisonings from a handful of tainted Tylenol capsules.

Homophobia led many decision makers to discount this epidemic, partly because they didn't care much about those who were sick, and partly because they believed that as long as they were straight, they themselves would never have to worry about it. The only real heroes were a few scientists inside the CDC, who lobbied early and often for more money to fight the epidemic, and a very small group of congressmen from California and New York, including Philip Burton, Henry Waxman, and Ted Weiss, whose openly gay staff members convinced them to take the epidemic seriously. Bill Kraus, a gay aide to Burton, and Tim Westmoreland, the gay counsel to a Waxman health subcommittee, were particularly important in sounding the alarm. In April 1982, Westmoreland wrote a statement for Waxman to read which declared, "There is no doubt in my mind that if the same disease had appeared among Americans of Norwegian descent, or among tennis players, rather than gay males, the responses of both the government and the medical establishment would have been different." In September of that year, the Congressional Research Service estimated that the National Institutes of Health had spent $36,100 per toxic shock death in fiscal 1982; $34,841 per Legionnaires' disease death in the most recent fiscal year; and just $3,225 per AIDS death in fiscal 1981 and $8,991 in fiscal 1982. Congressional staffers joked that NIH really stood for "Not Interested in Homosexuals."

Republican priorities were perfectly clear, right from the start of the Reagan government. One of the administration's first official acts was to propose a cut of nearly fifty percent in the appropriation for the CDC — from $327 million to $161 million. At the same time, Reagan asked for an immediate increase of $7 billion in defense spending and an additional increase of $25 billion for the following fiscal year — for a new annual total of $220 billion. Veneration for what Dwight Eisenhower had dubbed the "military-industrial complex" had never been higher. And although the Democratic House did a good job of resisting many of the Republican efforts to reduce spending on health care and research, the administration frequently retaliated by refusing to spend the moneys that Congress had appropriated.

Inside the Reagan administration — at the White House, at the Office of Management and Budget, and within the Department of Health and Human Services — there were no openly gay staffers, and therefore, very little will to attack the problem forcefully. In public, Reagan officials routinely pretended they had all the dollars they needed to fight the disease, while dissidents inside the administration secretly begged for more money.

The national press suffered from the same defect as the Reagan administration. Despite all the changes of the seventies, most newsrooms remained macho places where openly gay or lesbian reporters were almost nonexistent. Gail Shister believed that she became the first "out lesbian" at a major metropolitan daily when she revealed her orientation to her colleagues at the *New Orleans States Item* in 1975. Five years later, in San Francisco and New York, there were just two reporters at major dailies who had come out in their newsrooms — one at *The New York Post*, and one at *The San Francisco Chronicle*. There were none at *The New York Times* or *The Washington Post*. Nor were there any openly gay network television correspondents — and there still weren't any fifteen years later. The closeted reporters who did work in big city newsrooms were almost uniformly reluctant to lobby for "gay" stories, for fear of betraying their secret orientation. In 1982, the *Columbia Journalism Review* reported that "as gays see it, the prevailing attitude is a compound of hostility and ignorance that prevents gay journalists from openly acknowledging their sexual preference and thus virtually guarantees that coverage of . . . the lives led by the majority of gay men and women, will be inadequate and uninformed."

At *The New York Times,* a homophobic atmosphere continued to keep all gay employees in the closet, but there was an indication that the future might be more palatable.* In 1981, Arthur Sulzberger, Jr., the twenty-nine-year-old son of the paper's publisher, had moved from the Washington bureau to New York to continue his apprenticeship in the newsroom.

As children of the sixties, Sulzberger and his wife, the artist Gail Gregg,

---

*Early in the 1970s, two obviously gay men had come to the *Times* to be interviewed by a reporter in the culture department. As they sauntered out of the newsroom — but while they were still within earshot — Phil Dougherty, the paper's legendary advertising columnist, rose up from his desk, and shouted, "All right, everybody out of the closet!"

were fierce opponents of all kinds of prejudice; no one ever had to lobby them about the importance of diversity and equality. During his first two years in New York, Sulzberger did a remarkable thing: he met with every reporter whom he learned was gay. Over lunch, he told each one that he knew about his orientation. Then the future publisher assured all of them that this fact would have no effect on their careers at the newspaper. After a few moments of dumbfoundedness, these employees felt tremendously relieved. As long as they were willing to remain at the paper until after Rosenthal had retired, Sulzberger would make sure that they would never have to hide who they were, or suffer because they were gay.

Five years later, Rosenthal left the newsroom to become a columnist, and Sulzberger kept his word. Working with Max Frankel, who was Rosenthal's successor, one of the first things that Sulzberger accomplished was the lifting of a ban on the use of the word *gay* in the *Times*. During Rosenthal's tenure, the word could be used only if it was in the name of an organization, or part of a quotation. In a memo to Sulzberger's more old-fashioned father, who was still publisher of the paper in 1986, Frankel wrote, "Punch, I'm afraid you're just going to have to swallow hard, and let us use the word 'gay' in The Times." Coverage of gay issues and the treatment of gay employees improved dramatically during the Frankel regime, but the new executive editor was modest about this achievement.

All he had done, Frankel said, was to "let people know that whether they wanted to be openly gay, or whether they wanted to be relaxed, but not very openly gay, or whether they wanted to be secretly gay or lesbian, was their business, and essentially not mine." Frankel said he had never been attacked by anyone after the paper expanded its coverage of gay subjects, with one exception. "When we ran a picture of the two guys in Connecticut kissing — then you get a couple of stray letters saying, 'What the hell's going on? Are you going too far?'"

Within a few years, Sulzberger and Frankel had transformed one of the most homophobic institutions in America into one of the best places in the world for a gay person to work. And because of the influence of the *Times*, its example gradually had a huge impact on the way lesbians and gays were covered, and treated, at hundreds of other news-gathering organizations all over the country.

THE REPORTER WHO would make the biggest difference in the way the AIDS catastrophe was reported did not work at the *Times*. Randy Shilts was a product of the nation's heartland. He was born in Davenport, Iowa, and grew up in Aurora, Illinois, outside Chicago. As a teenager, this child of conservative and religious parents had founded a local chapter of the Young Americans for Freedom, which championed right-wing causes. But when he got to the University of Oregon in Eugene, he found himself.

At Oregon, Shilts studied journalism and became the managing editor of the student newspaper. Then he came out of the closet to head the Eugene Gay People's Alliance. After a stint as a writer at the gay news-magazine the *Advocate* and reporting jobs with two different Bay Area television stations, he learned that the *San Francisco Chronicle* was looking for an openly gay reporter, and he got the job.

Shilts was the kind of journalist who requested the night shift when he arrived at the *Chronicle* so he could spend his days finishing his first book, *The Mayor of Castro Street*, a fine biography of the gay city supervisor Harvey Milk, who was assassinated by a colleague in 1978. Shilts said gays "know they have somebody they can call up who won't make queer jokes when they hang up the phone. And within the paper I think a lot of dumb things that are written because of ignorance, not malice, don't appear because [colleagues] can come to me and feel like they're getting things in clearer perspective."

The young reporter inaugurated an admirable tradition of self-criti-cism among gay journalists. During his lifetime it brought him tremen-dous pain from the people he covered, but it would also inspire many of his gay colleagues to emulate him. "Writing about the gay community is like being a journalist in a small town," he once explained. "You get immediate reaction. I walked down the street and had people shout at me. . . . Self-criticism was not the strong point of a community that was only beginning to define itself affirmatively after centuries of repression."

Shilts was disgusted by how little attention the national media paid to the epidemic during its initial stages. In his landmark book about the first five years of the catastrophe, *And the Band Played On,* he was especially critical of reporters who ignored the politics behind the epidemic — among the scientists who were supposed to unravel it and between the legislative and executive branches in Washington.

It was true that none of the leading newspapers turned the story into a crusade, but a reluctance to write about homosexuals was only one of a number of reasons for that failure. Science writers are usually most com-fortable writing about new discoveries; as a result, American newspapers have never done a very good job of covering the politics of science.

Especially at the beginning of the epidemic, the paucity of knowledge about the nature of the disease made it logical for the press to be concerned about the danger of causing unnecessary panic — either among gay men, or the general population. Gay leaders expressed similar worries: the idea that too much publicity could lead to hysteria, or even quarantine for gay Americans.

Shilts himself was intimately familiar with these problems. When a report was leaked at the end of 1982 suggesting that at least one percent of the gay men in the city's Castro District were already infected with the disease, a gay activist pleaded with him not to report it. "They'll put barbed wire up around the Castro," said Randy Stallings, a senior gay leader in the Bay Area. "It will create panic." Shilts printed the story anyway. Later Shilts deduced that the real proportion of infected gay men in San Francisco at that moment was probably closer to twenty percent. Subsequent investigations indicated that a new viral agent had probably infected gay men for the first time in 1976 or 1977.

Shilts wrote that by the beginning of 1983, it was "virtually an article of faith among homosexuals that they would somehow end up in concentration camps." While most heterosexuals were baffled by these fears, Shilts thought they were perfectly understandable: "Humans who have been subjected to a lifetime of irrational bigotry on the part of mainstream society can be excused for harboring unreasonable fears," he wrote. "The general apathy that the United States had demonstrated toward the AIDS epidemic had only deepened the distrust between gays and heterosexuals."

The power of Shilts's book came from the author's willingness to be equally critical of greedy bathhouse owners, who resisted efforts to close their establishments long after it was clear that they were a breeding ground for infection, and lackadaisical blood bank administrators who pretended that the blood supply was safe and expensive testing was unnecessary for years after the first strong evidence that patients were becoming infected by transfusions. (Researchers at the Centers for Disease Control had predicted infections through transfusions as early as January 1982.)

One of the most chilling moments in Shilts's account occurs between a San Francisco bathhouse owner and Paul Volberding, the director of the San Francisco General Hospital AIDS clinic.

"We're both in it for the same thing," the bathhouse owner told Volberding. "Money. We make money at one end when they come to the baths. You make money from them on the other end when they come here." Volberding was too horrified to reply.

Bathhouse owners were among the most successful businessmen in the gay community. They were also among the most generous, lavishing contributions on gay political activists, as well as helping to finance early AIDS organizations like the San Francisco Kaposi's Sarcoma Foundation. Shilts suggests that particularly in San Francisco, some gay newspapers were corrupted by the money they received from bathhouses, which made them reluctant to give the epidemic the coverage it deserved.

In an excruciating irony, Shilts learned that he himself was HIV-positive the day he turned in the last page of his manuscript in 1987.

IN NEW YORK CITY, the first gay writer to become alarmed about the epidemic was neither a journalist nor an activist. Larry Kramer was a novelist and screenwriter. He had an elfin look, bouncing eyebrows, and boundless energy to excoriate enemies and friends alike. He had spent years in analysis to try to overcome the self-hatred typical of the gay men of his generation who had come of age in the fifties, but he still seemed deeply discontent much of the time. His first important success came in 1969 when he wrote and produced an excellent film version of D. H. Lawrence's *Women in Love,* which featured a famously homoerotic wrestling scene between the two male protagonists. For many years, that was his only visible contribution to the gay movement. "I certainly wasn't interested in gay politics," he wrote in 1989. "Like many others, when gay pride marches started down Fifth Avenue at the end of June, I was on Fire Island. Gay politics had an awful image. Loudmouths, the unkempt, the dirty and unwashed. . . . On Fire Island, we laughed . . . when we watched the evening news on Sunday night flash brief seconds of those struggling, pitiful marches."

Most gay activists were unaware of Kramer until 1977, when he published *Faggots,* an inflammatory account of upper-middle-class white gay life in Manhattan. Because he had so much contempt for the movement, the novel naturally did not acknowledge its existence, much less any of its achievements. Kramer thought he was writing satire on the level of Evelyn Waugh, but gay activists considered his graphic accounts of fist-fucking and every other sexual excess of gay culture a blood libel. Others simply found the book so overdone as to be unreadable.

"Why do faggots have to fuck so fucking much?" Kramer's narrator asked. "It's as if we don't have anything else to do. . . . All we do is live in our ghetto and dance and drug and fuck. . . . There's a whole world out there! . . . as much ours as theirs . . . I'm tired of using my body as a faceless thing to lure another faceless thing.

"I want to love a Person."

For thousands of young men mesmerized by their newly won sexual freedom, this notion was truly radical. As the gay psychologist Joe Brewer told Randy Shilts, "Stripped of humanity, sex sought ever rising levels of physical stimulation in increasingly esoteric practices," while Brewer's colleague Gary Walsh saw promiscuity as something more positive — "a means to exorcise the guilt . . . ingrained in all gay men by a heterosexual society."

In an interview published in 1982, the French theorist Michel Foucault explained the prevalence of promiscuity among gay men this way: "In Western Christian culture homosexuality was banished and therefore had to concentrate all its energy on the act of sex itself. Homosexuals were not allowed to elaborate a system of courtship because the cultural expression necessary for such an elaboration was denied them. The wink on the street, the split-second decision to get it on, the speed with which homosexual relations are consummated: all these are products of an interdiction."

Kramer's novel had focused on the emotional damage he thought had been inflicted by nonstop sex. But like Edmund White's pre-AIDS speculation about the possible cost of gay fantasies of San Francisco — "Did we know what price these dreams would exact?" — something else Kramer wrote would soon sound like an ominous prophecy. Everything had to change, said the narrator of *Faggots* — "before you fuck yourself to death."

Until the onset of the epidemic, almost everyone speaking publicly for the movement had assumed that an unfettered and unlimited sexuality was one of its most important achievements. For many, this was the main reason they were glad to be gay, and they reveled in their outlaw status. Gay people who had accepted themselves had created new lives by ignoring conventional advice. Thousands were addicted to danger; thousands more were addicted to sex. Unlimited access to sex was used like a drug to cure whatever ailed you. These attitudes deafened many gay men to the earliest warnings about the possible dangers of their behavior.

Philip Gefter recalled the Fire Island scene at the height of the seventies: "The Ice Palace in the Grove was the most fabulous disco I'd ever been to in my life because there were two thousand writhing, drugged, beautiful bodies dancing on this dance floor. By 6:00 A.M., we were outside around the pool, and we were dancing under the stars as the sun was coming up. And I believed at that moment in time that we were having more fun than anybody in the *history* of civilization had ever had. Because there was the combination of that sexual tension among all of these men, in concert with the drugs we were taking and the electronics of the music — and the sun coming up. It created a kind of *thrill* and excitement and sensation that I believe no culture had ever experienced before."

Then there was the Meat Rack — a sexual meeting ground in the woods between the two gay Fire Island communities, the Pines and the Grove. "The Meat Rack, basically, is this enchanted forest," said Gefter. "I remember walking through the Meat Rack, thinking, This was my *wildest* fantasy when I was in summer camp. There were either couples or *clusters* of men in various permutations of sexual activity. I remember once when I went there on the way back from the Ice Palace with Peter and Eric at 7:00 in the morning. And there were these three or four men, naked. They were all, like, playing with each other's hard-ons and sucking each other off, and sniffing an ethyl chloride rag. It's like poppers, but it's somehow more extreme. Basically it just renders you brainless. I never did it.

"So we were watching this cluster, and they just kind of reached out and grabbed us, drew us in. So we found ourselves — *six* of us in this cluster of men, in this *beautiful* path in the woods — with our pants down to our knees, in various permutations of sucking and fucking.

"That's kind of what the Meat Rack was like."

Faggots "angered everyone, of course," Kramer recalled, "particularly the gay political leaders who told everybody they should have as much love as they want." But Kramer thought that "having so much sex made finding love impossible. Everyone I knew wanted . . . a lover, and everyone was screwing himself twenty-four hours a day . . . to what turned out to be to death. . . . You could have sex twenty-three times just going to the market." After *Faggots* was published, it was made "pointedly clear" to him that he was "no longer welcome" on Fire Island.

At the beginning of the epidemic, because no one knew for sure whether AIDS really was a sexually transmitted disease, anyone recommending reduced sexual activity as a sensible precaution ran the risk of being attacked for "internalized homophobia" or "sexual fascism." And because Kramer had already attacked promiscuity for other reasons, he was particularly vulnerable to this criticism.

He went to his doctor three weeks after the *Times* article to ask him what he could do to avoid the new disease. "I'd stop having sex," his physician told him. One month after that appointment, his first warning about the epidemic appeared in the *New York Native*, a gay newspaper that pioneered coverage of the disease:

The men who have been stricken don't appear to have done anything that many New York gay men haven't done at one time or another. We're appalled that this is happening to them and terrified that it could happen to us. It's easy to become frightened that one of the many things we've done or taken over the past years may be all that it takes for a cancer to grow from a tiny something-or-other that got in there who knows when from doing who knows what. . . . Money is desperately needed. . . . This is our disease and we must take care of each other and ourselves. In the past we have often been a divided community; I hope we can all get together on this emergency, undivided, cohesively, and with all the numbers we in so many ways possess.

The attacks he received for this sensible appeal set the tone for the debate within the gay community during the first few years of the epidemic. On one side were those like Kramer who believed "*something* we are doing is ticking off the time bomb that his causing the breakdown of immunity in certain bodies," and therefore "wouldn't it be better to be cautious, rather than reckless?" On the other side were writers like Robert Chesley, who immediately skewered Kramer in the letters column of the *Native:*

> I think the concealed meaning in Kramer's emotionalism is the triumph of guilt: that gay men *deserve* to die for their promiscuity. In his novel, *Faggots,* Kramer told us that sex is dirty and that we ought not be doing what we're doing. . . . It's easy to become frightened that Kramer's *real* emotion is a sense of having been vindicated, though tragically. . . . Read anything by Kramer closely. I think you'll find that the subtext is always: the wages of gay sin are death . . . I am not downplaying the seriousness of Kaposi's sarcoma. But something else is happening here, which is also serious: gay homophobia and anti-eroticism.

Kramer later credited Chesley's attack with turning him into an activist. Kramer was the founder of two of the most important gay organizations spawned by the epidemic. The first one was Gay Men's Health Crisis, which grew out of a fund-raising meeting in Kramer's Fifth Avenue apartment on August 11, 1981, where he raised $6,635. Philip Gefter attended this first gathering with Jack Fitzsimmons; then Gefter volunteered to organize a follow-up fund-raiser on Fire Island over Labor Day weekend.

"Larry made this impassioned plea for us to focus all of our attention and our energy on this because this could become a major crisis," said Gefter, who was working as a picture editor at *Forbes* magazine at the time. "We went out to dinner after that meeting, and I remember Jack was panicked. I'd never seen him so panicked. He was a very controlled person and very even tempered. But he was really scared, much more than I was. I asked him, 'Why are you so scared?' And he couldn't answer. For six years he had an obsession about AIDS. Every time there was anything in the paper about it, he would call me and read me the story."

Gefter used the Xerox machine at *Forbes* to make several thousand copies of a six-page brochure about the epidemic, and a copy was placed at the front door of every house in the Pines and the Grove in September. The response was tepid.

"Nobody cared," Gefter remembered. "Nobody was interested. They'd just walk by us. I was profoundly disappointed in my community at that moment in time." A paltry $769.55 was collected during the whole weekend.

"They thought that this had nothing to do with them," Gefter continued, because "they were good clean middle-class men who in fact were the very men who hung out at places like the Anvil and the Mineshaft and the baths, so it had everything to do with them. But they just denied it. I didn't have a clue, but I thought it was sexually transmitted. I know that I had had syphilis, gonorrhea, and hepatitis in the previous six years. I thought it was a breakdown of the immune system. I didn't know how or why. I remember there were some kind of black comedic conclusions we had arrived at. At one point we thought it was the deer on Fire Island; years later we found out that the deer *did* carry Lyme disease. That was kind of a tongue-in-cheek conclusion. We thought it might have been the drugs we had been taking; we thought it might have been what we had been doing to our bodies; we thought it might have been just the general erosion of our immune system. Drugs, sex, the various illnesses we had had.

"Never once did I think this was some kind of divine retribution for what most of the world thought of as our sins, and what I thought of as a celebration. Partly, my conclusion about why I was a survivor may have to do with the general make-up of my body, for sure, but I also think that I never felt guilty about sex. I always thought that sex was a kind of celebration. That's not to say that there are not a lot of people who also felt that way who have since died. Guilt was never involved for me when it came to sex. I felt guilty about other things, but not sex and not about the amount of sex I had.

"Tom Johnston was the first person I knew who got sick. He was a friend of Jack's. He had a real gym body. He wasn't beautiful at all, but he had that Fire Island look. We shared a house in Water Mill in eighty-three or eighty-four. And I remember not knowing how to talk to him about having this disease. What did we call it then? GRID?* And just being terrified of it: any glass in the cabinet was somehow home to the virus. I was afraid to use the same toilet paper. Tom was trying all kinds of alternative treatments even then. I remember seaweed in the refrigerator. It was all so new and all so terrifying. We didn't know enough about the virus then, so that even though I assumed on some level that it was sexually transmitted, that didn't exclude the possibility of being exposed to it in any number of ways. I had also had parasites in the seventies, and you can get parasites from somebody else's water glass. So I thought that was possible with this virus.

"But I never thought this was moral retribution. I also bought into the conspiracy theories to some extent. I thought the world was hostile to this community and this is a concentrated community and here is some new disease kind of revolving within this community. I entertained the possibility that somehow something was planted by the government. I can't be more specific. I still think that's possible. It was too concentrated a community and too threatening to our society. Gay culture was becoming so visible at that moment in time. It was a period of time when being gay in New York was very chic — all these fashion designers, Studio 54. That whole nexus was written about in magazines and it seemed very exotic and appealing; ten years earlier it was still this hideous aberration. And that was very threatening to America: the established order.

"The party didn't stop for several years. By 1985 the party had stopped; but from 1981 to 1985 I don't think the party stopped at all. People were more and more terrified. I knew people who were afraid to go out and have sex. But I remember going to the Boy Bar in eighty-three or eighty-four, and it was packed. I remember going to The Bar from eighty-one to eighty-five, and it was always packed. And I continued to have sex. I did change it to some extent. I don't remember really using condoms until later. But I believe that one reason that I am a survivor is that whenever I was entered I came first, and the person who was inside me had to come out before he came. I would say that was true at least ninety-five percent of the time. They may have perceived me to be a selfish lover, but in the long run it turns out that that may be why I'm alive today."

ONE SCIENTIST outside the government was more important than any other heterosexual in New York City in sounding the alarm about the growing crisis. Her name was Mathilde Krim, and she was born in Italy in

*The first name given the disease was Gay Related Immune Deficiency. At a meeting in July 1982 about the blood supply, leaders of the blood industry, hemophiliac groups, gay community

1926, the daughter of a Swiss father and a mother of Austrian descent who had grown up in Czechoslovakia. When she was a child, her family moved to Geneva. In 1945, she made her first Jewish friends at the University of Geneva, and she was appalled by what Hitler had done to the Jewish population of Europe. To the dismay of her parents, she converted to Judaism and began to run guns to Menachem Begin's underground in Israel. After the Israeli War of Independence, she moved to Jaffa. Then she became a cancer researcher at the Weizmann Institute of Science. In 1956, she gave a tour of the laboratory to Arthur Krim, the chairman of United Artists, and a longtime Democratic party activist. In 1958, Arthur and Mathilde were married and she moved to Manhattan.

After playing an important role in the passage of the National Cancer Act of 1971, Dr. Krim continued to work as a cancer researcher. In 1980, Joseph Sonnabend, a former colleague who was now practicing medicine in Greenwich Village, told her that some of his patients had strange symptoms including swollen lymph glands. Three years later, Dr. Krim founded the AIDS Medical Foundation, which merged in 1985 with the National AIDS Research Foundation in Los Angeles to form the American Foundation for AIDS Research. From that platform she fought for funds to perform basic research.

With Elizabeth Taylor, Barbra Streisand, Woody Allen and Warren Beatty among her allies, Dr. Krim played a pivotal role in making the cause of AIDS respectable within the heterosexual community. People she knew "felt that this was a disease that resulted from a sleazy life style, drugs or kinky sex," she told George Johnson of *The New York Times* in 1988. They felt "that certain people had learned their lesson and it served them right. . . . That was the attitude, even on the part of respectable foundations that are supposed to be concerned about human welfare."

The reaction of many of her heterosexual friends reminded her of the stories she had heard about Jews during the war before she knew any herself, that they were dirty and evil and deserved to die. Dr. Krim was determined to prevent America from using AIDS to stigmatize homosexuals — and with the help of many of her famous Hollywood friends, she would be magnificently successful.

RANDY SHILTS BELIEVED that a Canadian airline steward named Gaetan Dugas had played a key role in spreading the epidemic across North

---

organizations, and representatives from the federal government agreed to rename it Acquired Immune Deficiency Syndrome.

America. Researchers called him "Patient Zero" because at least 40 of the first 248 gay men diagnosed with AIDS before April 1982 had either "had sex with Dugas or had had sex with someone who had." Eleven cases could be connected to a single tryst with the airline steward. A statistician at the Centers for Disease Control pondered whether it could be coincidental that 40 of the first 248 victims were all linked to the same man. He decided "the chance did not approach zero — it was zero."

Gay men had violently different reactions to the first reports about the epidemic. Some stopped having sex altogether: psychoanalyst Richard Isay reported that one of his patients even stopped masturbating because AIDS had made him feel so guilty about his sexuality. Other men sharply reduced their activity, but a third group continued to live their lives exactly the way they always had. Dugas was part of this third group — and like many other men in denial, he became furious whenever anyone suggested he might have a responsibility to stop having sex.

"Of course I'm going to have sex," he told a doctor who asked him to be more careful in April 1982. Then he directly contradicted himself: "Nobody's proven to me that you can spread cancer. Somebody gave this thing to me. I'm not going to give up sex." At the end of 1982, an AIDS hotline received repeated calls from men complaining about "a man with a French accent" who was having sex at the baths, and then calmly telling his partners afterward that he had gay cancer. Challenged again about his activity, Dugas articulated another notion that would become a popular, and criminally irresponsible, argument among some of those who knew that they had been infected by the virus — but remained determined to go on having as much sex as possible. "It's their duty to protect themselves," he said of his partners. "They know what's going on there. They've heard about this disease." Then he added guiltlessly, "I've got it. They can get it too." A San Francisco health official who confronted Dugas thought that he should have been locked up.

Howard Rosenman was an extremely active Fire Island visitor in the summers of the seventies. He never slept with Dugas, but he did have sex with a great many of the first AIDS patients on Fire Island, beginning with Enno Poersch, who was "German and six feet four, and one of the most beautiful men I have ever seen.

"He lived in the house right across from the one I had rented for the summer in the Pines. That was the house Randy Shilts wrote about. I didn't sleep with Patient Zero, but I slept with most of Patients One through Nineteen at sometime during the eleven years I had summered on Fire Island. Okay? *Most* of them. In the summer of 1980 they told us

Poersch's lover got cat scratch fever [he actually had toxoplasmosis; he died on January 15, 1981]. I was in medical school for three years, right? I remember saying to myself, cat scratch fever? That's really odd. That was the end of the summer of 1980, and that was the first time I knew something was rotten in the state of Denmark. I was at the zenith of my wildest time. And then I came home to California.

"Somewhere along the winter or the spring of 1980 I had a boyfriend named Reuven Levi-Proctor who was a rabbi drug dealer who Larry Kramer wrote about in *Faggots*. He was from Baltimore, Maryland, and his parents were very religious Jews. But in the summer of 1980, Reuven and I were now friends and he had a new boyfriend who came down with these marks on his body and died very, very quickly. And none of us knew what it was except Dr. Joel Weismann who treated him. Then Bronte Woodard, who was a writer who wrote *Grease*. He had been writing a screenplay for me. He was a bighearted guy from the south. He was like a big fat boy, bald. He used to give orgies that Nureyev used to attend in L.A., and he was also writing for Allan Carr. He got very, very, very sick with liver disease and other diseases." Woodard died August 6, 1980. His obituary gave the cause of death as liver failure.

Rosenman had been friendly with Larry Kramer until people whom Rosenman had told Kramer about in general conversations turned up as characters in *Faggots*. Kramer hadn't shown him the manuscript in advance. "He was dishonest with me," said Rosenman, "and I punched him out and I wasn't speaking to him. He modeled some of the characters in *Faggots* on people that were really close friends of mine. And I remember walking to the boat and Larry was sitting at a makeshift desk collecting money for gay cancer. And I remember saying to myself, 'Howard, whatever's going on here is really big-time and important. You've got to transcend your level of loathing for Larry and go for what he is representing and give him money.' And I gave him a hundred bucks. And I remember leaving the island and saying to myself, 'That fucking Larry Kramer. She may be one hysterical girl, but boy oh boy, is she committed!'"

In fact all of Kramer's instincts about how the community should have behaved at the beginning of the epidemic proved to be absolutely correct. When GMHC was founded, he felt exhilarated: "It was one of those rare moments in life when one felt completely utilized, useful, with a true reason to be alive." But Kramer continued to behave like a volcano that was never dormant, constantly spewing lava in all directions.

Because he was so lacking in any ability to get along with his colleagues, much less his adversaries, no one ever considered Kramer for GMHC's presidency. That job went to Paul Popham, a beautiful, closeted, ex–Green Beret, who worried that his mailman would realize that he was gay if he saw an invitation for a fund-raiser with Gay Men's Health Crisis as the return address. Popham constantly battled with Kramer about tactics and substance. Later, Kramer admitted that he had been somewhat in love with Popham.

One of the first arguments between Kramer and Popham was over whether GMHC should tell its members to stop having sex altogether, or reduce the number of their sexual partners. Kramer was adamant that they should be warned, but Popham and rest of the board opposed the idea. What if it was determined that there was *no* infectious agent? Popham asked. Then GMHC would look ridiculous.

The infighting came to a head in April 1983, after Kramer had repeatedly accused Mayor Edward I. Koch of an inadequate response to the health crisis. After months of violent attacks from Kramer, the mayor had finally agreed to a meeting about AIDS with ten representatives of gay groups around the city. But the GMHC board refused to send Kramer as one of its two envoys. Paul Popham was terrified of how Kramer might behave in a small meeting with the mayor. Kramer was stunned — and promptly resigned from the board. After that, GMHC rebuffed all of his subsequent efforts to rejoin the organization.

A decade later, Koch said that he regretted not meeting with Kramer sooner. "I read a letter from him in one of the magazines in which he was . . . denouncing me," Koch said. "I inquired and I was told that he had made a request for a meeting . . . I was told he was not held in high regard because of his vehemence and I should just ignore it. I'm sorry I took their advice, frankly. He is a very important force in the AIDS movement. . . . He has caused people to give this matter a lot of attention."

Despite all the internal dissension, GMHC grew rapidly into an extremely effective social service agency and lobbying group. Anyone with AIDS could come to the agency for help. After one of Kramer's periodic complaints about inadequate press coverage of the epidemic, the *Times* printed a glowing three-thousand-word feature story about GMHC at the end of 1983. Written by Maureen Dowd, then a rising star on the paper's metropolitan staff, the story described the agency as a "sophisticated social-service organization with growing political power, 12 paid staff members, an 8-member board of directors, 500 male and female volunteers, and a 1984 budget of $900,000" which was "currently helping 250 people with AIDS."

The story reported that GMHC had received a $200,000 grant from

New York State and $24,500 from the city, and credited the group with lobbying that helped to increase federal funds for AIDS from $22 million to $40 million. By this time, 1,261 New Yorkers had been diagnosed with AIDS, and forty-one percent of them had died. The number of AIDS cases had risen forty-eight percent in the first six months of 1983, compared with the same period a year earlier. Volunteers told Dowd a litany of horror stories — about government clerks who neglected AIDS cases "because they are afraid to be in the same room to fill out forms," about nurses and orderlies who refused to enter the rooms of AIDS patients, even a doctor who refused to clean off a patient's bloody face, and handed a GMHC volunteer a piece of gauze and told him to clean up the patient himself.

"Fighting a siege of death and prejudice, the community that was once characterized by a carefree and freewheeling spirit has evolved into a more mature and politically savvy population," Dowd wrote. The reporter also noted another effect of the crisis on the gay community: "Homosexual leaders . . . said it has drawn many young professionals out of the closet." A thirty-four-year-old psychologist named Ken Wein told Dowd, "I wouldn't have put myself on the line before. AIDS finally strengthened my will to confront my boss, who was biased against gays, and quit a job at a hospital where I worked. You get enraged at the feeling that the world thinks you're disposable because you're gay."

Dowd's story was one of the most favorable articles ever written about the gay community during the Rosenthal regime. "On the whole," she concluded, "homosexual leaders agreed the community has developed a new maturity in coping with the AIDS crisis."

NEW YORK had far more AIDS cases than any other city in America. For Howard Rosenman, 1982 was "already my last summer on Fire Island because there were people coming off the boat with IV things plugged into their arms, walking down the boulevard with those metal stands on which you hung the IV bag. And it was deathly, and people were dying, fucking getting sick left and right by eighty-two. I definitely think that the combination of gay liberation and the gay sexuality, the freedom of it, bred the matrix in which this epidemic could form — the way gays sanctioned promiscuity, innocently. In L.A., the 8709 was at the epicenter of this way of life because 8709 was the hippest bathhouse in the country. From that corner the disease spread. The epidemic started right there. In that 8709 came all those boys from New York, Chicago, and Miami. [A famous clothes designer from New York] would fly out to L.A. just to go there for a night. People would come out for weekends and go back to New Orleans and go back to Toronto and go back to Montreal. People would spend whole weekends at those baths. Ten years later I saw how destructive that was for me. But only ten years later.

"The price of this is so staggering. It informs every second of my life. I know 450 people that died of AIDS that I can count. Thirty to 40 of my close friends that I had made from 1967 to today, died from this disease. I've been through their deaths on a very personal level, in a big way. You know, I assisted them dying, did their errands, washed them, fed them, gave them their medicines. And then watched them die.

"I wake up in the morning and it's as if I'm outside of my body and I look at my body, and I say, 'How come this didn't happen to you? You were the wildest of all of your friends and you were a leader of all this. You said let's go to San Francisco for the weekend, all fifty of us, and we all went to party.'

"We had a group in California that came out to L.A. between 1972 and 1973, about fifty of us, that partied every weekend. Nando Scarffioti, who was a production designer for Bertolucci's movies, *The Conformist* and *The Last Emperor,* he was the rich one. He bought Brooke Hayward's house, which I turned him on to. In that house from 1972 to 1983 fifty of us that came from New York to get into the motion picture business partied every weekend, Friday, Saturday, and Sunday. And at the beginning we would buy a gram of coke and split it between all of us for the entire weekend. You just took one little toot at the very beginning. By the time the party was over, we would consume six ounces of cocaine in one weekend — and every other drug known to man. Of those fifty, there are six that are alive. Everybody else is dead. My closest friends in the world. People that I called every single day of my life for ten years in a row, who I holidayed with, who I New Year's Eved with, who I went to the Saint with, who I went to Fire Island with. Gay people, if they're not married and living in another city — especially out there, we form a tribe. It was a way of making a family. And we had our own traditions and we had our own worlds and our own celebrations and rituals. All of them are dead. It is beyond staggering to me. I do make friends, but I force myself to. I don't want to make new friends because it's, like, I don't want to make new gay friends because I think I'm going to lose them, you know? I'm on my fourth generation of people now that are dying.

"I feel that if I die it doesn't matter. I'm not that afraid of death anymore because maybe it'll be a relief, because the sense of loss is so overwhelming to me that I think that nothing is permanent. And it's made me cynical and sad and depressed. Now on the other hand, what I've replaced the sense of loss with is the sense of fulfillment that I get out of documentaries which mean something personal to me. I produce them without a fee." Rosenman produced *Common Threads,* an Oscar-winning documentary about the quilt invented by veteran San Francisco activist Cleve Jones to memorialize people who died of AIDS. Rob Epstein and Jeff Friedman directed the film, and Dustin Hoffman narrated. "If *Common Threads* transforms one straight person's homophobia into a more empathic way of viewing gay people, then I feel I have been successful in my life." Rosenman was also one of the producers of Epstein and Friedman's *Celluloid Closet,* the documentary based on Vito Russo's history of gay characters in film. "That's another film that shifts the homophobic curve downwards," said Rosenman. "That's what keeps me going."

IN 1985, Philip Gefter decided to leave New York and move to San Francisco. He and Jack Fitzsimmons were no longer lovers, but their relationship had evolved "in a way that I think many gay relationships evolve," Gefter recalled. "There was a kind of brotherly love with physical intimacy. But there was no commitment to an exclusive relationship. So I went to San Francisco in 1985. Jack came to visit me a lot — half a dozen times. And he would spend two weeks at a time.

"I met John McCarron in 1986. He was two years younger than me. He was thirty-three in eighty-six. I met him at a performance through mutual friends. My sexual habits had changed dramatically by then. I really didn't have very much sex at all. I might have gone on several dates between eighty-five and eighty-six, which is when I met John. So we were involved and we had a monogamous relationship for a year. I was working in Sausalito and he was living in the Castro. He was director of San Francisco Art Space, which was quite an influential arts center.

"When I moved there in 1985 it was like moving to the City of the Dead. I could walk down Castro Street, and there wouldn't be a soul on Castro Street. It doesn't mean that there weren't people in bars, but it didn't have the exuberance it had five years earlier. It felt like there was a pall over the city. I moved there to write. I didn't move there to have sex. But when I met John it seemed auspicious enough. So we were involved and we had a monogamous relationship for a year."

In April 1984, the federal government announced that it had isolated a virus that was the cause of AIDS. French researchers had actually made the original discovery, but it would take three more years and a lawsuit before they got part of the credit they deserved. In March 1985, a test finally became available that could detect antibodies that indicated exposure to the virus. But at this point there were still no effective treatments, and no one knew what percentage of the people who tested positive would ultimately get sick. As a result, thousands of gay men continued to resist testing. What was the point? they asked. If they learned they were positive, they would just worry themselves to death anyway.

Gefter had remained in close touch with Jack Fitzsimmons back in New York. "From 1981 to 1987, Jack is in superb health," Gefter said. But Fitzsimmons was one of the many who refused to be tested. "Some time in May of eighty-seven, Jack started complaining of shortness of breath," said Gefter. "He wasn't breathing as easily as he normally did. He went to a heterosexual doctor on Park Avenue who told him he had bronchitis. A month went by, and it was getting worse, not better. He was having greater difficulty breathing. He would call me from his house in Water Mill [on Long Island] on weekends when I was living in California, and saying that he really couldn't breathe. And I would say, 'Are you panicked about it? If you are, you need to go to the hospital. This is a problem.' And I remember him saying to me, it was a little better when he drove around, he could breathe a little better. So I remember telling him to please call his friend Lee Mindel, who was an architect with a house in the Hamptons. And maybe he would drive him to the hospital or something. So Lee takes him to the hospital, and it turns out that he has pneumocystis," a particularly virulent form of pneumonia.

Gefter flew in from California and visited Fitzsimmons at New York Hospital. "He had always seemed like he was in great health except for these two months. He called me from a Fourth of July party at Andy Tobias's in the Pines to tell me he was really having trouble breathing. So I spent a weekend sometime in late July, probably a week after Andy's party, visiting him in the hospital.

"So this is a horror story. He's on an oxygen mask. He tells me that he's terrified of going on a respirator. He takes off the oxygen mask and he's talking to me for two hours without it. The nurse walks in, and says, 'Oh, you really have to have the oxygen mask on. You can't be sitting there with the oxygen mask off.' So they put it on and they have to increase the dose of oxygen. When I got there, it was thirty-five percent. The next day it's something like ninety-five percent. He's having greater trouble breathing. Maybe they were giving him Bactrim. They really were not very sophisticated in 1987 about the medication. The nurse had come in three or four times before she noticed that he wasn't wearing the oxygen mask.

"He said to me that he really did not want to go on a respirator. It got to the point where he really couldn't breathe, even with the oxygen mask. And I could see that he was becoming somewhat delusional. So I went to the doctor, and I said something is wrong here. They said they were going to take him upstairs to make him more comfortable. And they put him on a respirator. They didn't tell us. Two hours later he was on a respirator, hands tied down, with a tube in his mouth. He couldn't speak." The next day he was still on the respirator, but his hands had been untied: "He could write, so I still have some of the things he wrote. I had to fly back to San Francisco because I was working full-time at the *San Francisco Examiner*. Jack was on a respirator and became comatose. He died two weeks later. Then I flew back for the funeral." One of Fitzsimmons's closest friends at his law firm was Susan Thomases — not yet famous as one of Bill and Hillary Clinton's confidantes. "Susan ended up being the person who organized Jack's funeral," Gefter remembered.

BACK IN SAN FRANCISCO, Gefter was still in a relationship with John McCarron: "I had been fucking John. And we were having unsafe sex. I fucked John for most of the relationship. At the end of the relationship he started fucking me. John maintained that he was HIV-negative. But he had never been tested. And this caused a rupture in our relationship over the course of a year. I had been tested twice, and I was HIV-negative at this point in time. When I questioned John about his sexual behavior, he maintained that he had had very little sex. And he was certain that he was HIV-negative.

"But there was no basis for this conclusion. *None.* In fact I was not convinced at all. Gina Kolata wrote a story in the *Times* about the fact that the virus could hide in macrophages in the system — for six months, or even much longer. And as a result, antibodies don't appear. So there might have been a lot of false HIV-negative results. I panicked. I thought, that is why I continue to be HIV-negative. In the article a doctor named Jay Levy is quoted extensively, and he is at UC in San Francisco. So I called him, and I said, 'I am a prime candidate for your study because given my history I am such a prime candidate to be HIV-positive, and I don't understand why I'm not.' And he does all these tests. The virus is nowhere to be found in my body. That's the result of his tests. I am simply clean. So I have all this documentation that I am HIV-negative. And I say, 'John, we are having unsafe sex. I am fucking you, I don't come inside you, but I'm in you, I could be exposed to the virus.' And he refuses to have the test.

"Then Jack [Fitzsimmons] gets sick and dies."

When Gefter returned to San Francisco from Fitzsimmons's funeral, he withdrew completely from John McCarron; within a month they had broken up. "The juxtaposition of Jack dying of AIDS and John refusing to be tested and my being HIV-negative scared me a lot."

Four months later, in January 1988, John came down with "a very severe flu. Jack dies in July of eighty-seven. And it turns out that John has the virus. He had very high fevers, and he had flu-like symptoms. He had pneumonia. It's pneumocystis and these are the first symptoms of the disease.

"I am mortified. But also really upset. I'm concerned about John — upset that he is sick. Mortified for myself. I had a relationship with him for a year. We were having unsafe sex. He kept assuring me that he was HIV-negative. And we broke up because he wouldn't have the test. And four months later he's diagnosed.

"I'm furious."

Like thousands of others in the epidemic, Gefter returned to his ex-lover after he got sick to take care of him. "I went to the hospital every day. The first time he saw me after the diagnosis, he burst into tears, and he apologized profusely. And he felt awful. A month later I went to be tested again.

"And I was negative.

"He was in and out of the hospital half a dozen times for a year. We were no longer boyfriends, but I would take care of him a lot. I would visit him. I would take care of him every day. When he got out of the hospital, I would bring him things. I was a very good caregiver. The horror story, though, with John is, when John got really sick, he disintegrated over the course of a year really quite rapidly. He died in January of eighty-nine. He had said to any number of people that he didn't want to die at the hospital, he wanted to die at home. Three days before he dies, it's very clear that there's no hope. The doctor tells me there's no hope. He says that he has exhausted every medical procedure and that if John wants to go home this is the opportunity to tell him. So the doctor says, 'Do you want to tell him this?'

"I say, 'OK.'"

Gefter told John there was nothing more the doctor could do for him. "If you want to go home, you have to let me know so that we can set up a full-time nurse at home.

"And he says to me: 'Are you telling me that I'm going to die?'

"And I say, 'Yes, that's what the doctor told me.'

"And he was furious, and he blamed me. He thought I was lying to him, he thought I was saying this just to make him feel horrible. He would not talk to me.

"That was it. And he died three days later.

"I continued to go see him, and I sat with him, and he became increasingly comatose, and I was there anyway. Basically what I did was play him music that he loved, like arias, and Mozart, and all that. But he wouldn't forgive me. So that was really quite horrible.

"A week later it's John's funeral. We have a funeral on a boat, which sails out from the piers into San Francisco Bay. It's at nine o'clock in the morning. I'm coming from Sausalito and I get on the Golden Gate Bridge at eight-twenty and there is bumper-to-bumper traffic — stalled. This is highly unusual. So it stalled for at least fifteen or twenty minutes. And I'm panicking because I'm going to miss John's boat.

"Finally I turn on the radio. It turns out the reason for the traffic is an ACT UP demonstration at the tollbooth of the Golden Gate Bridge. I am going to miss the funeral of my ex-lover who died of AIDS because of an ACT UP demonstration! It is really so perverse, I burst out laughing. Anyway, they hold the boat because several of us were late, and they figured out why. So we went out on the boat, and his ashes were poured into the bay. But it was just unbelievable.

"I would hear about half a dozen people who died over the course of three or four months. And then all of a sudden I would read someone's obituary in the *Times* and I would burst into tears. I mean five or six people would die and it would have virtually no effect on me. And then I read Tucker Ashworth's obituary in the *Times*. I didn't even know that he was sick. We had had an affair in the mid-seventies and I wasn't very close to him. But I read his obituary and I just burst into tears. There was a picture above his obituary and his cheeks were sunken and he didn't look like the man I knew.

"What would happen to me was an individual would serve as a symbol of all of the losses intermittently. So his death was a floodgate for me.

"It was worse in San Francisco than New York because it's a smaller city and everyone's death was more visible somehow. And it seemed to me that more people were dying in San Francisco than in New York, but I think it was just because it's a smaller place. The difference between San Francisco and New York is that San Francisco as a city and a community rallied admirably to the epidemic. They set up all kinds of home care programs. There was support on every level, medically, socially, and San Francisco to me was just such an enlightened model for the way human beings should respond to one another.

"I don't know if I feel guilty. I guess my behavior would exhibit a kind of survivor's guilt because over the years I have toyed with danger in terms of having unsafe sex and any psychologist will tell you that that's survivor's guilt. What I feel on some level is that there is some reason that I'm supposed to be alive. And I don't know what that is. But it's not that I feel like I'm being protected exactly, but I feel that it's not in my destiny to have this virus. And that's the best I can do. I don't know. I don't feel secure. I feel lucky. My doctor has said that there are some people who are resistant to the virus. It's that simple. Some people don't get colds. Some people don't get the virus."

Gefter's doctor's suspicion about the ability of some people to resist the virus is widespread in the gay community because many people who engaged in high-risk activity in the early eighties never became infected.

In 1996, there was apparent confirmation of this theory from a study that found that some people had CD4 cells that were pumping out ten times the normal levels of substances called chemokines, which can prevent HIV's reproduction in the test tube. The people with these unusual cells had remained uninfected despite repeated sexual contacts with carriers of the virus.

Two studies published in 1996 indicated that a small percentage of people carry certain genes that either prevent infection altogether, or create a much longer lag time between the moment they are infected, and the onset of the disease. Men with the best overall genetic profiles had lag times about seven years longer than men with the least favorable ones. At the time the study was published, half of the adults infected with the HIV virus developed the disease within ten years of infection.

Gefter believed that the overall impact of the epidemic had been to "make the community much more humane."

"It's unfortunate that it's taken something like this to bring the gay community closer together and enable it to operate from its humanity. It wasn't going in that direction pre-AIDS. It was actually going in the opposite direction.

"We were all objects to each other. I think because of AIDS we became human beings to each other."

ONE OF LARRY KRAMER'S most persistent complaints was about the failure of *The New York Times* and Mayor Edward I. Koch to make it clear from the beginning that AIDS was a crisis — and a communicable disease that gay men needed to avoid. But considering the degree of hostility that gay leaders encountered when they tried to make these points, it's unlikely that anything Koch could have said would have done much to influence the behavior of gay men. Dan William, a prominent gay New York doctor, was denounced as a "monogamist . . . stirring panic" just for suggesting that bathhouses should be required to post warning signs about the epidemic and the dangers of promiscuous sex. In 1982, according to Randy Shilts, "More gays were furious" at William "than at anybody in the Koch administration."

Kramer's most famous piece about the epidemic, entitled "1,112 and Counting," was printed in the *New York Native* on March 14, 1983, and reprinted in many other gay newspapers across the country. "If this article doesn't scare the shit out of you, we're in real trouble," Kramer wrote. "Our continued existence as gay men upon the face of the earth is at stake. Unless we fight for our lives, we shall die." It was one of his most effective polemics, and it included his usual criticism of *The New York Times* for what he considered inadequate coverage of the epidemic. But Kramer's piece was actually published five weeks *after* an extremely comprehensive, six-thousand-word analysis of the epidemic had been published in *The New York Times Magazine.*

The article, by the medical writer Robin Marantz Henig, was thorough, sensible and well written. Even though the precise method of AIDS transmission had not yet been finally determined, the fourth paragraph of the article stated, "The mysterious AIDS organism is generally thought to be a virus or other infectious agent (as opposed to a bacterium) and to be spread in bodily secretions, especially blood and semen."

This article contained everything a prudent gay man needed to know, if he was determined to avoid infection. "Some doctors hesitate to urge celibacy or monogamy on patients for whom casual sex is a way of life," Henig wrote, "but most seem to think the evidence is compelling enough to advocate just that."

> "I strongly recommend that my patients be very circumspect and cautious in their future sexual contacts," says Dr. Dan William, a Manhattan internist who treats primarily homosexual men. In his practice of some 2,000 patients, he has seen 24 cases of AIDS.
>
> "I tell my patients what the epidemiologists know — which isn't much," says Dr. William. "We are more or less convinced that we are dealing with a sexually transmissible agent. Large numbers of contacts — or a small number of indiscriminate contacts — increase the probability of exposure. In addition, a patient's susceptibility to any infectious disease is much greater." Dr. William counsels monogamy, and, he

adds, "It's important for a patient to emphasize to his sex contact that he must not bring any new diseases home with him."

Many doctors go even further. They urge patients to eliminate anal intercourse,* which frequently results in bleeding or trauma to the mucosal lining and is a possible source of AIDS transmission. They advise their homosexual patients to use condoms, which are thought to inhibit the spread of similarly transmitted diseases such as hepatitis B.

As a result of articles like this one, by the middle of 1983, any gay man sophisticated enough to be a reader of the *Times* already knew that unprotected anal intercourse was probably the most dangerous activity he could engage in. The worst blunder of the federal government was its failure to use television to reach people who weren't reading the *Times,* to make sure they knew about the dangers of the epidemic.

Reagan's alliance with the religious right, and its squeamishness about explicit descriptions of unsafe sex, combined to prevent the comprehensive sex education that young people desperately needed to avoid infection. Members of the Moral Majority believed that it would be worse to describe gay sex to young people than it was to deprive them of the information they might require to stay healthy. This attitude was another indication of the persistence of the myth that homosexuality was contagious — even though Reagan himself had publicly rejected that idea during the battle over the Briggs amendment that would have banned gay teachers from California's public schools.

Five years into the epidemic, one important member of the Reagan administration finally delivered a direct attack on the criminally irresponsible attitude toward AIDS education which the president's religious allies had encouraged. In October 1986, Surgeon General C. Everett Koop issued a blistering report.

"Many people, especially our youth, are not receiving information that is vital to their future health and well-being because of our reticence in dealing with the subjects of sex, sexual practices and homosexuality," the surgeon general wrote. "This silence must end. We can no longer afford to sidestep frank, open discussions about sexual practices — homosexual and heterosexual. Education about AIDS should start at an early age so that children can grow up knowing the behaviors to avoid to protect themselves from exposure to the AIDS virus."

Koop said AIDS education should begin "at the lowest grade possible"

*In the 1980s, the words *anal intercourse* had appeared in the *Times* only once before, in a review of *Time of Desecration,* a novel by Alberto Moravia.

in elementary school and be "reinforced at home" by parents. And he made it clear that anal intercourse — described in explicit detail in his report — had to be one of the activities young children were educated about for their own protection. But neither Reagan nor George Bush nor Bill Clinton would ever do anything significant to implement these extremely sensible recommendations.

The refusal to educate the young about the specifics of how this disease was transmitted was one of the worst scandals of the early years of the AIDS epidemic — and it persists, fifteen years after the epidemic began.

Another unconscionable mistake was the fierce opposition of the American Red Cross and other leading blood bankers to what they considered expensive tests, which could have protected the blood supply much earlier and prevented many AIDS infections through transfusion.

The miracle was that hundreds of thousands of men *did* change their sexual activities dramatically beginning in 1983 — changes that saved their lives. In big cities and small towns across the country, there were sharp drops in the rate of anal gonorrhea infections — the most reliable indicator of safer sex practices. And after the HIV test became available, the rate of new HIV infections among gay men declined for several years in a row.

As Kramer pointed out, the tragedy at the beginning was that so many people believed "that giving up careless sex until this blows over is worse than death." In the *New York Native*, he wrote, "How can they value life so little and cocks and asses so much? Come with me, guys, while I visit a few of our friends in Intensive Care at NYU. Notice the looks in their eyes. . . . They'd give up sex forever if you could promise them life."

Students of the epidemic assumed that once it became clear that most kinds of sex were relatively safe, while only one — unprotected anal intercourse — was frequently fatal, it would be fairly easy to convince the vast majority of gay men to abstain from that singularly lethal act. It was disheartening to discover that this kind of lifesaving behavior modification would be much more difficult to accomplish than anyone had suspected — because the emotions surrounding sex and survival are so complicated, especially during a sexually transmitted epidemic.

AS MORE AND MORE of their friends fell ill, the gay identity of some men began to merge with an AIDS identity, to the point where they felt that they weren't really gay unless they had also been infected. Charles Gibson was in this category.

Gibson had grown up in Louisville, and fell in love with New York City when he was twelve, during his first visit in 1964. Even at that age, he figured out how to take the subway by himself and how to use the Empire State Building as his "compass." He came back to live in New York seven years later and went to work for the Children's Television Workshop. There he met Richard Hunt, who was one of the original Muppets. Soon they began a long on-again, off-again affair.

"I met Richard the first year I worked at 'Sesame Street,'" Gibson remembered. "I worked in the mail room and after six months I was able to move into a position in the production department, as a script typist. On one of my first trips to the studio, I was distributing the scripts and I looked up and there stood Richard: the wonder boy from New Jersey.

"He was one of the principal Muppets: he was the back end of Snuffle-upagus, not a speaking part. He had a lot of roles. He was Gladys the Cow. He did a lot of the minor Muppet characters.

"What I remember is Richard calling me in the wee hours of the morning, most of the time waking me in my sleep, inviting himself down with a quart of orange juice and whatever drugs he had at the time. Probably pot. At that time I don't think cocaine was part of it. So he would arrive on the scene, and we'd get high and we'd drink our orange juice. And we'd go to bed, which was where we belonged. Richard and I belonged together in bed. We were *right* together in bed. The less said the better. He looked great. He was wonderful. All those basketball games: they did him good.

"This was probably 1972, the first year I moved to New York. Richard lived an exciting life. He knew celebrities. He was high, he was up and he was on. Things were happening. The Muppets were emerging. They were novel and exciting. They were big."

Once Rudolf Nureyev made a guest appearance on the Muppets. The first time he met Richard Hunt backstage, Nureyev looked him in the eye and introduced himself this way:

"You love to suck cock, don't you?"

Gibson was blond and good-looking and boyish, and he was completely open to the new world around him. He loved the New York men of the early seventies: "They were all unique," he recalled. "There were no clones at the time" — mustachioed men who wore identical uniforms of T-shirts and blue jeans. "They looked independent. They looked assertive. They stood their ground. They looked confident."

He was also in love with adventure: "the thrill of living, and the thrill of discovery. A feeling of being at the center of the universe: discovering a new planet. Extending the frontier. New York was energized. It was an education; it was like a university of life. It was a place where every person had something to say — and no matter how simple, whatever they were doing, it seemed exciting to me. Everybody was remarkable.

"There was nothing risky about sex that I can remember. I suppose there was some chance of falling in love, or it being one-sided. But you didn't think about those things. They always seemed to work themselves out. There was always the prospect that even if it didn't become something serious, that you stood to make a friend."

Gibson first found out about HIV sometime in the early eighties. By now he was living in California, and when he began to read articles about the virus, "It didn't make much sense to me. It was happening somewhere else: it wasn't happening in Sacramento. It wasn't happening in the Grand Canyon — or Death Valley [where he had also lived]. It was something that I read about that was happening somewhere else." Then he saw the picture of an old friend from New York, Mark Feldman, in a gay newspaper in San Francisco. The picture accompanied his obituary. Feldman was the first person he knew who had died of AIDS.

"What I remember is that I knew at one point that there was a risk of exposure, and I remember sort of making kind of a conscious decision not to take any precautions. I think I did bring it on myself. I don't know why I did that. It was almost like I was trying to beat the odds, perhaps. I don't know. I think that at that time I probably could have avoided exposure if I had . . . if I had really, really thought about . . . if I really had . . . if . . . if . . . if I had taken the time to, to really think about it. If I had, if I had talked to people, if I had listened. If it had somehow come home to me in a very dramatic way. I just didn't realize.

"I found out I was positive in eighty-six or eighty-seven. I had a pretty good idea that I was. I had a friend who was living in Sacramento at the time, a fellow I had become friends with when I was living in the Grand Canyon and we were going to get tested. I thought about it and I decided it was better knowing than not knowing. And I found out.

"My friend was negative. His name was Joe. We got tested together at a clinic and they did it anonymously. When we went back for the results, Joe went in to get his first. After having been taken out to be told the results of his test, he came back and he sat down. He told me he was negative.

"Then it was my turn, and I went in. And instead of coming back to my seat I was instructed to another room. To a counselor. Whose job it was to cushion the blow." Gibson laughed at his memory of that moment: "Some cushion. I didn't want to be cushioned. I thought I was probably positive because I knew what the risk factors were. And I knew that I had taken those risks.

"It's painful sometimes to find myself in a crowded bar [in 1991] and to look around me and to imagine myself ten years ago in that same place in those same circumstances, knowing how different it was. And the very dramatic differences for me. My perspective today, the realities.

"I've avoided intimate situations where you would feel an obligation to tell someone. If it was sex I was looking for, I would put myself in a situation where I could have sex without any commitments. Sex where I would be able to remain anonymous. And yet safe. But without feeling the same obligation to be forthcoming about my HIV status.

"Hopefully, you know, something will turn up. But it's hard to go on living with a smile, or go on living with any real enthusiasm, or any real joy. It's like with the frequency of people dying it's almost — it's so temporary: the pleasure, the joy, the thrill, the excitement, the enthusiasm.

"It's like my future consists of appointments to see doctors. I just see this progression. But who knows? Some part of me — that survivor part of me — likes to tell myself that somehow or other some miraculous thing is going to help me to come out of this relatively unscathed."

DAVID BARTOLOMI was born in Boston in 1965, which made him part of the generation that followed Charles Gibson. Bartolomi had fooled around with his best friend when they were both nine and again when they were twelve, and he had also had a couple of fleeting experiences in camp. But his first serious sexual encounter occurred when he was seventeen.

Bartolomi believed the main reason he avoided the epidemic was because his father always sold pornography in his smoke shop in East Boston. "Thank God," he said, "because it really did save my life.

"*Hustler* ran before-and-after pictures of this incredibly handsome man who looked like a model — one where he was young, beautiful, and healthy; the other one, emaciated, sickly, and old. The article didn't have a name for this 'gay disease' because AIDS still wasn't talked about in eighty-one. But it was enough to scare the life out of me. It burned its image into my brain. I knew there was this disease out there that affected gay men. I didn't know what it was called. And it seemed to be a sexually transmitted disease of some sort. I don't think I knew what kind of sex; I just knew that having sex with gay men was becoming risky. Maybe it did say anal sex because I knew it was anal sex. I wasn't that much in the closet about what was happening in the world. But if I'd never picked up those magazines, I never really would have been aware.

"In 1983, I met a guy in Filene's Basement," Boston's famous discount department store. "This handsome man — he was thirty-two — it turns out he was cruising me. I thought he can't be interested in me — I'm in my sweatpants and T-shirt. I haven't shaved. I look like a total slob. And I just had no idea that I could be attractive. And we exchanged phone numbers, and he called me, or I called him one night. I was still living at home. And we arranged for me to come over. I told my parents I had a night class — I was directing a show and I had to work on some scenes. He had a little railroad flat by the train station right at the bottom of Beacon Hill. It must have been the Red Line. I walked in the door, dressed like some greaseball kid from Brooklyn, with greaseball taste, with a guinea T-shirt on and a pair of tacky Jordache jeans. It turned out he was from my hometown — he was from East Boston. He was Italian. His name was Felix DeMarco. I walk into his place and we talked for a minute, and the next thing I know, he grabbed me. He kissed me — threw me down on the couch and had my clothes off so fast my head was spinning. And then he had my feet in the air.

"And I was like, 'Whoa! This is just happening way too fast.' He was fighting his way inside me. Trying so hard to get inside me. And I was just like, 'No, this ain't going to happen.' Like I'm not ready for that act yet. Psychologically I'm not ready for that. I know that there's this gay cancer. I just tightened up all my muscles until he finally gave up. Thank God. He said, 'OK, you can be inside me.' He was fine with it. He let me fuck him twice without a condom. Which leads me to believe that he didn't know he was sick. Because he didn't say, 'Put a condom on.' I was in and out, no problem. After sex, he said to me, 'I'd love to see you again.' And I was all nervous, and not ready to handle any sort of relationship with a man even if it was just sexual. But I had had the night of my life.

"So I pull in about eleven o'clock to my parents'. And I'm thinking, I pulled it off, I'm pretty cool, you know. And my father comes into my room to check on me. While we're talking, I begin to get undressed and ready for bed. As I'm hanging my shirt up, he says, 'Don't think I don't see that hicky on your neck! And I got one word for you: you just better be careful, mister!' And he walked out of the room.

"I froze. I'm *so* caught! What hicky on my neck? I didn't even know I had a hicky on my neck. But my dad saw through it all. He didn't know if it was a boy or a girl. He just knew obviously I'd had sex that night.

"So that year I moved to New York to attend NYU for film. One night my best friend from high school called to verify the name of my Filene's Basement one-night stand.

"'Why?' I asked — not a clue that anything could be wrong.

"'Cause I just read in the paper he's dead. He had AIDS.' And all of a sudden, my whole life flashed in front of me.

"Now I think to myself, if that night had been a little different: if he had either forced his way in you, or you had a few beers, chances are, you would have been infected. You would have come to New York, had sex with boys and girls, and because you would have been too scared to admit that you had unprotected sex or had AIDS, you would have infected other people. And oh my God — this is how it spreads among teenagers because the odds of getting fucked the first time are so tremendous. If it had been just a little different, my life might have been altered forever. When I hear teenagers still contracting HIV, you want to go, This is crazy because this can be avoided. They're still young enough to be educated."

IN 1984, Todd Alexius Long was twenty-three years old when he went on a blind date with Ethan Geto, who was then forty-one. Long was a recent graduate of Rochester Institute of Technology, where he had studied photography. Besides being a lot older, Geto was almost a foot taller than Long. "I said, Well, I could never go out with him," said Long. "But then I did right away. I liked him very much. I guess I felt like he really listened to me. We just seemed to have a lot in common right away." The blind date led to a long relationship, whose first phase lasted four years.

Three years later he decided to bury his past, and in 1988 he legally changed his name to "Xax" — because "I knew my Todd Alexius Long had nothing to do with me." Five years later, he discovered the Radical Faeries, which were started by Mattachine Society founder Harry Hay. One reason Xax appreciated Hay was because the Faeries' founder "points out that we're not male or female — and why should we even want to be? We're just something other — and that's why I changed my name to Xax. Because it had no gender connotation, it had no connotation of anything.

"It was almost even nonhuman — just like an object. And that way whatever came to be 'Xax' would just be whatever I became. It was a pure starting point. Because I always thought of myself as being omnisexual, omni . . . everything. Just completely inclusive."

The same year that he changed his name is when Xax believes he caught the HIV virus — during his first threesome.

"I met this guy at the gym. Got together with him and his lover. Had a great time. Rubber broke. And in retrospect I knew, because the guy was *really* upset about that. And I was like — it was the beginning, I wasn't really that concerned about AIDS yet. We didn't know much about it really. I was just like, I'm fine — nothing hurts me, I'm invincible. Blah blah blah. And he was just so concerned about it. In fact he would never talk to me after that. His lover kept in touch with me for a little while, I think just out of concern."

A few months later Xax came down with shingles, which is sometimes an early indication of the onset of an AIDS infection. "And I was *so* sick for six weeks. And the doctor said we have to test you right away. And that's how I found out" — in February 1989.

But Xax had a very unusual reaction: "I've always looked at that as the most positive experience of my life: finding out I was HIV-positive. Because it was such a blessing in disguise for me that it made me rethink my life: 'Oh, I do want to be alive — and these are the reasons.' Looking around and seeing that tree, 'Well, wow, that's a good enough reason. Oh, that friend of mine — well, that's a good enough reason.' It starts to build the one thing on the next, so you think, Wow, I guess there really is a reason. And I was always very determined to conquer it. Like if there's only one person who conquers AIDS, I'm going to be the one. I don't care if everybody else drops dead, nobody's going to put me in the box of you're-dying-tomorrow.

"I immediately went to all the meetings, and found out everything I could find out. I made up a newsletter called 'Save the Humans.' I took the Save the Whale things and scratched out 'Whales' and put 'Humans' on them. I sent it to all my relatives and friends. I said this is what I've got, this is what is happening. Don't believe all the crap you hear on the television. This is what's known, this is what isn't known. And I will not accept being stuck in a box. I just knew that thinking that way would kill me faster.

"I took Zovirax when I had shingles, although I didn't take it fast enough because I always procrastinated about going to doctors. So it was caught just in time.

"So then I was very healthy. I didn't take any drugs, I still thought drugs were terrible, I took lots of vitamins, health foods. I was macrobiotic.

"Until I found out I was HIV-positive, I didn't want to be alive anyway because I was so depressed. And then, I became HIV-positive, and it kind of forced me to make a decision. It was like, well, here you go, this is what you wanted: take it or leave it or something. It's like, well, you always wanted to be dead, so here you go. Is this what you want?

"And then I changed my mind. It made me see things differently; it made me make choices differently. Making choices toward living instead of against it."

NINETEEN EIGHTY-SIX brought gay people in New York City two glimmers of hope — one from politics and one from science — and one devastating defeat from Washington.

Hope sprang from the action of the New York City Council, where a gay rights bill had been introduced every year since 1971, only to be stymied by the council's majority leader, Thomas Cuite, who was a strong ally of the Catholic Church. "He was absolutely adamant against it," remembered Ed Koch. "There was nothing I could do to get him to change."

When Cuite finally retired at the beginning of 1986, Koch made a crucial deal: he agreed to endorse City Councilman Peter Vallone as Cuite's successor — in return for Vallone's promise that he would let the gay rights bill out of committee, even though Vallone did not support it himself.

Although Koch was frequently attacked by Larry Kramer and others for what activists considered a lackadaisical response to the AIDS crisis, the mayor had a strong record as a supporter of gay rights. In 1978, one of his first official acts as mayor was to issue an executive order prohibiting discrimination within the city government on the basis of sexual orientation. Most of the reporters in the city hall press room were horrified by this edict. Three years earlier, while serving as a congressman, Koch had been one of four cosponsors of a federal bill introduced by Representative Bella Abzug that would have prohibited discrimination in employment, housing, public accommodations, and federally assisted programs on the basis of "affectional or sexual preference."

Tom Stoddard, who by now was serving as the legislative director of the New York Civil Liberties Union, drafted the New York City bill that prohibited discrimination in housing and employment on the basis of sexual orientation. Stoddard "was an extraordinary lawyer," Koch remembered. "Even though he never retreated, he would find a way to explain, to placate and convince opponents that his approach was reasonable, rational and one they could accept. That's a gift."

Despite a huge last-minute push by John Cardinal O'Connor — who said the measure would offer protection to sexual behavior that was "abnormal" and a "sin" — the bill finally passed the council on March 21, 1986, by a vote of twenty-one to fourteen. Ethan Geto was one of the principal lobbyists on behalf of the legislation. The vote was greeted "by cheers and tears from supporters," Joyce Purnick reported in the *Times*.

"God, I can't believe it — after all this time," Stoddard told reporters.

The temperature dropped into the twenties that evening, but more than a thousand demonstrators gathered in Sheridan Square at the site of the original Stonewall riot to celebrate. "Psychologically, people can come out of the closet now," Christopher Mountain exalted.

The passage of the law encouraged thousands of New Yorkers to declare who they really were during the coming decade. Among journalists, for example, in 1980 Joe Nicholson was the only publicly gay reporter at a New York daily; by 1996 more than three hundred of his colleagues at other media outlets had emulated him.

The law also put an end to some blatant examples of discrimination. As late as 1992, the Board on Professional Standards of the American Psychoanalytic Association was still resisting pressure from analyst and activist Richard Isay to promise to accept lesbians and gay men as training analysts. In April 1992, Dr. Isay asked William Rubenstein, a lawyer at the American Civil Liberties Union, to write a letter to the association which pointed out that its continuing failure to promise not to discriminate was illegal under the New York City statute. Just one week later, the executive board of the Psychoanalytic Association finally passed a resolution stating that homosexuals were just as qualified as heterosexuals to become training analysts.

THE OTHER HOPEFUL DEVELOPMENT in the spring of 1986 was an announcement from the National Cancer Institute that a new drug called azidothymidine, or AZT, seemed to help some AIDS patients. Encouraging signs included "fewer fevers, the disappearance of infections, improved appetite and weight gain." In years to come the drug's effectiveness — and toxicity — would be fiercely debated within the gay community, but when AZT was first introduced, it was the only medical treatment that provided any optimism at all. Roy Cohn and the Broadway choreographer Michael Bennett were two of the first AIDS patients to be treated with it.

But most of the good feelings provided by the city council's action and this scientific development were blotted out three months later by a landmark decision by the United States Supreme Court.

In 1976 the Court had infuriated gay leaders by affirming a Virginia sodomy statute, without bothering to hear any arguments in the case.* Ten years later, activists convinced themselves that the national climate

*See page 252.

had changed enough to ensure a reversal. They also believed that they had found the perfect test case to use for a new challenge. Michael Hardwick had been at his home in Atlanta when a policeman barged in to serve him with a warrant to appear in court — because of a ticket for public drinking which Hardwick had already paid. After a roommate waved the policeman toward a back bedroom, the officer found Hardwick performing oral sex with another man and immediately arrested both of them.

At the end of March 1986, the Court heard arguments in *Bowers* v. *Hardwick*. Appearing on behalf of Hardwick, Harvard Law Professor Laurence Tribe told the Court that the Constitution protected private homosexual and heterosexual acts between consenting adults, while an assistant attorney general of Georgia countered that such a finding would undermine states' efforts to maintain "a decent and moral society."

When the justices first met privately to discuss the case two days later, there were five apparent votes in favor of striking down Georgia's sodomy law. John Paul Stevens was part of that initial five-member majority, even though he had told a colleague, "I hate homos."

The other justices who initially joined in that majority decision were William Brennan, Thurgood Marshall, Harry Blackmun, and Lewis Powell. Perhaps because Tribe's argument was considered so persuasive, rumors quickly spread through the gay community that a favorable decision in the case was likely. But less than a week after their first meeting on the matter, Justice Powell wrote a new memorandum to his colleagues indicating that he would probably reverse his vote, thereby providing a majority to *uphold* the antisodomy law.

When the Court rendered its decision on June 30, Justice Byron White took the unusual step of reading large portions of the five-to-four majority opinion from the bench. White was contemptuous of the arguments that Professor Tribe had offered. "To claim that a right to engage in [sodomy] is 'deeply rooted in this Nation's history and tradition' or 'implicit in the concept of ordered liberty' is, at best, facetious," White declared. Chief Justice Warren Burger enthusiastically agreed in a concurring opinion: "To hold that the act of homosexual sodomy is somehow protected as a fundamental right would be to cast aside millennia of moral teaching," Burger said.

But Harry Blackmun filed a fierce dissent: "The majority has distorted the question this case presents," Blackmun stated. The case was really about "the most comprehensive of rights and the right most valued by civilized men," namely "the right to be let alone" — as Justice Louis Brandeis had written in an earlier case in 1928. "The right of an individual to conduct intimate relationships in the intimacy of his or her own home seems to me to be the heart of the Constitution's protection of privacy," Blackmun continued. "Depriving individuals of the right to choose for themselves how to conduct their intimate relationships poses a far greater threat to the values most deeply in our Nation's history than tolerance of nonconformity could ever do."

A Gallup poll revealed that of the seventy-three percent of those who knew about the decision, forty-seven percent disagreed with it, while forty-one percent approved of the Court's action.

Tom Stoddard, who by now had become executive director of the Lambda Legal Defense and Education Fund, called the decision "a major disaster from our point of view." He continued, "For the gay rights movement, this is our Dred Scott case," referring to the 1857 Supreme Court ruling which held that blacks were not citizens and therefore could be slaves. Stoddard felt the Court's action rested on "nothing more substantial than the collective distaste of the five justices in the majority for the conduct under scrutiny." Justice Powell, who provided the key vote upholding the sodomy law, told an astounded clerk that he had never met a homosexual. Court historian David J. Garrow noted that Powell was "apparently unaware" that he had "already employed numerous gay assistants during his fifteen years on the Court."

A few years later, Justice Powell admitted that he had "probably made a mistake" in voting with the majority. "When I had the opportunity to reread the opinions . . . I thought the dissent had the better of the arguments," the justice admitted. Then he added, oddly, that it was a "frivolous case" because it had been brought "just to see what the Court would do," as if that distinguished it from dozens of other cases the justices heard every year.

Gay activists everywhere reacted with fury to the Court's decision. But a resounding vindication for the movement from the same Washington chambers was only a decade away.

THE AIDS COALITION TO UNLEASH POWER was founded in New York in 1987, after Larry Kramer gave another furious speech warning of imminent doom. While the Gay Men's Health Crisis continued to do a superb job of providing social services for AIDS patients and lobbying for more government money for treatment and research, Kramer perceived the need for another kind of organization that could focus a decimated community's anger and take it into the streets.

ACT UP was an instant success, driven by the energy of a new genera-tion of activists in blue jeans and combat boots, most of whom had barely entered elementary school at the time of the Stonewall riot. As forty other chapters formed across the country and around the world, these men and women in their late teens and twenties were joined by thousands of lesbians and gay men from preceding generations. As with the antiwar movement of the sixties, a life-and-death issue had been necessary to bring the generations together in a noble cause.

In fact it was their memory of the sixties which attracted some of the more seasoned ACT UP members to the new organization. Ann Northrop had "marched and demonstrated against the Vietnam war and for the rebirth of feminism," and it "really felt very nostalgic." Northrop was a former journalist turned AIDS educator who fell "totally head over heels in love at first sight" when she attended her first ACT UP meeting in 1988.

"All the goals appealed to me," she told the historian Eric Marcus. "They included everything from finding a cure for AIDS to doing the right education, which meant telling the truth, being explicit . . . and support-ing real protective health measures, as opposed to ineffective supposed moral standards. ACT UP was willing . . . to go out in the street and scream and yell."

Northrop got arrested during one of the Wall Street demonstrations, and she loved it. By going to work in the lesbian and gay community, she felt that she had liberated herself completely, "opening up my life in ways that I couldn't begin to imagine or anticipate. The proof of this was that I felt completely complacent about the idea of getting arrested."

ACT UP's charter described it as a coalition of "diverse individuals united in anger and committed to direct action"; one of its chants iden-tified it as "loud and rude and strong and queer." As the novelist David Leavitt put it, its members were determined to disprove the idea that a community in the grip of AIDS was "weak, ravaged [and] deserving only of charity." Instead, "they presented an image of a community pow-ered by anger and willing to go to almost any length in order to defend itself."

It was a fabulous combination of the practical and the theatrical.

Michelangelo Signorile was typical of the young people who were drawn to activism for the first time by the new organization; before he attended his first ACT UP meeting, the former theatrical press agent turned free-lance writer had never entered the Lesbian and Gay Commu-nity Services Center in Greenwich Village. Signorile was mesmerized by the Monday-night scene inside the former New York City school on 13th

Street, where the weekly meeting of 450 was facilitated by "the extremely handsome" David Robinson, who was wearing a dress, and Maria Maggenti, a "beautiful lesbian with long blond hair." Signorile reported, "Crying and yelling were almost rituals," and he was "exhilarated."

It was also a great place to pick up a date.

Signorile joined the media committee, which was meeting in Vito Russo's apartment, and started reading books by Larry Kramer, Martin Duberman, and other gay writers. "It was time to wake everyone else up too," he decided. The sidewalks of Manhattan were quickly covered with the organization's stenciled slogan, "Silence = Death."

The New York Stock Exchange was one of the first ACT UP targets, with protesters urging investors to sell stock in Burroughs Wellcome, the drug company that owned the patent to AZT and was charging an exorbitant amount for the treatment — as much as $10,000 a year.

"Die-Ins" in the caverns of Wall Street were succeeded by invasions of corporate headquarters. One day in 1989, four young men in business suits moved unchallenged through the front doors of the Burroughs Wellcome corporate headquarters, walked to the third floor, "ejected the startled occupant of an executive office and sealed the doors with metal plates and a high-powered drill," Cynthia Crossen reported on *The Wall Street Journal's* front page. On another occasion, ACT UP members forced Northwest Airlines to abandon its policy of forbidding passage to AIDS patients by staging a phone "zap," which flooded the airline with hundreds of false reservations.

"This is about constantly sticking it in the face of every single person you can stick it in," Vincent Gagliostro explained to the *Journal.* Less than three years after ACT UP's founding, Burroughs Wellcome had reduced the cost of AZT, and the organization's members had been invited to sit on many of the government panels they had attacked. "ACT UP has been my way of taking control of my life away from the AIDS virus," explained Peter Staley, an ex–bond trader turned activist. "The issues couldn't be more exciting — sexism, racism, needle exchange, homophobia, homelessness. These are the issues of our day."

"'The tribe'" has given way to a "'queer nation' which is assertively coed, multi-racial and anti-consumerist," David Leavitt wrote. "The closed club has become an open meeting. What I liked best about ACT UP was its joyousness. Here was a roomful of people who were refusing to accept the common wisdom that . . . they were necessarily doomed and hopeless, their lives defined by death. From the shellshocked landscape of the mid-1980s, they had stood up, dusted themselves off and gone to work rebuilding."

ACT UP's most controversial action was its disruption of Sunday Mass at St. Patrick's Cathedral in December 1989. John Cardinal O'Connor was the demonstrators' target because of his persistent opposition to explicit AIDS education and his lengthy battle against any law that would protect gay civil rights.

Some protesters lay down in the aisles while others handcuffed themselves to the pews. "We will not be silent," screamed Michael Petrelis, a veteran gay activist. "We will fight O'Connor's bigotry." Then the police arrested him and forty-two others inside the cathedral. Another sixty-nine protesters were arrested outside.

Ann Northrop explained her participation in the St. Patrick's action this way: O'Connor

> was telling the general public that monogamy would protect them from HIV infection and that condoms didn't work. As far as I was concerned, those were both major lies that were going to kill people . . . Every week he stands up in the church and during his sermon makes political statements about AIDS, abortion, [and] homosexuality . . . We believed we were entitled through our right of free speech to confront his political statements. Besides, by having the broadcast and print media in there on a regular basis, he had breached the limits of a religious service himself and was setting up a political event.

Cardinal O'Connor said it was "kind of ironic that I'm accused of not doing enough" because he had consistently advocated more government spending for AIDS care and research and because the archdiocese was devoting "10 to 12 percent" of its hospital beds to people with AIDS.

Alice McGillion was a deputy police commissioner who witnessed the demonstration from inside the cathedral. "People were horrified that they did it — particularly in a very Catholic police department," McGillion recalled. "But I did not think their manner was horrific: these were people who were under control. Some of the protesters were taken out on orange stretchers, and they were so frail, I could have picked them up myself. It was just one of the saddest things I've ever seen."

The demonstration created a sharp division within the gay community. One Catholic who opposed the St. Patrick's protest was Robert J. Anthony, a regional director of Dignity, an organization of gay Catholics. Anthony said that he understood the demonstrators' anger because he also considered the cardinal's position immoral: "No teaching whose net effect exposes thousands of young men and women to infection with the human immunodeficiency virus can be considered moral." But Anthony still objected to the disruption.

The Catholic activist explained that members of Dignity felt especially strongly about the right to worship without disruption because their own services had been interrupted when Dignity had been evicted from seven parish communities in the New York metropolitan area earlier in the decade. "The most notable example is the 1987 eviction by John Cardinal O'Connor of Dignity New York from St. Francis Xavier Church after eight years of weekly masses in that parish." All of the evictions had been ordered by the church hierarchy, "none by the parish communities" to which Dignity members belonged. "Therefore, Dignity opposes any such disruptions and asks other members of the lesbian and gay community to channel their anger and energy into other actions."

ACT UP's most important achievement was to make experimental drugs available much more quickly to people with fatal diseases. Johnny Franklin told *The Wall Street Journal* that the organization had saved his eyesight by getting him access to Gancyclovir while the drug was still working its way through the Food and Drug Administration's lengthy approval process.

Barely two years after ACT UP's founding, Anthony Fauci, the chief federal AIDS researcher, announced a new system that would permit rapid access to experimental drugs. Some researchers complained that Fauci's "parallel track" approach would make it harder to prove the effectiveness of new drugs in traditional trials, which required some patients to take placebos while others received the real thing. But the anger of AIDS activists had convinced federal researchers that it was immoral to offer placebos to anyone with a fatal disease, "a major shift long sought by those involved in the fight against AIDS," the *Times* reported.

One of the first drugs distributed under the new system was DDI, or dideoxyinosine, an antiviral drug manufactured by Bristol-Myers. Three months after Fauci's announcement, the FDA said DDI would be made available to some patients at no cost if they could not afford it — partly because of earlier protests about the high price of AZT. Federal officials said the decision was made after discussions that included ACT UP representatives. A Bristol-Myers official said the talks were "very polite," although the AIDS activists had clearly indicated their "mistrust of the pharmaceutical industry in general."

BY IMMERSING THEMSELVES in the minutiae of new medical developments and by constantly publicizing their cause through protests covered by everyone from the *Times* to "60 Minutes," these activists had achieved a revolutionary shift in the government's approach to experimental drugs.

This was an extraordinary achievement, and it would prolong thousands of lives into the new decade.

In the program notes for one of GMHC's earliest benefits, Paul Popham wrote, "I think the most impressive thing I've seen over the last year and a half is how affectionate men have grown. We are finding out who we are, what we can do under pressure. And that we're not alone. . . . Although we're paying a terrible price, we're finding in ourselves much greater strength than we dreamed we had."

For many straight Americans, the epidemic had transformed the prevailing image of gay men — from sex maniacs into caring, ingenious and grieving human beings. As the gay author Andrew Tobias put it, "It's pretty hard to hate people who have this run of bad luck."

Barney Frank, a congressman from Massachusetts, publicly declared his homosexuality during the sixth year of the epidemic. He told Jeffrey Schmalz of *The New York Times* that while he remained in the closet, his colleagues were often sympathetic when he lobbied them on gay issues, but they rarely took him very seriously. "The pain gay people felt was unknown," Frank explained. "We were hiding it from them. How the hell are they supposed to know when we were making damn sure they didn't?"

But once the dimensions of the epidemic became clear, many of Frank's colleagues "started voting pro-gay because they saw that life-and-death issues were at stake. They had to do the right thing, even though they thought it might hurt them politically.

"Then, guess what? It turned out not to hurt them politically very much."

VI

The Nineties

"New York is the best place on the face of the earth. There's the best of everything here. The best people. The best art. But when I moved here, I thought everybody was going to die."

— RICK WHITAKER

THE AIDS EPIDEMIC extinguished tens of thousands of lives and caused overwhelming anguish. But the seeds planted in the resulting wasteland would produce an era of amazing hope and progress.

While a small part of the country, inflamed by religious fundamentalists, portrayed AIDS as divine retribution for the immoral behavior of homosexuals, a much larger portion reacted generously. Because of the decency of millions of newly sympathetic heterosexuals, in hundreds of communities of all sizes, the nation's old ideals of tolerance and inclusiveness would finally expand to include what had long been its most hated minority.

The lesbians and gay men who survived this holocaust reached out to one another to strengthen their sense of legitimacy by founding hundreds of new organizations. Powered by a new generation, ACT UP received most of the attention from the mainstream media. But beyond this new brigade of street fighters, there was an explosion of every kind of organizational activity.

By the middle of the nineties, in the New York metropolitan area alone there were associations of gay journalists, bankers, lawyers, artists, runners, opera lovers, Irishmen (and women), Israelis, Venezuelans, academics, adolescents, and Yeshiva graduates; groups for gay fathers, gay youth (Hetrick-Martin Institute), gay seniors (SAGE), lesbian mothers, gay and lesbian analysts (and Gay, Lesbian and Bisexual Psychiatric Survivors), gay policemen and playwrights; a gay public high school with eighty students; seven chapters of Parents and Friends of Lesbians and Gays; groups for gay wrestlers, sailors, and scuba divers; Jewish Lesbian Daughters of Holocaust Survivors; lesbian computer hackers, gay Physicians and Medical Students of Color, architects, advertisers, and pet owners; Catholics, Jews, and Unitarians; Democrats and Republicans; Wonderful Older Women; and a Lesbian Sex-Mafia — for lesbians fond of sadomasochism.

In 1996, a browser on the Internet could find 62,902 documents mentioning "queers"; 251,592 about lesbians and 663,239 about "gays" — and everything from an Australian Internet service provider for gays called "Rainbow.net" to the Filipino Queer Directory and a Glasgow Bisexual Women's Group in Scotland. For millions of gays and lesbians living in small towns all over the world, the Internet eliminated the age-old problem of where to look for people just like themselves.

IT WAS Bill Clinton's success as a presidential candidate in 1992 which ratified a basic shift in American attitudes toward its gay citizens. For the first time, a major-party candidate who had cultivated gay voters would go all the way to the White House. Instead of an insurmountable handicap, gay support was perceived in 1992 as a potentially decisive advantage in a close race.

By the beginning of the presidential campaign, 230,000 Americans had been diagnosed with AIDS, and at least 150,000 were dead — more than the combined total of U.S. soldiers killed in the Korean and Vietnam wars. Over a million were believed to have been infected by the virus. Now forty-three percent of those polled said they knew someone who was a homosexual — double the number just seven years earlier.

Clinton came to the presidential campaign as an agnostic on gay issues; as governor of Arkansas he had never made a public comment in support of a gay cause. His only close gay friend was David Mixner, whom he had met at a 1969 reunion of volunteers from Eugene McCarthy's presidential campaign.

In 1992 Clinton was interviewed by Jeff Schmalz, a *Times* reporter who had been diagnosed with AIDS two years earlier, and then began to cover a newly created gay beat at the newspaper. Clinton told Schmalz that after his first important meeting with gay activists, he realized that "running for President would require me to think about things that I just didn't have to deal with as Governor."

The event that turned Clinton into a temporary hero of the gay community was his appearance at a Los Angeles fund-raiser. In May 1992, he told a gathering of the city's wealthiest lesbians and gay men, "If I could wave my arm for those of you that are HIV positive and make it go away tomorrow, I would do it — so help me God, I would. If I gave up my race for the White House and everything else, I would do that." Clinton promised a sharp increase in funds for AIDS research. He also endorsed an end to the ban on gays serving in the military — as did his four Democratic primary opponents, and, eventually, Ross Perot as well. A videotape of Clinton's Los Angeles appearance was replayed dozens of times at gay fund-raisers for Clinton all fall.

"The gay community is the new Jewish community," Clinton's finance director, Rham Emanuel, declared during the campaign. "It's highly politicized, with fundamental health and civil rights concerns. And it contributes money. All that makes for a potent political force, indeed."

The Democratic National Convention in New York City marked a coming of age for the movement, with 133 lesbian and gay delegates and alternates inside Madison Square Garden — and a winning candidate supporting their cause. In another testament to the establishment's new commitment to equal rights, the president of CNN, the executive editor of *The Los Angeles Times,* and the publisher of *The New York Times* all served as honorary cohosts of a reception held by the National Lesbian and Gay Journalists Association on the eve of the convention.

Roberta Achtenberg, a former head of the National Center for Lesbian Rights, who had become a member of the San Francisco Board of Supervisors — and an early Clinton supporter — and Bob Hattoy, a gay environmental lobbyist suffering from AIDS, both addressed the convention. When Hattoy exhorted the hall to "vote this year as if our lives depended on it," there were tears in the eyes of many delegates. And after a last-minute intervention by the gay adviser David Mixner, Clinton included gays in his list of those groups deemed outcasts in the politics of division.

Once again, the Republicans saw the open embrace of the gay cause by a Democratic candidate as an opportunity to exploit prejudice. But their reading of the electorate was finally out-of-date.

In March 1992, a senior Bush campaign adviser told a group of junior political appointees in the administration that the Republicans would use gay rights as a major dividing line in the election. All year, Vice President Dan Quayle described homosexuality as a "life style choice" — and a wrong one. President Bush said same-sex couples make poor parents, and his campaign demoted an openly gay staff member after fundamentalist groups objected to his prominence.

Gay bashing by a major-party speaker peaked when Patrick J. Buchanan addressed the Republican convention in August. Buchanan was a political pit bull who alternated stints as a communications specialist in Republican White Houses with a lucrative career as a newspaper columnist and commentator on CNN. When he decided to run for president in 1992, his status as ex-cohost of "Crossfire" made him very much a part of the Washington establishment, and most reporters shared a camaraderie with him which baffled gay Americans.

Typical of Buchanan's vituperative attacks throughout the eighties was a column he wrote at the beginning of the AIDS epidemic: "the sexual revolution has begun to devour its children. And among the revolutionary vanguard, the Gay Rights activists, the mortality rate is highest and climbing. The poor homosexuals — they have declared war upon nature and now nature is exacting an awful retribution." It was a theme he returned to frequently during his presidential campaign.

Although Buchanan's speech at the Republican convention wasn't surprising to anyone who had been following him on the campaign trail, his harsh tone was unfamiliar to millions of prime-time viewers. "There is a culture war going on in our country for the soul of America," Buchanan declared.

> It is . . . as critical to the kind of nation we will be one day as was the Cold War itself. . . . A militant leader of the homosexual rights movement could rise at the [Democratic] convention and exult, 'Bill Clinton and Al Gore represent the most pro-lesbian and pro-gay ticket in history.' And so they do. . . . Like many of you last month, I watched that giant masquerade ball at Madison Square Garden, where 20,000 radicals and liberals came dressed up as moderates and centrists in the greatest single exhibition of cross-dressing in American political history.

Many people assumed that this was just the ranting of a right-wing extremist. But Buchanan's speech was actually a carefully considered part of the Bush campaign's reelection strategy. Lesbian and gay activists were furious. "This is the most explicitly anti-gay campaign we've ever seen," said Urvashi Vaid, then executive director of the National Gay and Lesbian Task Force. "It's hateful."

Andrew Rosenthal reported in the *Times* that "behind the scenes, Republican strategists . . . unapologetically proclaimed their intention to follow Patrick J. Buchanan's declaration of a religious and cultural war with the Democrats." And the next day Jeff Schmalz reported that while

Republicans were cautious in their public remarks about gay issues, "Privately top Bush campaign officials said they would hit the issue hard in the campaign, portraying Mr. Clinton as a promoter of homosexuals."

Buchanan's speech marked another turning point in the history of the gay movement in America — but not in the direction the Republicans had anticipated. The day after his address, Congressman Newt Gingrich was practically the only prominent Republican who publicly defended him. Gingrich accused the Democrats of promoting "a multicultural, nihilistic hedonism that is inherently destructive of a healthy society."

Most mainstream commentators were appalled by Buchanan's tone, and even among those Americans who may have privately agreed with him, a majority were clearly uncomfortable with his strident articulation of an antihomosexual agenda. While traditional Values Coalition chairman Lou Sheldon thought that homosexuality still galvanized "Bible-believing Christians" even "more than right-to-life," it no longer seemed to have the power to bring mainstream voters into the Republican column.

As Washington political analyst William Schneider put it, "Upper-middle-class suburban voters are not wildly pro-gay, but they do not want to be associated with a party that is overtly bigoted." In a New York Times/CBS poll taken just ten days after the Republican convention, fewer than one in four voters said they were interested in hearing *anything* about legal rights for homosexuals. Reflecting their fundamental ambivalence about the subject, about eighty percent of those polled said gay people should have equal job opportunities, while fifty-seven percent favored the admission of gays into the military. But only thirty-eight percent described homosexuality as an "acceptable alternative lifestyle."

But because Buchanan's speech generated so many negative reactions, the Bush campaign never followed up on its threat to make homosexuality a leitmotif of the presidential contest. Even Bill Clinton's promise to lift the ban on gays in the military never emerged as a major issue, although Bush held the opposite position. "I think there was a thought that [gay people] would be the new Willie Horton," said the conservative political analyst Kevin Phillips, referring to the felon furloughed in Massachusetts who subsequently committed a rape — and became a nightmare for the Dukakis campaign in 1988. "But the Administration overdid it," said Phillips. "The gay-bashing turned people off."

The day after Clinton was elected, there was joy throughout the gay community. Pollsters estimated that Clinton had received about seventy-five percent of the gay vote, and lesbians and gay men had contributed

$3 million to his coffers. "This is a rite of passage for the gay and lesbian movement," said Urvashi Vaid. "For the first time in our history, we're going to be full and open partners in the government."

The most significant disappointment for the gay community on election day occurred in Colorado, where voters approved a ban on laws prohibiting antigay discrimination by the surprisingly large margin of 53 to 47. But even that result would ultimately be overturned because of Clinton's election. On the evening of January 20, 1993, gay activists held their own inaugural ball at the National Press Club. The new president did not make an appearance, but lesbian singing stars Melissa Etheridge and k. d. lang greeted the ecstatic throng from the balcony.

THOUSANDS OF GAY supporters of Clinton were disgusted by his failure to lift the ban on gays in the military as he had promised. Partly because the issue had caused so little commotion during the campaign, opponents of the ban had been lulled into a false sense of security about how easy it would be to change the policy after the election. But while gay supporters were basking in the Clinton victory, an impregnable alliance was forming among Georgia Senator Sam Nunn, Joint Chiefs Chairman Colin Powell, and the well-oiled political machine of the religious right. Having been humiliated in the presidential election, religious conservatives focused on gays in the military as the next great battle in the cultural war they were determined to perpetuate.*

It wasn't until February 1993 that Tom Stoddard moved to Washington to head the Campaign for Military Service, a hastily formed lobbying group organized by gay leaders to try to make the president keep his word. At that point, it was probably already too late to dislodge the committed majorities in the Senate and the House which opposed a lifting of the ban.

By now Stoddard was seriously ill with AIDS, but he threw himself into this final battle with all of his legendary energy. On April 16, 1993, he was part of the first publicly announced meeting of gay representatives with any president in the Oval Office. He found his fellow Georgetown graduate to be noncommittal but extremely charming.

Clinton was "completely sympathetic," said Stoddard. "Understood all the points that were raised. Was one of us, seemed one of us, of our generation, of our frame of mind. We were beguiled by him. I don't think any of us believed that we would necessarily prevail on any of these issues,

---

*For a detailed account of the gays-in-the-military fiasco, see *Perfect Enemies*, an excellent book about the gay movement and the religious right by Chris Bull and John Gallagher.

but we were beguiled personally. And it was thrilling simply to know that such a meeting had taken place and to be part of it. Symbols do matter, and this is a very important symbol."

Stoddard believed that had the president issued an executive order lifting the ban on the day he took office, "It would have been a political disaster because the Senate would have simply voted to overturn it and nothing would have happened." But he also considered the president's "don't ask, don't tell compromise" a serious legal setback for the movement: "First of all it codifies something that was not a statute before. You have to go back to Congress now. Second of all, it establishes a principal that is really obnoxious, and could worm its way into the law: the idea that anyone who speaks out is engaging in conduct and can be fired not because of sexual orientation discrimination, but because of indiscretion. And that idea, if it gains any headway in the law, would be disastrous in public and private employment because the whole purpose of this movement is to permit people to be openly gay, not just to be gay."

On the other hand, despite the outcome, Stoddard felt that the heated public debate had been good for the movement. He called it "the first national teach-in on gay rights. So I have no regrets about having participated in that."

Many gay activists would never forgive the new president for the new policy that kept thousands of servicemen locked in their closets — and seemed to do nothing to lessen the military's appetite for periodic witch-hunts of lesbian and gay soldiers, sailors and airmen.

But the controversy did have one significant benefit for the movement. Even the most vociferous opponents of gays in the military had acknowledged — either explicitly or implicitly — that lesbians and gays were entitled to serve in all other professions. The most persistent argument against allowing gays to serve in the armed forces centered on the horrifying prospect of openly gay and straight men showering together.

To gay activists, the 1993 battle was almost identical to President Harry Truman's fight to integrate black and white battalions after World War II. The main argument made by Pentagon generals against racial integration in the forties was the same one they made against sexual integration in the nineties: the idea that if blacks and whites — or gays and straights — served together it would "weaken unit cohesion." Although Stoddard succeeded in getting both the National Association for the Advancement of Colored People and the Leadership Conference on Civil Rights to endorse the lifting of a ban on gay soldiers, sadly the position of Joint Chiefs Chairman Colin Powell was much more important politically.

Powell asserted that "skin color is a benign, nonbehavioral characteristic," while sexual orientation is perhaps "the most profound of human behaviorial characteristics." The general strongly opposed permitting gay soldiers to serve openly — even though the Pentagon already prohibited all discrimination against its *civilian* employees based on their sexual orientation. As Chris Bull and John Gallagher, the authors of *Perfect Enemies*, put it, Powell, a black man already being treated by the press as a potential president, was able to "inoculate the pro-ban forces from charges of prejudice."

Despite the failure of the gay movement to change the military's practices, the debate produced some extremely unlikely converts to its cause. Even Abe Rosenthal, who had done so much to make his own gay employees uncomfortable when he was executive editor of the *Times*, took General Powell to task for his opposition to a change in policy. "The military may have greater need for discipline than civilian groups," Rosenthal wrote on the op-ed page six days after President Clinton's inauguration, "but its executives also have a lot more clout.

"So I have an answer for a question General Powell raised last month at American University — what can he tell a heterosexual youngster who comes in and says that in his private accommodations he prefers to have heterosexuals around him, not gays?

"General, I would ask him if he had been molested. If not, I would tell him exactly what an Army colonel commanding the R.O.T.C. wartime unit at City College suggested to me when I asked him some uppity question for the campus paper.

"'Boy,' he said, 'get the hell out of my office.'"

Three months later, *The National Review*, the bible of the Republican right for many decades, put the debate on its cover. Although it did not explicitly endorse a change in national policy, the magazine ran an article that included some startling conclusions for a conservative journal. "The truth is that without making a big deal about it most commanders tolerate homosexuals in the ranks," wrote A. J. Bacevich, a visiting fellow at the Paul H. Nitze School of Advanced International Studies. Having

> conformed to virtually every expression of cultural orthodoxy, the admirals and generals now argue that the military must preserve itself from contamination by 'unmilitary influences.' The argument will not wash. Having embraced the American experiment, the military cannot now on the specific issue of gays opt out of what that experiment has come to

signify — with regard to individuals, unfettered equality of opportunity; and with regard to sex, a permissiveness that approaches the absolute. Like it or not, an *American* military cannot arbitrarily exempt itself from either the first or the second.

So the generals and the admirals will lose on the issue of gays. Although some will find the adjustment painful, those in the ranks will quickly adapt themselves to the new order of things — which will prove soon enough to be all but indistinguishable from the previous order.

OUTSIDE OF THE MILITARY, Bill Clinton completed the decades-long process of prohibiting discrimination against gay people in every other federal agency. He also appointed nearly a hundred open lesbians and gay men to his administration, including Roberta Achtenberg, who became an assistant secretary of the Department of Housing and Urban Development. Despite Jesse Helms's attacks on her as a "damn lesbian," she was easily confirmed by the Senate by a vote of fifty-eight to thirty-one.

Frank Kameny, who had started the assault on federal discrimination against gays with a lawsuit back in the 1950s, was generally pleased with Clinton's record at the end of 1995. "I think he's gotten an enormous amount of criticism on the military issue," said Kameny. "But I think in the last analysis that's more a criticism for political ineptitude rather than for intentions." The veteran activist noted there are now organizations of gay employees in nearly every federal agency, including the FBI and the Agriculture Department. "That kind of thing I find tremendously rewarding and vindicating," Kameny said. "That sort of thing would be absolutely unthinkable in the sixties."

In 1996 the president enraged the gay community by signing the Defense of Marriage Act, which said that neither the federal government nor any other state would recognize a gay marriage performed in Hawaii or anywhere else. The law was probably unconstitutional, but Clinton's willingness to pander to the right on this issue infuriated his gay supporters, even though he had always publicly opposed gay marriage.

On the other side of the ledger, after Congress passed a defense appropriations bill in 1996 which would have compelled the armed forces to discharge everyone who was infected with the HIV virus, the Clinton administration managed to put together a new majority in Congress which repealed this heinous provision.

PROPONENTS OF THE BAN on gays in the military quoted copiously from the Bible. Writing in *The New York Times* in support of the gay activists' position, the novelist James A. Michener noted that Sergeant Major S. H. Mellinger had offered "an extreme expression" of the anti-gay position in the *Marine Corps Gazette:* "The Bible has a very clear and specific message toward homosexuals — 'those that practice such things are worthy of death.'"

"He is correct," Michener continued. "In Leviticus 20:13, it says: 'If a man also lie with mankind, as he lieth with a woman, both of them have committed an abomination: they shall surely be put to death; their blood shall be upon them.'" But then the eighty-seven-year-old author of forty books offered a wonderfully simple rebuttal to all those who used the Bible to perpetuate this prejudice:

> One must read all of Leviticus to understand the condition of the an-cient Hebrews when this harsh judgment was being promulgated. They lived in a rude, brutal, almost uncivilized place where abominations abounded. To read the list of the things the Jews were enjoined to stop doing is to realize that God had to be unusually strict with such an undisciplined mob. Women who had sexual intercourse with animals were to be put to death. "And if a man take a wife and her mother, it is wickedness: they shall be burnt with fire, both he and they." A father who had sex with his daughter-in-law "shall be put to death." On and on goes the litany of common abuses that the Jews must henceforth forgo.
>
> Two other verses from the same chapter of Leviticus bring into ques-tion the relevance of these edicts today. Verse 9 warns: "or every one that curseth his father or his mother shall be surely put to death." Would we be willing to require the death sentence for boys who in a fit of rage oppose their parents? How many of us would have been guilty of that act at some point in our upbringing?
>
> Just as perplexing is Verse 10: "And the man that committeth adultery with another man's wife . . . the adulterer and the adulteress shall surely be put to death." Can you imagine the holocaust that would ensue if that law were enforced today?
>
> The Old Testament condemnation of homosexuality must be seen as one law among many intended to bring order to human relationships. Because the Jewish community was in deplorable disarray, harsh meas-ures were required. As order was installed, the extreme penalties advo-cated in Leviticus were relaxed in the civilized nations that followed . . .
>
> Western society, reacting in its own way, has advanced far beyond the primitive days of Leviticus. We do not kill young people who oppose their parents or execute adulterers.
>
> So when zealots remind us that the Bible says male homosexuals should be put to death rather than be admitted to the armed forces, it is

proper to reply: "You are correct that Leviticus says that. But it also has an enormous number of edicts, which have had to be modified as we became civilized."

THE CONFIRMING EVIDENCE of the transformation of American attitudes toward the gay minority came in the nineties from corporate America.

Years after many of the Fortune 500 had promised to stop discriminating against gay employees, almost every major American corporation was still worried about any public identification with the gay market — just as every major presidential candidate had avoided courting any gay supporters for years after Stonewall.

Even as gay people prided themselves on being the secret tastemakers of Broadway and Seventh Avenue, they knew that any overt appeal to gay consumers remained almost unthinkable in what had been a relentlessly closeted society. In the early 1980s, Seagrams and Heublein were among a handful of alcohol manufacturers who had cautiously dipped into this market with print ads in gay publications. But before Bill Clinton's election, not even a master of homoerotic images like Calvin Klein had ever purchased a single advertisement in a gay magazine — seven years after Klein had surrounded a single naked woman with three naked men to sell the fragrance Obsession.

In the fall of 1992, all that began to change, largely because of the launching of *Out* magazine by Michael Goff and Roger Black. *Out* banned all sex ads to provide a more comforting environment for traditional advertisers, and the results were dramatic and almost immediate.

Out's first issue featured ads for Absolut vodka, Benetton clothes and Geffen records. Banana Republic, North American Philips Consumer Electronics, Apple Computer and Calvin Klein (with jeans and underwear modeled by Marky Mark) quickly followed, along with His & His (and Hers & Hers) double-signature traveler's checks from American Express. AT&T and Continental Airlines were both sponsors of the Gay Games held in New York City during the celebration of the twenty-fifth anniversary of Stonewall in 1993. A year later the Ikea furniture store became the first general marketer to use identifiably gay characters (two men buying a dining room table) in a television ad broadcast on mainstream media.

In 1995, even the big guns of macho American commerce had joined the trend, including units of General Motors, Philip Morris and Procter & Gamble. By the following year, the list included Tanqueray, Stolichnaya,

Dewar's, Johnnie Walker (Red and Black), Southern Comfort, Miller beer, Nike, Movado, Bacardi, Benson & Hedges, Carlton, Camel, Swatch, Hush Puppies, RCA Victor, Virgin Atlantic, Glenfiddich, American Airlines, Amtrak, Aramis, Gucci, Versace, Ralph Lauren, Ticketmaster (selling tickets for gay dances), and Baileys Original Irish Cream. "It all comes down to education," explained Sandra Lot, the publisher of *10 Percent*, another gay magazine. "We need to be like the Wizard of Oz and give them the courage to jump into the market."

Gay radicals who had taken satisfaction from the separateness of gay culture were understandably perturbed by this digestion of gay market share by the very institutions that had spent so many decades shunning lesbians and gay men. But the sharply dropping shock value of being gay — or appearing in the pages of a gay publication — was an unavoidable side effect of the movement's steady progress.

A BOOMLET for gay marriage was another portent of the mainstreaming of gay culture. It was also a very human response to the threat that AIDS continued to pose to the survival of gay culture. Just as marriage had been seen as a boon to the survival of the races by any number of ancient civilizations, some activists in the 1990s began to advocate marriage for exactly the same reason: they believed that anything that would help lesbians and gay men to focus on a single relationship would make it easier for gay culture to prosper in a new century.

Shortly after Hawaii's Supreme Court held that a state ban on gay marriage might be a violation of the state's constitution because it was gender discrimination, Tom Stoddard decided to marry Walter Rieman, his partner of five years.

Stoddard said the decision to solemnize their vows grew out of "a variety of converging factors," including the simple realization that both of them would enjoy wearing wedding rings. The ceremony would confirm their status as official domestic partners in New York City, but like gay marriages in every other state, it would not be recognized as the equivalent of a marriage between a man and a woman. "I realized my desire to wear a ring was at bottom a desire to show off my relationship," said Stoddard. "And we both decided that if we were going to wear rings, we wanted to wear them on the traditional wedding finger, and we wanted traditional wedding rings, to declare equivalency to heterosexual marriages."

John Boswell, a gay historian at Yale, had recently completed his book about gay marriages in ancient times, and he suggested to Stoddard and

Rieman that they could be the first couple in America to use one of the ancient ceremonies he had unearthed. Boswell said he had found eighty different ceremonies, "some written originally in Greek, some written in old Slavonic, and some written in Latin." But the ceremonies made the prospective couple uncomfortable "because all of them made considerable reference to Jesus Christ and to religious beliefs to which we do not subscribe." So they decided not to use any of the ceremonies and not to have anyone officiate "because part of the purpose was to create our own ceremony.

"We're not looking for approbation from the larger world. We're making our *declaration* to the larger world. So we composed a sentence that each of us would declare to the other and would precede the exchange of rings, and that's what we said to one another.

"The rings came from Tiffany's," said Stoddard. "I decided to go and buy a gift certificate for Walter, amounting to the total price of two rings, for our anniversary, which was in August. That was the very day I moved back from Washington, from the campaign [to permit gays in the military]. I was feeling sad, and sort of confused about things, but because we were having dinner in celebration of our anniversary, I wanted to present this gift certificate from Tiffany's to Walter that evening. I had only a few minutes to get to the store, and I was laden down with baggage, so I showed up at Tiffany's at quarter to six.

"I had trouble getting through the door because I had all this luggage. The salespeople thought I was just totally bizarre, and I made them very nervous. But eventually they escorted me over to the wedding ring counter, and I talked to the person behind the counter who sold me the certificate for $600. As she went away to process the transaction, another salesclerk, who was leaving, passed by. She said,

"'Talk about last minute!' She must have thought we were eloping. It was really funny."

When Stoddard returned with Rieman to get the rings fitted, he was delighted by the demeanor of their salesman. "I thought to myself, Gee, this is going to be real trouble, and he's going to be real uncomfortable in all this. And he *couldn't* have been better. He was courteous without being officious; he was not in the least uncomfortable. He just went through the transaction as if such things happened every day. I was pleased because I thought this was a sign of how much the world had changed, and disappointed at the same time because part of this thing was to make a fuss, to cause trouble on behalf of other people.

"When I went back to pick up the rings I saw the same clerk, and I said,

'I know this was an untraditional transaction. I really appreciated your businesslike attitude. It was a pleasure to deal with you.' And he had a big smile on his mouth, and he extended his hand. And I liked that. I thought that was very significant.

"We wanted to incorporate appropriate traditional elements in this ceremony while maintaining our individuality and our distinctness from a traditional ceremony. We filed for domestic partnership the week afterward. We did not have a cake with two male images, we thought that was absolutely ridiculous. But we did keep some traditional elements. The rings were presented to each of us by our oldest siblings. We had some form of ceremony and we dressed up. But we only wore suits."

Stoddard had tried for a formal wedding announcement in the *Times,* but the paper's editor said that would be impossible at least until the state had formally legalized gay marriage. But when another *Times* reporter learned he was getting married that weekend, he ended up with an announcement in the paper anyway — in the "Chronicle" section. "So I got, in some strange way, the wedding announcement that I wanted." *The New Yorker* also made the marriage the lead item in "The Talk of the Town." Both items also mentioned that Stoddard's partner had just been elected to a partnership at Paul, Weiss, Rifkind, Wharton & Garrison. That made Rieman nervous about how his fellow partners would behave at his installation, but Ted Sorensen, who was the master of ceremonies for the event, handled the recent publicity deftly.

"Now I'd like to bring to the dais Walter Rieman, whose wedding received more attention than anyone else's, except Donald Trump's," said Sorensen.

"That's all he said," Stoddard recalled. "It was just perfect. And then Walter came up, and among other things thanked me for supporting him as he became a partner. And then Sorensen got up after Walter spoke — and this still really affects me — and said, 'Congratulations, Walter, and welcome, Tom.' So he was welcoming me to the firm as a spouse — and that was very moving to me. Walter was euphoric."

Stoddard and Rieman had decided to conduct their ceremony at Chanterelle, which was their favorite restaurant in Manhattan. Rieman's brother and two sisters and Tom's gay brother were among the seventy guests. The ceremony took place in December 1993, which also happened to be the twentieth anniversary of Stoddard's coming out. "The comment which affected me the most was from Hendrik Uyttendaele,"* said Stod-

---

*A cancer researcher from Belgium

dard. "Hendrik seemed very moved by it and said that he thought that it was one of the most honest events that he'd seen in his life."

Each man declared, "I commit to you my life and my love for the rest of our days," put on their rings, and kissed. Then Stoddard's brother performed the traditional role of the best man by offering this toast:

"Tom and Walter have done something that gay people have dreamed of for thousands of years. Let's raise our glasses to Tom and Walter. May you continue your life together in a more perfect union, in good health, and always with adventure and purpose and love."

JANUARY 1996 BROUGHT inklings of the greatest hope the gay community had felt since the beginning of the AIDS epidemic fifteen years earlier. A new three-drug combination seemed to offer what Lawrence K. Altman described in the *Times* as "the most powerful AIDS therapy ever tested on infected patients." He quoted Dr. William Paul, the head of the federal office of AIDS research: "Patients need to know this is promising, all signs are optimistic."

For Charles Gibson, for Xax, and for thousands of others, it seemed it might possibly be that "miraculous thing" that would finally allow them to recover.

Xax, who had resisted all drug therapy for several years after he learned he was infected, was one of the first patients to start receiving one of the new treatments: protease inhibitors, in combination with D4T and 3TC.

"I started in the spring," said Xax. "Now I do know a lot of people on it. Then I didn't. Seeing these trials come along — one after another — and everybody's viral loads are dropping to undetectable levels. It took me about a month to go through the psychological change. And then taking them at the beginning was very hard too, because it was a very strong effect. You would feel it, like, coursing through your body. I would feel it washing through my brain. I would start to go unconscious and all of a sudden I'd snap to, like, where was I? And then in a few seconds I'd be back again, like, whoa, now where was I. And then all of a sudden I'd be knocked out and I'd be asleep. But then over like a few months, that stuff stopped. And I'd just have energy.

"And I'd just feel good. And that's a completely new phenomenon in my whole life.

"Now I feel great. For the first time people see the glimmer of a real cure. And so there's *life* ahead of them all of a sudden, instead of death. And like all the people who have unraveled their lives and prepared themselves to die, are suddenly like, 'Oh, I guess I'm going back to work. I guess I have a life again.'"

Other treatments had seemed to offer similar hope at earlier stages of the epidemic. But none had had such dramatic effects on so many people so quickly. In the first nine months of 1996, the number of deaths from AIDS in the United States dropped 19 percent.

"AIDS has been the best thing and the worst thing for the planet," said Xax. "Because I really think that AIDS is the crux of the change of the turn of the century: to force everyone on the planet to accept people who are different from themselves — of every kind. . . . It is our role as a sacred people to do this. Our culture has become so huge that it encompasses the whole world now — the huge media culture. We are all so connected now. So it's taken a very huge event to affect things on that scale.

"And I think that's why AIDS is here. I think that's why the cure is in sight now, because enough people have bonded together with a common goal. I have a friend who was doing medical research who stopped because there was no communication within the research world, everyone was so out to find their own discovery, everyone was so selfish, that nothing ever happened. AIDS, it forced people to finally come together to find something.

"And I think that's what the whole thing is about: it's about unity, it's about inclusion — and it's forcing everyone to wake up."

The Reverend Peter Gomes of Harvard sees America as it approaches the millennium this way: "The place for creative hope that arises out of suffering most likely now is to be found among blacks, women and homosexuals. These outcasts may well be the custodians of those thin places; they may in fact be the watchers at the frontier between what is and what is to be."

MORE QUICKLY — and more permanently — than any other federal institution, the Supreme Court has the capacity to set the tone for the treatment of any minority group — sometimes for decades at a time. Two and a half years after Stoddard's marriage, the country's highest Court rendered the decision that Stoddard had been hoping for since he first came out in 1970. In *Romer* v. *Evans,* on May 20, 1996, the Court voted six to three to throw out the Colorado state constitutional initiative that had forbidden protection for gay people from discrimination.

Very significantly, the decision was written by Justice Anthony M. Kennedy, an appointee of Ronald Reagan. Kennedy began by quoting Justice John Marshall Harlan's famous dissent in *Plessy* v. *Ferguson,* the 1896 case that subjected blacks to legally sanctioned discrimination for another fifty-eight years — until the precedent reversing *Brown* v. *Board of Education.*

"One century ago, the first Justice Harlan admonished this Court that the Constitution 'neither knows nor tolerates classes among citizens.' Unheeded then, those words are now understood to state a commitment to the law's neutrality where the rights of persons are at stake. The Equal Protection Clause enforces this principle and today requires us to hold invalid a provision of Colorado's Constitution.

"A state cannot so deem a class of persons a stranger to its laws," Kennedy continued. The Colorado provision had singled out the state's homosexuals as "a solitary class," creating a legal disability so sweeping, it could only be explained by "animus."

"It is not within our constitutional tradition to enact laws of this sort." Justice Kennedy said the Colorado amendment did not meet even the lowest level of scrutiny accorded an official action that is challenged as a violation of the constitutional guarantee of equal protection. Under that test, as Kennedy described it, "a law must bear a rational relationship to a legitimate governmental purpose, and Amendment 2 does not."

Justice Antonin Scalia filed a furious dissent for the three-member minority which included a concise description of the decision's huge significance: it placed "the prestige of this institution behind the proposition that opposition to homosexuality is as reprehensible as racial or religious bias."

Suzanne B. Goldberg, a lawyer with the Lambda Legal Defense and Education Fund, who was part of the winning legal team in the case, summarized the decision even more simply:

"This is the most important victory ever for lesbian and gay rights," she said.

THE DECISION FIT beautifully into Tom Stoddard's vision for the gay movement:

"It's about the tenor of a society which is intolerant of those people and those things that are different," he said. "There's no point in having a movement if you're just going to turn everyone into a suburban homemaker. The whole point is to celebrate difference. And there is something deeply offensive about a movement that only argues for its own people. The underlying idea behind the movement, to anyone's mind, it seems to me, is equality. If the idea is equality, it can't possibly be said that it should be equality for only one group of people. The idea of equality has to apply across the board, and therefore, it's not just that there ought to be inter-connectedness between the African American community and the Latino community and the gay community. It's that what motivates those movements is exactly the same thing. And it is a terrible thing to just promote one's own equality. It's what lawyers call special pleading. It's unprincipled and it's selfish — and it will never sell.

"We are engaged in the remaking of the culture in a way that benefits everybody. Martin Luther King, Jr., understood that: the significance of the black civil rights movement for white Americans. And he said it again and again. It wasn't just a device; he knew exactly what he was doing. It uplifted people. It not only touched them — because it made people listen to him who otherwise wouldn't — it made people feel better about them-selves and their culture. It moved them forward.

"We want a richer, more diverse, more compassionate culture, in which everyone feels the possibility of self-expression and self-actualization. And that is what it's about. I say that as a true believer because it was true for me. As I mentioned before, I would have a miserable, unhappy, meaning-less life if not for being gay and I would like for other people to experience that as well."

The day after the Court's decision in *Romer* v. *Evans* was announced, Stoddard felt "a sense of legitimization."

"It's a big deal both doctrinally and spiritually," he said. "But I worry that some people will decide that the Supreme Court is their savior and they therefore don't have to work hard politically. That's a very genuine danger, especially with the military issue and the marriage issue bearing down on us.

"The opinion was beautifully done — both a larger majority and a larger theory put forward than any of us expected. The theory being that animus is not a legitimate basis for distinctions among classes of people. And while the Court has said that before, it's especially important in this context — not just because it's us, but because we're an especially contro-versial group of people. And the majority was very political in its ap-proach. It cited very little precedent because there is very little precedent on this subject, unfortunately. And it went out of its way to dispose of the vile arguments on the other side — especially the special rights argu-ments. And it knew what it was doing in citing *Plessy* v. *Ferguson* at the beginning. That was a sign of the moral outrage of the majority. And just a wonderful thing to be on our behalf.

"I hope our people remember that this happened in part because a

Democrat is holding the White House [and appointed two of the justices who joined in the majority opinion].

"The point that I want to communicate is that this does not mean things are over and we can now sit safely at home. This is our christening or bar mitzvah.

"It's not our entry into heaven."

Acknowledgments

Whatever is good or useful about this volume is the product of the generosity of countless collaborators. My largest debt is to the extraordinary men and women who invited me into their homes and shared so much of their lives for the benefit of others. I made wonderful new friends, especially among my older subjects. Sandy Kern gave me inspiration when I needed it most. Arthur Laurents became my confidant and muse throughout the second half of this project. Paul Cadmus is the wisest and warmest ninety-two-year-old anyone has ever met.

Scores of friends provided hundreds of leads which shaped my investigation. No one was more generous than Ashton Hawkins, who led me to amazing sources and always provided excellent advice. Arlene Kochman introduced me to some of the most illustrious members of SAGE, the great private social service agency for older lesbians and gay men in New York City. George Trescher made a special contribution when he reminded me to consider the importance of the murder committed by Wayne Lonergan in 1943.

Bob Kaiser, Hannah Jopling, Cathy Kaiser, Andy Tobias, Lucy Howard, David Dunlap, Frank Clines, David Bartolomi, Andrew Morse, Henry Bloomstein, Thom Stoelker, Tema and Mark Silk, Ros Kaiser, Sarah and Bob Hyams, Rebecca and Tamara Kaiser, Dudley Greeley, Renata Adler, Steve Marcus, Martha Ritter, Roy Finamore, François Fortin, Andrew Jacobs, Didier Malaquin, Barbara Epstein, Marcia Chambers, Gloria Emerson, Steve Kay, Michael Lerner, Linda Healey, Tony Lukas, Mary Murphy, John Moore, Philip Gefter, Peter Kaplan, Lesley Stahl, Steve Rattner, Maureen White, Shelley Wanger, David Auchincloss, Ginger Crosby, Paula Kaiser, Blair Clark, Kirk Semple, Sarah Burke, John Flannery, Zarrina and Antony Kurtz, Christiane Audibert, Hope Kostmayer, Edward Flanagan, Michael Butler, Ellie Gelman, Maralee Schwartz, Elsie Bernice Washington, David White, Steve Friedman, Judy Hottensen, Colin Dickerman, Caleb Crain, Eddie Borges, Nick and Heyden Rostow, Jane Berentson, Bruce Knecht, Mary de Bourbon, Will Lung, Sharon and Charles Stouter, Alice McGillion and Martin Arnold all provided crucial support.

David Kaiser, David Garrow, John Herman, Gail Gregg, Arthur Sulzberger, Jr., Carl Chiappa, Mark Polizzotti, Roy Aarons, James Stewart and Judy Knipe read early versions of different portions of the manuscript, and each of them made valuable suggestions and corrections. David Kaiser also sets the standard for historical precision that I aspire to. Stephanie Lane and Nancy Lunney read nearly all of the book as it was being written, and they were unstinting with their advice and their enthusiasm.

When I was halfway through this project, I realized that my most important inspiration had been *Before Stonewall,* the first great television documentary about gay people in America, created by John Scagliotti, Greta Schiller and Robert Rosenberg. All historians interested in this subject owe a special debt to Michael Denneny because he has edited so many of the best books about gay life in America, including *And the Band Played On,* Randy Shilts's landmark volume on the AIDS epidemic.

The other books I found most useful were *Coming Out Under Fire,* Alan Bérubé's superb history of gays in the military during World War II; *Making History,* Eric Marcus's excellent oral history of gay activism since the war; *Christianity, Social Tolerance, and Homosexuality* by John Boswell; *Sexual Politics, Sexual Communities* by John D'Emilio; *City Poet* by Brad Gooch; *Liberty & Sexuality* by David J. Garrow; *Straight News* by Edward Alwood; *Being Homosexual* and *Becoming Gay* by Richard A. Isay; *Reports from the Holocaust* by Larry Kramer; *The Politics of Homosexuality* by Toby Marotta; *The Gay Militants* by Donn Teal; *Gay New York* by George Chauncey; *Sondheim & Co.* by Craig Zadan; *Perfect Enemies* by Chris Bull and John Gallagher; *The Long Road to Freedom,* edited by Mark Thompson; and all the books written or edited by Martin Duberman, especially *Stonewall.* Michael Cunningham's *A Home at the End of the World* remains *the* luminescent novel about New York life in the 1980s.

Kathy Robbins is much more than the best agent anyone ever imagined; she is also a fine editor, a great conceptualizer and a magnificent friend. All of her colleagues at the Robbins Office — especially Tifanny Richards and David Halpern — provided a powerful support system. Bill Clegg is my critic and collaborator in several important departments.

Dawn Seferian is an amazing editor, the kind who always manages to bolster an author's confidence. Jayne Yaffe's meticulous copy-editing improved many different sections of the manuscript. Robert Overholtzer produced an elegant design.

Murray Kempton was the dean of modern American iconoclasts; that made him a role model for all serious journalists. My favorite moment with him occurred during a magical dinner a couple of years ago in Barbara Epstein's apartment. Suddenly Murray leapt up from the table, darted to the bookcase and pulled down a volume of Auden; then he declaimed the couplet that became the opening epigraph for this book.

Because he believed the subject was important, Richard Slusarcyk volunteered four years ago to be my partner on this project. He contributed thousands of hours of research and made many important discoveries, including the *Journal-American*'s remarkable treatise on gay life during the Lonergan affair. This book could not have been written without him.

Elizabeth Lunney joined me at a decisive moment to bring order out of chaos;

she also offered many pithy and thoughtful suggestions. Raymond Geller enabled me to finally understand Judy Garland's importance. Linda Amster performed her usual roles as brilliant investigative reporter and wonderful friend. Anny Miller, Shields Remine and Duncan Arp transcribed hundreds of hours of interviews and offered constant encouragement.

Rob Boynton, a splendid colleague who defies categories, ended a four-year trauma by suggesting the perfect title for this book. For more than a decade, Ed Koch has been a devoted friend. I have tried (and probably failed) to insulate my judgments of his mayoralty from the effects of that friendship.

Media and Zoë Brecher, Sam Shapiro, Ben and Alex Goldberger, Adam Hirsh, Charles and Peter Gelman, Juliet and Arabella Kurtz, Nick Everett, Stephen Adler, Jonathan Erickson, Tito Bianchi, Ben Wheeler, Katie and Jeremiah Lane, David Crossland, Vanessa Vadim, Marc Stouter, Victoria Pringle, David Leonhardt, Jonathan Mallow, Will Bleakley, Abraham, Ezra and Isaac Silk, Zoë Coopridern, Mark and Ghita Levenstein, Tess and Ethan Hyams, Dana Greeley Artz, Delari, Tara, Margo and Garth Johnston, Jennifer Lunney, Theodore and Celia Rostow, Kate McNamara, and Arthur and Annie Sulzberger offer evidence every day that the twenty-first century will be more enlightened than the present one.

Michael and Laura Fisher Kaiser, Judy Barnett, Sal Matera, Ann Jensen, Steve and Nancy Shapiro, Eric Gelman, John Brecher, Dorothy Gaiter, Bill Carey, Eleanor Randolph, Peter Pringle, Janet Suzman, Rich Meislin, Hendrik Uyttendaele, Jean Vallely, Steve Weisman, Paul Goldberger, Susan Solomon, Merry McInerney, Michael Finnegan, Michael Anderson, and Judy Knipe nurtured the author through countless crises. Rick Whitaker helped me make many new discoveries about the gay metropolis.

I cannot even suggest how deeply my life was affected by all the men I loved who have already perished. Their deaths sometimes make me feel guilty to be alive; but my memories of their incredible accomplishments — especially Tom Stoddard's accomplishments — infused me with a sense of urgency to record our history as accurately as I could.

My parents shared all of their virtues, especially their flair for storytelling and their loathing for all forms of prejudice. Since the moment I first told them "I'm gay" they have traveled their own magnificent journey, from shock to discomfort to total support. For thirty-six years, our closest friends, Katie and Arthur Hustead, have been essential to all Kaisers.

Nephews and nieces play an especially large role in the life of an uncle with no children of his own. Emily Kaiser made a superb contribution to this volume when she discovered Christopher Isherwood's critique of *The City and the Pillar* among Gore Vidal's papers at the University of Wisconsin at Madison. Emily, Charlotte, Daniel and Thomas Kaiser give me more happiness than they can possibly imagine.

After nearly two decades, Joe Stouter remains my indispensable collaborator: the person without whom nothing important is possible.

— New York City, May 1997

Notes

EPIGRAPH

vi "Joseph, Mary, pray for those": W. H. Auden, "For the Time Being, a Christ-mas Oratorio," *Collected Poems*, 283.

INTRODUCTION

vii "When you were starting out": *James Baldwin: The Price of the Ticket* (documentary).
"If I had the power": Joseph Epstein, *Harper's*, September 1970.
viii "I think especially": "The Architecture of Community," 24th Jefferson Lecture in the Humanities, delivered in Washington, D.C., by Vincent Scully, May 15, 1995.
"We know our son": Author's interview with Richard Isay, July 7, 1996.
"Anglican over-soul" . . . "who knows me." Peter J. Gomes in Robert S. Boynton, "God and Harvard," *The New Yorker*, November 11, 1996.
ix "never contemplated a form": Peter J. Gomes, *The Good Book*, 102.
"Origin: a king's insistence": Author's personal archive.
x "almost everything about homosexuality": Author's interview with Richard Isay.
"Homosexuality is assuredly": Sigmund Freud, reprinted in Ronald Bayer, *Homosexuality and American Psychiatry*, 27.
xi "the official party apparatus": *Hidden from History*, ed. Martin Duberman, et al., 374.
"Hitler said afterwards": William L. Shirer, *The Rise and Fall of the Third Reich*, 220–25.
xii "a magic by-word": Donald Webster Cory, *The Homosexual in America*, 107–108.

I: THE FORTIES

3 "On any person who desires": E. B. White, *Here Is New York*, 1.
"I think the trick is": *James Baldwin: The Price of the Ticket* (documentary).
"We kids would stand" . . . "out of my head and heart": Author's interview
with Sandy Kern, June 29, 1993.

5 "In my world" . . . "very into *not* being gay": Author's interview with Otis
Bigelow, April 28, 1994.

7 The other man sharing: *New York Times*, January 10, 1989, and ibid.
"the silver and china queens": Author's interview with Arthur Laurents, June
14, 1995.
Bigelow, Merrick and Barr selected: Author's interview with Otis Bigelow,
April 28, 1994.

8 "It was a little bit": Author's interview with Murray Gitlin, February 26,
1993.
"It was like being under": Author's interview with Franklin Macfie, May 12,
1993.
"The city smelled totally different": Author's interview with Jack Dowling,
May 5, 1993.
"I had a tuxedo" . . . "I had to face": Author's interview with Otis Bigelow,
April 28, 1994.

11 "George was family to me": Author's interview with Philip Johnson, May 5,
1995.
While still a student at: *New York Times*, August 19, 1926, and March 5, 1974.
"gave the appearance": Author's interview with Paul Cadmus, October 29,
1992.
"stunning" . . . "I went back to school": Author's interview with Otis Bigelow,
April 28, 1994.

12 Hoyningen-Huene had been born: *New York Times*, September 23, 1968, and
William A. Ewing, *The Photographic Art of Hoyningen-Huene*, p. 13.
"You're doing all this moping": Author's interview with Otis Bigelow, April
28, 1994.
"gay society at that point": Ibid.
"fairies" . . . "gay hangouts": George Chauncey, Jr., "The Policed: Gay Men's
Strategies of Everyday Resistance" in *Inventing Times Square*, 323.

13 "very abrupt and candid": Tennessee Williams, *Memoirs*, 66, quoted in foot-
note in ibid., 419.
For speakeasies versus gay bars: George Chauncey, Jr., *Inventing Times
Square*, 325.
"You'd see a cop": Author's interview with Roy Strickland and William
Wynkoop, June 3, 1993.
For statistics on sex offenders: Donald Webster Cory, *The Homosexual in
America*, 56.

14 A red tie was sometimes . . . tone down their behavior: George Chauncey, Jr.,
Inventing Times Square, 326–27, and *Before Stonewall* (documentary).
"The sexual scene I'm sure" . . . "anything you want to": Author's interview
with "Stephen Reynolds," September 24, 1992.

15 "We were at that early": Author's interview with Jack Dowling, May 5, 1993.
"the naiveté of the public": Author's interview with Paul Cadmus, October 22, 1992.

16 "I grew up and came out": Author's interview with "James Atcheson," October 1, 1992.
"What seems to me": Richard Watts, Jr., *New York Herald Tribune*, June 14, 1942.
"Webb was playing the part": Author's interview with "James Atcheson," October 1, 1992.

17 "It'll ruin the party" . . . "consistency in music": Humphrey Burton, *Leonard Bernstein*, 41–43, 49.
The degree of protection . . . "the opportunity to commit suicide": for a comprehensive account of the Welles affair, from which these facts are taken, see Ted Morgan, *FDR*, 677–86.

19 As a result, when the: George Chauncey, Jr., *Inventing Times Square*, 324–25, and Donald Webster Cory, *The Homosexual in America*, 45.
"Biblical condemnations of homosexual behavior": John D'Emilio, *Sexual Politics, Sexual Communities*, 13.
"so sordid": *Newsweek*, November 8, 1943.
"a tall, powerfully built": Ibid.

20 "He was a gay one" . . . Ritz Tower apartment: *New York Journal-American*, October 25, 1943; *New York Post*, October 26, 1943; and *New York Times*, October 22, 1943.
Faced with imminent separation . . . Las Vegas: *New York Post*, October 29, 1943.
"neat souffle" . . . "door for him": Meyer Berger, *New York Times*, October 26, 1943.

21 But the unprintable details: Author's interview with Gore Vidal, January 14, 1994.
"he admitted he had killed": *New York Times*, January 3, 1946.
"I was in the army": Author's interview with Gore Vidal, January 14, 1994.
Although his uniform was covered: *New York Times*, October 29, 1943, March 29, 1944, and *New York Journal-American*, October 28, 1943.
"I raised my hand to knock": *New York Times*, March 29, 1944.
Lonergan ordered breakfast . . . "shouted in the District Attorney's office": *New York Times*, October 29, 1943, and *New York Journal-American*, October 28, 1943.

22 "You can't keep your eye": *New York Post*, October 25, 1943.
"openly labeled in newspapers": *New York Times*, October 29, 1943.
"For the first time in": *Time*, November 8, 1943.

23 "Psychiatrists Give Views": *New York Journal-American*, October 30, 1943.

25 "dubious joking about sexual": Richard Watts, Jr., *New York Herald Tribune*, June 14, 1942.
"Was he born or made?": *Time*, April 3, 1944.
"The majority of people": Author's interview with William Wynkoop, June 3, 1993.
On April 17, 1944: *New York Times*, April 18, 1944.

"civilly dead": Ibid., February 6, 1954.

Ten years after Lonergan: *New York Times,* February 6, 1954.

In 1965 Lonergan challenged: Ibid., August 14, 1965.

26 He died of cancer: Ibid., January 3, 1986.

"Just after I'd graduated" . . . "taken me to the doctor's": Author's interview with Roy Strickland, June 3, 1993.

27 Six months after the Japanese: Allan Bérubé, *Coming Out Under Fire,* 35.

28 To win their rightful place: *Coming Out Under Fire,* 8

Allan Bérubé reports: Ibid., 10.

On the eve of the: Ibid., 9.

29 "accepted and left alone": Ibid., 11.

"had carved out the": Ibid.

"an aspect of three": Ibid., 15.

In 1942, army mobilization: Ibid., 19.

30 "subject to ridicule" . . . "the male pattern": Ibid., 20.

"be on the lookout" . . . "machine-gunned": Ibid., 19–21.

was "very afraid that": Author's interview with Murray Gitlin, February 26, 1993.

"an awful lot of gay": Allan Bérubé, *Coming Out Under Fire,* 23.

"I wanted to go in" . . . "to hang in": Author's interview with "Leo Aultman," May 12, 1993.

32 "One of the worst": *Before Stonewall* (documentary).

"instantly called": Ibid.

"I never saw so many" . . . "paid again. Ever": Author's interview with "Leo Aultman," May 12, 1993.

33 "They brought him back": Allan Bérubé, *Coming Out Under Fire,* 197.

34 "This plane came overhead": Ibid. 197–98.

"all went to the plane": Ibid., 198.

"I got in my car" . . . "wonderful boys were killed": Author's interview with "Stephen Reynolds," September 24, 1992.

36 "It was a *great*": Author's interviews with "Leo Aultman," May 24, 1993, and March 28, 1994.

37 "My God!": Author's interview with "James Atcheson," October 1, 1992.

"The army set up a": Allan Bérubé, *Coming Out Under Fire,* 88–89, 97.

"Despite their hairy chests": *Life,* December 12, 1942.

38 "I was wandering" . . . "army was a strange place": Author's interview with Arthur Laurents, June 14, 1995.

"You are not fighting": Allan Bérubé, *Coming Out Under Fire,* 97.

"My sisters were all" . . . "was very hidden": Author's interview with Franklin Macfie, May 12, 1993.

39 "*anything* feminine" . . . "going too far!": Author's interviews with Jerre Kalbas, June 1, 1993, and March 27, 1994.

"People sort of did": Allan Bérubé, *Coming Out Under Fire,* 98.

"Manhattan parties got to be": Ibid., 113.

"During the war": *Gay Sunshine Interviews,* vol. 2, ed. by Winston Leyland, 213.

"New York in wartime" . . . "incessant": Author's interview with Arthur Laurents, June 14, 1995.

40 "Everybody was released": Author's interview with Gore Vidal, January 14, 1994.

"Just as I put on": Allan Bérubé, *Coming Out Under Fire*, 109–10.

"We never thought" . . . "not in my group": Author's interview with "Stephen Reynolds," September 24, 1992.

"The men who don": *Ebony*, March 1952 and March 1953, and Allan Bérubé, *Coming Out Under Fire*, 116.

41 "the first Mrs. Johnson" . . . "way to treat anybody": Author's interview with Philip Johnson, May 5, 1995.

"impeccable enunciation": Franz Schulze, *Philip Johnson: Life and Work*, 93–95.

42 "model of dignity": *The New Yorker*, May 4, 1940, quoted in James Gavin, *Intimate Nights*, 88.

"blacks and whites": Ibid., 87–88.

"general aura": Author's interview with Philip Johnson, May 5, 1995.

"Phillip [*sic*] Johnson": William L. Shirer, *Berlin Diary*, 213.

Kirstein biographical details: *New York Times Magazine*, June 20, 1982.

"I, Pvt Lincoln Kirstein": Franz Schulze, *Philip Johnson: Life and Work*, 164.

43 His salon included W. H. Auden . . . "tolerance, sympathy, and kindness": Author's interview with Paul Cadmus, October 29, 1992.

44 "On nights off I" . . . "several times after": Author's interview with Murray Gitlin, February 26, 1993.

45 "If you went in": Author's interview with William Wynkoop, June 3, 1993.

"We were in a building" . . . "living in New York": Author's interview with Roy Strickland, June 3, 1993.

46 "In those days you": Recorded interview with Jules Elphant, SAGE Archive.

"I was aghast": Author's interview with "Stephen Reynolds," September 24, 1992.

"A lot of my 'gay life'": Author's interview with Paul Cadmus, October 29, 1992.

"There was a tolerance" . . . "good battalion to be in": *Before Stonewall* (documentary).

47 "an extraordinary aspect" . . . "civilian life": Allan Bérubé, *Coming Out Under Fire*, 46, 50.

48 "the stigmatization of homosexuals": Ibid., 138–39.

"confirmed pervert" . . . "court-martialed and imprisoned": Ibid., 143–44, 147.

"gone down" . . . "have done to you": Author's interviews with "Leo Aultman," May 24, 1993, and March 28, 1994.

49 When the army moved toward . . . homosexuals were sick: Allan Bérubé, *Coming Out Under Fire*, 152, 148.

"in various military jobs": Ibid., 170–72.

50 "This study was the first": Ibid., 277–78. For the full text of these reports, see *Gays in Uniform: The Pentagon's Secret Reports*, ed. Kate Dyer.

"topped the average": *Newsweek,* June 9, 1947.

"is unrelated to job performance": Kate Dyer, ed., *Gays in Uniform: The Pentagon's Secret Reports,* ix.

"It was the most depressing": Author's interview with "Stephen Reynolds," September 24, 1992.

51 In 1945, they founded . . . "never lived together": Recorded interview with Jules Elphant, SAGE Archive.

52 In 1947, America was shocked: *New York Times,* January 17, 1947; February 11, 1949; September 1, 1947; and February 18, 1949.

But just weeks after: John D'Emilio, *Sexual Politics, Sexual Communities,* 34.

53 "religious background": Alfred C. Kinsey, *Sexual Behavior in the Human Male,* 3–4.

"no aspect of human biology": Dr. Alan Gregg in Ibid., v.

"To each individual": Ibid.

54 The questionnaire about homosexual: Ibid., 623–25.

"You started out shy": Author's interview with Otis Bigelow, April 28, 1994.

"gentle and quiet": Author's interview with Paul Cadmus, May 20, 1995.

55 famous zero-to-six: Alfred C. Kinsey, *Sexual Behavior in the Human Male,* 650–51.

"In view of the data": Ibid., 659–60.

56 "The judge who is considering": Ibid., 664–65.

"Homosexuality was thought": *Before Stonewall* (documentary).

Rusk biographical details: *New York Times,* November 5, 1989.

"end results": Ibid., January 4, 1948.

57 "we have the right" . . . "behavior of each human being": Ibid.

"degradation in American": John D'Emilio, *Sexual Politics, Sexual Communities,* 36.

"Lawrence Kubie was the prominent": Allan Bérubé, *Coming Out Under Fire,* 19.

"stuck a scalpel into": *Time,* June 14, 1948.

"The statistics based on the": *New York Times,* June 5, 1948.

"He was a celebrity": Author's interview with "James Atcheson," October 1, 1992.

"The implication that because": *New York Times,* June 5, 1948.

58 "Kubie ruined Tennessee": Author's interview with Arthur Laurents, June 14, 1995.

"All the so-called": Author's interview with "Nicholas Simmons," October 11, 1996.

"most of the sexual": *Time,* June 14, 1948, and *New York Times,* June 5, 1948.

"By revealing that millions": John D'Emilio, *Sexual Politics, Sexual Communities,* 37.

59 "even a member of Congress": Vidal, *The City and the Pillar,* 150–152, and ibid.

"You'd sit in the commissary": Author's interview with Gore Vidal, January 14, 1994.

Laurents had a four-year: Author's interview with Arthur Laurents, June 14, 1995.

"The studios didn't care": Ibid.

"You know, you're Farley's": Arthur Laurents interviewed by Larry Kramer in *The Advocate*, May 16, 1995.

"Hitch wanted Cary Grant": Author's interview with Arthur Laurents, June 14, 1995.

"I don't think the censors": *The Celluloid Closet* (documentary).

60 "It didn't matter whether": Author's interview with Arthur Laurents, June 14, 1995.

"I will not only not" . . . "for battle": Author's interview with Gore Vidal, January 14, 1994.

"A frightening glimpse": *New York Times Book Review*, January 11, 1948.

"The fact that it was a" . . . "this particular act": Author's interview with Gore Vidal, January 14, 1994.

61 "You spoiled it with": Gore Vidal, "Some Memories," *United States*, 1139.

"certainly one of the best" . . . "collective morale": Gore Vidal papers at the University of Wisconsin at Madison.

II: THE FIFTIES

65 "In that era of general": David Halberstam, *The Fifties*, x.

"Undergraduates seemed uniformly": Martin Duberman, *Cures*, 2.

"We are not living": Humphrey Burton, *Leonard Bernstein*, 229.

"The fifties was": Author's interview with Gore Vidal, January 14, 1994.

66 "No picture shall be" . . . "he immediately complied": Gerald Gardner, *The Censorship Papers*, xv, xx, 122, 207–10, 215.

67 "I Love Lucy" . . . suffer from morning sickness: Halberstam, *The Fifties*, 196–201.

"utter anomaly": George Chauncey, Jr., lecture at the Museum of the City of New York, June 22, 1995.

68 "Half of the nicest girls": David Halberstam, *The Fifties*, 201.

69 "homosexual panic": *New York Post*, July 10, 1950.

The *Washington Post* reported: Ibid., July 13, 1950.

According to Washington insiders: Ibid., July 15, 1950.

"At no point, whether": Ibid., July 14, 1950.

70 "spousal": Richard Gid Powers, *Secrecy and Power*, 171, 173.

"killer fruit": Truman Capote, *Answered Prayers*, 8.

"No one argues the question": *New York Post*, July 22, 1950.

"More drastically than anything": Ibid., July 12, 1950.

Hoover may have been too . . . "got to be born": Ibid., July 18, 1950.

71 "low, low, low general" . . . "this sort of thing": Author's interview with Benjamin C. Bradlee, April 6, 1995.

"the compulsive" . . . "their sex habits": *New York Post*, July 22, 1950.

72 Some of his friends believe: Victor Navasky, *Naming Names*, 75, 304.

"While other witnesses denounced": *New York Times*, May 6, 1953.

"so compliant": Navasky, *Naming Names*, 75, 304.

"He wasn't threatened" . . . "blacklist destroyed Hollywood": Author's interview with Arthur Laurents, June 14, 1995.

73 "something which tormented" . . . "saved my life": *James Baldwin: The Price of the Ticket* (documentary).

"I'd been a boy preacher" . . . Cole was "horrified": Ibid. and *The New York Times*, December 2, 1987.

74 "primary issue": *New York Post*, July 21, 1950.

"a preliminary sampling": Ibid., July 20, 1950.

"homosexual angle": John D'Emilio, *Sexual Politics, Sexual Communities*, 41–42.

"pervert problem": *New York Post*, July 17, 1950.

"[Maryland Democratic Senator]" . . . "homo who was jealous": Drew Pearson, *Drew Pearson: Diaries, 1949–1959*, 188–89, 190, 192.

75 "The portrait of the Wisconsin": *New York Post*, July 21, 1950.

"one of the boys": David Halberstam, *The Fifties*, 54.

"there was a lot of time": Author's interview with Benjamin C. Bradlee, April 6, 1995.

"wreck the Army": *New York Times*, August 3, 1986.

"real heart": Neil Miller, *Out of the Past*, 269–71.

76 "shamefully cut down" . . . "himself had practiced": Ibid.

"Bonnie, Bonnie and Clyde": *New York Times*, August 3, 1986.

"Anybody who knows me": Nicholas von Hoffman, *Citizen Cohn*, 132.

77 "The only thing I really": Author's interview with Gore Vidal, January 14, 1994.

"In Schine's case": Author's interview with "Bill Gillman," November 10, 1994.

"thrilling moments" . . . "a gay restaurant?": Author's interview with Ethan Geto, July 1, 1995.

"did not acquire" . . . "very busy man": Author's interview with "Bill Gillman," November 10, 1994.

78 "Roy was a lot of" . . . "growing up with him": Author's interview with Stanley Friedman, November 30, 1994.

79 "Homosexuals and other sex": "Employment of Homosexuals and Other Sex Perverts in Government: U.S. Senate document No. 241, December 15, 1950," quoted in Donald Webster Cory, *The Homosexual in America*, 272–77.

"sex perversion": Ibid., 276–77.

"Homosexuality became an epidemic": Lee Mortimer, *Washington Confidential Today*, 110–19, and Jack Lait and Lee Mortimer, *U.S.A. Confidential*, quoted in John D'Emilio, *Sexual Politics, Sexual Communities*, 43–44.

80 "sexual perversion": John D'Emilio, *Sexual Politics, Sexual Communities*, 43–44.

"U.S. Agency Box Score": *New York Times*, July 3, 1953, and February 24, 1954.

Joseph Alsop, the scion . . . his death in 1989: The facts for the Alsop account are taken from the *Washington Post*, April 13, 1995. It is also discussed in *Joe Alsop's Cold War*, by Edwin Yoder, Jr.; *Molehunt*, by David Wise; and a doctoral thesis, "Joseph Alsop and American Foreign Policy," by Leann Grabavoy Almquist.

82 "Perverts Called Government": *New York Times*, April 19, 1950; May 22, 1950; and September 17, 1950.

"psychiatric case histories": *Coronet*, September 1950.

"wide leather motorcycle" . . . "normal Saturday crowds": *New York Times*, August 1, 1954.

83 At the end of the decade: George Chauncey, Jr., lecture at the Museum of the City of New York, June 22, 1995.

"In those days it": Author's interview with "Sam Baron," December 12, 1991.

"The hustlers were mostly": Author's interview with Jack Dowling, May 5, 1993.

women were legally required: Author's interview with Sandy Kern, June 29, 1993.

84 "When a dead man": Author's interview with Joe Schoener, 1978.

"I always felt ugly" . . . "I loved it": Author's interview with Sandy Kern, June 29, 1993.

86 "We knew we were outside" . . . "place that was illegal": *Before Stonewall* (documentary).

"sex is beautiful" . . . "woman again, or a man": Author's interview with Sandy Kern, June 29, 1993.

89 "scientists, businessmen": Donald Webster Cory, *The Homosexual in America*, 161–62.

"homosexual creativity": Ibid., 161.

"a gay man who got married": Author's interview with Arthur Laurents, June 14, 1995.

"The *idea* of family": Author's interview with Stephen Sondheim, August 1, 1995.

90 "Jerry R. called today": Humphrey Burton, *Leonard Bernstein*, 187.

"I didn't want to write": Author's interview with Arthur Laurents, June 14, 1995.

"so-called Americans": Craig Zadan, *Sondheim & Co.*, 14–15.

Laurents recruited Sondheim: Author's interview with Arthur Laurents, June 14, 1995.

"We thought the same way": Craig Zadan, *Sondheim & Co.*, 15–16, and *New York Times*, October 21, 1990.

"Something's coming, it may": Humphrey Burton, *Leonard Bernstein*, 274–75.

91 "I remember all my collaborations": Ibid., 275.

"Originally, Robbins wanted only": Author's interview with Arthur Laurents, January 1, 1997.

"I twisted syllables": Craig Zadan, *Sondheim & Co.*, 20–21.

"Jerry continues to be": Humphrey Burton, *Leonard Bernstein*, 270.

"The idea was": Ibid., 275.

"I thought it would run": Author's interview with Arthur Laurents, June 14, 1995.

"It's such a shame": Craig Zadan, *Sondheim & Co.*, 26.

92 "We thought at that point": Ibid., 17.

Harold Prince was in Boston: Ibid.

Their gamble seemed worthwhile: Humphrey Burton, *Leonard Bernstein*, 273.

"Despite the triumphant": Ibid. and Craig Zadan, *Sondheim & Co.*, 25.

"It was extremely generous," Sondheim: Author's interview with Stephen Sondheim, August 1, 1995.

"The next day I went": Author's interview with Arthur Laurents, June 14, 1995.

93 "The purity of the music": Ibid.

The actor Alan Helms: Alan Helms, *Young Man from the Provinces*, 98.

In 1996, it was one: *New York Times*, March 26, 1996.

"It was never an issue": Author's interview with Murray Gitlin, February 26, 1993.

"There is one sensibility": Letter from Arthur Laurents to the author, August 21, 1995.

"boy-girl stuff": Author's interview with Gore Vidal, January 14, 1994.

"If you think that's": Author's interview with Sondheim, August 1, 1995.

94 "What we did was": Craig Zadan, *Sondheim & Co.*, 26.

"The radioactive fallout": Quoted in Humphrey Burton, *Leonard Bernstein*, 276.

"It was a big hit" . . . "The picture failed for me": Craig Zadan, *Sondheim & Co.*, 26–30.

95 "It was a rare sort": Quoted in Gore Vidal, *United States*, 447. From an essay first published in *The New York Review of Books*, June 13, 1985.

Michael Butler was the . . . "good arrangement for us": Author's interview with Michael Butler, March 10, 1996.

96 "there are no homosexual": Author's interview with Gore Vidal, January 14, 1994.

"What we can discuss": Edmund White, *States of Desire*, 259.

"any discussion of a group's": *New York Times Magazine*, June 16, 1991.

"you got very good" . . . "impersonating a gay man": *The Celluloid Closet* (documentary).

97 "At one point": Gore Vidal, *United States*, 443–44.

"so convinced of being": *City Poet*, 229, and *What Did I Do: The Unauthorized Autobiography of Larry Rivers*, with Arnold Weinstein, 228, 230, 232, 234.

98 "I wouldn't go to bed": Author's interview with Gore Vidal, January 14, 1994.

"repairing the three of us": Jack Kerouac, *The Subterraneans*, 53–54.

"It is hard now": Vidal, *United States*, 1136.

99 "So why all the fuss?": *New York Review of Books*, June 13, 1985.

"'Cause I was in love": Allen Young, *Gay Sunshine Interview* with Allen Ginsberg, 4.

"Neal [Cassady]": Ibid., 3, 4, 6.

"He had mixed feelings": Ibid., 7.

100 "That was eliminated": Ibid., 3–7.

"It took an enormous amount": *Before Stonewall* (documentary).

"In the forties": Ibid.

"We thought that we": *The Celluloid Closet* (documentary).

"There was a series": *Before Stonewall* (documentary).

102 "I loved the Puerto Ricans": Author's interview with Franklin Macfie, May 12, 1993.

"just had to become" . . . "loved to have fun": Author's interview with Murray Gitlin, February 26, 1993.

104 "I was twenty-one" . . . "the next fifteen years": Author's interview with Roy Aarons, December 12, 1991.

106 There was another famous cluster: Brad Gooch, *City Poet*, 194–96.

"Gay life was secretive" . . . "could talk to people": Author's interview with Jack Dowling, May 5, 1993.

107 "14th Street is drunken,": Frank O'Hara, "Homosexuality,"

After his adventures in the . . . "everybody bowed": Author's interview with "Stephen Reynolds," September 24, 1992.

110 "Truman lifted his cape": Author's interview with Paul Cadmus, May 20, 1995.

"He was so funny": Author's interview with "Stephen Reynolds," September 24, 1992.

111 "officially came out" . . . "moved a mountain": Author's interview with Franklin Macfie, May 12, 1993.

115 "sort of a village atheist" . . . "very cute country boy": Author's interview with Walter Clemons, November 9, 1992.

118 "I have noticed that straight men": Author's interview with Arthur Laurents, June 14, 1995.

"They would fix me up" . . . men had disappeared: Author's interview with Walter Clemons, November 9, 1992.

119 "It was vividly exciting" . . . "legs I've ever seen!": Ibid.

120 "a room with a lot": Author's interview with Murray Gitlin, February 26, 1993.

"It was before I": Author's interview with Walter Clemons, November 9, 1992, and James Spada, *Streisand*, 68.

121 "One day this girl": Arthur Laurents interviewed by Larry Kramer in *The Advocate*, May 16, 1995.

"It took me all day" . . . "wouldn't believe it": Author's interview with Jack Dowling, May 5, 1993.

123 "We didn't know" . . . "achievements of the homosexual minority": *Before Stonewall* (documentary), and John D'Emilio, *Sexual Politics, Sexual Communities*, 59–66.

gay friends: *Los Angeles Times Magazine*, June 10, 1990.

"She never treated": *New York Times*, November 22, 1996.

124 "Curiosity and empathy": *Los Angeles Times Magazine*, June 10, 1990.

"Every clinical psychologist": Eric Marcus, *Making History*, 24.

"gay men can be": Ibid., 24–25.

Although it would be: *New York Times*, November 22, 1996.

In the seventies: Ibid.

"how *terrible*": Author's interview with William Wynkoop, June 3, 1993.

125 It was published under the: Author's interview with Brandt Aymar, May 1, 1995.

The offending books: Ibid.

"It was well accepted": Ibid.

"American life as": Donald Webster Cory, *The Homosexual in America*, xiii.

"I said, '*This* is'": Author's interview with William Wynkoop and Roy Strickland, June 3, 1993.

"any facts about homosexuality": Donald Webster Cory, *The Homosexual in America*, xiv.

126 "deeply ashamed of": Ibid., xiv–xv.

"Passionate infatuations": Ibid., xv.

His final solution was typical: Author's interview with Brandt Aymar, May 1, 1995.

As the historian John D'Emilio: John D'Emilio, *Sexual Politics, Sexual Communities*, 33.

"is as involuntary": Donald Webster Cory, *The Homosexual in America*, 5–6.

To make money: Author's interview with Brandt Aymar, May 1, 1995.

127 "discrimination and social": Donald Webster Cory, *The Homosexual in America*, 47.

"social, legal or ecclesiastical": Ibid., 139–41.

"One of the reasons gay": Author's interview with Tom Stoddard, August 3, 1994.

"Tolerance is the ugliest": Donald Webster Cory, *The Homosexual in America*, 151.

128 "The prejudice of the": Ibid., 228.

"Sexual freedom is actually": Ibid., 232–33.

"All sexual activity": Ibid., 232.

"the dominant factor": Ibid., 6–7.

129 "Many homosexuals consider": Ibid., 230.

William Wynkoop was . . . "who was effeminate": Author's interview with William Wynkoop and Roy Strickland, June 3, 1993.

131 "Millions cannot be excluded": Donald Webster Cory, *The Homosexual in America*, 91, 243.

III: THE SIXTIES

135 "It was a marvelous time": *On The Edge: Images from 100 Years of Vogue*, 111.

"The thing that most": *Playboy*, March 1966.

"You do what's appropriate": Author's interview with Stormé DeLarverie, December 9, 1995.

"Queen power exploded": *New York Daily News*, July 6, 1969.

"Do you think homosexuals": Donn Teal, *The Gay Militants*, 36.

136 "the prototype of every": *Before Stonewall* (documentary).

As early as 1966: *Time*, January 21, 1966.

"I think the connections": *Before Stonewall* (documentary).

"America changed because": *The Question of Equality*, pt. 1 (documentary).

137 "of Levis, denim jackets": Thomas Powers, *The War at Home*, 24–25.

"and no one ever bothered": Author's interview with David Kaiser, November 7, 1995.

"Dial-a-Demonstration": Andy Warhol and Pat Hackett, *POPism*, 255.

the antiwar movement convinced: Charles Kaiser, *1968 in America,* 78.

138　"I fought my way" . . . "not financially stable": Author's interview with Frank Kameny, October 21, 1995.

139　"The worst effect of slavery": Letter from Jack Nichols to the author, December 12, 1995.

In November 1961: Author's interview with Frank Kameny, October 21, 1995.

"As we got into things": Ibid.

"Our opponents will do": John D'Emilio, *Sexual Politics, Sexual Communities,* 152.

Kameny was speaking: See, for example, *Mattachine Review,* vol. V, no. 6, June 1959, which included a "Critique" by Albert Ellis, Ph.D. "Homosexuals will only harm themselves immensely to the degree that they do not admit that fixed homophilism (as distinct from occasional homosexual acts) is invariably a distinct sickness." Eight years earlier, Ellis had written the introduction to *The Homosexual in America,* presumably because he was one of the most sympathetic psychologists Edward Sagarin could find.

140　"I do not see the NAACP" . . . "in which they live": John D'Emilio, *Sexual Politics, Sexual Communities,* 153.

In the summer of 1963: Author's interview with Jack Nichols, January 15, 1996.

"discriminatory": Author's interview with Frank Kameny, October 21, 1995.

"homosexual scandal" . . . declined further comment: *New York Times,* October 16 and 28, 1964.

141　"The mental attitude": John D'Emilio, *Sexual Politics, Sexual Communities,* 163.

"no homosexual problem": Donald Webster Cory, *The Homosexual in America,* 228.

"It remains to be proved": Ibid., 85.

142　"He could get very nasty": Author's interview with Frank Kameny, October 21, 1995.

"The entire homophile movement": John D'Emilio, *Sexual Politics, Sexual Communities,* 164.

"You have fallen": Ibid., 167.

"It is very much": Ibid., 168.

"These demonstrations created": Letter from Frank Kameny to the author, December 19, 1995.

"Is God Dead?": *Time,* April 8, 1966.

143　"God's continuing and progressive": *New York Times,* November 26, 1964.

The following year, even: Ibid., June 8, 1965.

But the Catholic Archdiocese: Ibid., July 23, 1965.

"per se" . . . "effeminate and identifiable": Ibid., November 29, 1967.

In October 1968: Mark Thompson, ed., *The Long Road to Freedom,* 5.

"Homosexuality is not": Donald Webster Cory, *The Homosexual in America,* 36.

At the same time, the: *New York Times,* June 20, 1984.

144　"that everybody, including": Thomas Powers, *The War at Home,* 204–206.

"Who needs jazz": *New York Times Magazine,* May 14, 1967.

145 "the love generation": Thomas Powers, *The War at Home,* 209.

"coming of the psychedelic": Author's interview with Roy Aarons, December 12, 1991.

After Bobby's killing: Norman Mailer, *Miami and the Siege of Chicago,* 15.

"one of those liberal": *James Baldwin: The Price of the Ticket* (documentary).

After King was killed: Charles Kaiser, *1968 in America,* 148–49.

Under pressure from: *New York Times,* April 2, 1966.

Harold Bramson, a thirty-three-year-old: Author's interview with Harold Bramson, March 4, 1994.

146 "apparent homosexuals": *New York Times,* November 7, 1967.

"a general and an admiral" . . . "television personality": *New York Times,* March 3, 1966, July 24, 1966, and May 17, 1967.

"the fundamental human right": Ibid., May 3, 1967.

147 John Koch was an Iowa: Author's interview with John Koch, June 6, 1995.

"I understood the psychodynamic" . . . "us from every source": Letter from Frank Kameny to the author, December 19, 1995.

148 "crypto-Nazi": Mark Thompson, ed., *The Long Road to Freedom,* 31.

"homosexual bill of rights": Letter from Frank Kameny to the author, December 19, 1995.

"History indicates that": *The New Republic,* September 7, 1968.

149 "must always be regarded": *New York Times,* November 29, 1967.

"modern technology was": Karla Jay and Allen Young, *Out of the Closets,* xvii–xviii.

"The difference was": Author's interview with Frank Kameny, October 25, 1995.

In April 1969, *Playboy: Playboy,* April 1969.

"And I know no better": *New York Times,* August 11, 1967. Thirty years later, Ms. Hauser declined to comment on her revolutionary point of view.

"I was scared to death": Author's interview with Dan Stewart, October 10, 1991.

150 "releasing of moral and cultural": *New York Times,* March 8, 1964.

"It's at that age when": Author's interview with Bob Dylan, November 13, 1985.

Their beguiling public persona: Peter Brown and Steven Gaines, *The Love You Make,* 58.

"We were more confused": *The Beatles Anthology,* pt. 3, first broadcast in America on ABC, November 23, 1995.

151 "They exuded exuberance": George Martin with William Pearson, *With a Little Help from My Friends,* 31.

"While I was watching": *A Hard Day's Night* (documentary).

"You didn't take your eyes": Ibid. The executive producer, Walter Shenson, reported that after the first screening of the film, George Harrison was the first to speak. He told Shenson it was very good; then the rest of the Beatles agreed with him.

"undisputed troubadours": *Weekly News* (Miami), December 20, 1995.

"In the age of Calvin": Gore Vidal, *United States*, 448.

"male as sex object": Ibid.

152 "The Beatles provided": *Sgt. Pepper's Lonely Hearts Club Band* (documentary).

"It was four guys": *The Beatles Anthology*, pt. 3, first broadcast in America on ABC, November 23, 1995.

"metamorphosis from the ugly": Jim Miller, ed., *Rolling Stone Illustrated History of Rock and Roll*, 276.

"It was Ginsberg": *Playboy*, March 1978.

Ginsberg was in the studio: *The New Yorker*, October 24, 1964.

"Listen," exulted Ginsberg: Ibid.

153 "Thanks," said Bogarde . . . "or we don't": Dirk Bogarde, *Snakes and Ladders*, 201–202.

"It was the first film": Vito Russo, *The Celluloid Closet*, 126.

"If only these unfortunate" . . . "antiquated law": *Victim*, directed by Basil Dearden, produced by Allied Filmmakers/Parkway/Rank, written by Janet Green and John McCormick, 1961.

154 "I do not believe": *Newsweek*, July 7, 1965.

Dr. Arthur M. Ramsay: Ibid., June 7, 1965, and *New York Times*, July 5, 1967.

155 "which had never before": Vito Russo, *The Celluloid Closet*, 128.

"candid and clinical": *New York Times*, November 16, 1961.

"We came out": Author's interview with Murray Gitlin, February 26, 1993.

Ironically, the censorship office: *New York Times*, October 4, 1961, and Gerald Gardner, *The Censorship Papers*, 191.

"a coyly sensational": quoted in Vito Russo, *The Celluloid Closet*, 131 and 126–27.

156 "too many people": *New York Times*, February 20, 1966.

Six years later: Ibid., October 12, 1986.

One of the first things: Gay Talese, *The Kingdom and the Power*, 354.

157 "homosexual haunts" . . . "homosexual destiny": *New York Times*, December 17, 1963.

159 "truly psychotic inverts": Ibid.

160 "No sponsor wanted": Author's interview with Mike Wallace, November 6, 1995.

The first version: Ibid. "I went to Fred's eightieth birthday party last Friday night," said Wallace. "I told this story, which of course convulsed the audience. And Fred said, 'That's true, that's right!'"

But after Friendly . . . sensationalism: *Variety*, March 8, 1967; C. A. Tripp, *The Homosexual Matrix*, 209–10; author's interviews with Edward Alwood, November 6, 1995, and with Mike Wallace, November 6, 1995, and December 28, 1995; and Edward Alwood, *Straight News*, 71.

161 forty million prime-time viewers: Edward Alwood, *Straight News*, 73.

"not interested in": "The Homosexuals, CBS Reports," March 7, 1967.

"He's nervous": Author's interview with Mike Wallace, November 6, 1995.

"terribly frightened" . . . "please my father": "The Homosexuals, CBS Reports," March 7, 1967.

163 "I can't imagine": Author's interview with Jack Nichols, November 7, 1995.

"Mike said I had": Ibid.

"It seems perfectly": Author's interview with Mike Wallace, November 6, 1995.

"The day after the program: Edward Alwood, *Straight News*, 74.

"The fact that someone": Ibid.

164 "I don't think it's easy": *New York Times*, December 24, 1995.

"homosexual acts are not": "The Homosexuals, CBS Reports," March 7, 1967.

"Is it not time to": *Newsday*, May 27, 1965.

"Every American citizen": "The Homosexuals, CBS Reports," March 7, 1967.

165 "Writers feel they": *New York Times*, November 5, 1961.

"three of the most": Ibid., January 23, 1966.

166 "Stanley had this absolutely": Author's interview with Jack Kroll, September 7, 1995.

"disgusting article": *New York Times*, June 16, 1991.

"People make the mistake": Author's interview with Arthur Laurents, June 14, 1995.

"theory which one reads": "The Homosexuals, CBS Reports," March 7, 1967.

167 "He won't even mention": Author's interview with Mike Wallace, November 6, 1995.

"It is now widely": Gore Vidal, *United States*, 443.

"It seems to me": Author's interview with Stephen Sondheim, August 1, 1995.

"Somebody would become successful": Author's interview with Gore Vidal, January 14, 1994.

"faced with the contrary": Gore Vidal, *United States*, 443.

168 "horror at the fact": Author's interview with Arthur Laurents, June 14, 1995.

"You know, everybody": Arthur Laurents interviewed by Larry Kramer in *The Advocate*, May 16, 1995.

"In Hollywood, you have": *Time*, January 21, 1966.

"Oh, I don't mean it": Author's interview with Arthur Laurents, June 14, 1995.

"even in ordinary": *Time*, January 21, 1966.

169 "anti-homintern hysteria": Author's interview with Gore Vidal, October 14, 1993.

"It seems to me" . . . "An outsider": "The Homosexuals, CBS Reports," March 7, 1967.

170 "Jesus Christ!": Author's interview with Mike Wallace, November 6, 1995.

171 "It's not a question" . . . "out in that way": Ibid.

In September 1967: Mark Thompson, ed., *The Long Road to Freedom*, xvii–xx.

172 "Babe had said" . . . "unbelievable": Author's interview with Katharine Graham, July 10, 1995.

173 "as spectacular a group": *New York Times*, November 29, 1966, and the personal archive of Katharine Graham.

It *was* an amazing list: *New York Times*, November 29, 1966.

"I'd never seen anything like": Author's interview with Katharine Graham, July 10, 1995.

"experience an instant inflation": *New York Times,* December 8, 1966, quoted in Gerald Clarke, *Capote,* 379.

174 "I really did": Author's interview with "Stephen Reynolds," September 24, 1992.

"There was such a": *Esquire,* November 1991.

"Don't you see whom": Ibid.

"So," Capote asked: Gerald Clarke, *Capote,* 379.

"I'd never met Jack": Author's interview with Katharine Graham, July 10, 1995.

"Truman said he didn't": Author's interview with Paul Cadmus, May 20, 1995.

"Completely" . . . "I never was": Author's interview with Katharine Graham, July 10, 1995.

175 "That's really why": Author's interview with Walter Clemons, November 9, 1992.

"Any writer suspected": Author's interview with Gore Vidal, January 14, 1993.

"I always thought those guys": Author's interview with Jack Kroll, September 7, 1995.

176 "My mother was planning" . . . "do with anything": Author's interview with Walter Clemons, November 9, 1992.

177 "Writing for Walter": Author's interview with Jack Kroll, September 7, 1995.

"Jack's the best editor": Author's interview with Walter Clemons, November 9, 1992.

"I always assumed": Author's interview with Jack Kroll, September 7, 1995.

"I had never gotten" . . . "read you a passage": Author's interview with Walter Clemons, November 9, 1992.

178 "The first person he knew": Charles Simmons, *Wrinkles,* 93–94.

"So Chris read me": Author's interview with Walter Clemons, November 9, 1992.

179 "certainly a way" . . . "by the minute": Author's interview with Christopher Lehmann-Haupt, April 11, 1997.

"Absolutely no recollection": letter from A. M. Rosenthal to the author, May 5, 1997.

"I had gone to *Newsweek*": Author's interview with Walter Clemons, November 9, 1992.

180 "very religious life" . . . "and my yarmulke": Author's interview with Howard Rosenman, December 20, 1995.

182 "How to begin?": Humphrey Burton, *Leonard Bernstein,* 183–184, 186.

183 "fabulous . . . Leonard is an iconic": Author's interview with Howard Rosenman, December 20, 1995.

In the fall of 1948: Humphrey Burton, *Leonard Bernstein,* 183–85.

"The idea of resurrection": Ibid., 365.

"Mrs. Leonard Bernstein": Author's interview with Howard Rosenman, December 20, 1995.

184 "a look of almost": Humphrey Burton, *Leonard Bernstein,* 365.

"He was incredible" . . . "turned on to it": Author's interview with Howard Rosenman, December 20, 1995.

185 "problem" . . . "detriment of others": *New York Times,* January 1, 1966.
"with a sugarcane" . . . "boys in the band": *New York Times,* October 21, 1993.
186 "What I *am*, Michael": Mart Crowley, *The Boys in the Band.*
"I can't send this": *New York Times,* October 21, 1993.
"It worked as a play": Author's interview with Murray Gitlin, February 26, 1993.
Crowley told colleagues: Author's interview with Howard Rosenman, December 20, 1995.
187 "transforming": Author's interview with Murray Gitlin, February 26, 1993.
"You Don't Have": *New York Times,* September 29, 1968.
"You think they'll": Ibid., October 21, 1993.
"The Clothes The Boys": *Women's Wear Daily,* May 9, 1968.
Seven months into: *New York Times,* November 6, 1968.
"As Christians": Ibid., November 11, 1968.
"The thing I always hated": Ibid., May 12, 1968.
"these were people": Author's interview with Murray Gitlin, February 26, 1993.
"by far the frankest": *New York Times,* April 15, 1968.
188 "the shot heard round": Author's interview with Stephen Sondheim, August 1, 1995.
"I thought it was": Author's interview with Howard Rosenman, December 20, 1995.
"did for plays what": *New York Times,* October 21, 1995.
"have fun": Ibid., May 12, 1968.
"Bored with Scandinavia": Mart Crowley, *The Boys in the Band.*
"I knew a lot of": *The Celluloid Closet* (documentary).
189 "You are a sad" . . . "if you try": Mart Crowley, *The Boys in the Band.*
190 The play was a hit: Author's interview with Murray Gitlin, February 26, 1993.
Just a year after: Mark Thompson, ed., *The Long Road to Freedom,* 28–30.
"grimly visible": *Time,* October 3, 1969.
"very pretty": E-mail from Harvard undergraduate to author, May 18, 1997.
Jack Nichols and his lover: Letter from Jack Nichols to the author, December 12, 1995, and from Frank Kameny to the author, December 19, 1995. Kameny emphasized that he wasn't actually acting *in response* to Crowley, "of whom and of whose play I probably had not heard at the time I coined the slogan."
191 "have learned to hug": *New York Times,* December 10, 1972.
"We're not like that": Ibid., October 21, 1993.
"He was one of" . . . "he was a star": Author's interview with Murray Gitlin, February 26, 1993.
192 "What's more boring": Mart Crowley, *The Boys in the Band.*
"a combination of absolute": David Shipman, *Judy Garland,* 74.
"I believe in doing what": Noel Coward, "If Love Were All."
"without doubt": Dirk Bogarde, *Snakes and Ladders,* 196, 199.
After Peter Lawford: Gerold Frank, *Judy,* 516–17. Liza Minnelli said she witnessed this routine (from her mother's end of the line) regularly in 1962 and 1963. Shipman relates the same story, 392.

"There was a vulnerability": Liza Minnelli interview with *The Advocate*, September 3, 1996.

Garland loved men: David Shipman, *Judy Garland*, 138–40.

193 "girl and boy next door": *New York Times*, August 12, 1993.

"She is at bottom": David Shipman, *Judy Garland*, 408.

She was born Frances: Anne Edwards, *Judy Garland*, 12, 14.

"worked, slept, ate": Ibid., 39.

"I sort of grew up": Author's interview with Walter Clemons, November 9, 1992.

"the American people": Anne Edwards, *Judy Garland*, 62.

"I don't seem to": Ibid., 60.

Garland made a halfhearted: David Shipman, *Judy Garland*, 205–206.

Two years later: Gerold Frank, *Judy*, 451, and David Shipman, *Judy Garland*, 390–91.

194 "I think she beat": Author's interview with Arthur Laurents, June 14, 1995.

"She ate up music": David Shipman, *Judy Garland*, 457.

"Here is my heart": Gerold Frank, *Judy*, 469.

"because with Streisand": Author's interview with Arthur Laurents, June 14, 1995.

"the range of her talent": Author's interview with Judy Barnett, December 4, 1995.

"I saw staid citizens": David Shipman, *Judy Garland*, 405–406.

"I could never cheat": Dirk Bogarde, *Snakes and Ladders*, 199.

In April 1961: David Shipman, *Judy Garland*, 407.

She arrived at her Carnegie: Ibid., 409.

195 3,149 other fans: Liner notes, *Judy at Carnegie Hall*, Capitol Records, CDP 7090014-15.

Outside, scalpers were: David Shipman, *Judy Garland*, 409.

Garland opened the show: *Judy at Carnegie Hall*, Capitol Records, CDP 7090014-15.

Then she proceeded: David Shipman, *Judy Garland*, 410.

"office boy in some": Anne Edwards, *Judy Garland*, 188–89.

"I don't know why": *Judy at Carnegie Hall*, Capitol Records, CDP 7090014-15.

"Well, you know": Anne Edwards, *Judy Garland*, 190.

twenty-seven songs: "Almost Like Being in Love" and "This Can't Be Love" were part of one medley, and "You Made Me Love You," "For Me and My Gal," and "The Trolley Song" were part of another.

"You really want more?": *Judy at Carnegie Hall*, Capitol Records, CDP 7090014-15.

Judith Crist saw tears: Anne Edwards, *Judy Garland*, 189.

196 At a Christmas party: David Shipman, *Judy Garland*, 501.

Three months later: Ibid., 504.

Three months after that: Ibid., 507–508.

"The greatest shock": Vincent Canby, quoted in Ibid., 507.

Liza Minnelli remembered: Gerold Frank, *Judy*, 632.

197 Frank Sinatra wanted: David Shipman, *Judy Garland*, 509.

"Don't I look": Gerold Frank, *Judy*, 633.

For a day and a night: Ibid., 634–35, David Shipman, *Judy Garland*, 509, and (for Valentino) *Encyclopaedia Britannica*, 1974, vol. 10, 337.

Minnelli requested that no one: Anne Edwards, *Judy Garland*, 303.

James Mason began: David Shipman, *Judy Garland*, 509.

All anyone knows: Martin Duberman, *Stonewall*, 198.

"I had been in combat": *Newsday*, June 20, 1994.

But the crowd was unusually: *Weekly News* (Miami), June 2, 1994.

"free-wheeling anarchy": Martin Duberman, *Stonewall*, 181.

198 Like nearly all gay bars: Martin Duberman, *Stonewall*, 181.

Because the "inn" was: Ibid., 184.

"Judy Garland" and "Elizabeth Taylor": Ibid., 187

unlikely gold mine: Ibid., 185.

The bar had often been: Ibid., 194.

After checking for: Ibid., 195.

Several spectators agreed: Ibid., 196.

"The cop hit me": Author's interview with Stormé DeLarverie, December 9, 1995.

The police were pelted: *Village Voice*, July 3, 1969.

"This is your payoff": *The Question of Equality*, pt. 1 (documentary).

Morty Manford remembered: Eric Marcus, *Making History*, 201.

The raiders quickly: *Village Voice*, July 3, 1969.

199 "They fell down": *New York Newsday*, June 20, 1994.

Believing he could intimidate: *Village Voice*, July 3, 1969.

"Grab it, grab": *Rat*, July 1969, quoted in Toby Marotta, *The Politics of Homosexuality*, 73–74.

"Gay Power!": Martin Duberman, *Stonewall*, 197.

Now one of the attackers: *Village Voice*, July 3, 1969.

"The homosexuals were usually": *New York Newsday*, June 20, 1994

"It was that close": *Village Voice*, July 3, 1969.

As the TPF waded: Ibid.

"Oh my God": *The Question of Equality*, pt. 1 (documentary).

200 "black guy, a queen": Author's interview with Randy Bourscheidt, February 26, 1993.

"Stonewall was just": Author's interview with Stormé DeLarverie, December 9, 1995.

"I got up and I" . . . "laughed at, scorned": Author's interview with Roy Strickland and William Wynkoop, June 3, 1993.

"We are the Stonewall": Martin Duberman, *Stonewall*, 200–201.

201 "totally spontaneous": *Rat*, July 1969, quoted in Toby Marotta, *The Politics of Homosexuality*, 74.

By four A.M.: *New York Times*, June 29, 1969.

"Gay Power! Isn't that": *Screw*, July 25, 1969.

When the *Voice* hit: Donn Teal, *The Gay Militants*, 17.

"Sheridan Square this weekend": *Village Voice*, July 3, 1969.

"Homo Nest Raided": *New York Daily News*, July 6, 1969.

The very first gay-authored: *Screw*, July 25, 1969.

"If you are tired": Ibid.

201 "The revolution in Sheridan": Ibid.

IV: THE SEVENTIES

205 "The 'homosexual problem'": *New York Times Magazine,* January 17, 1971.
"It is one thing": Ibid.
"This was a very idealistic": Eric Marcus, *Making History,* 204.
"To Victory!": *New York Times,* January 6, 1986.
206 "It was like fire": *The Question of Equality,* pt. 1 (documentary).
"I am a great believer": *New York Times Magazine,* October 10, 1971.
"It's amazing when you": Author's interview with Arthur Laurents, June 14, 1995.
"Gay and lesbian liberationists": Toby Marotta, *The Politics of Homosexuality,* 322.
207 "I do remember featuring" . . . "biggest sin of all": Author's interview with Phil Donahue, April 26, 1996.
208 In 1972, Hal Holbrook: Mark Thompson, ed., *The Long Road to Freedom,* 79.
"the California suburban": Frank Rich, *Esquire,* November 1987.
"the evil flower": Anne Roiphe, *New York Times Magazine,* February 18, 1973.
"as important a moment": Margaret Mead, *Time,* January 22, 1973.
"the ultimate soap opera": Ibid.
209 "an unfettered, guiltless": *Esquire,* December 1969.
210 "really celebrated homosexuality": *The Celluloid Closet* (documentary).
"final crumbling": *Weekly News* (Miami), June 22, 1994.
"Come to Us Because": Author's interview with Philip Johnson, May 5, 1995.
When Paul Cadmus visited Germany: Author's interview with Paul Cadmus, May 20, 1995.
In *Cabaret,* Liza Minnelli: *New York Times,* April 28, 1973.
"You are like me": *Cabaret,* directed by Bob Fosse, produced by Cy Feuer, screenplay by Jay Allen, music by John Kander, lyrics by Fred Ebb. Allied Artists and ABC Pictures Corp., 1972.
"creative process": Michael York, *Travelling Player,* 217.
211 "one of the best-edited": Ibid., 217, 231.
"long, extraordinary day": Ibid., 220.
"Screw Maximilian!": *Cabaret,* 1972. Allied Artists and ABC Pictures Corp.
"People take this attitude": Mark Thompson, ed., *The Long Road to Freedom,* 121.
Forster had read *Maurice:* Author's interview with Paul Cadmus, October 29, 1992.
212 "his sensitively drawn": *New York Times,* November 11, 1970.
"through the sixties": Author's interview with Judy Barnett, December 4, 1995.
"In the fifties I never": Author's interview with Dan Stewart, October 10, 1991.
213 During most of the seventies: Author's personal knowledge.

"We both turned around": Author's interview with Roy Aarons, December 12, 1991.

"alternative": Edward Alwood, *Straight News*, 91.

"This was in the early" . . . "that kind of thing": Author's interview with Philip Johnson, May 5, 1995. Johnson has given different dates for his dinner with Barbara Walters in different interviews. He told me that it took place in the 1980s; in an interview with Martin Filler for the *Times*, June 2, 1996, he placed it in the 1970s.

214 "I came to realize": Humphrey Burton, *Leonard Bernstein*, 434–40.

215 "When we first started": *The Question of Equality*, pt. 1 (documentary).

Nine months after Stonewall: *New York Times*, March 3, 1970, and David Deitcher, ed., *The Question of Equality*, 21.

"This cop is the nicest": Author's interview with John Koch, June 6, 1995.

"I would like to know": Donn Teal, *The Gay Militants*, 124.

"It takes real balls": Ibid.

"Everybody was very interested": Author's interview with "Edward Stone," October 11, 1996.

216 "I think there are": Toby Marotta, *The Politics of Homosexuality*, 157–58.

That same month: Ibid., 159.

"Not long ago": *New York Times*, June 29, 1970.

217 "The main thing": Ibid., July 5, 1970.

Similar festivities were held: Ibid., June 29, 1970, and January 17, 1971.

Less than four months later: Ibid., June 6, 1970, and October 27, 1970, and *New York Times Magazine*, January 17, 1971.

"Today we know not": Marotta, *The Politics of Homosexuality*, 157–60.

"The idea of a 'homosexual'": *New York Times*, May 17, 1971, and June 27, 1971.

"right in the middle" . . . "flabbergasted": Author's interview with Ethan Geto, July 1, 1995.

221 "catcalls from the balcony": Author's interview with Robert Abrams, July 10, 1995.

"We were flooded": Author's interview with Ethan Geto, July 1, 1995.

222 The *Washington Post* columnist: *Washington Post*, March 16, 1973.

"The old-style Chinese": Quoted in Edward Alwood, *Straight News*, 153.

"While I am pleased": Author's interview with Nicholas von Hoffman, June 25, 1996.

"the cultural majority": *Village Voice*, February 6, 1978, and author's interviews with ABC employees, February 27, 1996. In 1996, Greenfield did not respond to repeated requests by phone and letter to comment on these subjects.

223 "homosexuality is spreading" . . . "pain of the earth": *Harper's*, September 1970.

225 "'I look into myself'": Toby Marotta, *The Politics of Homosexuality*, 181.

Nevertheless, Morris refused: Ibid, 182.

"civilized, intelligent": Donn Teal, *The Gay Militants*, 269.

"serious and honest": Toby Marotta, *The Politics of Homosexuality*, 184.

By the end of the: Donn Teal, *The Gay Militants*, 269.

"That was a *dreadful* article": Author's interview with Frank Kameny, February 20, 1996.

"chronic affliction of *Harper's*": Donn Teal, *The Gay Militants*, 267.

226 "civil rights for homosexuals": *New York Times Magazine*, November 12, 1967.

"Damn it" . . . "I'm a homosexual": *Columbia Journalism Review*, March/April 1982.

"Is it true?" . . . "directors, myself": *New York Times Magazine*, January 17, 1971.

227 "I was on leave in Paris" . . . "basically decent": *New York Times*, October 10, 1971.

228 "rage" . . . "ever believed it": Ibid., November 24, 1985.

229 "several dozen homosexuals": Willie Morris, *New York Days*, 197.

"Parents Aren't Always": *New York Times*, February 10, 1971.

"Being a nice human": Ibid., October 10, 1971.

"the vast majority": Ibid., February 28, 1971.

230 "turn the penis": Author's interview with *Times* reporter, February 27, 1996.

"I love my stories actually" . . . "very unhappy": Author's interview with Jane Brody, March 13, 1996.

231 "there was a lot" . . . "So I'm outta here": Author's interview with "Sarah Waters," January 6, 1996.

235 "in full force" . . . "homosexuality is a disease": *New York Times*, October 10, 1971.

"an attribution of mental": Author's interview with Frank Kameny, October 21, 1995.

236 "It was a very dramatic": Eric Marcus, *Making History*, 253.

"In those days": Author's interview with Frank Kameny, October 21, 1995.

In 1969, Hooker was part: *New York Times*, October 21, 1969.

"Why are you here?": Author's interview with Arthur Laurents, June 14, 1995.

Marmor had always been: *New York Times*, May 11, 1969.

237 "appalled by the stereotypic": Eric Marcus, *Making History*, 252–53.

"It was a very": Ibid., 253, and *New York Times*, November 10, 1973.

"Right there we wrote": Author's interviews with Frank Kameny, October 21, 1995, and February 20, 1996.

238 Marmor thought his side: Eric Marcus, *Making History*, 253.

"regularly cause emotional": Mark Thompson, ed., *The Long Road to Freedom*, 104.

"psychiatrists call it": Eric Marcus, *Making History*, 254.

"aghast": Ibid.

"His rhetoric has not": Author's interview with Frank Kameny, October 21, 1995.

239 "it would be a serious": Ibid.

"We were ecstatic": Mark Thompson, ed., *The Long Road to Freedom*, 105.

Still Socarides refused: Author's interview with Frank Kameny, October 21, 1995.

"They claimed the whole thing": Ibid.

"I don't in any way": Eric Marcus, *Making History,* 254.

240 "We stated that there was": Ibid.

"the pleasure of most": Author's interview with William Wynkoop, June 3, 1993.

"totally straight": Author's interview with John Koch, June 6, 1995.

The rent was a bargain . . . "he had turned gay": Ibid.

242 "My view of the world" . . . "the Anvil": Author's interview with Philip Gefter, December 3, 1991.

244 "Weimar Germany": Author's interview with Tom Stoddard, August 3, 1994.

"I remember long lines" . . . "time of my life": Author's interview with Philip Gefter, December 3, 1991.

245 "The Anvil was like" . . . "Saturday night": Author's interview with Howard Rosenman, December 20, 1995.

246 "The people seemed crazy": Author's interview with Tom Stoddard, August 3, 1994.

"huge orgies" . . . "electrifying for me": Author's interview with Howard Rosenman, December 20, 1995.

247 "she did not want": *New York,* July 9, 1973.

248 On December 26, 1978: *New York Times,* December 27, 1978.

"very much a repressive": Author's interview with Tom Stoddard, August 3, 1994, and *New York Times,* February 13, 1997.

"very cute" . . . "go along with us": Author's interview with Tom Stoddard, August 3, 1994.

252 "with the quiet conviction": Eulogy delivered by Richard J. Meislin, March 19, 1997.

"I guess I'm still" . . . "rebel and conservative": Author's interview with Tom Stoddard, August 3, 1994.

253 Studio 54 was the brainchild: *Money,* September 1978.

"double-knit three-piece" . . . "bridge and tunnel": Ibid.

"we want it to": *Vanity Fair,* March 1996.

"the revenge of the nerd": *Esquire,* November 1987.

254 "overwhelming . . . like a Sodom": *Vanity Fair,* March 1996.

Later, Rubell dated: *Wall Street Journal,* December 2, 1977.

Depending on which story: *New York Times,* April 27, 1977; *People,* July 31, 1978; *Money,* September 1978; *Wall Street Journal,* December 2, 1977; and *Vanity Fair,* March 1996.

"had an impeccable eye": Author's interview with Howard Rosenman, December 20, 1995.

"need to be liked": *Money,* September 1978.

Inside the club were Andy: *Vanity Fair,* March 1996.

"Turn some of these princes": *Wall Street Journal,* December 2, 1977.

255 "hot spot of the universe": Author's interview with Ethan Geto, July 1, 1995.

"the greatest club of all": *Vanity Fair,* March 1996.

"Roy would have an entourage" . . . "how to market": Author's interview with Stanley Friedman, November 30, 1994.

Times reporter Robert McG. Thomas: Author's interview with Robert McG. Thomas, Jr., September 23, 1996.

"There's these mobs" . . . "doin' that in public": Author's interview with Ethan Geto, July 1, 1995.

256 "We started to lean": Author's interview with Philip Gefter, December 3, 1991.

257 Waiters at Studio 54: *Wall Street Journal,* December 2, 1977.

"Usually men": Author's interview with Alec Baldwin, *Interview,* October 1989.

"You needed something" . . . "wasn't my scene": Author's interview with Howard Rosenman, December 20, 1995.

258 "to be there as a peon": *Esquire,* November 1987.

The excluded establishment . . . $400,000 in taxes: *New York Times,* August 25, 1979, August 29, 1979, and May 27, 1980.

259 "They stopped everything": Author's interview with Ethan Geto, July 1, 1995.

Diana Ross was there: *Vanity Fair,* March 1996.

Later the club owners': Ibid.

"consummated the country's": *Esquire,* November 1987.

"The gay physical ideal": Ibid.

260 "I said, 'I can't'" . . . "on the GAA side": Author's interview with Ethan Geto, July 1, 1995.

262 "Will you talk to" . . . gay organizations in America: Eric Marcus, *Making History,* 242–49.

"We all trudged out": Author's interview with Jeff Katzoff, September 30, 1994.

"She saw for the first": Author's interview with Frank Kameny, October 21, 1995.

263 "packed to the gills": Author's interview with Philip Gefter, December 3, 1991.

"I walked in, and I": Author's interview with Arthur Laurents, June 14, 1995.

"very high ceiling": Author's interview with Jeff Katzoff, September 30, 1994.

"This was before SoHo" . . . "the way I did": Author's interview with Ethan Geto, June 1, 1995.

V: THE EIGHTIES

269 "I don't think people's": Author's interview with John Fairchild, May 2, 1995.

"San Francisco is where gay": Edmund White, *States of Desire,* 30.

"What everyone had wanted was": Randy Shilts, *And the Band Played On,* 20.

"Out of the closets and": Author's personal knowledge.

"a watershed": Author's interview with Ethan Geto, July 1, 1995.

270 By 1980, in response: Author's article in *Entertainment West,* July 15, 1979.

The National Gay Task Force: *New York Times,* May 24, 1979.

"I was more interested": Larry Kramer, *Reports from the Holocaust,* xv.

After the tennis star: *New York Times Magazine,* May 2, 1982.

"from getting involved in a public": *Columbia Journalism Review,* March/April 1982.

271 "so dangerous that they": Edward Alwood, *Straight News,* 184–85.

"It was a very decadent": CBS transcript, "Gay Power, Gay Politics."

"It's shocking that CBS News": Edward Alwood, *Straight News,* 187.

"gay window advertising": *New York Times*, May 2, 1982.

Randy Alfred, a free-lance: E-mail from Randy Alfred to the author, June 5, 1997.

273 The election also meant: *New York Times*, October 10 and 13, 1980.

"We must affirm the dignity": Ibid., October 30, 1980, and Randy Shilts, *And the Band Played On*, 43.

274 Another senseless shooting . . . remained incarcerated in 1996: *New York Times*, November 20 and 21, 1980, and July 27, 1981.

276 "From this blow": Theodore H. White, *The Making of the President, 1968*, 36.

"Homosexuals want your children" . . . "two-to-one margin": Randy Shilts, *The Mayor of Castro Street*, 229–30.

After Mrs. Reagan's sixtieth: *Washington Post*, March 18, 1984.

277 "a trim, precisely groomed man": *New York Times*, September 28, 1980.

"perennial bachelor": Ibid., July 10, 1981.

Six autographed pictures of Reagan: *Washington Post*, May 7, 1985.

"generous nature, great warmth": *New York Times*, December 19, 1981.

"He's all man": *Newsweek*, July 21, 1980.

"White House wasn't that homophobic": Author's interview with Steven R. Weisman, June 6, 1995.

"best-little-boy-in-the-world" . . . "not have been a problem": Author's interview with Philip Gefter, December 3, 1991.

278 "The inherent tragedy": Donald Webster Cory, *The Homosexual in America*, 230.

279 "Doctors in New York": *New York Times*, July 3, 1981.

281 "I was in a state" . . . "throw of the dice": Author's interview with Howard Rosenman, December 10, 1995.

282 A federal study at the beginning: Randy Shilts, *And the Band Played On*, 132.

283 (By comparison, less than three): According to John Ellis's *World War II Data Book*, 16,354,000 Americans served in World War II, and 450,000 Americans were killed.

"a time when the streets": *New York Times Magazine*, July 9, 1989.

"completely unpredictable": Author's interview with nurse, 1988.

"All your other blood work": Author's interview with "James Blair," February 4, 1993.

284 A typical disaster: *New York Times Magazine*, June 16, 1991, and *New York Times*, May 9, 1994.

285 In April 1982, Westmoreland: Randy Shilts, *And the Band Played On*, 143, 186–87.

One of the administration's first: Ibid., 55, 173, and *New York Times*, February 16, 1981.

286 "as gays see it": *Columbia Journalism Review*, March/April 1982.

287 "let people know": Author's interview with Max Frankel, 1992.

He was born in Davenport: *New York Times*, February 18, 1994.

288 At Oregon, Shilts studied: Ibid.

"know they have somebody": Ibid., October 31, 1987.

"Writing about the gay": Randy Shilts, *And the Band Played On*, 20.

289 "They'll put barbed wire": Ibid., 253–56.
      "virtually an article of faith" . . . "between gays and heterosexuals": Ibid., 228,
      253–56, 541.
      (Researchers at the Centers): Ibid., 116.
      "We're both in it": Ibid., 422.
290 In an excruciating irony: *New York Times,* June 18, 1994.
      "I certainly wasn't interested": Larry Kramer, *Reports from the Holocaust,* xvi.
      "Why do faggots have to": Larry Kramer, *Faggots.*
291 "Stripped of humanity": Shilts, *And the Band Played On,* 90.
      "In Western Christian culture": "Sexual Choice, Sexual Act: An Interview
      with Michel Foucault," *Salmagundi* 58–59 (Fall 1982–Winter 1983): 10–24.
      Quoted in Richard A. Isay, *Being Homosexual,* 133.
      "before you fuck yourself": Larry Kramer, *Faggots.*
      "The Ice Palace in the Grove" . . . "Meat Rack was like": Author's interview
      with Philip Gefter, December 3, 1991.
292 "angered everyone, of course": *Larry Kramer* (BBC documentary).
      "The men who have been": Larry Kramer, *Reports from the Holocaust,* 8.
293 "*something* we are doing": *New York Native,* December 21, 1981–January 3,
      1982, reproduced in *Reports from the Holocaust,* 14.
      "I think the concealed meaning": Larry Kramer, *Reports from the Holocaust,*
      16.
      "The first one was Gay: Ibid., 13.
      "Larry made this impassioned plea": Author's interview with Philip Gefter,
      December 3, 1991.
294 "A paltry $769.55 was collected: Larry Kramer, *Reports from the Holocaust,* 15.
      "They thought that this" . . . "why I'm alive today": Author's interview with
      Philip Gefter, December 3, 1991.
295 Her name was Mathilde Krim . . . deserved to die: *New York Times,* February
      14, 1988.
297 "had sex with Dugas": Randy Shilts, *And the Band Played On,* 147.
      psychoanalyst Richard Isay: Richard A. Isay, *Being Homosexual,* 69.
      "Of course I'm going to": Randy Shilts, *And the Band Played On,* 83, 138 147,
      200.
      "German and six feet four" . . . "other diseases": Author's interview with
      Howard Rosenman, December 20, 1995.
298 death as liver failure: *New York Times,* August 8, 1980.
      "He was dishonest": Author's interview with Howard Rosenman, December
      20, 1995.
      "It was one of those": Larry Kramer, *Reports from the Holocaust,* 23.
299 Later, Kramer admitted: Randy Shilts *And the Band Played On,* 120.
      "I read a letter from": *Larry Kramer* (BBC documentary).
      "sophisticated social-service" . . . "with the AIDS crisis": *New York Times,*
      December 5, 1983.
300 "already my last summer" . . . "what keeps me going": Author's interview
      with Howard Rosenman, December 20, 1995.
302 "in a way that I think" . . . "not convinced at all": Author's interview with
      Philip Gefter, December 3, 1991.

304 "Gina Kolata wrote a story": *New York Times,* June 7, 1988.

"And as a result, antibodies" . . . "don't get the virus": Author's interview with Philip Gefter, December 3, 1991.

307 In 1996, there was apparent: *New York Times,* April 4, 1996, and August 9, 1996.

"make the community much more": Author's interview with Philip Gefter, December 3, 1991.

308 "monogamist . . . stirring panic": Shilts, *And the Band Played On,* 182.

"If this article doesn't": Reprinted in Larry Kramer, *Reports from the Holocaust,* 33.

"The mysterious AIDS organism" . . . "diseases such as hepatitis B": *New York Times Magazine,* February 6, 1983.

309 "Many people, especially" . . . "reinforced at home": *New York Times,* October 23, 1986. The *Times* underplayed this story, printing it not on the front page, where it belonged, but on page A24.

310 "that giving up careless": Reprinted in Larry Kramer, *Reports from the Holocaust,* 46.

Gibson had grown up . . . "relatively unscathed": Author's interview with Charles Gibson, December 5, 1991.

313 David Bartolomi was born . . . "enough to be educated": Author's interview with David Bartolomi, May 6, 1996.

315 In 1984, Todd Alexius Long . . . "instead of against": Author's interview with Xax, September 18, 1996.

317 "He was absolutely adamant": Author's interview with Edward I. Koch, July 25, 1995.

"affectional or sexual preference": CRS Report for Congress, July 18, 1996.

"was an extraordinary lawyer": *New York Times,* February 13, 1997.

"abnormal" . . . "sin": Ibid., March 17, 1986, March 21, 1986, and author's interview with Edward I. Koch, July 25, 1995.

318 As late as 1992: Richard A. Isay, *Becoming Gay,* 170–72.

"fewer fevers, the disappearance": *New York Times,* March 14, 1986.

Ten years later, activists: Most of this account is taken from David J. Garrow's *Liberty and Sexuality,* which provides an extremely detailed description of the Court's deliberations in *Bowers* v. *Hardwick* (653–67).

319 "a decent and moral": *New York Times,* April 1, 1986.

five apparent votes: David J. Garrow, *Liberty and Sexuality,* 660.

"I hate homos": Ibid.

The other justices who initially: Ibid.

"To claim that a right": *New York Times,* July 1, 1986.

"The majority has distorted": Ibid.

320 A Gallup poll revealed that: *Newsweek,* July 14, 1986, quoted in David J. Garrow, *Liberty and Sexuality,* 665.

"a major disaster from our": *New York Times,* July 1, 1986.

"apparently unaware": David J. Garrow, *Liberty and Sexuality,* 658–59.

"probably made a mistake": Ibid., 667.

321 "marched and demonstrated" . . . "getting arrested": Eric Marcus, *Making History,* 483–84.

"loud and rude": *New York Times Magazine,* July 9, 1989.

"weak, ravaged [and] deserving": Ibid.

322 "extremely handsome" . . . "everyone else up too": Michelangelo Signorile, *Queer in America,* 54–58.

"ejected the startled occupant": *Wall Street Journal,* December 7, 1989.

On another occasion, ACT UP members forced: *New York Times Magazine,* July 9, 1989.

"This is about constantly": *Wall Street Journal,* December 7, 1989.

"'The tribe'" has given way: *New York Times Magazine,* July 9, 1989.

Some protesters lay down: *New York Times,* December 11, 1989.

"was telling the general public": Eric Marcus, *Making History,* 485–86.

"kind of ironic": *New York Times,* December 11, 1989.

"People were horrified": Author's interview with Alice McGillion, October 15, 1996.

324 "No teaching whose net effect" . . . "energy into other actions": *New York Times,* January 4, 1990.

Johnny Franklin told *The: Wall Street Journal,* December 7, 1989.

"a major shift long": *New York Times,* June 26, 1989.

"very polite": Ibid., October 21, 1989.

325 "I think the most impressive": Randy Shilts, *And the Band Played On,* 283.

"It's pretty hard to hate": Author's interview with Andrew Tobias, December 27, 1996.

"The pain gay people": *The New York Times Magazine,* October 11, 1992.

VI: THE NINETIES

329 "New York is the best": Author's interview with Rick Whitaker, July 2, 1996.

330 By the beginning of . . . "potent political force, indeed": *New York Times Magazine,* October 11, 1992.

331 The Democratic National Convention: Chris Bull and John Gallagher, *Perfect Enemies,* 85.

"vote this year as if": Ibid., 85–87.

"life style choice": *New York Times,* November 7, 1992.

332 "the sexual revolution has begun": Quoted in Randy Shilts, *And the Band Played On,* 311.

"There is a culture war": Chris Bull and John Gallagher, *Perfect Enemies,* 88.

"This is the most": *New York Times,* August 20, 1992.

"behind the scenes": Ibid., August 19, 1992.

333 "Privately top Bush": Ibid., August 20, 1992.

"a multicultural, nihilistic": Ibid.

"Bible-believing Christians": Chris Bull and John Gallagher, *Perfect Enemies,* 84.

"Upper-middle-class suburban": *New York Times Magazine,* October 11, 1992.

"I think there was": Ibid.

334 "This is a rite of passage": *New York Times,* November 5, 1992.

voters approved a ban on: Chris Bull and John Gallagher, *Perfect Enemies,* 119.

For a complete account of the battle over admitting gays into the military, see Ibid., 125–61.

"completely sympathetic" . . . "participated in that": Author's interview with Tom Stoddard, August 3, 1994.

336 "skin color is a benign": Ibid.

"inoculate the pro-ban forces": Chris Bull and John Gallagher, *Perfect Enemies*, 134.

"The military may have greater": *New York Times*, January 26, 1993.

"The truth is that without": *National Review*, April 26, 1993.

337 "damn lesbian": *New York Times*, May 25, 1993.

"I think he's gotten an enormous": Author's interview with Frank Kameny, October 21, 1995.

On the other side of: *New York Times*, February 11, 1996, and April 26, 1996.

338 "an extreme expression": Ibid., March 30, 1993.

339 In the early 1980s, Seagrams: *New York Times Magazine*, May 2, 1982.

Out's first issue featured ads . . . Baileys Original Irish Cream: *Out*, February 1996 and April 1996.

340 "It all comes down to": *New York Times*, February 23, 1994.

"a variety of converging" . . . "purpose and love": Author's interview with Tom Stoddard, August 3, 1994.

343 "the most powerful AIDS therapy": *New York Times*, February 2, 1996.

"I started in the spring" . . . "have a life again": Author's interview with Xax, September 18, 1996.

344 the number of deaths from AIDS: *New York Times*, July 15, 1997.

"AIDS has been the best" . . . "everyone wake up": Author's interview with Xax, September 18, 1996.

"The place for creative": Peter J. Gomes, *The Good Book*, 141.

345 "One century ago, the first" . . . "racial or religious bias": *New York Times*, May 21, 1996.

"This is the most important": Response to author's question at press conference held at Lesbian and Gay Community Center in Manhattan, May 20, 1996.

345 "It's about the tenor of" . . . "entry into heaven": Author's interview with Tom Stoddard, May 26, 1996.

Selected Bibliography

Abell, Tyler, editor. *Drew Pearson: Diaries, 1949–1959*. New York: Holt, Rinehart and Winston, 1974.

Albury, Simon, and John Sheppard, producers; Ron Caird, executive producer. *Sgt. Pepper's Lonely Hearts Club Band* (documentary). London: Grenada Television, 1987.

Almquist, Leann Grabavoy. "Joseph Alsop and American Foreign Policy."

Altman, Lawrence K. "Rare Cancer Seen in 41 Homosexuals," *New York Times*, July 3, 1981.

Alwood, Edward. *Straight News*. New York: Columbia University Press, 1996.

Aspinall, Neil, executive producer; Chips Chipperfield, producer; Geoff Wonfor, director; Bob Smeaton, series director and writer; Andy Matthews, editor; interviews by Jools Holland and Bob Smeaton. *The Beatles Anthology* (documentary). First broadcast in America on ABC, November 23, 1995.

Auden, W. H. *Collected Poems*. Edward Mendelson, editor. New York: Random House, 1976.

Bacevich, A. J. "Gays and Military Culture," *The National Review*, April 26, 1993.

Bayer, Ronald. *Homosexuality and American Psychiatry*. Princeton: Princeton University Press, 1987.

Bennett, Stephanie, and Patrick Montgomery, producers; Stephanie Bennett and Jeannie Sakol, executive producers; David Silver, writer. *The Compleat Beatles* (documentary). Delilah Films, 1982.

Bérubé, Allan. *Coming Out Under Fire*. New York: Plume, 1991.

Bogarde, Dirk. *Snakes and Ladders*. London: Chatto and Windus, 1978.

Boswell, John: *Christianity, Social Tolerance, and Homosexuality: Gay People in Western Europe from the Beginning of the Christian Era to the Fourteenth Century*. Chicago: University of Chicago Press, 1981 (reprint).

——. *Same Sex Unions in Premodern Europe*. New York: Villard Books, 1994.

Boynton, Robert S. "God and Harvard," *The New Yorker*, November 11, 1970.

Brown, Peter, and Steven Gaines. *The Love You Make: An Insider's Story of the Beatles.* London: Pan Books, 1984.

Bull, Chris, and John Gallagher. *Perfect Enemies: The Religious Right, the Gay Movement and the Politics of the 1990s.* New York: Crown, 1996.

Burton, Humphrey. *Leonard Bernstein.* New York: Doubleday, 1994.

Capote, Truman. *Answered Prayers.* New York: Plume, 1988.

Chauncey, George, Jr. "The Policed: Gay Men's Strategies of Everyday Resistance." In *Inventing Times Square: Commerce and Culture at the Crossroads of the World,* William R. Taylor, editor. New York: Russell Sage Foundation, 1991.

Clarke, Gerald. *Capote.* New York: Simon and Schuster, 1988.

Cory, Donald Webster. *The Homosexual in America: A Subjective Approach.* New York: Greenberg, 1951.

Crowley, Mart. *The Boys in the Band.* New York: Samuel French, 1968.

Deitcher, David, editor. *The Question of Equality.* New York: Scribners, 1995.

Demaris, Ovid. *The Director: An Oral Biography of J. Edgar Hoover.* New York: Harper's Magazine Press, 1975.

D'Emilio, John. *Sexual Politics, Sexual Communities.* Chicago: University of Chicago Press, 1983.

Doty, Robert. "Growth of Homosexuality in City Provokes Wide Concern," *New York Times,* December 17, 1963.

Dowd, Maureen. "For Victims of AIDS, Support in a Lonely Siege," *New York Times,* December 5, 1983.

Duberman, Martin. *Cures, A Gay Man's Odyssey.* New York: E. P. Dutton, 1991.

———. *Stonewall.* New York: E. P. Dutton, 1993.

Dyer, Kate, editor. *Gays in Uniform: The Pentagon's Secret Reports.* Boston: Alyson Publications, 1990.

Edwards, Anne. *Judy Garland: A Biography.* New York: Simon and Schuster, 1975.

Ellis, John. *The World War II Data Book.* London: Auvum Press, 1993.

Epstein, Joseph. "Homo/Hetero: The Struggle for Sexual Identity," *Harper's,* September 1970.

Epstein, Rob, and Jeffrey Friedman, producers and directors; Rob Epstein, Jeffrey Friedman, and Sharon Wood, writers; Armistead Maupin, narrator; based on the book by Vito Russo. *The Celluloid Closet* (documentary). Sony Classics, 1995.

Ewing, William A. *The Photographic Art of Hoyningen-Huene.* New York: Rizzoli, 1986.

Frank, Gerold. *Judy.* New York: Harper and Row, 1975.

Gardner, Gerald. *The Censorship Papers: Movie Censorship Letters from the Hays Office, 1934 to 1968.* New York: Dodd, Mead and Company, 1987.

Garrow, David J. *Liberty and Sexuality: The Right to Privacy and the Making of Roe v. Wade.* New York: Macmillan, 1994.

Gavin, James. *Intimate Nights: The Golden Age of New York Cabaret.* New York: Grove Weidenfeld, 1991.

Gomes, Peter J. *The Good Book: Reading the Bible with Mind and Heart.* New York: William Morrow, 1996.

Gooch, Brad. *City Poet.* New York: Alfred A. Knopf, 1993.

Goodman, Fred. *The Mansion on the Hill: Dylan, Young, Geffen, Springsteen, and the Head-on Collision of Rock and Commerce.* New York: Times Books, 1997.

Halberstam, David. *The Fifties.* New York: Fawcett Columbine, 1994 (reprint).

Hall, Radclyffe. *The Well of Loneliness.* New York: Anchor Books, 1990.

Helms, Alan. *Young Man from the Provinces.* Boston: Faber and Faber, 1995.

Henig, Robin Marantz. "AIDS: A New Disease's Deadly Odyssey," *New York Times,* February 6, 1983.

Isay, Richard A. *Becoming Gay.* New York: Pantheon Books, 1996.

———. *Being Homosexual.* New York: Farrar, Straus, and Giroux, 1989.

Jay, Karla, and Allen Young, editors. *Out of the Closets: Voices of Gay Liberation.* New York: New York University Press, 1992.

Kaiser, Charles. *1968 in America: Music, Politics, Chaos, Counterculture, and the Shaping of a Generation.* New York: Weidenfeld and Nicolson, 1988.

Kerouac, Jack. *The Subterraneans.* New York: Grove Weidenfeld, 1989 (reprint).

Kinsey, Alfred C., Wardell B. Pomeroy, and Clyde E. Martin. *Sexual Behavior in the Human Male.* Philadelphia: W. B. Saunders, 1948.

Kramer, Larry. *Reports from the Holocaust: The Making of an AIDS Activist.* New York: St. Martin's Press, 1989 (reprint).

Lait, Jack, and Lee Mortimer. *U.S.A. Confidential.* New York, 1952.

Laurents, Arthur. Larry Kramer interview, *The Advocate,* May 16, 1995.

Leavitt, David. "The Way I Live Now," *New York Times Magazine,* July 9, 1989.

Lerner, Max. "Washington Sex Story," *New York Post,* July 10, 12, 15, 17, 18, 20, 21, 22, 1950.

Leyland, Winston, editor. *Gay Sunshine Interviews,* vol. 2. San Francisco: Gay Sunshine Press, 1982.

Mailer, Norman. *Miami and the Siege of Chicago.* New York: New American Library, 1968.

Marcus, Eric. *Making History: The Struggle for Gay and Lesbian Equal Rights, 1945–1990, an Oral History.* New York: HarperPerennial, 1993.

Marotta, Toby. *The Politics of Homosexuality.* Boston: Houghton Mifflin, 1981.

Martin, George, with William Pearson. *With a Little Help from My Friends: The Making of Sgt. Pepper.* Boston: Little, Brown, 1994.

Meiran, David, executive producer. *The Question of Equality* (documentary). Produced by Testing the Limits for Independent Television Service. Program One, "Outrage '69," Arthur Dong, producer, director, writer; Program Two, "Culture Wars," Tina DiFeliciantonio and Jane C. Wager, producers, directors, editors; Program Three, "Hollow Liberty," Robyn Hutt, producer, director; Program Four, "Generation Q," Robert Byrd, producer, director.

Michener, James A. "God Is Not a Homophobe," *New York Times,* March 30, 1993.

Miller, Jim, editor. *The Rolling Stone Illustrated History of Rock and Roll.* New York: Random House, 1980.

Miller, Merle. "What It Means to Be a Homosexual," *New York Times Magazine,* January 17, 1971.

Miller, Neil. *Out of the Past: Gay and Lesbian History from 1869 to the Present.* New York: Vintage Books, 1995.

Morris, Willie. *New York Days.* Boston: Little, Brown, 1993.

Morgan, Ted. *FDR.* New York: Simon and Schuster, 1985.

Mortimer, Lee. *Washington Confidential Today.* New York: Paperback Library, 1962.

Navasky, Victor. *Naming Names.* New York: Viking Press, 1980.

On the Edge: Images from 100 Years of Vogue. Introduction by Kennedy Fraser. New York: Random House, 1992.

Powers, Richard Gid. *Secrecy and Power: The Life of J. Edgar Hoover.* New York: Free Press, 1987.

Powers, Thomas. *The War at Home.* New York: Grossman Publishers, 1973.

Rich, Frank. "The Gay Decades," *Esquire,* November 1987.

Rivers, Larry, with Arnold Weinstein. *What Did I Do? The Unauthorized Autobiography of Larry Rivers.* New York: HarperCollins, 1992.

Russo, Vitto. *The Celluloid Closet: Homosexuality in the Movies,* revised edition. New York: Harper and Row, 1987.

Scagliotti, John, executive producer; Greta Schiller, director; Robert Rosenberg, codirector. *Before Stonewall* (documentary). Before Stonewall Inc., in association with the Center for the Study of Filmed History, released by David Whittier Promotions, 1985.

Schulze, Franz. *Philip Johnson: Life and Work.* New York: Alfred A. Knopf, 1994.

Shilts, Randy. *And the Band Played On: Politics, People and the AIDS Epidemic.* New York: St. Martin's Press, 1987.

———. *The Mayor of Castro Street: The Life and Times of Harvey Milk.* New York: St. Martin's Press, 1982 (reprint).

Shipman, David. *Judy Garland: The Secret Life of an American Legend.* New York: Hyperion, 1992.

Shirer, William L. *The Rise and Fall of the Third Reich: a History of Nazi Germany.* New York: Simon and Schuster, 1960.

Signorile, Michelangelo. *Queer in America.* New York: Anchor Books, 1994.

Simmons, Charles. *Wrinkles.* New York: Farrar, Straus, and Giroux, 1978.

Skeet, Brian, producer. *Larry Kramer* (documentary). London: BBC, 1992.

Spada, James. *Streisand: The Intimate Biography.* London: Little, Brown, 1995.

Talese, Gay. *The Kingdom and the Power.* New York: World Publishing Company, 1969.

Teal, Donn. *The Gay Militants.* New York: Stein and Day, 1971.

Thompson, Mark, editor. *The Long Road to Freedom.* Foreword by Randy Shilts. New York: St. Martin's Press, 1994.

Thorsen, Karen and William Miles, producers; Douglas K. Dempsey, coproducer; Karen Thorsen and Douglas K. Dempsey, writers. *James Baldwin: The Price of the Ticket* (documentary). Nobody Knows Productions, 1987.

Timmons, Stuart. *The Trouble with Harry Hay: Founder of the Modern Gay Movement.* Boston: Alyson Publications, 1990.

Tormé, Mel. *The Other Side of the Rainbow: With Judy Garland on the Dawn Patrol.* New York: Galahad Books, 1970.

Tripp, C. A. *The Homosexual Matrix.* New York: McGraw-Hill, 1975.

Vidal, Gore. *United States: Essays, 1952–1992.* New York: Random House, 1993.

Von Hoffman, Nicholas. *Citizen Cohn.* New York: Doubleday, 1988.

Wallace, Mike, correspondent, and Harry Morgan, producer. *The Homosexuals,* (documentary). New York: CBS Reports, 1967.

Warhol, Andy, and Pat Hackett. *POPism: The Warhol '60's.* New York: Harcourt Brace Jovanovich, 1980.

White, Edmund. *States of Desire: Travels in Gay America.* New York: E. P. Dutton, 1980.

White, E. B. *Here Is New York.* New York: Warner Books, 1988 (reprint).

White, Theodore H. *The Making of the President, 1968.* New York: Atheneum, 1969.

Williams, Tennessee. *Memoirs.* New York: Bantam, 1976.

York, Michael. *Travelling Player.* London: Headline Book Publishing, 1991.

Young, Allen. *Gay Sunshine Interview* with Allen Ginsberg. Bolinas, Calif.: Grey Fox Press, 1974.

Zadan, Craig. *Sondheim & Co.,* 2d edition, updated. New York: Harper and Row, 1989.

Index

The author is grateful for permission to quote from:

Vincent Scully, Sterling Professor Emeritus of the History of Art, Yale University, "Jefferson Lecture in the Humanities: The Architecture of Community," Kennedy Center, Washington, D.C., May 1995. Donald Webster Cory, *The Homosexual in America: A Subjective Approach.* Reprinted by permission of the Estate of Edward Sagarin. John D'Emilio, *Sexual Politics, Sexual Communities,* The University of Chicago Press, copyright © 1983 by the University of Chicago. All rights reserved. Allen Bérubé, *Coming Out Under Fire: The History of Gay Men and Women in World War Two,* reprinted with the permission of The Free Press, a Division of Simon & Schuster. Copyright © 1990 by Allan Bérubé. Gore Vidal, *United States, Essays, 19521992.* Copyright © 1993 by Gore Vidal. Reprinted by permission of Random House, Inc. Max Lerner, "Washington Sex Story," *New York Post,* July 10, 12, 20, 21, 22, 1950. Eric Marcus, *Making History: The Struggle for Gay and Lesbian Rights, 1945–1990.* Copyright © 1992 by Eric Marcus. Reprinted by permission of HarperCollins Publishers. Inc. Randy Shilts, *And the Band Played On: Politics, People, and the AIDS Epidemic.* Copyright © 1987 by Randy Shilts. Reprinted by permission of St. Martin's Press Incorporated. A. J. Bacevich, "Gays and Military Culture," *The National Review,* April 26, 1993. Copyright © by National Review, Inc. Reprinted by permission. CBS Reports, "The Homosexuals," 1967. Reprinted by permission of CBS News, a Division of CBS Inc. Christopher Isherwood letter to Gore Vidal, 1948. Reprinted by permission of Don Bachardy. Frank Rich, "The Gay Decades," *Esquire,* November 1987, © Frank Rich. Aaron Latham, "An Evening in the Nude," *New York,* July 9, 1973. Reprinted by permission of Aaron Latham. Larry Kramer interview with Arthur Laurents, *The Advocate,* May 16, 1995. Reprinted by permission of Larry Kramer. Jules Elphant, interview in the SAGE Archive. Reprinted by permission of Jules Elphant. James Michener, "God Is Not a Homophobe," *New York Times,* March 30, 1993. © 1993, reprinted by permission of the *New York Times.* A. M. Rosenthal, "General Powell and the Gays," *New York Times,* January 26, 1993. © 1993, reprinted by permission of the *New York Times.* Maureen Dowd, "For Victims of AIDS, Support in a Lonely Siege," *New York Times,* December 5, 1983. © 1983, reprinted by permission of the *New York Times.* Lawrence K. Altman, "Rare Cancer Seen in 41 Homosexuals," *New York Times,* July 3, 1981. © 1981, reprinted by permission of the *New York Times.* Robert C. Doty, "Growth of Overt Homosexuality in City Provokes Wide Concern," *New York Times,* December 17, 1963. © 1963, reprinted by permission of the *New York Times.* Robin Marantz Henig, "AIDS: A New Disease's Deadly Odyssey," *New York Times Magazine,* February 6, 1983, copyright © Robin Marantz Henig, 1983. Merle Miller, "What It Means to Be a Homosexual," *New York Times Magazine.* Copyright © 1971 by Merle Miller. First appeared in *The New York Times Magazine.* Published by The New York Times Magazine. Reprinted by Curtis Brown, Ltd. David Leavitt, "The Way I Live Now," *New York Times Magazine.* Copyright © 1989 by David Leavitt, reprinted with the permission of the Wylie Agency, Inc.